BETWEEN WOMEN

BETWEEN WOMEN

Biographers, Novelists, Critics, Teachers and Artists Write about Their Work on Women

Edited by Carol Ascher
Louise DeSalvo, Sara Ruddick

Beacon Press   Boston

Beacon Press books are published under the auspices
of the Unitarian Universalist Association of
Congregations in North America,
25 Beacon Street, Boston, Massachusetts 02108
Published simultaneously in Canada by
Fitzhenry and Whiteside Limited, Toronto

Printed in the United States of America

(hardcover) 9 8 7 6 5 4 3 2 1
(paperback) 9 8 7 6 5 4 3 2 1

Library of Congress Cataloging in Publication Data
Main entry under title:

Between women.

1. Feminism — United States — Addresses, essays, lectures.
2. Women authors — United States — Addresses, essays,
lectures. 3. Women in literature — Addresses, essays,
lectures. I. Ascher, Carol, 1941–   . II. DeSalvo,
Louise A., 1942–   . III. Ruddick, Sara, 1935–   .
HQ1426.B47   1984   305.4′2′0973   83-70651

ISBN   0-8070-6712-1
ISBN   0-8070-6713-X (pbk.)

PHOTOGRAPHS AND ART

Grateful acknowledgment is made to the following for permission to reprint: Grace Warnecke for her photo of Alix Kates Shulman; *The Ann Arbor News* for their photo of Ding Ling and Yi-tsi Feuerwerker; William Padilla for his photo of Louise DeSalvo; Henry W. and Albert A. Berg Collection, The New York Public Library, Astor, Lenox and Tilden Foundations for the photo of Virginia Woolf accompanying Louise DeSalvo's essay; John C. Vaught for his photo of Bonny Vaught; Moorland-Spingarn Research Center at Howard University for photo of Charlotte Forten Grimké; Joan Tedeschi for her photo of Elizabeth Wood; BBC Hulton Picture Library for their photo of Dame Ethel Mary Smyth; *Helicon Nine* for permission to reprint page 6 from *Helicon Nine* #4, Spring 1981; Robert Pittenger for his photo of Carol Ascher; Niepce/Photo Researchers, Inc. for their photo of Simone de Beauvoir; Gloria T. Hull for photo of Alice Dunbar-Nelson; Barbara Klutinis for her photo of Lynda Koolish; Margie Adam, Elsa Gidlow, Ruth Ann Crawford, Slim TeSelle, Susan Leigh Star, Dobie Dolphin, Susan Raphael, Carolyn Kizer, Paule Marshall, Alice Walker, Judy Grahn, June Jordan, Audre Lorde, and Adrienne Rich for their individual photos taken by Lynda Koolish; Sara Krulwich for her photo of Sara Ruddick; Alfred A. Knopf, Inc. for photo of Virginia Woolf from *Lady Ottoline's Album* by Lady Ottoline Morrell, edited by Carolyn Heilbrun, copyright © 1976 by Julian Morrell Vinogradoff, reprinted by permission of Alfred A. Knopf, Inc.; Ian Kamal Fisher for his photo of Myrtha Chabrón; Rhoda Nathans for her photo of Hannah Arendt; Katherine St. Clair for her photo of Leah Glasser; Manuscripts Department, University of Virginia Library for their photograph of Mary Wilkins Freeman; Thomas Victor for his photo of Janet Sternburg; Peter Beard for his photo of Isak Dinesen; Miriam Billig for her photo of Jane Lazarre; National Portrait Gallery, London, for their reproduction of the print of Charlotte Brontë; Fritz Senn for his photo of Erlene Stetson; Schomburg Center for Research in Black Culture, The New York Public Library, Astor, Lenox and Tilden Foundations for photo of Georgia Douglas Johnson; Leo Baeck Institute, New York, New York for photo of painting (artist unknown) of Bertha Pappenheim; Linda Cunningham for photos of May Stevens and Alice Stevens; Librairie Artheme Fayard for photo of Simone Weil; Susan Forrest for photo of J.J. Wilson; Mercury Gallery, London, for self-portrait of Dora Carrington; Alice Bissell for photo of Meredith Tax; Collections of the Library of Congress for photo of striking shirtwaist workers; Lawrence A. Gale for photo of Bell Gale Chevigny; Picture Collection, Branch Libraries, New York Public Library for photo of Margaret Fuller; Midge Mackenzie for photo of Jane Marcus; Jill Craigie for photo of a suffragist demonstration; Colleen McKay for photo of Blanche Wiesen Cook; United Nations for photo of Eleanor Roosevelt; Barbara Murphy for her photo of May Sarton with Martha Wheelock at the premiere of *World of Light: A Portrait of May Sarton;* Estate of Carl Van Vechten, Joseph Solomon, Executor, for photo of Zora Neale Hurston; Zora Neale Hurston photo courtesy of The Collection of American Literature, the Beinecke Rare Book and Manuscript Library, Yale University.

POETRY AND PROSE

Grateful acknowledgment is made to the following for permission to reprint: In "This Is Who She Is to Me" by Lynda Koolish — The lines from "Paula Becker to Clara Westhoff" by Adrienne Rich are reprinted from *The Dream of a Common Language, Poems 1974–1977* by Adrienne Rich, by permission of the author and the publisher, W.W. Norton & Company, Inc., copyright © 1978 by W.W. Norton & Company, Inc. In "She Is the One You Call Sister" by Leah Glasser — The sections from "The Mirror in Which Two are Seen as One" from *Poems, Selected and New 1950–1974* by Adrienne Rich, are reprinted by permission of the author and the publisher, W.W. Norton &

For Our Mothers

Ellen Ascher Bergman
Eleanor Willcox Loop
Mildred Sciacchetano

This is the time at which to think more of her, to think her further, to let her live and grow older as other people do. It was negligent sorrow that made her almost disappear, imprecise memory, vague knowledge. Understandable enough. Left to herself she was gone; that was always the way with her. At the last moment, one has thought of working on her.

Under a sort of compulsion, to be sure . . .

the compulsion to make her stand and be recognized.

Useless to pretend it's for her sake. Once and for all, she doesn't need us. So we should be certain of one thing: that it's for our sake. Because it seems that we need her.

Christa Wolf, The Quest for Christa T.

It seems then that men and women are equally at fault. It seems that a profound, impartial, and absolutely just opinion of our fellow-creatures is utterly unknown. Either we are men, or we are women. Either we are cold, or we are sentimental. Either we are young, or growing old. In any case life is but a procession of shadows, and God knows why it is that we embrace them so eagerly, and see them depart with such anguish, being shadows . . .

Such is the manner of our seeing. Such the conditions of our love.

Virginia Woolf, Jacob's Room

It was impossible for me to cry when I saw the field full of weeds where Zora is. Partly this is because I have come to know Zora through her books and she was not a teary sort of person herself; but partly, too, it is because there is a point at which even grief feels absurd. At this point, laughter gushes up to retrieve sanity.

It is only later, when the pain is not so direct a threat to one's own existence, that what was learned in that moment of comical lunacy is understood. Such moments rob us of both youth and vanity. But perhaps they are also times when greater disciplines are born.

Alice Walker, "Looking for Zora"

CONTENTS

CONTENTS xiii

ACKNOWLEDGMENTS

This book has become, over time, the collective vision of its editors. We came to it separately, with different aims; our debts, too, are various.

In the first glimmering of this book, I envisioned women telling personal stories about their reading and writing on Virginia Woolf. Collectively, I thought, we could unnerve the critics who doubted our seriousness or Woolf's greatness; at the same time, the multiplicity of our voices would attest to the partiality of any single perspective on her work. However, the book soon broadened to include women working on the variety of subjects you see before you.

From the outset, I needed collaborators. J. J. Wilson was the first to lend her blessing and counsel. Louise DeSalvo quickly became an enthusiastic coeditor. Later Carol Ascher joined us and saved the project from succumbing to our fatigue. I have been endlessly grateful to both Louise and Carol for taking on a demanding, unpredictable project and making it live.

Among friendly counselors and invigorating conversationalists too numerous to list four stand out. Evelyn Keller encouraged my early absorption in Woolf and gently criticized my first attempts to write about her. Pamela Daniels directly inspired this book by making indispensable in my life the pleasures and struggles of collaboration. As usual, Marilyn Young spurred me to complete a project I would otherwise have abandoned, criticizing my words and cajoling my wayward spirit. In this case, she also secured and helped edit two of our essays. Finally, Elizabeth Coleman insisted that I could talk and write about Woolf although I was not trained to do so. At the New School for Social Research, she created a version of Woolf's "New College," the Seminar College where faculty and students were urged to "discover what new combinations make good "wholes in human lives."

In *Working It Out*, I thanked my children for a "self-reliance" that made the book possible. At the time, this was a kindly construction of their moody, ambivalent support for work that took me away from them. Now they do better than cheerfully keep out of my way. I first publicly talked about this book at my son's college. His sturdy feminism along with his respect for feminist women lightens my days. My daughter has become my liveliest, if sternest, critic. By introducing me to her heroine — Charlotte Brontë — she forced me to confront the limitations of mine.

William Ruddick was a partner in my work, providing, in his many distinctive ways, the practical and emotional foundation on which I built my project.

Sara Ruddick

Some time in 1979, Jane Marcus called me to ask if I would be interested in collaborating with Sara Ruddick on a sequel to *Working It Out* — Sally (as we all know her) was looking for a coeditor, and Jane suggested me.

I cried. Of course I was interested.

I was two years out of graduate school, an adjunct instructor, awaiting the publication of my first book. I was terribly depressed, wondering whether any of my dreams of becoming a member of a community of scholars would come true. Sally's wanting to collaborate with me lifted the gloom. Sally took the same chance that Jane Marcus had taken earlier when she invited me to write an essay for *New Feminist Essays on Virginia Woolf*. I thank them both for helping me join the community of feminist scholars. Blanche Cook, Jane Lilienfeld, Susan Shapiro, Susan Squier, and Martha Wheelock are among that community, and I thank them for their support.

Carol Ascher's joining our project gave it a new direction and a new spirit. I thank her for it.

When we began this project, my son Jason DeSalvo was several inches shorter than I. He is now tall enough to pat me on the head, and he calls me Munchkin. I want to thank him for his encouragement of my work. I am delighted that he has become a feminist without having been coerced. When we began this project, my son Justin DeSalvo could barely write his name. He is now writing eloquent science fiction fantasies. I thank him for smiling when he sees me at the typewriter and for being willing to wait (almost always) until I finish the sentence I'm working on instead of scowling, which is what I would do.

My husband, Ernest DeSalvo, has done more than encourage my work. He has been willing to abandon the privileges accorded the Italian male and become nurturer-in-chief. I am delighted to report that we have successfully lived through a feminist revolution in our own household.

My parents and parents-in-law, Louis and Mildred Sciacchetano and Fran and Don DeSalvo have made sure that our children have had care and comfort and outings and wonderful home-cooked meals when we were unable to provide them. They have been willing to accommodate themselves to a new kind of daughter and daughter-in-law, and I thank them for it.

Frank McLaughlin gave me the confidence to write in my own voice. Tony Prete read an early version of my essay for this book and told me I was on the right track.

Kate Probst has been my friend for twenty years. Everything I accomplish is due in part to the sustenance that her friendship provides me. She is now completing her own dissertation on Seamus Heaney and the time has come, at last, when I can help take care of her.

Louise DeSalvo

Involvements often have more than one beginning. In 1980, while writing my book on Simone de Beauvoir, I had come up against irrational resentments toward this woman on whom I was spending so much time. I spoke to Sara Ruddick, who not only seemed thrilled at my troubles but anxious to have me write about them for a book she was conceiving. Knowing well the healing power of writing, I set my conflicts to the page. Sally was pleased: "It's just right!" Since my book was of a personal sort, and I was clear about wanting to describe what goes on behind the scenes of biography or literary criticism, I included "Clearing the Air — A Personal Word" in my *Simone de Beauvoir: A Life of Freedom.*

Meanwhile, I continued to hear about the collection on which Sally was working, now with Louise DeSalvo, and in the spring of 1981, having experienced the public reception of my personal explorations in "Clearing the Air," I enthusiastically joined their project. I thank Sally and Louise for bringing me on. Our work together on *Between Women* has been good-spirited, stimulating, and creative.

Several friends have stood by supportively and without complaint during the busy period of editing this book: Muriel Dimen, Irena Klenbort, Bell Chevigny, and Suzanne Ross.

I also thank Robert Pittenger, my husband, who has walked with good nature around piles of paper and put up with urgent phone calls at the oddest times.

Carol Ascher

As editors, we have together incurred many debts. A number of people read parts of the manuscript or took an interest in the project and advised us about it: Gail Bragg, Bell Chevigny, Margaret Comstock, Carolyn Heilbrun, Jane Lilienfeld, Sarah Snyder, Bonny Vaught, and Marilyn Young.

Sari Broner not only took charge of pictures and permissions but also helped us with editing and myriad other tasks in the last stages of our project. Her judgment, patience, creativity, and cheer were invaluable.

We want to thank Joanne Wyckoff, our editor at Beacon Press, who conveyed her excitement when she heard of the project and sustained us lovingly as we collected the essays for the book. We also thank our designers, Deborah Taylor and Jane Carey, who blessed us with their artistic creativity on both the inside and outside of the book. No book enters the world without the enormous efforts of a publicity director: For her generosity of time and spirit, we want to thank Judy Rosen.

Finally, we thank our contributors. Although each of them probably shares some of our hunches and commitments, they all contributed blindly to a collection they had not yet seen. They gave us a chance to expand our thinking by revealing the personal stories behind their work.

Carol Ascher
Louise DeSalvo
Sara Ruddick
December 1983

INTRODUCTION

It is a rainy Monday evening. We three are scurrying to the Lion's Head Café on Sheridan Square in New York City to have dinner and an editorial session about our book, *Between Women*. We are feeling slightly self-conscious that we have chosen this Village literary haunt. Other meetings have taken place in our homes and across oaken tables in other Greenwich Village places — a health food restaurant, a fast-food bagleria. But now that the book is nearing completion, we have chosen the Lion's Head for a celebration. We have become more and more sure, as the months progress, that we will, in fact, really finish this book.

We arrive carrying briefcases, dripping umbrellas, shopping bags, manuscripts, lists, queries, permission forms. Each of us has brought triplicates of the latest versions of articles received from our contributors. The amount of paper we exchange across the table is staggering. We will all have an enormous amount of reading to do. Carol has just returned from Italy, and she has brought Sally and Louise posters of Virginia Woolf in Italian. The posters are unfurled and admired. Other diners turn and stare. We smile at one another. As we begin to order drinks and food, the collaboration, on this rainy March Monday, feels very good.

Of course, it was not always that way. But it was that way some of the time, even much of the time. Meetings at the Lion's Head in the closing stages of our project came to epitomize our enthusiasm and good will, toward each other and toward our contributors, whose manuscripts filled our table with their strong presence.

Our project had grown out of our own literary relationships to the particular women on whom we had worked. This connection to a distant stranger had shaped our work, politics, and loyalties. We were struck by the power of our experiences and wanted to share them. Sometimes we were puzzled and uneasy about our own intense feelings: Could other women who also had literary relationships with women enlighten us? When we talked to other women, we found that they too had interesting experiences and puzzling, intense feelings. Their stories and ours seemed to have larger implications for feminist attempts to find authority in women while remaining respectfully independent of all authority.

Once the idea for a collection had taken root, we, the editors, asked women who had worked on women simple questions: How did their projects begin? Why did they turn to a woman or women for study? Who encouraged, who dispirited them? What did they hope their work would do for them or their readers? What doubts arose about themselves, their projects, or the women they worked on? How did they change in the course of their work? Did they come to judge themselves or their subjects differently? Were they transformed as writers, activists, teachers, artists, lovers, mothers, daughters, feminists?

In answer to our questions, we heard from women who have worked on a variety of women subjects: composers, writers, artists, slaves, workers, activists, philosophers, political theorists, mental patients. Although the majority of our contributors use writing as their primary means of creating their vision of another woman or women, we are pleased to include a photographer, a painter, and a filmmaker. Largely because we are three urban, intellectual, literary women, those women who knew and trusted us sufficiently to write for this volume had many of the same qualities.

Their answers to our questions came largely in personal stories. Like us, most of our contributors did not feel ready to generalize from their own idiosyncratic experiences. What truths they offer are those trapped inside their narratives and then sprung loose in a moment of insight about themselves — or their subjects — along the way.

Although the tone of these essays is personal, and the details specific, they do raise general issues. Because work on women is one kind of intellectual or artistic work, these essays speak generally about the place of chosen work in women's lives. Or again, because they are about women's relations to the women they study, the essays clarify feelings of protectiveness, jealousy, competition, and overidentification, which trouble so many relations between women. Finally, over and over in the following pages, our contributors ask: How are we to represent justly and generously the complicated lives of the women we honor?

For some women in this collection, the process and rewards of work, rather than their literary relationships, are the major themes. This makes *Between Women* a kind of sequel to *Working It Out*. These essays reveal women struggling with themselves and their environment as they work, but the stories they tell are remarkably often ones of achievement. We read about the thrill of research or of developing a photograph, the elation of dating a manuscript, finishing a thesis, or correcting a mistaken interpretation. The essayists attest to the joy they have taken in their work, the self-knowledge it has given them, the moral strength they have earned and hope to share, and the political insight that continues to challenge them. In fact, most of the contributors write at moments of triumph, and so the tone of their essays may mitigate against the very real, often long, periods of difficulties that have been part of their achievement.

Yet nearly all write about one or more serious external obstacles. Often their chosen work must be supported by other, more grueling labor; responsibilities to children, lovers, husbands, and political causes create conflicting — and for long periods overriding — demands. Specific barriers are set up by unemployment, academic taskmasters, publishers, estate executives, copyright law, and control of information; more global barriers are generated by misogyny, racism, and desperate economic need. One author writes of carrying around a single microfiche on her working-class women subjects that she did not read for several years because of the pressure of nine-to-five jobs combined with single motherhood. Another found herself nearly unable to contribute to this volume — to write in a leisurely, open, personal style — when so much of Black women's lives and writings has been destroyed.

Some contributors also speak of subjective obstacles to their work, the "raging demons" of doubt and fear that lead to "self-sabotage." Women ask whether their work is any good, whether old angers stand in their way, whether their love for their woman subject is foolish. They wonder what "people" (reviewers, parents, lovers) will say. Doubts about their own worth become mixed with doubts about the worth of their subject: Is she too minor? Is she cruel? Is she crazy? Among these inner problems, two stand out. One is the internalization of external discouragement, whether in the form of personally aimed admonishment from family or teachers or of an almost generic silencing of creativity because of one's race, class, or gender.

> Because of my not-very-good college; because I couldn't afford to attend Mount Holyoke; because I am a mulatto from Jamaica, a colored immigrant to America, the child of a colonized society; because I am a female — all those pieces that fit together to form a pattern of difference, of outsiderhood, made me insecure about my mind.

The second type of inner difficulty that emerges in these pages is the sense of being lesser than, inferior to, even swamped by the woman the writer or artist is studying. Literary criticism, biography, and, as our photographer reminds us, portrait making, are all kinds of work in which self-loss is a liability. "My main difficulty in working on your writings is my fear or wish that the boundaries between us will simply disappear. That I will become a witness to you, who is 'no one.' "

In addition to speaking of external and internal impediments to their work, many essayists tell us how their very labors on women helped them to overcome these obstacles. In some cases, their subjects provided models for the discipline of work and for the place of work in human life. Several of the subjects revealed to our contributors the way that writing can be a healing process. Similarly, many of our contributors report on healing moments during the life of their projects — a meeting with a subject, a visit to her home, an attempt to place a gravestone on an unmarked grave. It has been especially gratifying to us that several essayists wrote (and many more told us privately) that contributing to *Between Women* "cleared the air" and enabled them to move on.

Finally, it may be, as some contributors suggest, that difficulty in working is partly the result of masculinist conceptions of work. One essayist compares the retrieving of women's lives and the rereading of their texts to the "invisible mending" her mother and aunts engaged in, celebrating rather than repudiating our female heritage. Another emphasizes the importance of thinking *in the world,* stressing the political significance of intellectual independence and courage. Along with redefining work comes a demand for new institutions. Several contributors reject both the style and the morality of the academic, publishing, and literary worlds. Women want to invent new types of criticism, alternative forms of cooperation that will suit the unabashed seriousness of their ambition. Several ask that work be both more and less: less compulsive, aggressive, lonely, competitive; more communal, caring, and integrated with love and politics.

The study of other women is also a pursuit of inspiration and guidance. Our contributors "look for affinities" or "search for authority" in women. They speak of conversion — "Virginia Woolf changed my life" — and express gratitude — "She has been very good to me, this woman." The subjects act as talismans in time of change, guides and mentors. They challenge, give ideas or comfort, serve as warnings. Some contributors are helped by their subjects in working through life crises or troubling relations with mothers, sisters, children, lovers, husbands, and fathers. In turn, many essayists feel that they give to their subjects. Literally or metaphorically, they witness, nurse, rescue, and memorialize.

Few would even have begun their projects had they not been prompted by some as yet misty, if puzzling, element of identification with their subjects. "Why so involved with a person from another century? From another race?" Identification has entailed different feelings for different contributors: strength and renewal, confusion, exhilaration, odd discomfort, pleasure, defensiveness. Studying the lives and work of women appears to offer something like the transference in psychoanalysis:

> I dream about the people I write about — they enter my conversations, intrude on the privacy of my bath, join me in the ocean and the garden. They tell me stories, give me feedback, disagree, suggest new sources. I listen very carefully. Frequently a great flirtation emerges.

For some, relationship with a distant woman, one usually mediated by the printed word, the painting, the musical score, allows a particular calm and safety from which to examine their own desires and needs. As in other transferences, this one also leads many contributors to crystallize in their subjects unrealistic expectations about themselves and other women. Many writers speak of individuation and separation, of learning to distinguish their own needs from those of their subjects. Others describe relinquishing idealization so they can see "the conflicted, realistic sister of our common past."

Clearly, identification is not static; it is a process through which our essayists and their work develop. Although it may be tempting initially to fight for distance and impartiality, most contributors relax and let the stages of identification occur. It is as if they believe that "there might be a way of engaging our identification with our subjects with so little qualification or inhibition that one would emerge at the far side of the experience with a greater clarity than usually accompanies objectivity." Consequently, one way of looking at some of these essays is as a report of the process of women's identification with their subjects. If we submit to identification self-consciously and reflect on the process rather than fighting it, what do we learn?

Looked at from one vantage point, the project of discovering and making available the lives and works of women is one of myth-making — the creation of a tradition that can sustain women personally and give them a rich and lively social world. Setting down a record with energy and love is the primary task. But to be strong, this record must be accurate.

Creating an accurate record can be arduous. One of our contributing editors spent seven years reconstructing and interpreting an early manuscript of her subject. Another essayist writes of the difficulties in merely securing the documents needed to give reliable and enriching detail to a life. A third, who has turned to fiction, describes the importance to her of communicating accurate information about her working-class women to her prospective working-class readers: "A book should be well made, like a good coat."

Many contributors fear compromising their work by the fierceness of their loyalty and compassion. They are aware that when they turn to women's lives and works out of hunger for guidance or a need to witness and rescue, they may project their desires onto their subjects, idealizing the work of their foremothers so that it can inspire their own. Whatever the philosophical difficulties of seeing the world as it is, our essayists want the past they are creating to be sturdy, and this means they must be responsible interpreters.

The question of how to evaluate the women they work on, however, is not an easy one for our contributors. Should they present attitudes or events in the woman's life that in their eyes dishonor her? Should they tell about episodes or relations that the subject or her survivors would want concealed? Should they accept conventional assessments of their subject's "greatness"? If not, by what new criteria should her work be judged? What place should they give to the subject's own evaluation of her life and accomplishments? Given the hardships women have suffered, particularly if they are poor or persecuted, how should their choices be assessed? How can the political usefulness of a woman's story be balanced against a more ambiguous, potentially subverting reality?

Answers to these questions change over time, and confidence comes in odd ways: through dreams, conversations with a daughter, reading a musical score, a visit to the subject's home or country. Some of our contributors work on living subjects; their judgments and interpretations are partly responses to vivid personal encounters. Most must check their findings indirectly, through diaries, manuscripts, contemporary memoirs, as well as published works. All of our essayists are aware that, however carefully they work, their portraits are ultimately their creations — a blend of their subjects' lives and their own.

Somewhere toward the end of our project, we decided to ask our contributors to provide us with photographs of their subjects and themselves. Around that time, we also asked a photographer to share her portraits of women and her thoughts about them. The photos we have collected are a visualization of several of our aims. They bring our contributors and their subjects to life in a way not possible through the printed word alone. Moreover, because the contributors selected the photographs of their subjects (and, when they had a choice, picked the age, mood, and setting), we see the subjects as the women who studied them see them. In her essay, our photographer celebrates both the subjectivity of her work and her passionate attempt to portray women "as they really are." She emphasizes the double truth that photographs too are a blend of artist and subject and that they reflect, nonetheless, a commitment to their subject's reality.

The photographs of our contributors should remind readers that this book is, after all, primarily about the women who study, write about, and otherwise depict other women. Some readers may be tempted to make interesting associations about the relationship between the characteristics of the contributors and those of their subjects. Certainly, our book is an attempt, as one contributing editor phrased it, to "put the portrait painter into the painting." More important still is our wish to avoid the self-abnegation too common among those who celebrate and work on heroines. Only when all parties feel present, visible, and attended to will love and good will exist between women.

Emma Goldman

Alix Kates Shulman

Alix Kates Shulman

LIVING OUR LIFE

There is a certain tidal pool in the rocks on a nubble in Maine that teems with bivalves and crustaceans. For years I have gone to the pool to collect mussels, knowing I can usually find all I want there, but in all the times I've gone musseling, I have been almost unaware of the profusion of small crabs that inhabit the green seaweed surrounding and trailing into the mussel pool. Recently when I went crabbing in the rocks and wound up at the same pool, I barely noticed the large clusters of blue mussels waiting there to be picked. This didn't surprise me; by now I've learned that when I go down to the sea on a quest with all my senses tuned I generally find what I'm looking for. Background and foreground alternate, like blue mussels and green crabs, in perfect balance with each other and with my needs.

Something similar happens when I write. Once I have settled on a subject to write about, it seems as if, almost magically, everything I see and hear bears crucially on the work I am doing. I have only to open a newspaper or turn on a radio to find half a dozen stories that seem to have been planted there like green crabs to answer my needs. Every word I hear seems relevant; every event I witness is a sign; even what is unsaid or unseen, like blue mussels on crabbing days, contributes to my work. This, I take it, is what it means to be in harmony with your environment: you look for what you can find and find what you're looking for.

So with my relation to Emma Goldman (1869-1940), the magnetic anarchist, feminist, radical activist, speaker, editor, writer, theorist, midwife, free lover, and general troublemaker, who was the subject of several of my earliest (and, as you can see, latest) writings. Although I am primarily a novelist, I have written a biography of Emma Goldman, edited two collections of her works, written essays and given talks and interviews about her, and I feel I will never tire of thinking about her. From the time I first began to study her, I have been finding in the rocky pool of her life and work precisely what I've needed to know. I, her biographer, have shaped her life, and she, my subject, has shaped mine. For better or worse, we're a couple. (Nonexclusive, naturally; she insists passionately on free love!) The major themes of my work are there in hers — or shall I say the major themes of hers are there in mine? — and it is clear to me too that in working on Emma (we have long been on a first-name basis) I developed skills, attitudes, and insights that might seem to an outsider to have little to do with hers but that I know to be inspired by hers, skills and attitudes which have been crucial in shaping my life as a writer. Not only the subject of her works and the substance of her life but also her process of self-reflection and the form of her work have affected the process and form of mine. Whether this is because I was seeking what she had to show me or because I am following a path she led me on, I can't say. Both. One.

I had been writing for about a year before I started to work on Emma in the late 1960s. When my children entered nursery school, after a lifetime of working and playing with other people's written words I began composing words of my own. Into stories, fictions. During that first year of writing I completed (but had not yet published) my first book, *Bosley on the Number Line,* a mathematical fantasy for children, and several stories for adults. Between finishing my first book, in which I had put no female characters, thinking that the adventures of a boy were much more interesting and publishable than those of a girl, and beginning my second, *To the Barricades: The Anarchist Life of Emma Goldman,* I attended my first meeting of the young Women's Liberation Movement. That event changed my life. From then on, the new, transforming illuminations of feminism allowed me to bring into the foreground, where I could catch them, from the background where they had lived as invisibly as crabs, ideas and events of sexual politics. Like every important work of theory or art, feminism began to make visible to me what had previously been invisible; from then on, I focused my attention on the lives, works, and history of women, and I became a fighter in our movement.

When an opportunity to write a biography of a "forgotten woman" for T. Y. Crowell's *Women of America* series was presented to me by a friend, I seized it. Here, I thought, was a chance to walk ahead on both feet of my new life: the writer (my right foot) and the feminist (my left). But that hope proved premature — it's not so easy to learn to walk. Until then, my two feet had been in unsteady alliance: instead of working smoothly together to carry me forward, sometimes they threatened to get in each other's way, causing me to falter, stumble, even trip. In the beginning phase of the Women's Liberation Movement, there was an undercurrent of suspicion directed at writers. To many feminists, writers were seen as individualists, elitists, opportunists, ready to advance themselves by exploiting the movement, particularly if they wrote about feminism, and accusations flew. I watched and listened. I certainly didn't want to alienate my comrades or see my efforts work against the cause of feminism, to which I already owed so much, but I didn't want to stop writing either. I listened to the debate, neither accepting nor rejecting the charges.

I personally had escaped suspicion, at least temporarily, because at that time much of my work was for children, and in those days the world of children was one in which many young feminists had at best a negative interest. My writing, therefore, seemed to them unimportant. (Ironically, it was writing for children that had also enabled me, before my feminist awakening, to slip behind the lines of male literary hegemony without encountering the big guns I believed were leveled at every woman writer so arrogant as to claim authority in print. To the literary establishment, then as now, writing for children, like housework, was usually considered women's work — no challenge, no threat, hardly worth wasting ammunition on.) But the movement, ever expanding, soon raised its consciousness about writing for children: months before my first book was actually published, I and a dozen other women organized the pioneering Feminists for Children's Media to develop a feminist critique of children's literature. Every week for many months we met at my apartment to examine children's books, both trade and text, until we had produced an article, a slide show, and a bibliography ("Little Miss Muffett Fights Back"), which we presented under the title "Sexism in Children's Literature" to a stunned American Library Association. Subsequently, our work was taken up by many other groups and expanded to include critiques of TV, film, toys, and other media.

The Crowell *Women of America* series was ostensibly aimed at "young adults" — a step up from children, but still not elevated

enough to make my work as a writer suspect, either in the movement or out. Under the double cover of *selfless work* and *insignificance*
since I was helping to restore to view a "forgotten" woman whose
works had long been out of print and since I wrote for the young,
I hoped to walk on both feet straight into print. Far from limiting my
stride as a writer, my special young audience challenged me to
stretch my talents as I might not have done writing for "old" adults.
Before I began the book I made certain vows. Assuming that there is
nothing young people are incapable of understanding if it is presented carefully enough, and assuming that my readers knew
nothing about the history or ideas of Emma Goldman's time, I knew
I had to make everything I wrote extremely clear. To be able to
explain to the young such concepts as anarchism, socialism,
feminism, sexual repression, revolution, as well as the complicated
and exciting events of those earlier social movements, I would have
to understand them so well myself as to be able to convey them with
utter simplicity — a task as difficult for a writer as writing with
complexity. Then, too, writing for an audience notorious for its low
threshold of boredom, I decided to lure my young readers' interest
by lingering over my subject's formative years. Emma's childhood
in a Russian village, her response to her father's cruelty, her love of a
devoted teacher, her pleasures in dancing, in reading, the first
glimmerings of her intellectual and social awakenings — such
experiences could do much, I thought, to make sense of a life to
young readers. This decision turned out later to be invaluable to me
as a novelist because it led me to search for the social and psychological roots of character. I felt that once I succeeded in capturing my
readers' interest I could hold it most readily by telling my story in
dramatic scenes (vowing, however, not to present a single word,
feeling, or action for which there was no explicit, citable evidence)
— another valuable novelistic technique. In fact, the only restriction
I imposed upon myself because of my special audience was to use
simple sentences instead of complex ones; but I refused to fudge any
issues or rule out any subject matter, particularly the sexual, as
inappropriate to youth.

   With fine intentions, then, but ignorant, inexperienced, and confused, I approached Emma Goldman: ignorant about history,
inexperienced as a writer, confused by the conflicting factions of the
early Women's Liberation Movement. With little confidence in my
abilities and much trepidation about my ambitions as a writer, I
signed a contract to write a book, determined to make my work
serve, not subvert, feminism. I assembled Emma's works and began
to read. And what, to my amazement, did I find? I found in Emma's

words and deeds, life and times, a veritable mirror of every problem and paradox that we — I — in the young women's movement were wrestling with. Her concerns, conflicts, passionate struggles exactly paralleled ours, mine. The problems of individualism, dissent, minority voice, authority, hierarchy, which were at the heart of the movement's quarrel with the world, with its own adherents, and with writers, were examined by Emma in essay after essay, event after event. Our great subjects — the relation between the sexes, the organization of society, and, most profoundly, the connection between the two — were also her great subjects. She even wrote one essay, "Intellectual Proletarians," that explicitly examined the question of the writer's relation to revolution. (Obviously, she herself was a writer whose political commitment was above suspicion.)

Not that my conclusions or my emphases were the same as hers: I did not even consider myself an anarchist. But of what teacher and student is identity ever required? A good teacher helps you develop in your own direction, helps make you aware of the variety of life in the tidal pools that you can harvest as you choose. Our differences, our many quarrels, were quite as instructive as our agreements, since they invariably focused on the same crucial questions to which our separate times, lives, and ways had, astonishingly, led us. Her times became my school, her books my text and commentaries, just as, in the progress of my book, retrospectively mine became hers.

Thinking about Emma's ideas forced me to deepen and expand my own. And since she, who lived her packed life at the center of the great political and social upheavals of her time, recognized the patriarchal family, capitalism, and the state as equal united forces against liberty, she gave me a greatly expanded context in which to analyze the gender relations around which my social awareness had flowered. In the Women's Liberation Movement I had discovered how the personal was not petty but political; from Emma, who tried always to live by her principles, I learned how the seemingly great, the "political," was personal. She embraced with the passion of principle such concerns and activities as free love, midwifery, contraception, children's schools, literature, and magazine editing with no less ardor than she brought to her participation in the Russian Revolution and the Spanish Civil War. When I reflected on her life, a life in which selfless participation was indistinguishable from self-assertion and fulfillment, a life so much longer and larger than mine, I began to understand the connections between authority and oppression, individual and society, anarchism and feminism, sex and politics — the very connections our movement was struggling with and I had discovered were so necessary to social under-

standing. By leading me to explore relations I had not previously
thought to explore, Emma led me to a method of analysis that gave
me the confidence and therefore the courage to write with conviction. And the method was this: Through anarchist doctrine and its
practice in Emma's life, I learned to question authority, all authority,
including the movement's. Soon I realized that despite the movement's suspicions, not only was there no conflict between the writer
and the feminist in me (I was in fact a feminist writing), but there
was nothing I could not study and think about deeply enough to
write about if I chose. In this way, she led me into the world.

And not only through her ideas. Through her actions too. By
example, she taught me to trust my ideas and to act with courage. In
her life she was frequently considered a pariah. She was arrested
countless times, shunned, persecuted, chased from country to
country. (She was proud to be the first political deportee from the
United States.) Yet her resolute rejection of authority, which left her
with only her own feelings and principles, her integrity, to rely
upon, turned each persecution into a kind of strength. "The more
opposition I encountered," she crowed, "the more I was in my
element." With Emma constantly demonstrating to me that courage
strengthens, at least when it is cushioned by a movement, how
could I continue to coddle my own small terrors? I had to fight them.
The first time I faced a furious crowd at a political demonstration,
the first time I defied a police order, the first time I published an
article under my own name instead of a pseudonym, the first time I
triumphantly overcame my shyness and insecurity and dared to
speak before an audience or teach a class, I felt the encouraging
hand and smiling nod of Emma behind me.

In this way, Emma's essays and exploits formed, as it were, my
lesson plans. But I also discovered in her work more esoteric
lessons, not only of content but of form, lessons important to my
development as a writer. In addition to her essays, speeches, books
on political and social subjects, Emma wrote a long, detailed first-
person account of her own life, rich in personal interpretation and
speculation, her 1,000-page autobiography, *Living My Life*. Reading
this astonishing specimen of biography when I was about to write a
biography myself was like discovering crabs at the mussel pool.
Although I must surely have read many other biographies and
autobiographies before *Living My Life*, Emma's was the first one I
remember reading with a writer's eye, as much aware of the writer as of
the subject of the book. Until then I hadn't needed such dual awareness.

Here I must say that ever since I began writing I have been unable
to read "innocently"; I approach most of what I read as a writer

primarily observing another writer's techniques for conveying the subtleties of meaning. I read most self-consciously when the book is fiction, since I write mostly fiction. I can no longer lose myself in a novel and can lose myself in a work of nonfiction only when it is in a form or on a subject I don't usually tackle in my own work.

For my new work I needed to know how to interpret a life. How did one begin to reflect upon the fluid multiplicity of experiences that comprise a life? I was puzzled less about how to discover what happened than about what the happenings meant; how could one draw conclusions about the motives, actions, intentions behind events, even supposing one knew the events? Just as I sank myself into these questions, I read *Living My Life,* and there was Emma freely demonstrating before my eyes one way to do it, teaching me how to squeeze the meaning from the events of a life. Taking as her subject a life she knew well, her own, she unabashedly used her own clear, all-embracing vision, her anarchism, to guide her through the swarming events of her life and help her decide which events were most significant, which required reflection, how to interpret for herself and her readers her experience. Reading her life, I not only glimpsed her living it, but I saw her mind and character at work writing it. And I saw that my own vision might be able to guide me through a different set of events.

Even without corroborating her reports of events from other sources (a task on which, eventually, I spent most of my research time), I discovered that I had to read Emma on two levels at once, observing what she revealed consciously and what again unconsciously. Sometimes her reports were convincing, sometimes suspect; here she seemed self-serving, there cautious, elsewhere overgenerous or defensive or mean. Like all of us, she championed her version of the "facts" and let her passion and temperament color her judgment. (The summary running heads at the top of each page of *Living My Life* are themselves as revealing as they are entertaining. A brief sample: "I enthrall my audiences; I speak on patriotism; Ben satisfies my deepest yearning; Donald betrays our comrades; I disseminate birth-control propaganda; I am arrested; Billy Sunday nauseates me; I help sexual unfortunates; we triumph in San Diego; I talk atheism to theologians; I begin to grow weary of Ben; I relax at Provincetown; the benefits of reading; the Fourth of July in prison; the liberals disgust me; I disagree with Frank Harris; Ben and I break for good.") But her unconscious disclosures were no less expressions of character than were her explicit boasts and confessions. The interplay of hidden influence, chance event, intention, opportunity, desire, which together with the whole of history make up character, paraded past as Emma consciously and unconsciously revealed her life.

Now, portraying or revealing character through event is precisely
what a novelist does too. Studying Emma's autobiography, I incidentally learned what it means to present a life in the first person,
with all the powers and limitations of that point of view. And as I
tried to understand her life "objectively," I found myself relying on
what is ultimately, after all the research has been done, the novelist's
chief method for creating character: introspection. You enter into
the life of your subject, your character, by *becoming* your character.
You put yourself in the precise situation your character is in and
observe your own reactions and feelings. To be able to do this,
naturally you must know every possible detail of the situation, large
and small, distant and close, hidden and apparent; you must master
all the facts you can of your character's time, place, heredity, environment. But this process only facilitates the final step: to know
your subject from inside, through an act of empathy, of introspection.

Perhaps because *Living My Life* was written by a woman whose
concerns so closely paralleled mine, I found myself putting myself
into her situation with relative ease. Naturally, I read everything I
could about her and her times; but before I could begin to write
about Emma with any confidence, I had to develop what I later
discovered to be my main method of writing fiction, a method that
might for all I know horrify most historians: checking my subject's
feelings against my own.

Of course, writing a nonfiction life, a biography, demands a
different relation to the names and "facts" than fiction requires.
Different conventions govern, different rules must be followed.
Whereas in fiction you try to imagine an event to convey your
meaning, in biography you usually try to imagine a meaning to
illuminate an event. But biography and autobiography are no less
fictions than novels are. Character must be imagined, significance
imposed, events interpreted, and from a flowing stream of
moments some must be diverted by the writer to cut a new bed.

Emma's was the first life aside from my own that I undertook to
interpret. It was an all but forbidding task, so formidable that I
found the restrictions imposed by the rules of biography reassuring
and even comforting. Since the form of my book was, in a sense,
given, I felt as if I were taking a limited risk as a writer. It was not
only the genre, with its givens, that made me feel relatively secure; I
felt Emma there ready to talk over with me every problem, every
idea. As it was her life I was writing, not mine, she shared my risk:
Every tentative statement I made, I could support with a quote from
her. Under her guidance, with her own story as model and inspiration, I was able to exercise my powers of reflection, interpretation,

and imagination one muscle at a time, without the risk of collapsing, until eventually I was ready to throw off the bonds of biography, loose my imagination, follow my bent, and undertake to write a novel. A year after I finished *To the Barricades* I felt I had sufficiently mastered the process of introspection and interpretation — in other words, I had learned enough empathy and confidence — not only to walk on my two feet but to march, to dance.

And I had learned how to give shape to a life. Beginning, middle, climax, end. Intimation, development, resolution. The elusive working out of a destiny. It was no accident that my first two novels were cast in the form of fictional autobiographies: first-person fictions, each telling the life of a single central character. I had learned to reflect on a life in the workshop of Emma Goldman.

When I finished *To the Barricades* and was selecting my next subject, I briefly considered writing a biography of Emma's long-time lover and business manager, Dr. Ben Reitman. A complicated and colorful character, once elected King of the Hobos, he was criticized by Emma's friends as politically suspect and rejected by them as unworthy of her. Like Emma, I found him fascinating and sexy; besides, I was still caught up in Emma's life and wanted to champion her right to choose her own lovers. (There were too many people in our own movement who wanted to dictate to others the correct way to live, and I wanted to present them with Emma's defiant response. "Censorship from comrades had the same effect on me as police persecution; it made me surer of myself," she wrote.) But the year was 1969. A great new audience of women hungry to know about women was gathering. Many of us in the movement believed that it would be a diversion from our urgent cause to devote our major energies to men when so many remarkable women were unknown and needed to be heard. I could not in conscience choose a man for my next subject. Emma had had a hand in rescuing me from what seemed like a dangerously passive life; the least I could do was carry on the rescue operation. Following Emma's lead, I undertook to edit a collection of Emma's speeches and essays, some of which I had found in manuscript and discovered had never before been published, others of which had not been published since Emma published them herself in her magazine *Mother Earth* early in the century. By making these works available in my collection *Red Emma Speaks* (Random House, 1972; Schocken Books, 1983), I hoped that others might get the same boost from reading Emma that her work had given me; I also hoped to repay some of the debt I owed her for lending me her life as a subject and for helping my career. (She of course would scoff at the idea of a debt; as an anarchist, she thought ideas and assistance ought to be free to anyone who could use them and never even bothered to copyright *Mother Earth*.) And when that book was done, I decided to drop the shield of the past and the protective distance granted an editor and a biographer and to write what I most wanted to write: a novel, set in the present, about ourselves.

My first adult novel, *Memoirs of an Ex-Prom Queen* (Knopf, 1972), is the story of Sasha Davis, a private middle-class midwestern girl with no political awareness at all, whose main concerns are beauty and boys. As such it may seem very far from the history Emma presents of a born Russian rebel who spends her life all over the Western world publicly promoting reform and revolution. Mine is a comic novel; Emma's story is earnest and energetically pedagogical. Perhaps no one but the authors could see the connection. Yet I know that the underlying impulse behind the book, to show the way ideology and social forces become a kind of destiny for the heroine, was inspired by Emma.

From the time Sasha enters kindergarten until she is ready to pack up her children and leave her second husband, she thinks that if she is everything her society expects her to be she can somehow escape her destiny. We see her as a prude and a sexpot; dumb and cunning; beautiful, popular prom queen, devoted wife and mother. But of course, Sasha always winds up facing another impossible bind.

Emma might well miss the essential irony of my novel and be impatient with my Sasha, hopelessly unconscious and middle class; patience was never one of Emma's virtues. Nevertheless, as a tribute to her inspiration and for the authority her words confer on my subject, I opened my novel abut the adventures of a high school beauty queen with the following epigraph from Emma's *Living My Life:*

> On the Sunday of my first lecture a sealed note was left at my hotel for me. The anonymous writer warned me of a plot against my life: I was going to be shot when about to enter the hall, he assured me. . . . I walked leisurely from the hotel to the meeting-place. When within half a block of it I instinctively raised to my face the large bag I always carried. I got safely into the hall and walked towards the platform still holding the bag in front of my face. All through the lecture the thought persisted in my brain: "If I could only protect my face!" Surely no man would think of his face under such circumstances. Yet I, in the presence of probable death, had been afraid to have my face disfigured! It was a shock to discover in myself such ordinary female vanity.

Yes, even in Emma Goldman!

My second novel, *Burning Questions* (Knopf, 1978), bears a much more obvious connection to Emma's work. This book, I like to think, Emma would have approved and enjoyed. Another first-person "memoir," the story of the evolution of a contemporary radical feminist, the novel almost parodies the genre Emma wrote in, the revolutionary memoir. Starting with Emma's own, I searched out and studied all the autobiographies of revolutionary women I could find, from the pre–Russian Revolutionary martyrs to such American radicals as Mother Jones, Mother Bloor, and Elizabeth Gurley Flynn, in order to distill the elements common to them all for the "autobiography" of my heroine, Zane IndiAnna.

Zane comes from a small midwestern town in a time when, as she says in her own preface, "my generation seemed to consist of nothing but jocks, grinds, and the contented" — worlds and aeons away from the seething childhoods of most of her revolutionary predecessors. Unlike the nonfictional revolutionary memoirs I studied, in which irony seems to be all but impermissible, my book is filled with irony. Still, the form of Zane's memoir, the transforming events she recalls of her youth, the details she chooses to emphasize, the shape of her life, and the very title of her book (*My Life as a Rebel*) closely parallel those of her models. Like them, Zane leaves home seeking adventure and a life of significance, follows her passions, gives herself to her movement, proudly recounts her running battle with the police (Zane gleefully presents her readers with her own FBI dossier), and even manages to find good sex. She carries on a running dialogue with her heroes, including, of course, Emma, and there on the reading list with which Zane naturally ends her own book is — what else? — *Living My Life.*

Even my third novel, *On the Stroll* (Knopf, 1981), though written in the third person rather than the first and begun a full decade after I began writing about Emma, owes a good deal to Emma. *To the Barricades* was, after all, written in the third person; writing that book I had to learn to become a narrator with a point of view separate from that of my subjects and characters and to write with authority different from that of my sources. The story of a teenage prostitute named Robin, a shopping-bag lady named Owl, and a pimp named Prince, *On the Stroll* draws on Emma's concern with society's outcasts in more ways than I can name. From the time I first read Emma's essay on prostitution, "The Traffic in Women" (which I included in both my anthologies and, as part of a feminist action, read into the record of a New York City legislative hearing on "victimless" crimes), I wanted to write about a prostitute. And Ben Reitman's only published book, *The Second Oldest Profession,*

published by Emma's Mother Earth Publishing Company, a pioneering if quirky study of pimps (whom he served as physician),
sparked my early fascination with the relationship between prostitutes and pimps. At least as far back as the 1969 New York Radical
Feminist Prostitution Conference, prostitution and sex were issues
that divided the women's movement, even as they had in Emma's
day. Like Emma, I always found the puritan strain within our
movement as distressing as puritanism without. (I left that organization after the Conference.) Although my interest never led me to
try to turn tricks as Emma did on one occasion (if there's one thing
she can't stand it's a competitive attitude among comrades), I did
want to take a stand, as Emma had.

One night in the mid-1970s, something happened that convinced
me to write my own book about a prostitute. When the Democratic
National Convention came to New York City, the mayor ordered the
police to get the prostitutes off the streets. A group of feminists
decided to fight such police harassment of women by taking up
positions on the street corners of the Stroll (the part of the city where
the prostitutes walk), warning the police that if they arrested any
women for just standing around, they'd be charged with false
arrest. I joined the group. And a strange thing happened to me that
night. As I stood around on the Stroll, the people who until then had
usually inspired fear in me, like the men who hang out in the streets,
suddenly became my allies; and those whom I didn't ordinarily fear,
like the police and the men in business suits (the prostitutes' main
potential customers), began to appear threatening. I resolved then
to try to convey this illuminating experience to others and understood that to do so I would have to explore this life from the
inside — a vantage point I might never have dared without Emma
there before me.

Not only Robin the prostitute and Prince the pimp but my bag
lady too derives partly from my work on Emma. Though Owl
doesn't know it herself, never having had much interest in politics,
she has Emma Goldman's physique, tenacity, spectacles, and
something more.

Would I have learned similar lessons about the shape of a life and
about narrative approaches if I had written a biography of someone
else? Probably. When I go looking for crabs, even in the mussel pool,
I find crabs. And I might have learned introspective empathy and
gained the necessary confidence to write about someone else, since
these were the skills I needed at the time. As I said, by the time I
discovered Emma I had already begun to question authority: I'd
been writing for a year and had been startled awake by the new

feminist movement. But if I had signed a contract to write about someone whose puzzles and passions less clearly mirrored my own, it might have been harder for me to cultivate the habit of empathy; and if my subject had been less egalitarian and libertarian, less feminist and questioning than Emma, or if my first subject had happened to be a man, I'm not sure I would have gained the confidence I needed to risk exposure in print.

Let's say I was lucky in choosing Emma as my first subject, not least because I was able to see confirmed in her life what I had already begun to know in my own: that an idea, a cause, a movement could give meaning to a life. Maybe I would have learned different lessons with a different teacher, maybe not. I don't know. I can't say I'm dissatisfied.

One could do worse than have Emma as a guide to how to end life as well as how to live it. "My fiftieth birthday I spent in the Missouri penitentiary. What more fitting place for the rebel to celebrate such an occasion? Fifty years! I felt as if I had five hundred on my back, so replete with events had been my life." Shortly after that birthday, she was deported from the United States to the Soviet Union, where she launched a new round of dissent. In the next decades she wrote her memoirs in France, fought fascism in Spain, and in Canada at the age of sixty-five had a love affair with a man of thirty-six with whom she found "complete harmony in ideas . . . and complete fulfillment of my woman soul." Until the day she died, at seventy, she kept on fighting, questioning, loving.

Can it be that once again Emma seems to know just what I need to learn? Or is it rather that I want to learn what she has to teach? I'm afraid after a couple has been together as long as we have such questions become impossible to answer.

Yi-tsi Mei Feuerwerker and Ding Ling

Yi-tsi Mei Feuerwerker

IN QUEST OF DING LING
(IN QUEST OF MYSELF)

On January 2, 1981, an unlikely day that I had grimly dedicated to the task of cleaning out my office for whoever would be occupying it during my leave of absence, the letter from Ding Ling arrived. The ragged beige envelope (it had been traveling by land and sea since October 4) was postmarked Peking, the undulating English letters of its address in marked contrast to the vigorous Chinese signature in the lower left-hand corner. That name now leapt at me; I tore open the envelope with unsteady hands and a beating heart. "Dear Ms. Mei Yi-tsi," began the four-page letter. "Your letter of July moved me deeply, let me thank you." This was my first direct contact with "my writer," the subject who had been the focus of my life, work, and waking thoughts (or so it seemed) for the past five years. I told myself that I held in my hand tangible proof that Ding Ling was indeed alive; now I could really believe that she had come back to life.

When, as the result of a series of historical accidents, I chose the analysis of Ding Ling's fiction as my dissertation topic, I had no idea whether she was still in the land of the living. She had been expelled from the Chinese Communist party when she was branded a rightist in 1958, presumably had been exiled somewhere for labor reform, and immediately faded away to become a nonperson. Her writings were completely banned, her name was never mentioned in public; histories of modern Chinese literature produced during the next twenty-odd years gave no indication that one of China's most prolific and prominent women writers had ever written or had ever existed. Up to the late 1970s any writer ostracized by the Party was rarely heard from publicly again; so I assumed with good reason that my scholarly investigations would be restricted mainly to Ding Ling's completed oeuvre, a group of self-contained narrative texts. But the death of Mao Zedong and the fall of the Gang of Four in 1976 ushered in a period of relative liberalization, and in the same month that I completed my dissertation, Ding Ling was officially rehabilitated. Indeed, the very day in June 1979 that I received my degree, the news that she had been named a member of the Chinese People's Consultative Conference, the first clear signal that the Party had completely reversed its former verdict against her, was published in the *New York Times*.

What happened on that June day in 1979 was by no means the first seemingly miraculous coincidence that has marked my relationship with my subject. Nor was it to be the last. Because of such recurring coincidences, I have come to believe that I have been fated, "chosen" even (but by whom is the question) to study Ding Ling the writer. Certainly my choice of subject and the events that resulted have profoundly changed my life. They have not only determined what I was to do and how I was to spend my time, but they have also affected my ways of thinking about myself.

In retrospect it is difficult to say whether I would have voluntarily elected to study Ding Ling if certain events had not converged. I had come to the United States to study English and then comparative literature. In my choice of profession I was, rather unimaginatively I suppose, following in the footsteps of my parents, who had studied for advanced degrees in literature in American universities, before returning to China to teach. My father died in 1945, but he had often expressed the hope that I would come to America for advanced study. So with the financial help of some of his former colleagues I found myself in America, and at the very same graduate institution my parents had attended, receiving my M.A. exactly twenty years after my mother received hers. Somewhere in the back of my mind as I continued through graduate school was the idea that to really make it in the United States, to prove that I could be a worthy scholar and could compete with members of the male academic establishment on their own ground, I would have to write on a truly "significant subject." I never thought that that subject would be a Chinese woman writer.

The choice of a thesis topic soon lost whatever urgency it might have had. I was married three weeks after passing my general exams, and I spent the next fifteen years rearing two children, fulfilling social duties as wife of the director of the University of Michigan's Center for Chinese Studies, and teaching part-time. Challenging and rewarding in themselves, these responsibilities did little to advance my professional career, as I realized much too late when I began seriously to aspire to have one.

I became involved again in research and writing by chance, when a colleague of mine had lunch with an editor in Ann Arbor and suggested me as a contributor of an article on women writers for a volume on women in Chinese society. This was an entirely new subject of inquiry for me; I had not paid more than passing attention to the Chinese women writers of the 1920s and 1930s because in my view, as well as in the view of the critics, they had not established themselves as writers good enough for intensive literary analysis. Now as I began to look closely at them as a group, I saw more clearly the established literary tradition against which they had to struggle and their anguished search for the new self-definitions necessary if they were to write at all. It was this anguish and this search that became their primary subject matter, which at times seemed only half-processed into finished literary products. They were extraordinarily self-absorbed; to keep up with their changing lives, the lives they were struggling to bring into being, they wrote over and over the story of their own lives. And out of this personal and limited art that nevertheless speaks to us with great immediacy came new insights into the tragedy of woman's condition and a momentous expansion of the realm of literature.

But the careers of most of these women writers of the 1920s and 1930s were extremely brief. My attention was drawn to Ding Ling because she alone actively pursued a serious literary career for more than three decades. In 1974, when a conference on modern Chinese literature was organized and the Czech scholar who was to contribute a paper on Ding Ling was providentially (from my point of view) denied an exit visa, I was called upon to replace her. The more I read of Ding Ling the more interested I became in the way her fiction continued to develop within a changing historical and ideological context. Although she had begun, like the other women writers, by focusing on the subjective concerns of young women, she soon moved beyond to write about their social and political world. While certain critics had given up on her because she had joined the Chinese Communist party and saw nothing but artistic decline in her post-conversion writings, I felt that it was precisely this abiding political commitment, which accounted for her lifelong efforts to balance or reconcile her dual allegiance to the conscientious practice of literature on the one hand and to the party on the other, that made her an exemplary subject for study. I decided to expand the conference paper into a larger study of Ding Ling's fiction to examine the relationship between ideology and narrative practice. Having found this new subject, I put away the half-finished chapters, the drafts, the voluminous notes of my dissertation on the traditional novel of manners, which I had begun much earlier, to start on this new one.

If it was Ding Ling's resilience as a writer, her tenacious commitment to the literary enterprise that had provided me with a challenging field of investigation, it is harder to say how much that tenacity rubbed off on the investigative process itself. To work on the thesis was one thing — I had had plenty of practice — but to work on it *and* carry it through to completion, I discovered, was an entirely different matter. It clearly would not do to permit success to come lightly. Working against success were two raging demons within me, both difficult to appease. One wanted to continue to address my husband and the male-dominated world he represented: "See how you have made me fail!" The other wanted to address my mother: "The more you want me to accomplish this for you, the more must I prove I am unable to do it." Self-sabotage took excruciating, near fatal physical forms as well. I developed bleeding uterine fibroids, requiring drugs to induce contractions to stop the bleeding, then drugs to stop the pain of the contractions; I manifested infections, requiring antibiotics and then antihistamines to relieve allergic reactions to the antibiotics. Symptoms seemed to spiral and multiply in spectacular ways as my work on the dissertation neared completion, culminating in an exquisitely timed attack of pain the night before the last part of the manuscript was to be handed over to the typist, a night that could well have been spent in the hospital's emergency room if my cries to be taken there had been heeded.

Yet through all the turmoil, somehow the chapters got done one by one and were placed gingerly in manila envelopes and sent out every four or five weeks from Ann Arbor to my advisors in Cambridge. The deadline was met, but barely. In my pocket I had an airplane ticket to Boston for the day the dissertation was due, just in case it required last-minute delivery in person.

It is easy to scoff at the self-destructive demons, especially when somehow they turned out to have been less than completely successful in their work. But how much more difficult it is to identify the factors that finally enable one to bring off the miracle, because every completed work of writing is, for me, a miracle in the end. In looking back, not just to the days of the dissertation but to the beginning of my life, I am surprised to find that now I can acknowledge with gratitude the pressures I so often resented from my mother. In despair over my own failure, I would suspect my mother of all the worst motives of vainglory and self-compensation, and I was bitter that, in spite of all the evidence, she refused to give up on me.

My mother, Ida Lee Mei, belonged to the generation of women that made the breakthrough in China's transition from traditional to modern. When in 1921 National Central University became coeducational for the first time, she was one in that pioneering class of eight female students. Soon after graduation she became head of a women's normal school. Then she married my father, who had been her professor at Central University, and both came to the United States — she to attend graduate school, he to teach. For one of her courses my mother wrote a series of sketches based on a first-century B.C. Chinese text, the *Lienü zhuan* (Biographies of Eminent Women). Her professors were so impressed that they urged immediate publication. However, our family was returning to China and my father advised her to do some revising and checking on dates first. Children — there were to be four in all — further delayed the project and then the manuscript was lost during World War II. My mother's missed opportunity to become a published author was one of the tragic tales I grew up on. Then, quite by chance, some forty-five years later, a carbon copy of certain parts of the manuscript was found among the papers of a Radcliffe classmate who had helped with the typing. My mother began to revise and put the sketches into publishable form. She also began writing articles for the neighborhood page of the *Ann Arbor News*, an undertaking born of a secret resolve; although we lived very close to each other and communicated daily, I had no inkling of her writing until I looked at the paper one Saturday morning and saw her first piece. Thus, during the last stages of my dissertation my mother and I were engaged in parallel efforts to write. I had before me the example of ambition and determination set by a woman publishing her first book (*Chinese Womanhood*)[1] at age eighty. It appeared six months before mine.

Furthermore, an absurd but, I think, sustaining fantasy kept me at it; it was a daydream, yet versions of it would appear in night dreams too. At a time when there seemed to be little prospect of the United States normalizing relations with China, or of my traveling to China, when my thesis had as yet no form or shape and Ding Ling was, as far as could be ascertained, either dead or never to be seen again, I began to dream of one day returning to the country I had left some thirty years ago, of finding Ding Ling somewhere (often it appeared to be a jail) and saying in a low voice, "I have written a book about you . . ." I always stopped there because I never knew how I would finish the sentence. This absurd fantasy — groundless, shameless, impossible as it seemed at the time — is the only fantasy in my life that has ever come true.

Ding Ling began writing in the late 1920s, as a member of the May Fourth generation, the iconoclastic, breakaway generation that initiated the era of the new Chinese literature. Except for the period when she was silenced, she continued to write for more than fifty years. Taken together, her writings as they have developed from one phase to another provide a telescopic history of modern Chinese literature. Her personality and temperament seem to have conspired with certain accidents of history and biography to place her constantly in the center of whatever was going on. Time and again, she has been actively involved in the literary issues and controversies of the past half-century.

Ding Ling was born in 1904 into a once wealthy gentry family in Hunan, the home province of many of China's revolutionary leaders. She was named Jiang Bingzhi and later created the pen name Ding Ling. Her grandfather and great-grandfather had been officials under the Manchu dynasty; indeed, when Ding Ling was born, there was still a Manchu emperor on the throne, a reminder that the tremendous upheavals in China have taken place only within her lifetime. By the time Ding Ling's parents were married, the family had entered a period of precipitous decline, producing, as families will at such times, a generation of degenerate males who whiled away their days in gambling, opium, and keeping fancy horses. Ding Ling's father was such a man, but he suffered from ill health and died when Ding Ling was three. Her mother was the great influence on her life, a woman, Ding Ling has often said, much greater than herself. When Ding Ling's father died leaving her mother with a host of debts and two small children — one an infant son who died soon after — the young widow moved back to her hometown of Changde and took the bold step of attending a normal school to prepare herself for a teaching career. She later became a pioneer educator and founder of elementary schools.

In an unfinished novel entitled *Mother*, Ding Ling gives an account of her mother's experiences as a student, including a moving description of how her mother "let out" her bound feet, a process almost as painful as the initial binding. She soaked them daily in cold water to speed up the process and insisted on enduring the pain of running in gym class, even though she could have been excused. The unbound feet become a central image in the novel, symbolic of the mother's heroic efforts to break out of the bonds of the past. With the example provided by her mother, Ding Ling became a precocious activist. When only thirteen, she was demonstrating with other female students at the Hunan Provincial Assembly demanding equal rights for women. With her mother's support she broke off an arranged marriage in a stormy confrontation with her uncle, the head of the family, later publishing an article denouncing her uncle and the whole social stratum to which he belonged. This was her "first taste of the power of the pen." She soon left home, an "exiled insurrectionist," for the semi-Westernized metropolis of Shanghai to try out the life of a liberated woman in the China of the 1920s.

Ding Ling's feminist concerns can be said to belong to those of the "second generation" in that the pioneering battles against the most flagrant institutionalized forms of oppression — arranged marriages, foot-binding, denial of education — had already been fought and won for the daughter by the mother. What she was to explore in her own life and early writings were the dilemmas of young women who had broken away from traditional social structures and conventional modes of behavior and had found themselves living on the fringes of society, up against the hostile world on their own.

In Shanghai, Ding Ling sporadically attended classes — she never finished high school — studied painting and Western literature, hobnobbed with anarchists, then moved to Peking with the idea of getting into the university. There she met a fledgling poet, Hu Yepin: a "rare person," she was to write some twenty years after he was killed, "with the most perfect qualities, yet a piece of completely uncut, unpolished jade." Soon they were living together, a life of almost idyllic young love, literary aspirations, and precarious poverty.

The story that established Ding Ling's name and made her the most famous — or notorious — woman writer of her time was "The Diary of Miss Sophie," published in 1928, an account of a tubercular, high-strung woman's infatuation with a young man who has the handsome "exterior of a medieval knight" but a despicable soul. It exploded, in the words of contemporary critics, like a bombshell, shattering the quiet of the literary scene. No one in Chinese literature had ever described in such frank and impassioned terms the sexual fantasies of a young woman. Because this is Ding Ling's best-known story, she has been unfortunately identified with its central character; a constant refrain in later political campaigns, when she was attacked for her sexual immorality, was that she was the "incarnation of Sophie." As the history of Marxist criticism in China has shown, fictional characters are an infinitely malleable source of damning evidence for the political purpose of excoriating the writer, since authors are "responsible" for what their characters do. Such critically naive or politically calculated blurring of the distinction between life and literature plagued Ding Ling throughout much of her career.

While Ding Ling's early stories won recognition for the unprecedented audacity and sensitivity with which she depicted the psychology of modern young women, more recent criticism has focused on the social context of the dilemmas of her characters. Although liberated in the sense that they have broken with traditional authority, they lack the economic means and social support needed for any genuine independence. They might be free of the institutionalized oppression of fathers or husbands, but they become all the more vulnerable to the pain of betrayal by lovers or by their own fluctuant emotions. Sophie uses the diary form for a relentless investigation of the self caught in this predicament; her apparent liberation from the constraints of social structures leads her to feel that she has no one to blame but herself for what she is doing or suffering. She is therefore all the more anxious to analyze and understand her own behavior. Yet as spectator and self-conscious actor in her own drama, she often catches herself playing a part, making it difficult for others to give her the true understanding that she craves, while sabotaging at the same time her own efforts to evolve an intelligible and authentic image of the self to cope with her personal crisis. By the end of the diary Sophie has become disillusioned with both herself and the diary as a means toward self-understanding. Thus the story in theme and form is a provocative inquiry into the limits of subjectivism in modern literature and foreshadows Ding Ling's readiness to move into a broader arena for her fictional explorations.

External events also politicized Ding Ling's fiction. During the late 1920s both the Kuomintang government's persecution of writers and the radicalization of literature were proceeding apace. Shanghai, where Ding Ling and Hu Yepin were living, had become the center of intellectual life because its foreign settlements and less than totally efficient police allowed a political opposition to exist with some degree of impunity. Hu Yepin joined the League of Left-Wing Writers and became increasingly active in the Chinese Communist party. While he was busy attending meetings, Ding Ling stayed home writing stories about the conflict between love and revolution. Their first child, a son, was born in November 1930. Two months later, on January 17, 1931, Hu Yepin was arrested while attending a meeting and, along with twenty-three or twenty-four alleged

Communists, was executed in Longhua prison on February 7. The brutality of the summary executions aroused widespread protest within China and abroad, and the Five Martyrs — there were four other young writers among the victims — soon became one of the most powerful emblems of literary persecution in history.

Modern Chinese literary history is strewn with the dead bodies and broken lives of martyred writers. This heartbreaking fact is premised on a belief in the power and seriousness of literature, a belief apparently shared by those who undertake the risk of writing and those in power who persecute them for doing so. It is this same belief that led Ding Ling to commit herself even more fully to the cause for which her husband had been killed. She soon joined the Communist party and assumed the editorship of its major literary journal. Her own writings also took a sharp leftward turn. Instead of focusing on introspective and alienated young women, she expanded her subject matter to striking factory workers, awakened peasants, social injustice, and the coming socialist revolution.

On May 15, 1933, she was arrested, or rather abducted since it was an illegal operation, from her home in the International Settlement by government agents, imprisoned, and presumed to have become another martyr. The main purpose of her arrest apparently was not to execute her but to persuade her to renounce the Communist party and to place her talents at the service of the Kuomintang government. She refused to cooperate, but as time went by the conditions of her detention ameliorated; she had a daughter, her second child, while in captivity. Three years later, in September 1936, she managed a daring escape to the Border Regions in northwest China, where the Communist party then had its base. For part of the journey she disguised herself as a Manchurian soldier, which meant riding on horseback for the first time in her life, but she made it through the treacherous terrain and arrived to a heroine's welcome. There was a banquet, and Chairman Mao Zedong composed two poems to commemorate the occasion. Two years later her children, who had been in the care of her mother, were sent to the Border Regions to join her.

When the War of Resistance against Japan broke out in 1937, Ding Ling organized and directed the Northwest Front Service Corps and spent several months with her dramatic troupe traveling through the backward mountain villages of the area, performing plays and songs to spread the message of uniting to fight Japan. One important member of the troupe was the writer Chen Ming, twelve years her junior; despite much criticism of their relationship, they were married in 1942.

At the time when Ding Ling arrived at the Border Regions, the Chinese Communist party did not look like much more than a bunch of stragglers who had barely escaped the encirclement campaigns of the Kuomintang and survived the Long March to reach one of the poorest and most backward areas of China. Yet it was from such an improbable base that the party carried out the most dramatic expansion of a revolutionary movement in history and established thirteen years later its government over all of China. There in Yanan the party forged the revolutionary techniques that were to carry it to power, and Mao Zedong formulated his vision of the Chinese revolution as above all a process of mass consciousness-raising. One question that was debated urgently and that directly involved Ding Ling was the role of art and literature within such an engrossing effort. Although the stories about war and revolution from her Yanan period emphasized heroic characters and positive outcomes, she did not believe that support of collective goals precluded all negative criticism. It was over this matter of whether literature should mainly underscore the "bright side" and play down the "dark side" that she came into open conflict with the party.

Ding Ling was at the time the editor of the literary page of the party's newspaper, the *Liberation Daily,* and in that capacity she called for critical essays on society, literature, and art, publishing several that exposed the dark side of Yanan reality. She herself contributed an essay, "Thoughts on March 8," published on March 9, 1942, in which she wrote that although women in the liberated areas under Communist control were much better off than women elsewhere in China, the bitter contradictions of their existence remained. They were forever the objects of attention or criticism, damned if they married or didn't, had children or didn't, stayed home or didn't. Divorce was usually initiated by the man; if the woman wanted it, "then there must be something even more immoral and it is entirely the woman who should be cursed." Then the woman grew old and lost her attractiveness, never having escaped the fate of being "backward." In traditional society she might have been considered "pitiful" or "ill-fated"; now that she was supposedly equal and had choices, if she suffered it was "her own doing," it "served her right":

> I am a woman myself, I understand women's shortcomings better than most, but I understand even more their suffering. They cannot be above their times, they are not ideal, they are not forged of steel. They are unable to resist society's temptations and silent oppressions, they all have a history of blood and tears, they have all had lofty emotions (whether

they have risen or fallen, are fortunate or unfortunate, still struggling alone or have joined the crowd). To say this about women comrades who have come to Yanan is not unjust. Therefore it is with a great deal of leniency that I consider those who have sunk to become female criminals. I hope that men, especially men in high positions, and women themselves will see the shortcomings of women more as based in society.[2]

For such criticism, Ding Ling and the several writers whose essays she had published were attacked by the party and required to confess their mistakes. Mao Zedong's famous "Talks at the Yanan Forum on Literature and Art," given in May 1942, were in large part directed against Ding Ling and other "petty bourgeois" writers who, like her, had come to join the revolution at the Border Regions. An important turning point in the history of Chinese literature, the Talks state explicitly once and for all that literature and art must be subordinate to politics and claim for the party the right to direct, control, and intervene in the literary process. Although the principles stated by Mao have been applied with varying degrees of stringency, they have remained the fundamental scripture of party policy toward literature for the past forty years.

Having been responsible, in part at least, for precipitating the confrontation and bringing down on literature and art the authoritative pronouncements of Mao Zedong, Ding Ling underwent public self-criticism, worked in the party school and in the countryside, and did not write for the next two years. In 1944 she wrote several sketches of model labor or production heroes based on uplifting real-life incidents and was congratulated by Mao for embarking on this new literary path. When the People's Republic of China was established five years later, she was for a time one of the most prominent members of its cultural hierarchy, vice-chairperson of the Writers' Union, editor of important literary journals, and head of the training school for writers. For the first time in her life she traveled abroad, leading delegations to the Soviet Union, Hungary, and Czechoslovakia.

In 1951 she was awarded the Stalin prize in literature for her novel on land reform, *The Sun Shines on the Sanggan River*. The Stalin prize may or may not in itself be a guarantee of literary excellence, but this award, along with her other honors and positions, indicates that Ding Ling was then one of the most acclaimed writers in the People's Republic of China. The events of the novel take place over some twenty-one days during the early phase of radical land reform in a small village of about two hundred families in northern China.

Ding Ling managed within these limits to provide in microcosm the quintessential Chinese revolutionary experience. While land reform was an important policy that helped win over the peasantry in the Communists' war against the Kuomintang government, its main purpose was the total destruction of the traditional rural structure of economic and political power, and it took place even where landlords were not the problem. Through participation in the land reform process and the activated mass struggle, the peasants' consciousness was raised; for the first time they saw that their centuries-old poverty and oppression could indeed be lifted and their world transformed into one where hope and a new beginning were suddenly possible. Whether Ding Ling's novel is historically accurate is beside the point. As a fictionalized treatment of an ideological version of the past, it is a celebration of the dream of revolution come true at this special moment of awakening for the humble individuals in small villages.

The Sun Shines on the Sanggan River showed, in its sweeping vision of China in revolution, the vast distance, in both ideology and technique, that Ding Ling had traversed in her writing since her early stories about young women involved in lonely crises of love, sex, and identity. While this literary development confers interest and complexity on Ding Ling's works, it did not assure her continuing status in a volatile revolutionary society. Her prestigious position lasted but a few years. In 1957 she was the prime target of the antirightist drive and was denounced in a nationwide campaign. She was attacked for her superiority complex, for her sexual immorality, for ideological failings, for maligning the peasant masses in her fiction, and for traitorous conspiracy against the party. She was further charged with setting up literature in opposition to party leadership, by subscribing to the bourgeois view that the achieved literary work was an individual creation that could secure for its author profit and fame, a view her critics called her "one-bookism." The party saw it as necessary to wage the struggle against her to "protect the socialist line in art and literature."

Could her literary activities indeed have constituted such a threat? The history of political campaigns against writers in the People's Republic of China — and indeed there have been waves of them since 1949 — is painful to contemplate. Factional feuds, some of which can be traced back to the 1930s in Shanghai, when vituperative debate and adroit quoting out of context became the fashion, were an important continuing impetus. The campaigns were exploited as opportunities for rivals to take over literary journals and propel themselves into high positions in the cultural bureaucracy.

There were of course genuine ideological uncertainties over the latitude that should be conceded to such refractory and extravagant pursuits as literature and art under conditions of scarcity. Should not only the literature that could clearly demonstrate its usefulness for the attainment of collective goals be accepted? Utilitarianism and philistine moralism, which historically have been the enemies of art everywhere, found in revolutionary China a powerful ally in fundamentalist political ideology. In Ding Ling's case this mix of motives was reinforced by the expediency of making an example of one of China's most prestigious writers.

One suspicion often voiced is that Ding Ling was a more obvious target because she was a woman. While this may be difficult to ascertain, once the campaign was under way it followed the familiar pattern of criticizing a woman not so much for what she writes or does, but for what she is, for what is presumed to be her personal character, which then is quickly narrowed to the question of sexual conduct. Sexual conduct becomes a relevant and inflammatory issue because the double standard makes women particularly vulnerable. Ding Ling's stories were combed for her glorification of sexual immorality; they were cited as further evidence of what were claimed to be their author's own violations of the chastity code. Her specific feminist concerns were criticized as divisive and undermining of collective goals, for it was held it was the reactionary class that suppressed women's liberation, not men in general.

The sessions of mass criticism against Ding Ling went on from June 6 to September 27, 1957, but apparently she was not repentant enough and in 1958 she was expelled from the party. Information about where she was or what had happened to her did not emerge until after her official rehabilitation twenty-one years later.

She had been sent to a state farm for labor reform in the Great Northern Wilderness, the northeast corner of China just south of the Heilongjiang River bordering Siberia. The first year she acquired much expertise in raising poultry while trying to adjust to the harsh climate and frontier conditions. Her situation improved somewhat when she was given the task of teaching adult literacy classes. Although there seemed little chance of publication, she did try to take up writing again. But with the onset of the Cultural Revolution in 1966, her "days of fear" began. Having been labeled a rightist, she was an available target for anyone during this period of near anarchy when ideological fanaticism held sway. Her home, a thatched hut seven meters square, was raided dozens of times by groups of Red Guards; all her manuscripts, diaries, notes, scraps of paper with a single word were taken away, torn up, irretrievably lost. During "struggle-and-criticism" sessions she suffered much physical abuse. Then she was forced to perform menial labor under the "supervision of the revolutionary masses" for up to fourteen hours a day. In 1970 she was returned to Peking in shackles and put in solitary confinement in the notorious Qincheng prison, where she remained for five years. Only the day after her release in 1975 did she learn that her husband, Chen Ming, had spent that same time in the same prison, one cell away. After three more years of restricted freedom in a mountain village in Shanxi, she was allowed to return to Peking.

Official rehabilitation in 1979 finally permitted Ding Ling to resume her writing career. The ban on her books was lifted; both new and old works were again available to the public. A piece about a model heroine, written in 1966 but destroyed during the Cultural Revolution and then rewritten, was published in July 1979. It was her first work to appear since 1956. To make up for lost time, she has been very prolific, writing critical essays, a sequel to her land reform novel, and reminiscences of her friends, many of whom she discovered had died during her imprisonment. In the fall of 1981 she came to the United States for the first time, spending two months at the International Writing Program at the University of Iowa and two months touring and lecturing on college campuses. Her tour included a talk at the University of Michigan and, incredibly it seems when I recall the circumstances at the time I began to write about her, a stay at my house in Ann Arbor.

She had promised me this visit, she and her husband Chen Ming, when we said good-bye in China at the end of my stay there in 1981.

I had decided that I should go to China when I unexpectedly learned, just as I was concluding my dissertation, that its subject was after all still alive. My objective was first to see her, of course, and to find out what had happened during those twenty years of silence. I wanted to check over and bring up to date my analytical study of her fiction and perhaps collect material for a full-scale biography. I applied for a grant from the Committee on Scholarly Communication with the People's Republic of China (which is funded by the National Endowment for the Humanities) and, as a research scholar in its National Program for Advanced Study and Research in China, went for six months. I wrote my first letter to Ding Ling when I knew that I had been accepted in the program and, to fulfill the terms of the fantasy, when I learned that my manuscript had been accepted for publication. Her answer was very, very long in coming because, as she explained, she had been recuperating outside

Peking from a mastectomy and, because she was enclosing a recent book about her, her letter was not sent airmail.

I had left China before the revolution to attend college in the United States and, except for a month in 1973 when I accompanied a U.S. scientific delegation, was now returning after an absence of thirty-three years. Eager as I was, I had many misgivings about the trip. How would I, an apostate outsider by now, be received by a writer who was attempting to reestablish herself in a somewhat liberalized yet still unstable political situation? I had anxieties about how I would find Ding Ling, now that I had learned about her surgery. She was seventy-seven, her problems of ill health and old age exacerbated by the hardships she had suffered in labor reform and solitary imprisonment. In spite of the cordiality of her letter, I was acutely conscious of the basic presumptuousness of my pre-senting myself to her at all.

I arrived in Peking to find that Ding Ling was some three thousand kilometers away in a convalescent home for party cadres on an island off the southeastern coast of China. I cannot describe the mixture of expectation and anxiety I felt as I took the seventy-two-hour train ride that passed through seven provinces. It was late March, and I was journeying from winter to spring, watching the seasons change rapidly through the train window — from the bleak, brown landscape of the north to the lush greenness of the semitropical south, where the rice seedlings were already tall enough to be transplanted. Ding Ling's husband, Chen Ming, was there to meet the train, but when I saw Ding Ling the emotional scenario I had so often envisioned for our first meeting flew out the window, in part because I had forgotten all my prepared speeches and in part because of the officious presence of the cadre from the municipal foreign office. The next day, however (and I do not know who suggested or arranged it), I was moved from my hotel for overseas Chinese visitors into a building adjacent to Ding Ling's, and so began my "magic mountain" existence as an inmate in the convales-cent home.

Mornings were always set aside by Ding Ling for her writing. Every afternoon at three o'clock, when she had had her nap and was done with her various therapies, I was to go over to talk. She said graciously that she would answer questions, but she never "authorized" a biography, constantly reiterating that an author's personal life was much less important than the relationship between the literary works and their time. An indefatigable talker with a vivid memory, she would describe in memorable detail even the weather conditions surrounding events that had taken place when she was a child. As I listened, I was deeply moved by the sense of being involved simultaneously in two kinds of time: The experiences within her fiction that had for so long taken on a contemporary reality for me were now being placed within the context of a long personal history, distanced yet made all the more intimately true. There were moments when she seemed to relive as she talked emotions that had gone into the writing of stories forty or fifty years before. How could I possibly take in, much less set down, even a small portion of that rich, intense, and fully lived life of which I was just beginning to get a glimpse?

Our stay at the convalescent home was cut short because Ding Ling had to return to Peking for the memorial service of the writer Mao Dun. We took the train north. The city by then was resplendent with flowering trees. I interviewed writers, publishers, and critics, met other Ding Ling scholars, and scoured libraries trying to read everything she had ever written, including short pieces in ephemeral periodicals or local newspapers, pieces that she herself had long forgotten. In June I went to Shanghai to do the same things. Then toward the end of my stay, another unexpected yet perfectly timed opportunity arose.

Ding Ling decided to visit the state farms where she had spent her twelve years in exile and labor reform, and she thought I could join her entourage of writers and editors for the trip. But because I was a foreign citizen my application for a travel permit to this closed border area was turned down. I reapplied, wrote letters, and, somehow, someone in the Public Security Office relented. About a week before Ding Ling and her group were to leave, I was told, in just enough time to join them, that I had been given permission to go along.

All of us were most anxious to learn something about Ding Ling's experiences while she had been in the Great Northern Wilderness, to get a visual impression of this unique place, and to talk with those who had known her and what it had been like there during the unimaginable time when the Chinese revolution was living through its darkest nightmare. For the twenty days that we traveled and lived intimately together, often in the harsh conditions of a still developing frontier area, I gained some insight into the dynamics of small-group relationships in contemporary Chinese society. But even more instructive was the opportunity to observe the charismatic personality of Ding Ling, as she greeted the people who had known her during this difficult period of her life. Those who had maltreated her were not much in evidence now that she was returning as a celebrity — there were a couple of reporters and a TV camera crew in our group. Those who had befriended her and risked persecution themselves to help her were the ones she wanted me to meet. Most of what we learned about her suffering during her years of exile was not obtained from her but from talking to her acquaintances there. Because Ding Ling had determined — and her return visit to her place of exile was in itself an indication of that determination — to see the horrendous experience of the past twenty-one years in as positive a light as possible.

She sees her unjust persecution by the Party as a temporary, although extended aberration. Now having acknowledged its mistakes about her and other "rightists" as well, the Party can be restored at last to its authentic self, as a true carrier of the revolutionary ideal. Ding Ling's adoption of this attitude, difficult as it may be for us to sympathize with, is no doubt psychologically necessary for her to come to terms with what happened to her in light of her lifelong commitment to the Party, a commitment that had already, in the days of her youth, required the sacrifice of her husband. Were the martyrdom of Hu Yepin and her own subsequent pain and perilous struggle to have been for nothing? Her positive stance also has much to do with her self-image as a writer and the writer's vital role in Chinese society. What became evident to me in our travels was the tremendous moral authority, inconceivable in America, that the writer radiated. Without an alternative ideological system — and there is none visible on the horizon for China today — Ding Ling believes it is up to the writer to affirm the goals of the system that exists.

I felt privileged indeed to be permitted to witness these scenes of the writer among the people, to share the emotional reunions and the memories of past injustices and suffering. Why had I been granted this privilege? I believe that Ding Ling gave a partial answer to my unvoiced question when, during a welcoming dinner at the first state farm we visited, she explained to our hosts who I was: "She is Chinese, not just because of her roots and origin, but in her thinking and feelings. Otherwise I would not have brought her along." Surrounded though I was by a tableful of strangers, I could hardly hold back the tears these sudden remarks brought on, because I took them to be a statement of confidence in me and of what she thought we had in common. She meant, I believe, that I could in some way be trusted to understand the reality of recent Chinese history, what people there had all so agonizingly passed through, a history in which, because of my long absence from China, I had never participated. She meant too that I could be trusted to accept and understand her representation of that reality. This national or cultural identity, which could not but include the political system now embodying it, was her way of expressing what constituted our essential bond.

My quest for Ding Ling has ended up contradicting what her reputation abroad is principally based on. She has been portrayed as a literary dissident who has courageously stood for artistic independence in opposition to party control or a feminist whose life exemplifies what has been called the "uneasy alliance" between a feminist consciousness and a socialist revolution. Ding Ling has refused to make it easy for her Western admirers by going along with these perceptions of her. To accept them would be to contravene her abiding commitment to China's revolution. She continues to say that she is first a member of the Communist party and only second a writer. She had contemplated leaving out of her collected works, when they were republished in 1981, her essay "Thoughts on March 8," which has been taken up by feminist movements in France, Japan, Iran, and Mexico, among others. It is ironic that she should have considered omitting a piece for which she is so well known. In spite of all disclaimers, her life and work, as I have tried to stress, have an undeniable message for women and therefore deserve to be known.

Having satisfied some basic academic requirements with a study of the relationship between ideology and narrative in Ding Ling's fiction, my next project, an attempt to reach that perhaps mythical intelligent lay reader, will be a less scholarly narrative of her life, surely one of the most dramatic of our time. It was fortunate, as I told her, that our discussions, while enabling me to fill in useful details, had not necessitated any revisions in my interpretations of her fiction. But my trip to China has taught me how inadequate liberal Western notions are when applied to Ding Ling's story. Through writing about her I had already been restored to work; through visiting her I had returned, in more ways than one, to my country. If our mutual understanding is indeed based on her perception of me as someone who has, in spite of everything, remained Chinese, then I should ask myself what that cultural identity means to me. I have learned that to understand more fully the meaning of her life in its Chinese context, I must at the same time rethink my own.

Notes

1. Ida Lee Mei, *Chinese Womanhood: A Small Gallery of Chinese Women* (Taipei, Taiwan: China Academy, 1982). A second book, an autobiographical account of her work as an educator in China, to be published by the same publisher, is now in press.
2. Ding Ling, "Sanbajie you gan" (Thoughts on March 8), *Jiefang ribao* (*Liberation Daily*), 9 March 1942, p. 4. A translation of this article is included in Gregor Benton, "The Yenan Literary Opposition," *New Left Review* 92 (July–August 1975): 93–106.

The Stephen children, Thoby, Adrian, Vanessa, and Virginia

Louise DeSalvo

Louise DeSalvo

A PORTRAIT OF THE *PUTTANA* AS A MIDDLE-AGED WOOLF SCHOLAR

The year is 1975.

I am thirty-two years old, married, the mother of two small children, a Ph.D. candidate, on a charter flight to England with a friend to do research on Virginia Woolf at the University of Sussex in Falmer. This is the first time in my whole life that I am going away by myself. I have no idea where Falmer is, except that it is near Brighton. We have no hotel reservations. We have no idea how we will get to Brighton. But we are gloriously drunk on our third sherry, free from the responsibility of our children for awhile. (We have already had enough sherry so that each child can have her or his own little sherry bottle as a souvenir when we return home.) We are, at long last, grown-ups, going to do *real* research. The next generation of Woolf scholars, in incubation. We are formidable.

★

I come from a family, from a cultural heritage, where women simply don't go away to do things separately from men. That is not to say that men don't go away to do things separately from women. They do. And often. But in the land of my forebears, women sit around and wait for their men. Or they work very hard and watch their children and wait for their men. Or they watch their children and wait for their men. Or they make a sumptuous meal and they work very hard and watch their children and wait for their men. But they don't go anywhere without their men. Or do anything for themselves alone without their men. Except complain. To their children or to anyone else who will listen to them. About their men and about their bad luck in having been born female.

A few years ago, I decided, like everyone else, to explore my ethnic roots. It lasted a very short time. I bought a pasta machine. Learned how to combine the ingredients for pasta, to roll out the dough, and cut it. Word got out that I was a terrific pasta maker.

Then I began to realize that you can tell how enslaved the women of any country are by the kind of preparation their traditional foods require. Any recipe that begins "Take a mortar and pestle . . ." now drives me into a feminist frenzy. Well, pasta making is something like that. Women who really care about their families make it fresh every day. Purists insist that if the sacred pasta dough is touched by metal pasta machines (i.e., twentieth-century labor-saving devices), it becomes slightly slippery — a quality in pasta that is akin to infidelity in wives. Oh yes, I now remember what women who do anything without their husbands are called. *Puttana.* Whores. I remember hearing stories in my childhood about how women like that were stoned to death in the old country.

Well, given a background like that, you can imagine the way I felt as we flew high above the Atlantic. There I was, a *puttana,* alone at last.

★

Early on in my work on Virginia Woolf, I thought that I would devote the rest of my life to carefully considered scholarly essays and books on every aspect of her life and art. Those were the heroine-worship days when I blanched at the sight of her manuscripts, when I did not dare to think that she had an outhouse, much less that she and Leonard used the typescripts of her novels instead of toilet tissue, that she could be hardy enough or human enough to walk across the Downs in her beloved Sussex. I saw her as an earlier generation of critics had painted her for me — frail, weak, crazy, tortured, looking out of windows, vacant, probing the inside of her troubled psyche, like the wistful adolescent on the edge of the family in the picture I have chosen for this volume.

I loved the sight of myself, briefcase in hand, walking up the steps of The New York Public Library, past the lions Patience and Fortitude (I would have preferred lionesses), thinking that the kid who grew up on the streets of Hoboken, New Jersey, was now walking past the painting of Milton's daughters taking down the immortal words of his verse, now walking down the third floor corridor to the Berg Collection, now pressing the buzzer. And they were actually letting me into the sacred recess where I would soon sit next to all those famous literary scholars whose work I had read and do work of my own.

The American Dream.

And as I sat there, beginning my work, I thought that if only I could have the good fortune to be able to sit over a glass of sherry at the Algonquin, or even over a cup of coffee at Tad's Steak House down the block, with someone really famous to talk about Virginia

Woolf, life would be so sweet, so very sweet, and I would ask for
nothing more in this universe.

★

I got into Woolf scholarship quite by accident. (Or so I thought at
the time.) When I was in graduate school at New York University, I
took a course with the Woolf scholar Mitchell Leaska. He was in the
throes of his work on *The Pargiters,* his edition of the earlier draft of
The Years. I was enthralled with his classes. I'll never forget the day
that he brought in his transcription of Woolf's holograph, the
handwritten draft of that novel. I changed my mind about what I
would be doing with my scholarly life in the moments it took him to
read to us from Woolf's earlier version of *The Years.* Here was a more
political, less guarded Woolf. I had never known that earlier versions of literary texts were available. It had never occurred to me before
that one could inquire into the process of the creation of a novel and
learn about the writing process and the process of revision. It sounded
like detective work. It was meticulous. It required stamina. Drive. It
was exciting. I too would be working with manuscripts. I think I
understood that I required a grand consuming passion in a project.

I soon decided to work with the manuscript of *The Voyage Out,*
Woolf's first novel, because I wanted to catch Virginia Woolf in her
beginnings where I thought she might be least guarded.

★

The Voyage Out is about Rachel Vinrace, a young, inexperienced
woman, who accompanies her father on a trip to South America. On
her father's ship, the *Euphrosyne,* she resumes a relationship with
her aunt and uncle, Helen and Ridley Ambrose, and she meets
Richard Dalloway, a former Member of Parliament, and his wife
Clarissa. Rachel becomes involved with two parental surrogates —
Helen and Clarissa — but the relationship with Clarissa is complicated because Rachel is sexually attracted to Richard. During a storm
at sea, Rachel and he embrace. That night she has a dream that she is
being pursued.

Later, when she is at Santa Marina, a South American port city,
she meets Terence Hewet, who is spending his holiday there. They
fall in love and decide to marry. But both are extremely reluctant
lovers. Rachel dies of a mysterious illness before the couple can marry.

What I had no way of knowing when I decided to work on *The
Voyage Out* was that I would have enormous difficulty keeping the
problems that I was having in my life separate from the issues that

Woolf was discussing in the novel. I had reached that moment of
sexual reevaluation that often occurs at about thirty. Although I was
married, I went through a time when I identified with Rachel so
strongly that I believed I shared her distrust of intimacy. It was
simpler for me to see myself in terms of Woolf's character than it was
to look at my own problems. I vacillated between thinking that
Rachel — and by extension I — were typical of all women, and
thinking that her hesitations (and mine) were pathological. It took
many years for me to separate myself from Rachel Vinrace. It took
many years for me to understand that part of the reason for Rachel's
hesitation was her submerged rage at the misogyny and brutality of
the men in her life — all disguised through the artifice of civilization, to be sure, but there nonetheless. In the process of separating
myself from Rachel, I learned not to make disparaging judgments
about Rachel's behavior — or mine — but to look for the causes of
that behavior in familial and societal histories. I also saw that I was
letting this very close identification with Rachel hold me back, keep
me in check, because my work was making me feel very powerful.
And I was terrified of feeling powerful.

I wake up in the middle of the night from a dream. The dream is
easy to describe, difficult to comprehend. Ishtar — the many-
breasted goddess — with a face vaguely like that of Virginia Woolf
but resembling my mother, in profile, has placed her hands under
my armpits and has picked me up. Her face is impassive. She does
not look at me, does not recognize me, stares past me. She begins
shaking me — not violently, but powerfully and rhythmically. As
she shakes me, all the things that define me as a woman fall off.
They form a pile beneath my feet. As she continues to shake me, still
staring beyond me, impassively and without emotion, what is left of
me begins to shrivel into the baby doll that I remember having in my
childhood. The only openings I have, now, are the hole in the
middle of the little red mouth where you put the toy bottle and the
one where the water runs out, between the legs. I begin saying, in
the doll's voice that I remember, "Mama, mama." Ishtar stares
impassively ahead. But she stops shaking me.

★

Working on Woolf's composition of *The Voyage Out* was my first
long project. One that would take years. It terrified me and it thrilled
me. Sometimes I would feel immensely powerful, feel that I, single-
handedly, might change the course of Woolf scholarship. Or I
would feel impotent, wondering how could I make any contribution
to our knowledge of Woolf.

I learned what it is humanly possible to do in one day; what one cannot do; that one must trust the times when no work is getting done, because it is in those fallow periods that the unconscious mind is working. I had to change the way I thought about time. I had to scale down my expectations to a human level. All of this was very hard for me to do. Every time I sat down to the project, my infantile power fantasies reared their ugly heads. I always thought that I would get more done in one day than it was possible to do. Then my feelings of potency would turn into feelings of powerlessness and despair. I slowly learned that the work could proceed only as quickly as it could proceed. (I have not entirely learned that lesson yet.) I learned that I have the same trouble that anyone else has in working, in writing comprehensible sentences, in revising them, but that if I worked every day, the work would get done. I gradually realized what working on *The Voyage Out* for seven years must have been like for Virginia Woolf. I too was working on a project that was taking a very long time. There was the temptation, too, to work constantly, without interruption, to get it done more quickly. There was the temptation to work incessantly — days, nights, weekends — at the mountain of manuscripts, at the letters, diaries, and journals that Woolf had written while composing the novel.

From time to time, my husband reminds me of a moment in the days preceding our marriage. He was at work. I was at our apartment. The place was filthy. I was trying to clean it so that we could move in. All the stores in the neighborhood were closed because of some holiday. I decided that I would clean all the tiles in the bathroom. The only thing I had that would do the job was a toothbrush. So, instead of waiting for him to come back to help me, instead of waiting for the next day to get a scrub brush that would speed the work, I took the toothbrush to the tiles. When he came to pick me up, I was exhausted and miserable, but also triumphant because I had finished.

At the beginning, much of my work on Virginia Woolf's composition of *The Voyage Out* was like that day with the toothbrush.

★

One day, after two years of work, I went to the Berg Collection to begin work, as usual, and discovered to my chagrin that the manuscripts of the novel were not now in the order in which Virginia Woolf had written them. Why I had not noticed this before is beyond me. The Berg Catalogue clearly states that each of the manuscript groups was composed of various drafts. On the day I realized that I would have to sort, sequence, and date the thousand or so pages of manuscript, I became slightly sick. I even believed that I was being punished for having been grandiose in my expectations. I knew nothing about dating manuscripts.

I spent that summer taking an inventory of the manuscripts, noting the watermark on each sheet, the color of the ink, how many perforations it had — anything that might help me sort the manuscripts into drafts. Although I read about the dating of modern manuscripts and certainly learned from the experience of experts, I was also secretly grateful that I had voraciously read Nancy Drew detective books when I was a girl, that I had learned, through her, to be alert to every possible clue. I went back and reread the thousand or so letters that I had read before, searching now for clues to the dating of those sheets.

One night, at about four in the morning, I awakened from a dream in which I saw Woolf using pages from earlier drafts of the novel in later drafts. I had overlooked that possibility. I suddenly realized that if I used the watermarks as a guide, assuming that Woolf had used different kinds of paper during the several years the novel was in progress, I might be able to sort the manuscripts into drafts. I also realized that there was a code to the two sets of page numbers that were on several hundred sheets, now scattered throughout the manuscripts. The paginated sheets might represent one draft — one set of page numbers indicating the placement of the sheet within the draft, the other, the page number within a given chapter.

There it was, happening to me — my very own "Ah ha" experience. Just like in the textbooks. I rushed upstairs to my desk and in the space of an hour or so, I had figured out the order of four earlier drafts of the novel. Now I could proceed to study the stages of the novel's development, although I still had to date the drafts.

One morning, on the way to the Berg, I discovered that I had forgotten my see-through ruler, the one I used to measure the sheets of the manuscript. I was passing a stationery store, hesitated, but went in and bought another one. On that day, as I was reading Woolf's letters to Violet Dickinson, searching for clues to date the manuscripts that I had already sorted, I was fiddling with the ruler. I put it beside the letter I was reading and suddenly realized that the sheet was the same size as the paper Woolf had used in one of the drafts. I quickly checked the watermark. Sure enough. The letter was dated. That accident enabled me to date, to my satisfaction, one of the major drafts of the novel.

Now I was ready to do what I had always wanted to do: analyze the composition of the novel in conjunction with the events that were occurring in Woolf's life.

I remember sitting in the Berg, surrounded by a thousand sheets of paper, while the rest of the world was swimming and sunning themselves, thinking, "This is where I belong. I am in my element."

★

As I recorded the progress of Virginia Woolf's days to figure out what she was doing as she was writing *The Voyage Out*, I started realizing that this was one hell of a woman, filled with incredible energy, so different from my original impression of her. Reading about her life in London, her visits to the British Museum, the books she read, the jaunts down to Sussex on weekends, the trips to St. Ives, to Wells, to the Lizard, to Lelant, Cornwall, the walks, the work, the lived life, fruitful beyond my wildest imaginings, her engagement with the most important political and social issues of her day, her teaching of working-class people, I began to revise my picture of her and my hopes for myself. I decided that it would be foolish of me to spend endless days alone inside libraries working on Woolf when the great woman of my dreams had spent no small portion of hers walking around the countryside, cultivating important relationships, particularly with women, taking tea, learning to bake bread, teaching, getting involved in politics, becoming an essayist, a novelist, integrating work and pleasure, and having what seemed to me, in contrast to my confined scholarly life, a hell of a good time.

That's when I bought my first pair of hiking boots and started walking, first around the lower reaches of New York State and then, at long last, through Woolf's beloved Sussex and Cornwall and later through Kent, Cumbria, Northumbria, Yorkshire. I retraced the trips she took while she was writing *The Voyage Out*; visited the places she visited; read the books she read; began having important friendships of my own with Woolf scholars; started teaching; began writing essays; started writing poetry; wrote a novel.

In 1975 I was on my way from Brighton to Sevenoaks to see Knole, Vita Sackville-West's ancestral home, delighted by the likelihood that Virginia Woolf herself had travelled these very roads to see Vita Sackville-West when she was writing *Orlando*. We had just come through a small stretch of moor that smelled powerfully of damp and peat when we saw a road sign that read, simply, "Sevenoaks," the village in which Knole is located. When I saw that sign, I began weeping, inexplicably and uncontrollably, filled with a sense of myself newly born, capable of working and of having fun, capable of enjoying my life's work. This was released somehow by that sign and the sense it inspired of the flesh-and-blood reality of the Virginia

Woolf who had passed, a long time ago, by that very spot to go see a friend, another woman.

I thought that I would like to write about these two women, about their friendship, about their love affair, about their work. I thought about how the creative act has been misconstrued as a solitary, solipsistic act and how we must correct that misapprehension; we must write about the creative act as it is nurtured by loving friendships.

★

1976.

I am sitting outside a speech therapy room, balancing Lyly's *Euphues: The Anatomy of Wit* on one knee and a yellow pad of paper and some note cards on the other. What I am trying to figure out as I sit here, waiting for my four-year-old son, Justin, to finish his session, is whether any part of Virginia Woolf's conception of *The Voyage Out* may have been due to her knowing this work. After all, she *did* say that *Euphues* was the germ of the English novel. Is there any evidence that *Euphues* may have been the germ for hers?

I open the book. I am delighted to find that there is a character called Lucilla in the work and that, for Euphues, she is an inconstant woman (another *puttana*). In Virginia Woolf's 1908 draft of her novel, one of the central characters is called Lucilla, and I become convinced, as I sit here, that it was no accident.

I glance, occasionally, through the one-way mirror and watch the therapist working with Justin. Every time he sounds a letter correctly, which is virtually impossible for him to do, he gets an M&M candy. Today, because they are working on *s*, the most difficult sound for him to produce, because he cannot hear it, he is angry because he hasn't gotten very many M&Ms and he *loves* M&Ms and this is the only place where he is allowed to have them (the therapist's amazingly successful strategy). I know I am going to have my hands full when his session is over. Maybe an ice cream cone will help. Chocolate chip mint, his favorite.

★

A while ago we had been told that Justin's hearing is severely impaired. Or rather, *I* had been told. One of the teachers at his nursery school had called and told me that Justin responds to commands only after he sees other kids doing something. I was too unconscious in those days of my own needs to understand that taking your child to a specialist to find out whether he is handicapped is not something you should do by yourself, even if you are a tough woman.

And so there I was, on a rainy day, in the elevator, on the way to the appointment my husband had made with the specialist, by myself, holding Justin's little hand, thinking, maybe he *is* hearing impaired and not emotionally disturbed. I had been secretly afraid that this extraordinarily difficult child, who had been an absolute angel as a baby, who never cried, who slept all night almost from the beginning, had become the way he was because I had gone back to graduate school. I shared my private fantasy with no one, partially because to share it would have been to admit that something might really be terribly wrong, and in admitting that something might be terribly wrong, I might have to confront my fantasy that I had caused it. Sitting in the doctor's office, holding Justin on my lap, I listened as the doctor said, "Yeah, we seem to have a deaf one on our hands."

I will never forget those words. I will never forgive that doctor his callousness. I will never forget choking back my tears, swallowing my vomit, as I sat, by myself, holding this child on my lap, thinking, I must not let this child see me crying about him, not here, and not yet, hating myself, hating the doctor, hating my fate yet again.

But on the way back to the car, we walked, Justin and I, through a rose garden adjacent to the hospital, and, by now, the rain had stopped, and the sun had come out, and the sun was hot, and the roses were so beautiful, and Justin tugged at my hand and looked up at me, as I touched his tangle of red curls, and I thought to myself, "What do I do now? What's to become of him now?" And he said in his garble that only I could understand, "Mommy, mommy, so happy, the sun," and I knelt down, and hugged him, and cried and cried and cried, but I knew he was going to be all right, and I knew that it hadn't been my fault.

What strikes me now, although it did not strike me that day in 1976, is the insane incongruity of my reading *Euphues,* the most esoteric and highly cultivated prose in the English language, while my son struggled to utter his first comprehensible sounds, while a Vietnam veteran, a multiple amputee, struggled, in the room next to Justin, to let go of his rage and speak again, while a woman who had had cancer of the larynx struggled, in the room on the opposite side, to belch up her first sound. What I do know now was that taking Justin there day after day and week after week, admitting that he *was* hearing impaired, and seeing people who were so much more severely handicapped than he was, helped me.

In the acknowledgments to my dissertation (which became my first book), I wrote, in a kind of code, about how Justin had been a model "of persistence and patience for me to emulate," how, during the years when my study was in progress, I had watched "Justin learning to express himself." And I printed, in very large letters that he could understand (because by now, in 1980, he was eight years old, and chattering away, and able to read), in his very own copy of my first book (which he insisted that I give him), "Thanksgiving Day, 1980. For Justin — Who was near me while I was writing this whole book and who learned a lot in that time. I love you. Mom."

What I didn't write to him overtly then, but what I write now, is how much I *learned* from him; how, in watching the struggles of a little boy with a voice that no one could understand, I learned to be less angry about the impediments to my own expression. Finding my own voice was, after all, not so difficult a task compared to what I saw him and others experiencing. If he had the guts, surely I did too. After all, he was made out of the same stuff that I was. As he found his voice, I too found mine.

★

I finished my dissertation and converted it into a book, *Virginia Woolf's First Voyage: A Novel in the Making*. My next big project became the editing of an early version of *The Voyage Out* (*Melymbrosia*), one of the versions I had studied and written about in the dissertation. An early version of the first novel of one of the greatest literary stylists of this century might prove useful, not only to scholars but also to common readers. I had been immensely excited when I first read through the pages of this submerged draft, seeing how different it was from the version that Woolf chose to publish. It was more radical politically, more lesbian, more contemptuous of men.

The work of editing the draft went like this: I would go to the Berg Collection and hand-copy pages of Woolf's typescript of the earlier version. There were 414 pages that had to be copied. I could copy about 15 or so pages on a good day, but I always expected myself to do better, to do more, as if I were in competition with my own limitations. The work taught me what it was like to be a medieval scribe. It was dreadful. The work couldn't be done from Xeroxes because there were many sets of corrections on the sheets in various ink colors, made at different times, and I was using only the earliest ones. After I copied a day's pages I would take my transcription home and type it. Then I would take my pages back to the Berg and proofread them against the original. Again I would take the typescript home, make corrections, then bring the corrected typescript back to the Berg and check that the corrections were correct. Next I would write textual notes, indicating where my text was different from Woolf's. Then I would type the textual notes; proof them against the original; make changes; bring the changes back to make sure they were correct; and so forth. I began to imagine myself in purgatory.

I come to the breakfast table one morning during this time, trying to shake the effects of a night of work. My twelve-year-old son Jason (he was six when I began), usually cheerful in the morning, is sitting at the table in a foul, rotten mood. He glares at me. I ask him what is troubling him. He tells me that they had a discussion in his English class about the generation gap. Do I realize that he is the only child in the class who sees his mother less than he sees his father? Do I realize that my work is killing him? That he hates it? That he can't stand to have me up at my typewriter when he comes home from school? That the sound of the typewriter keeps him up all night? That he needs his sleep? He begins sobbing. I want to hold him but he won't allow it. I recall that the only time this child has ever had an uncontrollable temper tantrum was on the day he overheard me talking about beginning my second book. He looked at me and said, "Second book?" Then he threw himself off his chair onto the floor, began shrieking and beating his fists against the floor. When I calmed him enough so that he could talk, he told me that he thought that when I finished the first book, he would have me back again.

I understand why he is so angry. My work takes me away from him far more often than he would like; yet at twelve, he is beginning to want to separate himself from me. I ask him if he thinks anything that I have done has rubbed off on him. I love his compositions. He writes the most wonderful works of fiction. I am delighted, thinking that something of me has lodged itself in him. He says no, emphatically no. Nothing at all about my work has ever done him any good.

He calms down as quickly as he has flared up. He asks if I'd be interested in hearing the latest thing he has written. I say I am. He pulls a sheet of paper out of his notebook. It is the biography of an imaginary character, John C. Lectica. As Jason reads it to me, I think to myself "A chip off the old block."

Autumn 1978.

I receive a copy of *Virginia Woolf Miscellany* in the mail. There is an article by Quentin Bell, entitled "Proposed Policy on Virginia

Woolf's Unpublished Material." (An editor later tells me that originally it had been entitled "The Bottom of the Barrel" as in "scraping the bottom of the barrel.")

It reads, in part: "A short time ago a reputable scholar suggested the publication of an earlier version of one of the novels [I am sure Bell is referring to my work on *Melymbrosia*], not only because it would be of interest to other scholars but because it could be offered as — in effect — a new novel to the 'generalist Woolf reader.' This, I must say, arouses acute misgivings — suppose that the reader agrees with Virginia in condemning the earlier version, suppose that it is below her usual standard? Then, surely it is unfair to give it currency. Some such deflation of values follows any inflation of published matter [and] must surely be apprehended. Scratch the bottom of the barrel and you will come up with impurities."

In the last six years of my life, I have probably spent more time working with Virginia Woolf's works than I have doing anything else. My work has become more important than my life. As I face the possibility that *Melymbrosia* might never be published, I must look back over my life to try to salvage something of myself, to try to see clearly what of my past I have tried to bury in my work.

★

I am thirteen years old. I have begun my adolescence with a vengeance. I am not shaping up to be the young woman I'm supposed to be. I am not docile. I am not sweet. I am certainly not quiet. And, as my father has told me dozens of times, I am not agreeable: if he says something is green, I am sure to respond that it is orange. I have mastered every conceivable method of turning my household into turmoil. I have devised a method of looking up at the ceiling when my father lectures me that instantly drives him into a frenzy.

In the middle of one of these fairly frequent outbursts, I run out of the house, feeling that I am choking, the tears hot on my cheeks. It is nighttime. I have no place to go. But I keep running. There are welcoming lights a few blocks away. It is the local library. I run up the stairs. I run up to the reading room with its engulfing brown leather chairs, pull an encyclopedia down from the shelf, and pretend to read so that I won't be kicked out. It is cool and it is quiet. My rage subsides. I think that if there is a heaven, surely it must resemble a library. I think that if there is a god, surely she must be a librarian.

★

It is 1957.

I am fourteen years old, standing behind the window of the bakery where I work to earn my spending money. Inside the bakery, I have to control my appetite or I will eat everything in sight and become grotesque and obese. You can't let yourself do that because boys only like attractive girls and attractive girls are always slim. What I do inside the bakery is fold paper boxes before I put the pastries and cakes inside. And then I tie up the boxes with the red and white string that always tears into my flesh. What I'm doing is putting my appetitive self, which I am afraid will run out of control, into neatly packaged, antiseptic, pure boxes — containing it and tying it up.

Across the street, through the window, I see my friends playing endless games that involve laughing, touching, rolling on the grass. I am behind the plate-glass window, looking at life, looking at them having fun, locked away, earning money by putting buns in bags and cakes in boxes.

On Halloween, children come and paint the plate-glass window. They paint witches and goblins in black and in primary colors. Now I can't even see what is going on in the park across the street. But I still put the buns in boxes. It never occurs to me to even fantasy breaking through the window while I'm working or to wash the paint away. Or, more simply, to open the door and cross the street to the playground. Work is work. And work permits no play. I have to work. That is the way it is. Opening the door to let in the sound of laughter while working, crossing that street to the playground after work, learning to enjoy work and learning to be able to play will take many years. And psychoanalysis. And work on Virginia Woolf.

★

Autumn 1963.

I am a senior at Douglass College. In 1963 Douglass College is the kind of school a bright young working-class woman can afford. Douglass, I think, is filled with brilliant women, and I have never

seen brilliant women before. I have studied Shakespeare with Doris
Falk, the novel with Anna Wells, philosophy with Amelie Rorty. I
now have Twentieth-Century Fiction with Carol Smith.

Carol Smith is lecturing on Virginia Woolf's *To the Lighthouse*. She
is talking about the relationship between Mr. and Mrs. Ramsay in
"The Window" section of the novel. I have never in my life heard
such genius. I am taking notes, watching her talk, and watching her
belly. She is very pregnant. She is wearing a beige maternity dress. I
take down every word, while watching to see when the baby she is
pregnant with will kick her again.

I learn to love Virginia Woolf. I observe that it is possible to be a
woman, to be brilliant, to be working, to be happy, and to be
pregnant. And all at the same time.

★

I am interviewed about how an Italian-American woman like me
became a Woolf scholar. I search my memory, think of studying
with Carol Smith, and suddenly remember my fascination with the
figure of Cam Ramsay in *To the Lighthouse*. Cam Ramsay, the child
Mrs. Ramsay virtually ignores, so busy is she with her son James;
Cam Ramsay, the child who is "wild and fierce." The child who
clenches her fist and stamps her feet. The child who is always
running away, running away. The child who will not let anyone
invade the private space that she has created to protect herself in this
family with a tyrannical father who strikes out with a beak of brass.

I remember my own adolescence. Could it be that I have seen
something of myself in Cam those many years ago and that in trying
to understand the relationship between Cam Ramsay and her
creator, Virginia Woolf, I am also trying to learn something about
my own past? Aren't I now in the middle of a long essay about
Virginia Woolf as an adolescent, reading her 1897 diary, a tiny
brown gilt leather volume, with a lock and a key, that must be read
with a magnifying glass, so tiny and spidery is the hand, an essay
that has given me more satisfaction to write than anything I have
written yet about Virginia Woolf? And haven't I been stressing
Woolf's capacity to cope, rather than her neurosis, in that difficult
year? Could it be that in concentrating on Woolf's health, I am also
trying to heal myself?

★

1968

I am married, and enduring my husband's medical internship as best I can, on next to no money, with a baby who never sleeps and who cries all the time. Although I am twenty-five, I look fifty. I have deep circles under my eyes. I have no figure. I am still wearing maternity clothes.

I had put my husband through medical school. (According to him, I *helped* put him through medical school — his parents paid his tuition and gave him a small allowance, and I worked as a high school English teacher and paid for everything else.) In that internship year, we came very close to a divorce. Your basic doctor-in-training-meets-gorgeous-nurse-and-wants-to-leave-his-wife-and-small-baby story.

★

One day, I look into the bathroom mirror and decide that I will either kill myself or that I will go back to graduate school and become economically independent as quickly as I can. I look into the medicine chest, thinking that if my husband leaves me with this baby, I will probably be young, gifted, and on welfare. After wondering whether you could kill yourself by taking a year's supply of birth control pills and fantasying that, with the way my luck is running, I might grow some hair on my chest, but I probably wouldn't die, I decide that I will go back to school, get a Ph.D., and go into college teaching. I also realize that I might buy some time by squelching the young-doctor-leaves-his-young-wife-for-nurse script, at least temporarily, by announcing to my husband that if he leaves me, *he* can have the baby. Then he and his sweet young nurse can contemplate how romantic their life together will be with this baby who cries and throws up all the time.

He tells me he doesn't believe that I can part with my child.

I say, "Wanna bet?"

Shortly thereafter, he decides to hang around for a while longer.

★

The way I write this now, the "tough broad" tone I take, is of course a disguise for how hurt I was, for how seriously betrayed I felt. And I really don't know now what I would have done if he *had* left me. Unlike many of my friends, my husband *did* stay. I had done everything I was supposed to do. Clipped coupons. Made casseroles from *Woman's Day* with noodles and chopped meat and cream of mushroom soup for all his friends. I had laughed at the story of how Doctor X had fucked Nurse Y in the linen room adjacent to the O.R. and how the surgeon couldn't figure out where the grunts and groans were coming from, without paying too much attention to how Mrs. X or Nurse Y might feel about having this sexual conquest the subject of our dinner table conversation. And I didn't think at all then about how hospitals institutionalize the sexual and economic servitude of women.

I had done everything you were supposed to do, the way you were supposed to do it, and he still wanted to leave me. And that profound disillusionment, that rage at the preposterous hoax that society tries to play on young women by convincing them that if they do everything right for their men, their men will stay with them forever, stays with me to this day.

I had been a high school teacher early in our marriage, but that wasn't a career. I now wanted a career. And my own money. And access to the public world. I wanted to carry a briefcase. I wanted to carry a briefcase while walking down the path at a college, with students to my right and to my left, engaged in serious, important, intellectual discussions about literature. And I never wanted to depend on a man again as long as I lived.

★

When I first learned that Virginia Woolf had spent seven years in the creation of *The Voyage Out*, her first novel, I thought that surely she must have been mad for that, if for no other reason. But as I carted off copies of *Melymbrosia*, my reconstruction of the earlier version of that novel, to the Editor's Office of The New York Public Library some seven years after *I* had begun working with her novel, I reflected that I have come to share a great deal with this woman. I have come to be a great deal like her in her attitudes toward the male establishment and art and feminism and politics; have learned from living for seven years with her to take the very best from her while managing, through the example of her life and her honesty about it, to avoid the depths of her pain.

She has been very good to me, this woman.

*

In looking back over my life, I realize that my work on Virginia Woolf has helped me make some important changes.

Before I worked on Virginia Woolf, I wasn't a feminist. Before I worked on Virginia Woolf, I didn't know how strong a woman I was. Before I worked on Virginia Woolf, I whined a lot, like my Italian foremothers, about how men got all the breaks and about the ways they abused their women, like I felt I had been abused, but I didn't really understand that there was a social structure that was organized to keep men dominant and women subservient, and I really didn't understand how important it was for women to be economically independent and the potentially horrifying consequences if they were not.

Before I worked on Virginia Woolf, I would ask the young doctors who came to our house for dinner if I could get them another cup of coffee, being careful to wait until there was a break in the conversation. Now my husband, Ernie, and our children — Jason and Justin — get up to cook me breakfast. Virginia Woolf has, in many ways, created a monster in me, and I am proud to give her partial credit for it. I like to think that she would have been pleased that my reading *A Room of One's Own* has been a very important part of my emancipation from the tradition of the suffering woman. Now I am a hellraiser, a spitfire, and I buy and wear "Mean Mother," "Nurture Yourself," and "I Am a Shameless Agitator" buttons. And I have recently started to pump iron (much to the amusement of fifteen-year-old Jason — the would-be writer, the one who used to throw up all the time, who has turned out to be a very nice kid after all — and eleven-year-old Justin, who has something to say about everything I do). But sometimes, when I'm feeling really good and have the time, I make them a bread pudding.

*

I think of what Virginia Woolf has done for our generation of women, of Woolf scholars. I think of what she has taught us.

There are the political and the feminist messages in *A Room of One's Own* and *Three Guineas*. The antiauthoritarian, antipatriarchal stance. The exposure of the inequities between the way men are treated and the way women are treated. The difficulty of being a woman and being a creator. Woolf has unleashed our anger. Allowed us to use it constructively. She has taught us the value of work; the necessity of art; the necessity also of a feminist politics. She has taught us to express ourselves as women — in our lives, in our work, in our art.

Woolf was interested in the writer behind the work, in what she or he was like — what kind of house she lived in, what her writing schedule was like, what she ate for breakfast, how she dressed for dinner. She was concerned with what literature and memoirs revealed abut the history of the times, its morals and mores. The pages of her essays and her notebooks are filled with questions and answers about the human beings behind the works of art, about the implications of art for humanity. Woolf taught us that writers are human beings, that writing is a human act, that the act of writing is filled with consequences for a society and for its readers. No "art for art's sake." Instead, "art for the sake of life."

She understood that literature by its very nature is a powerful didactic instrument and, therefore, as potentially dangerous as it is edifying. Literature teaches us when we are young about the way we are supposed to behave and about the consequences of certain kinds of behavior. Woolf reminds us of how profoundly influential literary texts can be in the formation of character and in the formation of a nation's character.

I imagine Woolf thinking, "What one must do is write a literature of one's own."

*

28 March 1941.

Virginia Woolf commits suicide by walking into the River Ouse with rocks in her pocket. My mother is three months pregnant. The fact that she is pregnant with me when Virginia Woolf dies is of no significance to her. Many years later I ask her if she remembers hearing abut Virginia Woolf's death on the radio. She says no. Maybe she read Virginia Woolf when she was pregnant with me? *The Years?* It was a very popular novel. She says no. She never heard of Virginia Woolf until I started talking about her.

The fact that Virginia Woolf and my mother were alive at the same time, breathed the same air, so to speak, is mysteriously significant. The fact that my mother was pregnant with *me* when Woolf killed herself seems laden with meaning. What can explain the fact that I am devoting a very large part of my life to this woman with whom I have absolutely nothing in common? She is English, purely and highly bred. I am more Italian than American, rough, tough, a street kid, out of the slums of Hoboken, New Jersey. We have absolutely nothing in common, except for the fact that we are both women.

And that, I realize, is quite enough.

Charlotte Forten Grimké

Bonny Vaught

Bonny Vaught

TRYING TO MAKE THINGS REAL

Charlotte Forten came into my life ten years ago. Dates in brackets [1837-1914] could not contain this woman; her journal touched me, made me catch my breath in sympathy as I read it for the first time. Though she had begun writing her journal when she lived in Salem, Massachusetts, Charlotte Forten suddenly was alive in my home in New Mexico more than a century later.

A ninety-five-cent paperback edition of *The Journal of Charlotte L. Forten* had caught my eye in a local bookstore, partly because it was subtitled *A Free Negro in the Slave Era.* Before moving to Albuquerque in 1969, I had taught in a California high school with a predominantly Black student body. Social studies curricula were just beginning to acknowledge the Black men and women in American history, so I had been a white teacher sharing my students' frustration about those missing Black people. Where were they to be found?

My interest in Black history had continued — grown, in fact — and now Ray Allen Billington's edition of Charlotte Forten's journal looked as though it might provide interesting information. I was totally unprepared for the impact those pages would make on me. Feelings of understanding and sympathy overwhelmed me when I began to read the journal. Even the setting remains vivid: When I looked up from the book I saw late afternoon sunlight forming patterns on the carpet. For a moment I became aware of the actual distance between myself and this woman who seemed mysteriously close.

What began as a chance meeting has deepened into a close, vital relationship. Charlotte Forten Grimké (you will note that she married since we first met) has become a remarkably important person in my life. When asked to describe her I speak in the past tense: "She was a free Black woman born into a wealthy Philadelphia family in 1837. Forten was well educated, talented, and uncompromising in her commitment to the antislavery movement. She taught freed slaves in the Sea Islands experiment during the Civil War. Later she married Francis J. Grimké, a mulatto nephew of the white abolitionist sisters Angelina and Sarah Grimke."

Given the slightest encouragement, I go on to tell of her happy marriage and the couple's lifelong commitment to racial equality: "Charlotte Forten Grimké and her husband believed that communication between Black and white people was essential." I quote the Grimkés lifelong friend, Dr. Anna J. Cooper: "Their verbs they conjugated mostly in the active, not the passive voice."

It is all in the past tense when I speak. And yet, for me, over the past ten years Charlotte Forten Grimké has become a vital presence. By now she seems as alive to me as any friends I see face to face. It is no wonder that my perplexity has kept pace with my growing involvement with this woman. Why am I so attracted to her? Why so involved with a person from another century? From another race?

At times, pondering my strange affinity for Charlotte Forten Grimké, I have tried to find some parallels between her life and mine. But parallels do not emerge. What I find instead are some preferences and personal traits we have in common.

In both of us — Charlotte and me — there seems to have been a constant curiosity about the world we began to observe. She lived in a large city but was turned away (often meanly rebuffed) from many of the classes, exhibitions, and lectures Philadelphia offered only to its white citizens. I had no access to these possibilities because I lived in a small midwestern town. Yet the hunger to explore a larger world persisted in both of us.

On the surface, our families seem quite dissimilar. Her mother died when Forten was a small child, so her father and the extended Forten-Purvis families were the people who nurtured and cared for her. Both my parents raised me; unlike Charlotte, I had no siblings. Quite the opposite of the network of grandparents, aunts, uncles, and cousins Forten enjoyed, I could claim only eight living relatives.

But perhaps there is a familial similarity between this nineteenth-century woman and me, inverted over many decades. Each of us struggled in her own way to reconstruct a family heritage. Like any "motherless child," Forten had a special need to know her background. Robert Bridges Forten, her father, was often distracted as he sought answers for his own problems. My family was small, somewhat isolated, and surely not extroverted. I too was continually trying to reach out for more information, more contacts, as I sought my own heritage.

Charlotte Forten's journal pages intrigued me. I never felt I was reading *about* someone. A peculiar, immediate understanding made her someone I knew very well — someone I liked very much. It was not only because we had done similar work; the rapport extended even to finding her using a word I might have chosen in my own writing. When she "luxuriated" in a beautiful day, I thought I might have done exactly the same thing and used exactly the same word to describe it.

In one aspect of her life we have obvious ground for understanding. My husband was a Lutheran pastor during the early years of our marriage. Consequently, I find her years as a minister's wife far more comprehensible because of my own experience. Still, it was that young woman excitedly beginning her journal in Salem in 1854 who captivated me.

I responded to her eagerness and openness to learn, no matter how badly she had been rebuffed in Philadelphia because of the color of her skin. Forten's enthusiastic plunge into her studies made me enjoy her very much. Her single-mindedness appealed to me every time I saw it expressed.

Charlotte Forten's abolitionist beliefs not only were quietly confided in the pages of her journal; they were actively tested in her attempts to persuade other women of the urgent need for the end of slavery. I responded to the clear-cut antislavery commitment underlying her life and at the same time appreciated her frustrations and disappointments. On every page I found a person who was energetic yet uncertain, filled with vitality yet wrestling with illness — deeply involved in living out all the contradictions of her life.

I felt enormous empathy for this young woman who was caught between two worlds. She was Black, identified and categorized simply because of her color. However, rather than being a slave, she was a free Negro in Philadelphia before the Civil War. It was not a comfortable position for any free Black person who lived in the North at that time. Forten's situation was further complicated by her family's wealth, by her own education, and by her passionate commitment to abolitionism.

Though I had not fully realized it at the time, the experience of teaching Black students at that high school in California was to affect all the rest of my life. Without that experience, I might have seen

Charlotte Forten only as a distant individual from another century. She could not have made such a strong impression on me had I not been sensitized by my students in Oakland.

When Forten left her Philadelphia-Salem-Boston world to teach in the Sea Islands during the Civil War, she had her first encounter with people of her own race whose skin color had not been diluted by intermarriage with whites. Coming from the North, from a society where her mulatto skin made her a shade more acceptable to whites, Charlotte Forten stepped into a world of dark-skinned newly freed men and women who even spoke a different language. Gullah must have been as foreign to her ears as French or German before she had learned those languages.

As I read her journal, I vividly recalled my first visits to classes at the school where I would soon be student-teaching. Black students swirled around me in the corridors as they changed classrooms; I heard a language that was new to me, though surely not so foreign as the Gullah with which Forten was greeted. For a few minutes I was the only white person in sight. Suddenly I had the discomfiting awareness of "white visibility." It was to become, years later, another tentative connection with the woman in the journal.

I read Forten's description of schoolmates in Salem who spoke to her in the classroom but pointedly avoided recognizing her on city streets. Charlotte recorded time after time when she anticipated acceptance but was turned away; when she expected to be admitted but was denied access. I found the diary a poignant reminder of a certain Black girl in Oakland. One rainy morning Jennifer had rushed into class angry and upset. Riding to school on a city bus, she had been on the window side of a double seat. As the bus filled with white people she looked up, expecting someone to sit beside her. Nobody moved toward Jennifer. Remarks began to come from several white people; soon they jeered loudly about sitting next to a Black person.

"What's wrong with me?" Jennifer asked her friends in the classroom. "I'm not so terrible they couldn't sit next to me for a few minutes!" She began to cry as others tried to comfort her. It was only one of the cruel situations those Black students had to face every day of their lives. In a quiet room in my Albuquerque home, that specific memory of Jennifer's anguish merged with Charlotte Forten's writing.

What happened on the bus may seem like a small incident. It is quite possible that on another day Jennifer herself might have handled it differently. The point is that she should never have needed to handle such cruelty. Moreover, if such incidents are dismissed as "minor," continuance of the cruelty gains tacit endorsement.

Clearly, Charlotte Forten and those young Black students had lived in equally harsh circumstances, though separated by an entire century. I felt both angry and helpless at recognizing repeated, daily suffering down through all those decades. Here were the parallels that could not emerge between my life and Charlotte Forten's. Parallels were to be found between those Black students and Charlotte Forten. The parallels existed in Black Americans' experience.

Still, something in addition to teaching those students in Oakland made me reach back across the decades to Charlotte Forten. Living in Albuquerque for more than four years gave me another reason. Does the lifestyle of a middle-class white woman in 1969 seem totally unrelated to Charlotte Forten's existence one hundred years earlier? This experience yielded a peculiar tie between us.

It would be fair to say that the women's movement had not begun to flourish in Albuquerque when we moved there in the summer of 1969. Newcomers "learned their place." People who came in from the outside — everywhere else was perceived as outside by Albuquerqueans; we/they without end — immediately faced demands for appreciative comments about the locale. But I had loved living in Berkeley; we moved only because my husband, John, was offered a transfer that advanced his career.

During five weeks of intense heat in a motel room, waiting for our house to be finished and wondering what had possessed us to make the move, we had one bright spot in the blistering desert heat — Herb Caen's column in a San Francisco newspaper. Unfortunately, or so it turned out, I wrote him a letter to say that his column brought a touch of the real world as I coped with this unreal new location. My comments about Albuquerque were acerbic, and Caen printed them in a Sunday column. That column set in motion a series of events that followed us and doomed us for the entire time we lived in Albuquerque.

To be sure, these were *my* comments above *my* name. Neither the letter nor the column carried any mention of my husband or his employer, a major corporation. Yet the Monday after my letter appeared in Herb Caen's column, irate reactions came crackling over the phone from California division headquarters to the Albuquerque plant manager. On Tuesday my husband was informed that he might as well forget any future with that company. On Wednesday he was told to get an apology from me (presumably to the people of Albuquerque) and was told to have me write a second letter to Caen denying the first. He was gallant through the whole affair, giving a firm, flat no to his superiors.

By Thursday — four days after the original column was in print — word had gone cross-country to the corporate offices in New York.

Organization chart titles came to life. The executive assistant to the president called the Albuquerque plant manager. The message from New York was terse: "Tell Vaught to get his wife under control."

If all this seems incredibly Victorian, especially in light of the women's movement, remember that I was sitting in the middle of the desert in 1969, certain that I had ruined my husband's career beyond repair. If it seems the least bit funny to think of a whole town reacting so strongly, try to realize how seriously Albuquerqueans took this. Herb Caen's column was soon printed in a local paper. It appeared under a new title ("Bonny's Little Love Letter to Albuquerque") and the editorial comments following my words were quite clear. If I didn't like the Land of Enchantment, why didn't I get out?

It may be that desert heat burns memories into people — or it may be that I had hit too many nerves. At any rate, my husband and I were suddenly the Albuquerque equivalent of untouchables. I cannot even describe the isolation resulting from that newspaper column. Invitations we had received were withdrawn; tentative acquaintances abruptly cut off further contact; anticipated friendships never even began. Angry Albuquerqueans wanted nothing to do with someone who had maligned their city.

I wrestled with feelings of guilt. (Why did I even think of writing to Herb Caen?) At times the humor of the situation was clear. (Was it really so bad to note that Albuquerque rhymes with turkey?) I wondered what I could do to redeem myself. (Why didn't it help now when I tried to be tactful?) Nothing made any difference. I had been condemned. There was to be no act of redemption during our entire stay in Albuquerque.

Now, ten years later, I can remember the situation ruefully and sometimes even laugh about it. But I will never forget it. That day in Albuquerque when I read Charlotte Forten's words, I had some idea of how she felt when she was rejected before people even met her. If my "crime" had ben criticism that hurt local pride, hers was the "crime" of having skin that was not white. My isolation was presumably temporary and would end whenever we were able to leave that particular city. But imagine the scope of her burden — for Charlotte Forten was to have no relief from white racism through her entire lifetime.

My experience cannot possibly be equated with — set parallel to — the experience of any Black woman during any time in our country. I do believe, however, that being ostracized in Albuquerque made me more sensitive to the pain in Charlotte Forten's life when I first met her. Coming so soon after teaching

Black students (where I had seen the parallels in painful abundance), the experience in Albuquerque led to consideration of a far greater issue: What breaks down — and what facilitates — communication when anger and hurt have predominated? Taking the next step: How can Black people and white people communicate with each other?

Frederick Douglass, writing in 1860, believed that "consciously or unconsciously, almost every white man approaches a colored man with an air of superiority and condescension." Even for persons who might protest this point, Douglass's next words strike home: "The relation subsisting between the races," he wrote, "at once shows itself between the individuals, and each prepares, when brought together, to soften the points of antagonism. The white man tries his hand at being a negro, and the negro, to make himself agreeable, plays the white man. The end is, each knows the other only superficially."[1]

Might it be possible, though, to break through some barriers by enabling a Black woman of the nineteenth century to speak to people of the twentieth century? We know that it is often more possible to listen to truths when they come to us once removed. Could Charlotte Forten Grimké's life itself become that form of truth if she came alive in a biography? I began to believe it was possible.

However, we lived in Albuquerque and essential Forten manuscripts were at Howard University in Washington, D.C., and I saw no possibility of writing Charlotte Forten Grimké's biography. She stayed in the back of my mind while I went on to other work, writing in entirely different fields.

I remember that when we moved to the East Coast in 1974 — again making a move connected with my husband's work — I thought of going to Howard University to see those manuscripts. Predictably, when the distance no longer was prohibitive, all my other questions came to the surface.

How could I, no matter how empathic, a white woman in the twentieth century, truly understand the experience of a Black woman in the nineteenth century? Had I the right to rely on my husband for total support during all the months (years?) it would take to carry out the project? What made me think I could possibly handle such an enormous task?

I wrestled simultaneously with all my doubts and all my desires. Perhaps I wasn't capable of such a project; yet Charlotte Forten was now someone I wanted other people to know. Still diffident, I went to Howard's archives. At this point I actually met the woman whose journals had already spoken to me so strongly. Meeting her face to

face with no ellipses in the manuscript, seeing those simple notebooks with that precise handwriting in ink now turned copper
brown, I encountered a far more complex person than I had anticipated.

Comparing the original journal texts with Billington's edition, I
found his choices consistent. He had presented a particular period
of Forten's life, focusing on her days in Salem and her teaching in
the Sea Islands during the Civil War. But now, reading further
details in her journal and also learning about her husband, I began
to form a more complex picture. Once again Charlotte Forten
seemed alive—this time as a more realistic, less distant embodiment.

I caught intense flashes of anger when she had been patronized.
Sometimes the words conveyed her pain when the journal read
"Dear A."—Dear *Ami*—her only friend at that moment. I began to
form a more complete picture of her family. No longer did I idealize
them although their courage as abolitionists never failed to impress
me. Now they became human.

No wonder Charlotte had trouble. She was definitely not the
enthusiastic teacher often mentioned in anthologies. She was a
young woman trying to reach out to her own race — and if that
meant teaching, so be it. She would serve and serve well; her journal
was at hand to record the words she forbade herself to speak out
loud. Disillusionment, anger, despair: The qualities often hidden by
those earlier ellipses now balanced my original picture of Charlotte
Forten. Her anger was not always righteous; she could be petulant.
At times she was inflexible and demanding, far beyond the sweet-
ness and light of a docile portrayal. But I liked her more than ever.
She was human after all.

During that crucial week at Howard University, Charlotte's personality emerged from the old letters and papers. Now I became
firmly committed to telling her story. I wanted people to meet her.

I did not seriously consider anything other than a scholarly biography. My training had been in political science, but I was undaun-
ted by the need to learn historians' methods. In retrospect, I think
that dealing only with the established facts offered tantalizing security. Although I would be shaping her life by what I chose to
emphasize, there would be a comfortable certainty in footnoting.
My book, then, would be the definitive biography of Charlotte
Forten Grimké — a model of scholarship, gracefully written. (At
least I knew what to aim for.)

Now, writing this essay, I'm tempted to launch into a description
of my unswerving, unwavering, steadfast commitment to the task I
had set for myself. I want to say that reaching into the nineteenth

century, becoming involved in Charlotte Forten Grimké's life, somehow made any obstacle surmountable. I want to tell about the mystical connection that bound me to another person and made the work invigorating. I must, instead, write the truth.

I knew that the pleasure of research has undone many a writer. I might have known that the allure of New York City's resources could be my own downfall. "Never mind any tight schedule. I'll concentrate on today's facts," I told myself. There seemed never to be a day of research that did not yield exciting, meaningful details that would round out this study of Charlotte Forten Grimké. I became hooked on pure research.

I completely disregarded one of the most important lessons I had learned about my own writing: Never, never should I have only one project going. At least two writing projects could move simultaneously, I knew, each stimulating and enriching the other. For me to concentrate every bit of energy on an elusive, long-range project meant depriving myself of some intermediate satisfactions. I should have had articles to write at the same time I worked on the Forten research. This was a nearly fatal mistake.

The imbalance continued for many months. Research was real; I was brimming over with ideas: "You'll never guess what I found at the library today!" My files were filling with facts. I worked efficiently day after day. But the research had no counterweight: No book was taking shape. Rather than abandon the whole idea, I decided that if I could stay with research long enough, I would eventually reach the writing project. I felt frightened.

Gradually, almost imperceptibly, I came to feel so close to Charlotte Forten that her problems became entangled with my own. Like many women of my generation, I had expected that raising a family would be the most important thing I would ever do. Now I was facing the fact — an irrefutable fact — that I would never have children of my own. As luck would have it, I was in my early forties, looking at Charlotte Forten Grimké in her early forties. When she mourned the loss of her only child, a little girl who lived for just six months, somehow my own sense of loss was heightened. My depression became entangled with hers in a way I still do not fully understand. It may have been a classic identification of biographer with subject, but I suspect the coincidence of our ages made it uniquely personal.

At any rate, I began to think Charlotte's life had ended when little Theodora died. No matter that the Grimkés had a long, productive life together following their daughter's death. Charlotte's writing after 1880 (the year of her child's birth and death) was more often prose than poetry. It seemed to me that my subject had ended almost all activity when she was forty-three years old. How could I write about half a life? What to do with thirty-three more years?

Whatever blinded me to Charlotte Grimké's subsequent activity also made me think that I might have no further work. No children, no future — or so the equation seemed to balance out. For someone who had come late to making the commitment to write, this was a devastating time. Although I had written two books published in the sixties, my standard comment had always dismissed them. "I'm not a writer," I would say. "I just did those two books."

No enlightening parallels-across-the-decades came to me during this time. As I lost sight of the intense, charming young Charlotte Forten, her image seemed transformed into a sad, childless woman of middle age. It would have been difficult to go through my own midlife transition in any case. Adding the weight of another woman's life and another century's problems brought me nearly to a halt. Again I experienced the entangling of Charlotte's life and mine. Searching for the shape of my own existence, I felt baffled in assessing hers. She was elusive, no matter how much factual evidence overflowed from desk to table in my study. I wavered between using the research as an anchor and suspecting that research itself had become a ruse.

Interludes of free-lance editing gave me some breathing space. When I worked on another person's book manuscript, I could reaffirm my own skill with words. Each time a call came from the New York publisher for whom I edited, it was a relief to know I would be dealing with something tangible.

Reality entered in another form when, early in 1976, I signed a contract to write a book for a Philadelphia business firm celebrating its 140th anniversary during the bicentennial year. For nine months I traveled, interviewed a variety of people with the company, dug into business records, and finally produced the agreed-upon book. Not surprisingly, I had approached the project as a biography of the company. *Measuring/Merging/Emerging* gave me some satisfaction when I saw the first bound copies in December 1976.

It seemed legitimate, of course, to set aside the Forten project for a specific number of months. Forten had receded into the background, but with the other finished book in my hands I felt strong and ready to build on a new momentum. Now was the time for Charlotte Forten Grimké's biography. My own life was in clearer focus; hers seemed infinitely clearer too.

Once again, in writing this essay, I want to give a glowing account of obstacles overcome — and once again the truth intrudes. This time no midlife transition troubled me; no self-doubts about my commitments of time and energy were plaguing me. But for several months I had been troubled by bewildering physical changes. My hands had become quite useless; my stiffened, swollen fingers simply would not move for me. I suffered from intense headaches. Pain began at the base of my skull, radiating to my shoulders and arms, culminating in muscle spasms that gripped my entire body.

I thought of Charlotte Forten Grimké's agonizing headaches, but this time I knew I did not have some mystical identification with my subject. Difficult, exasperating, infuriating doctors announced their diagnoses in solemn terms. Some pontificated; each new one was positive.

Yet it was nearly a year before I learned that the basic problem was a ruptured cervical disk. By then I had pain from pinched nerves, muscle spasms, damaged joints (and three doctors who said, "Do you *really* like your work?") Surgery was not an alternative, the neurosurgeons declared. I began a rigorous year-long program of treatment.

I write these words almost two years to the day after I began the so-called twelve-month program. Although the pain is still intense, it is at a more manageable level. By now I have faced the likelihood that I will live with a permanent disability for the rest of my life. (Contrary to popular belief, accepting the fact that one is disabled does not necessarily make life run more smoothly.) Nevertheless, within this new setting I have returned to my involvement with Charlotte Forten Grimké.

In recent months I have laboriously retrained myself to focus on her life. Each day is delicately balanced. Every movement is restrained to prevent further neurological damage. Describing my life today, I form a tiny box with my hands. But the turning point has come: Within that box, I am determined to live as well as possible. Not simple to exist, but to live well.

Working carefully — painstakingly! — I am gradually becoming productive again. And once again, this time to my amazement, Charlotte Forten Grimké is a different woman than ever before. I see the shape of her life quite differently. Where closeness may have blurred the facts, increased objectivity now lets me see her wholeness.

I had been jolted out of further research when I could no longer use my hands to type or write. Even as I began to consider using a tape recorder and finding someone to transcribe the notes, my pain became mind-numbing. Work in nearby New York libraries was out of the question. What, then, could protect and yet maintain the connection with Forten? The only possible answer: reading.

Intending to read around her life, I searched for accounts written by people who had traveled in America in the mid-1800s. Since Harriet Martineau had visited the home of James Forten (Charlotte's grandfather) on Christmas Day 1834, I was not surprised to find myself making a connection between Martineau's words and Charlotte Forten's world. (No matter that Martineau's visit occurred three years before Charlotte was born; I could make allowances.) But then I discovered that whether the accounts were written by Argentine diplomat Domingo Sarmiento, British feminist Barbara Sleigh Smith Bodichon, or even Charles Dickens, these books seemed to be an invitation for me to meet Charlotte Forten herself. Without my expecting her, she moved in and out of scenes these writers described.

Occasionally a work of fiction was a wonderful find. I devoured *The Garies and Their Friends,* Frank J. Webb's novel portraying problems of free Negroes in Philadelphia in 1857. Charlotte Forten was twenty years old that year. It was impossible not to see her together with his fictional characters.

Please do not misunderstand: This was not my first glimpse of nineteenth-century life. Yet this reading stood apart from all the rest. For earlier visits to the 1800s I had issued myself a work permit stamped *Researcher.* This time I went back into the nineteenth century with a travel permit stamped *Visitor.* I relaxed and enjoyed the visit.

Not assessing or evaluating or making weighty comparisons — not even searching for what was relevant to my own twentieth century — I was free to savor nineteenth-century ambience. I was grateful when the reading was absorbing enough to set me free from my immediate situation. Places became vivid; people began to stand out clearly against their own backgrounds.

Catherine Drinker Bowen said that a biographer needs to "go on reading until one hears the people talking." In this instance I noticed that words and phrases from the mid-1800s began to sound familiar. Printed pages gradually seemed elegantly worded rather than stilted. The fiery abolitionist arguments no longer seemed impeded by convoluted phrasing. I had indeed begun to hear the people talking.

Ironically, this escape did more than shield my research. I had feared losing Charlotte Forten Grimké. Instead, my attempt to read around her life led to another stage in our relationship. I was surprised to find that Charlotte was a personality firmly, steadfastly anchored within the stream of my own life.

Why did I feel surprised? Because during a protracted, painful illness the body imposes its own logic. Pain asserts itself. Familiar patterns of thought and work cannot break through. It was as if thought had been turned off — completely off — for long weeks and months. I sometimes was a sponge when I read, absorbing but doing nothing more. Not making connections, not enjoying sparks from one idea to another. Only soaking up what I read.

Not until the pain had receded to a more manageable level did I find that a deeper instinct must have been at work during all those months of reading. Shaping, reshaping, patterning bits and pieces of information, my mind had taken advantage of the time. We — Charlotte Forten Grimké and I — had become separate entities.

Total entanglement of our lives had been deadly — for me, for her, for the entire writing project. Now our separateness is invigorating. Charlotte is herself; I am myself. We meet in a new way. We have several experiences in common; often our concerns intersect; but all of this happens within an accurate framework. Each of us now stands within her own context.

It was essential for me to step back from the journals of Charlotte Forten to see her life take shape. When Charlotte Forten Grimké is etched against the panorama of all her years, 1837 to 1914, the wholeness of her life becomes apparent.

Consider the prejudice she abhorred so passionately. The racism never ended; her struggle with it never abated. She was relentless in protest, staunch as she insisted on equality. Think of the education Forten relished when she was young. She found ways to go on learning and growing for the rest of her life.

What of the worries stated in her diary about marriage ("for me, I must achieve my destiny — alone")? Charlotte finally met and married a man with the qualities she had so longed to find — and wed him in spite of hurtful comments about age. (She was forty-one, he was twenty-nine the year they married.) The Grimkés built a loving partnership that would be considered outstanding in any period.

Did she continue to struggle with sickness and loneliness? Like many other nineteenth-century women she was frequently enervated and drained by illness. Yet husband and friends said that she was "young and buoyant in spirit in her old age," as she had been in youth. The loneliness of earlier years was not forgotten. Charlotte transformed it by building long-standing, rewarding relationships that cut across racial barriers. "She was absolutely loyal to her friends," wrote Francis Grimké. "[They] could depend upon her with absolute assurance." Friends were moved as they remembered occasions when she had written spiritedly in their defense.

Charlotte was, of course, a woman of her own day in many respects. She was also unique. "There never was a sweeter, gentler, purer nature," wrote her husband. "And yet . . . she was a woman of great strength of character. She could take a stand and hold it against the world."

A phrase in her journals has come to haunt me. Thrust into a new, bewildering experience, the young Charlotte once wrote that she was sorting out conflicting impressions, "trying to make things real." These words, it seems to me, capture the essence of her life. Beginning with the abolitionist movement, she believed that impressions — ideas and ideals — were meant to be changed into reality. She persisted, forever "trying to make things real."

The more vivid she becomes, the more I discern a shift in my own aims. I am no longer concerned with establishing credentials for writing a scholarly biography. It seems far more important that Charlotte Forten Grimké come alive for the reader. Much as I value well-written biography, I have become convinced that fiction can provide the best form for this woman's life. In other words, I no longer intend to prepare a historical document. I don't even want to preach a sermon. I want to tell her story.

Then what of my misgivings? They will always be part of this project, and rightly so. My body now imposes physical limitations that cannot be ignored. Worse yet, they cannot always be accurately anticipated. In addition, the color of my skin imposes limitations that must always be held in mind. Although it is a double set of physical hindrances, in a curious way accepting this greater uncertainty has led to still another stage in my relationship with Charlotte Forten Grimké.

It requires a peculiar leap of faith for me to write about a nineteenth-century Black woman. I think of Ralph Ellison saying, "I will not Jim Crow my imagination."

She waits.

I find my way back to her again.

And now at last I prepare to write, thinking of the way Charlotte Forten Grimké lived her life: trying to make things real.

Note

1. *Douglass Monthly,* quoted in Jane H. Pease and William H. Pease, *They Who Would Be Free: Blacks' Search for Freedom, 1830–1861* (New York: Atheneum, 1974).

Bibliography

Forten, Charlotte L. *The Journal of Charlotte L. Forten: A Free Negro in the Slave Era.* Edited, with an introduction and notes, by Ray Allen Billington, 1953; reprint (New York and London: Norton, 1981).
Forten, Charlotte. "Life on the Sea Islands." *Atlantic Monthly* 13 (May 1864): 587-96; (June 1864): 666-76.
Olney, James, ed. *Autobiography: Essays Theoretical and Critical.* (Princeton: Princeton University Press, 1980).

Dame Ethel Smyth

Elizabeth Wood

Elizabeth Wood

MUSIC INTO WORDS

From earliest childhood, I heard my mother's violin, my aunt Gwenyth's Responses on the organ of our Presbyterian church, and my grandmother's piano accompaniments to her three daughters — and their daughters — as we all harmonized around the family upright in Sunday night singsongs. Our Welsh forebears sang in *eisteddfodau*. Grandfather Charles built pipe organs. Sometimes he agreed to carry me off on his repair and tuning trips around Sydney, Australia. I held down the white ivory notes while he hummed and crouched high above me, lost to sight in the silvery forest of pipes that crowned the organ loft.

When I became proficient on piano, I was expected to prepare Uncle Frank's latest piano compositions to perform them for him in private concert. He would listen attentively, clap with delight, and thank me for the gift of sound. I loved music, not so much because it was central to Sundays and family activities, but more, I think, because it offered a private, magical space for work and pleasure.

In the cramped, rented apartment where I grew up after my family moved to Adelaide in South Australia, my "room of my own" was the borrowed piano — we could not afford to buy one — and its long, polished bench stuffed with scores of Bach, Mozart, Brahms, Schumann, and Debussy. Only there, when I settled into hours of practice, did I find the solitude, in a respectful silence accorded musical work, normally begrudged me by anxious and intrusive parents.

My school, a Church of England girls' college where my mother worked as a secretary, encouraged all the arts as admirable amateur accomplishments. Piano, violin, and rudimentary ear training were taught; there was no orchestra, no theory. At fifteen, I was composing. My music, when it was not paraphrasing Bach, sounded dissonant and ungainly because it knew no rules. My willing performers were the Youth Fellowship Choir at church and a group of school friends I formed into a Choir Guild. After one music club concert, when we successfully navigated one of my tricky chorales, a beloved teacher stopped me outside on the asphalt playground. She must have assumed the piece was the wretched work of some obscure Australian man, for first she demolished "his" unnatural techniques and then she warned me, "Elizabeth, don't try impossible things like that again. Stick to real music."

I decided I had better concentrate on piano playing. I missed the comradeship of choirs, the thrilling terror of conceiving a new musical score. I also doubted I had the necessary talent and temperament to become a solo concert artist. It made me feel sick to perform. I opted for playing organ in church or conducting when I could. Each step seemed at the time a slow retreat.

By the time I left high school, I contended not only with my onstage nerves but with offstage poverty and downright family opposition. I had to support myself financially if I insisted on going to university. A musical career for me was unthinkably insecure. I found a bed-sitter and varieties of day and night jobs, began a degree in English literature, and played my friends' pianos for fun and relaxation. Two decades later, in 1977, the distinguished American composer Vivien Fine talked with me about Ruth Crawford's mentor role in her early career. Fine said that there is a crucial time when you need someone who says "You, too, can compose." I understood the manna of timely encouragement. A kind of residual hunger still gnaws at my composing and conducting ambitions.

I did have an intellectual mentor who had taught me in my final year at high school. Fay Gale was the first woman to receive her Ph.D. at Adelaide University were she is now its first and only female full professor. Her specialty was then Aboriginal culture and society. When I was seventeen, she invited me on an anthropological field trip to inland mission settlements to interview Aborigines. Observing her and listening to Aboriginal women recount their lives stirred in me the first interest in my own culture, in our fallow as well as fertile history.

Toward the end of that first degree, I married an engineer. Within six years, four children were born and I had returned to university for advanced keyboard lessons and a fresh degree in musicology. Although my husband claimed he was tone-deaf, he appreciated my intellectual interests, and Fay gale urged me to pursue research. At the age of thirty, when my last child was born, I was teaching music history to undergraduates, writing concert reviews, broadcasting on educational radio, and completing master's degree courses before starting on my doctorate. I felt I had boundless energy. A family, far from creating obstacles, seemed to provide an increasingly supportive base as the children grew more independent and close-knit among themselves.

Of course, I had to adapt. The "doctoral decade" was rarely serene. On my interstate research trips, I breast-fed the baby between archival stacks and changed diapers on the lids of grand pianos. Indexing and filing could be sandwiched between kindergarten committees, sports' days, measles and meals. Wherever I worked, my space was cluttered with children. The sound of the typewriter or the opening bars to a sonata announced an irresistible fanfare: fingers on the keys imitated mine; toys jammed the action; peanut butter smeared the score. With grim good humor, I improvised. I bought instruments to occupy them while I played Mozart: Our "Toy Symphony" of maracas, marimba, tambourine, bongos, and didjeridu made disorderly — if exhilarating — harmony out of those cacophonous themes of motherhood, domesticity, and creative work.

In retrospect, I think the research task I undertook provided an ideal apprenticeship. I chose my doctoral subject, Australian-made opera, in part because it was an unknown field but mostly because I found the very idea of this synthetic bloom, this curious hybrid of Western European music oddly heroic in its determination to survive the blighted muscial and intellectual deserts of nineteenth century Australia.

My primary sources were scattered and in disarray. What was not lost or mutilated lay uncataloged in cardboard boxes in library basements; handwritten letters, original manuscripts, old programs, newspaper clippings filled family trunks and attics, country organ stools, cupboards in theaters, city halls, and universities.

Once I had cataloged some four hundred musical theater works dating from early convict theaters of the 1840s to works-in-progress in 1970, I decided to expand my thesis into a cultural history and set the operas in their sociological, political, and artistic contexts. Taken chronologically, they suggested to me patterns in cultural history applicable to the development of other colonially based cultures and to other art forms. I was sure of my perspectives but floundered for appropriate ways of presenting them. There were few scholarly guides; musicology was mainly devoted to "life and works," single-composer monographs with performing editions of "great music." I still remember the excitement I felt when I discovered the work of pioneer American music historians such as Oscar Sonneck, Irving Lowens, and Gilbert Chase and read a paper on American music and musicology by Richard Crawford. Here was the validation of my work; here was my intellectual base.

Australian composers who shared their scores and personal experiences with me became close friends; they, more than academic colleagues, cheered my enthusiasms and ideas. I joined an opera company chiefly because I wanted to promote revivals of some of the operas I had unearthed and to prod managers to com-mission new ones from my friends. It was as if the act of retrieving lost works of art were fueling my own creativity, and my scholarship was becoming audible and alive through performance. For part of my concern was practical: Most of the early operas had not survived intact; only one of the most recent works had been recorded. To "hear" the works I analyzed, I had to learn to read scores with my inner ear. I wanted to see how they worked and how they might affect an audience.

I was eager to enter the public arena after years of solitary research and absorption with young children. In the early 1970s, I was reading feminist books that helped put into focus the reason for my intellectual frustration and loneliness and drew me to join the women's movement. I looked for ways of directing my work closer to my sense of identity and my personal interests. Two of the operas I helped revive were composed by women: One was by Peggy Glanville-Hicks (born 1912), an expatriate then living in Greece; the other was by Margaret Sutherland (born 1897), then doyen of Australian composers, who invited me to meet her and study her scores in her Melbourne home.[1]

I noticed all her work in manuscript on the shelves beside her piano. Could I see the complete catalog? "No one ever made one," she smiled. Which pieces were commissioned? "None," she said. I nibbled on a hot buttered scone she had produced for afternoon tea. Well, how had she made her living? "Scrounged," she said without bitterness. "Some of my larger works did get published, but if they knew the composer was a woman, they usually rejected them. The world at large, you see, thinks that a woman can't be creative. My musical life has been a frustration of half-performances, then bad performances, then no more performances. I used to wait years to get a first performance, but by then I could not profit from what I had heard, because I had moved along to other areas and passed that by."

Whether she knew it or not, Sutherland articulated feminist principles. However she may have managed to accommodate her feelings, after that interview I was both angry and elated. There had been a handful of women composers in Australia before her. It appeared from the scant traces of their lives and work, that most had simply stopped composing after marriage or failure to have their music played or had disappeared into impoverished and anonymous music teaching careers. Sutherland and Glanville-Hicks had won scholarships to study abroad, a vital step for isolated Australian artists whose distance from musical sources undermined their chances for recognition "at home" and the confidence and opportunity they needed to make their work internationally relevant and contemporary. Sutherland returned home, married, raised two children, yet contrived to make composition central to her life. She was the first woman composer I knew to be defined by her work.

I have never met Glanville-Hicks although we still correspond, and she has now returned to Australia where she composes and cajoles Australians to cherish their young composers. She had lived in New York for twenty years, taken American citizenship, and won international acclaim while Australia virtually forgot her. At the time I was examining the impressive scores of her operas in the Melbourne archives, I thought of her as a woman I might have wanted to be, had I her tenacity and talents. She had done exciting and unusual things: enthnomusicological field trips to Asia and the Aegean; promotion of her own as well as other people's music in concerts, recordings, and music reviews for the New York *Herald Tribune;* and collaboration in her stage works with the writers Thomas Mann, Lawrence Durrell and Robert Graves. Her fellow critic and composer Virgil Thomson had described her as "thin, passionate, tireless, and insistent (for Australian women can indeed insist) . . . she believed, on some evidence, that the world was out to crush women composers . . . She complained, she stormed, she telephoned . . . She continues to fulminate and to be useful."[2] Whereas Margaret Sutherland had led a short-lived Australian avant-garde movement in the 1930s, the music of Glanville-Hicks belonged to a more significant and experimental American avant-garde of the 1950s and early 1960s.

I was still struggling with my thesis when a visiting American professor of music read my work and invited me to get away, to finish writing about my country at a suitably "objective" distance. I was awarded a Fulbright travel grant, but at first I fought accepting it and all it promised and threatened. Like those earlier women composers, I believed myself tied to homeland (through work and identity) and to family. But, in fact my marriage was dying, my children were old enough for me not to feel overwhelming guilt if I were to leave them for a while, and my work, like myself, was already in transition, ready to leap into new directions. Two years after it was offered me, I took the Fulbright and flew to New York. It was 1977.

As a visiting scholar, free to choose whatever I should do, I wanted to investigate American music and American feminism. The freedom, the release of energy, was intoxicating. The intellectual compulsion to come to America was rewarded at once by the feeling that I was no longer alone and that the work I had been doing was part of a wider and more generous vision. I listened avidly, followed every clue that seemed to have relevance, with senses flooded with new sounds. I made a list of women composers working in Manhattan and began to interview them. I felt I moved in familiar yet transforming landscapes; in a few weeks I had heard extraordinary musical variety and vitality and had recorded twenty different musical lives that ranged from Berlin to Bennington and Soho and across the spectrum of contemporary styles and genres.

One year before I arrived, Doris Hays and Beth Anderson had presented their "Meet the Women Composers" series at the New School; composers Ruth Anderson and Annea Lockwood had taught their first course on women in music at Hunter College; Marnie Hall had brought out her first recordings of women's art music. I met and worked with the team of CUNY women bibliographers who were compiling thousands of sources on American women composers, performers, educators, and benefactors. A dozen doctoral theses were viewing women's musical history; old and new music was performed at the annual Women's Interart Center festivals. Grand Old Ladies ran venerable clubs that still actively sought money and recognition for women composers.

Apart from supportive composers in Australia, I had come from a small, disinterested academic community to whom my work was, and largely still is, irrelevant. American women musicologists who worked on women's music shared some similar experiences. Few of us held full-time or tenured teaching posts; fewer had been able to teach courses in our specialty. Most waited for grants, squeezed their research papers into the back rooms of professional conferences, and their agendas for change in the small-print columns and footnotes of musical societies and scholarly journals.

I knew that at the distance of 13,000 miles I could complete my Australian narrative and then begin new work that would focus on women's music. That was the promise. The threat was more immediate. I had to make several more Pacific journeys before the major leap was accomplished — terrible and painful journeys of severance and salvage, through divorce, two bitter custody trials, and the resettlement of all the children with me in America. Sometimes I felt myself to be a woman without her shadow. My children gave substance and dimension to the missing parts of my Australian past.

When we arrived in New York with two suitcases each, we carried private talismans, whether a favorite book, a teddy bear, a cricket bat. In my bag, I packed the picture of a musical and feminist pioneer, the British composer, conductor, writer, suffragist, and bombshell, Dame Ethel Mary Smyth.

Ethel Smyth died in 1944 at the age of eighty-five but I often feel as if she were still alive. I have imagined her striding to greet me off the Seventh Avenue bus. I anticipate her reactions to people and events. When I speak of her or write about her music, I experience something of her galloping energy, the power and vibration she brought to everything she did. A woman who loved tough competitive sports — the hunt, tennis, golf, cricket — she always took the sporting chance. She seems to have impelled herself, as well as her performers and sponsors who stayed the course, over obstacles in her career and hurdles in her music as she would urge her horse over hedgerows or her companions over alpine peaks, charging ahead in her sturdy shoes, her tweeds, her cocky Napoleonic hat.

She had an acute ear for the clamor of approaching battle. An army general's daughter, she fought for women's equality and freedom of expression, her artillery no less the stones she threw at politicians' windows with Emmeline Pankhurst than the petitions she hurled at conductors, managers, and committees in the musical *Male Machine* to unblock their "gangway" and ensure that her music would be performed and that women would be hired, paid a fair wage, and professionally trained and treated. She spent two months behind bars in Holloway Prison after one of her more flamboyant forays with the suffragists. Later in life, she won honorary degrees and knighthood — more, she laughed, for her ferocious tennis game than for her musical scores.

More than anyone I have known or studied, Ethel Smyth's indomitable presence is imprinted on much of what I do and care for. Unlike so many of the Australian men and women in music, she left reams of evidence about herself and her work, far more than most women ever bequeathed in and to history. She published nine books, wrote diaries, broadcast speeches, exchanged letters, copied and rearranged her scores of six operas and various chamber, vocal, and orchestral works.

Others found her so memorable (but called her an eccentric, virile, outrageous, tweedy old battleax) that many affectionate as well as acid portraits of her survive in gossipy anecdotes that border on myth. Virginia Woolf, guilty of both, wrote best. She felt as "a little sailing boat might feel which follows in the wake of an ironclad . . . [for] she is of the race of pioneers . . . [who] drew the enemies' fire and left a pathway for those who come after her."[3]

At an early stage in her friendship with Woolf, Smyth lent her her private letters. Woolf considered writing Smyth's biography and mused aloud that there has "never been a woman's autobiography . . . Nothing to compare with Rousseau . . . Chastity and modesty I suppose has been the reason." Clearly, Smyth was refreshingly free from both restraints, yet Woolf urged her to tell the inner, underlying truths about herself: "I should like an analysis of your sex life, as Rousseau did his. More introspection. More intimacy."[4]

I want to write the life Woolf might have, that she imagined, then transposed into her portrait of Miss La Trobe in *Between the Acts*. Woolf and others who fictionalized Smyth did not know how to take her music seriously, and while Smyth wrote her own legend, she was neither introspective nor an intellectual. Like all performers and good sports, Smyth could play to the gallery. I respond as much to her vibrant personality as to her music — to the music because of its creator, who, as a woman rather than a composer, was more consciously, daringly, intelligently rebellious than any before and few since.

Few musical biographies can show me the way. One is novelist Wolfgang Hildesheimer's speculative study of Mozart, where he describes the biographer's art: "To express it musically: we have before us a score consisting of only two staves — the melodic line (Mozart's music) and the bass (his external life). The connecting middle voices are missing — his unconscious, the dictates and impulses of his inner life, that which governs his motives and behaviour."[5] Smyth *has* provided some connecting inner lines in her "illuminating confessions," and with these parts I am concerned not to tamper or distort even when her confessional mode alerts me to self-delusion. I take care when I add my own conjectural cadenzas to her revelations and insights so far as she takes these. I will not improvise on what I do not know. Yet I wonder where her realities lay.

When, for example, I scan the "staves" of Smyth's private life and sexuality, I find, first in her memoirs, that she was astoundingly frank, on the surface, about her passionate lesbian love affairs and her anguish when they ended in betrayal or rejection. Second, in her letters, I find at times a hesitant exploration of a nurturing maternal desire. Yet in her opera libretti, I am confronted with conventional romantic passion and heterosexual longing. If I imagine that autobiographical themes run, symbolically at least, behind her dramatic texts, I recall Smyth's reply to Woolf's insistence that she should write more intimately about her sexual experiences. Smyth reminded Woolf of the perils of the déclassé: that to succeed in a man's world as a woman composer, she had to identify with men. Can her memoirs or her letters offer explanations beyond helping us to see her as she wished to present herself?

The scenarios of her operas pale beside her account of the chief romantic experience of her youth in Germany, where she was a composition student for seven years, beginning in 1877 at the age of nineteen. She was infatuated with musician Elisabeth (Lisl) von Herzogenberg, who was a friend of Brahms, the wife of Smyth's composition teacher, and the sister of Julia, the languid wife of philosopher Henry Brewster. Smyth "lost" Lisl, whom she calls Mother, when she "won" Brewster's love and thereby managed to alienate the entire family and many friends. Brewster became her librettist, closest friend, mentor and even, possibly, her lover; he offered marriage which she flatly refused. Scenes of recrimination, sacrifice, silence, death haunted Smyth for the remainder of her long life. They spill like bitter leitmotifs through the two operas she wrote with Brewster before his death (*Der Wald* and *The Wreckers*) as well as in countless letters and variations on her memoirs. In their endless refrain, Smyth did not subject her own "performance" to self-analysis but clasped the proud innocence of a victim and martyr. This belies her courageous candor toward most other dramatic and tragic events in her life.

Connections, disconnections, facts, fictions become less problematic for me when I face the music. Perhaps I can know Smyth more intimately in and through her musical voice, an art at once more conscious and more abstract than writing. At least, I want to test this hypothesis. In music, I know I am less likely to skew or blur through too near and rosy an interpretation. I have a trained ear. In her scores, in the conscious techniques discernible in a musical line, her creative impulses and inner motives may be more profound and more accurate than memoir.

Ironically, Smyth was literally deaf for half of her professional life. She believed she heard in her music the music of a deaf Beethoven. Poignant and heroic though her identification seems, I hear as well the music of Brahms, of Wagner, of her detested Elgar, among the hearty bugle calls and hunting horns that echo her raucous childhood, and among the English folk tunes that she remembered and renewed in her musical vocabulary. There is sheer genius in her major opera, *The Wreckers,* in her dramatic setting of social and religious bigotry and the relentless rhythms of the sea that engulf human love and hatred. There is promise and prophecy in her two final operas, *The Boatswain's Mate* and *Fête Galante,* and a robust humor in her comic texts.

In these works, Smyth thought she had found the key to open a renaissance in British opera. In the context of British opera in the 1920s, her voice *was* fresh and original. In terms of what was then revolutionizing Western European music, which had come to the limits of tonality as it had been practiced for centuries, and from my present perspective, I quibble with Smyth, for I also hear where her aim overshoots her technique, where her experiments with neo-classical form become mired in nineteenth-century romanticism, where her humor is both temporal and insular, and where her promise is not fully realized. She could be wrong about her music as she was wrong about Webern and Schoenberg. I can know this in her music as well as in her forthright opinions. In her last years, her music was trapped in her musical past, symbolized in her final settings of the "Last Post." Perhaps by then she was too old and deaf to hear her own retreat from the new music of her time.

In writing about her music, I do want to bring others closer to it. I am hampered by my inability to conjure its sound. There is only one, discontinued recording of a short excerpt of her work, yet it is music that demands to be played and heard. I want my work to stimulate performances as it did for Australian operas. Again, I write about Ethel Smyth from many of the same impulses that led me first to study Australian culture. In Smyth, I encounter connections between music and writing, women and history, feminism and scholarship, activism and private work, and between community and sexuality. These connections matter in my own life.

Smyth stood for a way of working that I espouse. Her genius for the pursuit of friendship was daily counterpointed by her wish for solitude, her diligence and discipline, her care for the smallest details of orchestration and texture as well as for the long-term, large-scale vision, her control and perspective over the entirety of structure, style, and personal expression. Her habits of work, her qualities of wit and feeling, and the audacity of her ambition inspire me. She has been a mentor for my way of life. Her daring to live in public the life of a lesbian was a symbol of courage to me in my transition from marriage, through the courts, to lesbian parenting.

On the other hand, the company of a Smyth has its burdens. Should I identify with her, I measure difference. I played cricket but never hunted! She did not marry. She never sought the company of children. When my father refused to help me go to university, I ran away from home and took jobs to pay for night classes. Smyth's father boxed her ears and forbade her to travel alone to Leipzig to study music, so she locked herself in her room and went on strike until he was forced to relent. If *her* teacher criticized too harshly some tricky counterpoint and harmony, Smyth did not give up. She found another teacher. When an opera director made cuts in the final scene of her opera, she ripped all the parts off the orchestral stands and tore around Europe to find another who would produce her work with integrity. My patience and adaptability were not part of her vocabulary.

But, I console myself, Smyth was not perfect. If she took fewer wrong turns than I, and refused to be diverted by a setback (failure, for Smyth, was in another's execution, never in her vision), she could be cavalier about another woman's success. She could be mean toward a rival. When she insinuates that the alluring Irish-born composer Augusta Holmès owed some of her fame to "songs and seduction," and when she scarcely mentions other women composers in her musical and political tirades, I fear she echoes the very "male machine" she had so properly attacked for its greedy, jealous prejudices against creative women. Virginia Woolf advised Smyth that her advocacy for women's equality in music might be more effective if she were to give facts and figures about women other than herself lest readers assume she merely held a personal grudge: "You will say, 'Oh, but I must cite my case because there is no other.' But my dear Ethel, your case is that there are a thousand others." Woolf's advice was ignored.

I am as impatient as Ethel Smyth with attitudes that have silenced women. However, I am equally disheartened by those women I meet who scramble to have their music performed on all-women concert programs, yet dread the whiff of female segregation as much as feminist bonding. Smyth refused to succumb either to the attitudes that have produced women's fears or to sympathy with their victims. She did admit to shyness on the stage and discomfort in the glare of the publicity she nonetheless craved. I am probably more nervous than she with my own and other women's failures of nerve and will, but more generous toward their triumphs.

Another compelling reason for my work is that other women in music have lacked and longed for mentors because the historical narrative we inherit has so often obliterated female precursors. I interviewed an octogenarian Boston composer who had the temerity at twenty to take herself to Paris to study, but met and married a

man who soon persuaded her to research his scientific papers. She
proudly shows me the books her husband and her daughter wrote.
When I ask if I might see her manuscripts, she produces an
unfinished string quartet begun fifty years ago. I don't know if I
want to cry or to shake her, and then I am ashamed because I
remember a part of myself that shriveled on a school playground. If
only she had heard, en route to Paris, a performance of Ethel
Smyth's oratorio *The Prison* or her speech to the Women's Social and
Political Union. For Smyth did have musical as well as political
models to sustain her. Clara Schumann, for one, respected her raw
talents. The old woman in Boston tells me she felt alone; she knew
no other women who composed.

As much as Ethel Smyth, it is the women I know who compose
music today who inspire my vision. My own work is electrified by
their daring and innovative freedom of voice and by their belief that
an imagined future is more than the known past, that a future can be
imagined and then expressed in sound. It is through contact with
avant-garde composers that I remember to keep open and inclusive
my critical responses and keep visible and fearless my interpretation
of a Smyth, of a musical past and present.

The experiments of women composers with the articulation of
musical sounds sharpens my ear for language and the texture and
timbre of words. A sculptor of sonic environments chops a salad for
lunch while I interview her. In the background, I hear her tape of an
earlier piece. My own tape captures our conversation, the crisp cut
of celery and lettuce on a wooden board, the percussive sounds of
her music, as we shred and toss experience. When I return home, I
hear how we have just created a new composition, a chance impro-
visation between two women meeting for the first time to talk about
music. It is composers such as these who have taught me what to
ask, what to make of what I hear, and how to write what I have learned.

Notes

1. The Australian composers Peggy Glanville-Hicks and Margaret Sutherland and
   the British composer Ethel Smyth appear in *New Grove Dictionary of Music and
   Musicians* (New York, Macmillan, 1980). Also see Glanville-Hicks, "Technique
   and Inspiration," *The Juilliard Review* 5, no. 2 (Spring 1958): 3–11; George Antheil,
   "Peggy Glanville-Hicks," *American Composers Alliance* 4, no. 1 (1954): 2–9;
   Laughton Harris, "Margaret Sutherland," in *Australian Composition in the Twen-
   tieth Century,* ed. Frank Callaway and David Tunley, (Melbourne, Australia:
   Oxford University Press, 1978), 29–36; James Murdoch, *Australia's Contemporary
   Composers,* (Melbourne, Australia: Macmillan, 1972), 102–7, 181–86.
2. Virgil Thomson, *Virgil Thomson* (New York: Da Capo Press, 1966), 344–45.

3. Virginia Woolf, "Speech Before the London National Society for Women's Service, January 21, 1931," reprinted in *The Pargiters: The Novel-Essay Portion of "The Years,"* ed. Mitchell A. Leaska (New York: Harcourt Brace Jovanovich, 1978), xxvi–xliv.

4. Virginia Woolf, letter to Ethel Smyth, 24 February 1940, reprinted in Christopher St. John, *Ethel Smyth: A Biography* (London: Longmans, Green, 1959), 232–33. Jane Marcus is preparing an edition of the Smyth-Woolf correspondence for The Women's Press, London.

5. Wolfgang Hildesheimer, *Mozart,* trans. Marion Faber (New York: Farrar, Straus & Giroux, 1982), 11.

Simone de Beauvoir

Carol Ascher

Carol Ascher

ON "CLEARING THE AIR": MY LETTER TO SIMONE de BEAUVOIR

In June 1980, while writing *Simone de Beauvoir: A Life of Freedom*, I stopped to compose an imaginary letter, which I then somewhat brazenly included as a chapter, "Clearing the Air — A Personal Word."[1] The following is a slightly shortened version.

Dear Simone de Beauvoir,

I am in the midst of writing my book about your ideas, and I have been badly troubled by you — by my book on you — over the past weeks. Often in the morning as I go to my desk, I feel resentful, begrudging, sick of the lack of reciprocity between us. I know that if I am to convey to others what is admirable about you, I must do more than mechanically edit out my off-balance sentences. Besides, continuing on mechanically seems to me a kind of "bad faith." So I shall sit here until I have put down on paper what has happened to me in relation to you over the past years, but particularly over the last months of intensive reading and writing about your work.

I first heard of you when I was twenty years old and, ignoring my immigrant parents' hopes that Vassar College would turn me into a dignified and socially prominent young woman, had just transferred to Barnard College in New York City. In the deteriorated rooming house where I settled, one of several students in my suite was a dark-haired Brooklyn girl with hazel eyes. In my first memory of her, she is standing against my doorway in jeans and a black turtleneck, holding a ragged paperback with a naked lady draped across its cover. I look at the book fearfully: it reads *The Second Sex* by Simone de Beauvoir. This was 1961. Somehow this new sophisticated roommate must have told me what the book was about. I know she remarked, in the offhand way she assumed at the time, that she was a feminist, as was her mother. I had never even heard the word before. I certainly did not want to read the book.

My other early memory of the woman, who would become one of my dearest friends, is of her going everywhere for an entire semester carrying a canary yellow–jacketed book with *Being and Nothingness* striped boldly in black. A high-strung person, she nervously tore off the corner of each page and twisted it into a ball as she read; and I recall *Being and Nothingness* growing as ragged over the months as *The Second Sex* had been.

It amazes me to imagine how rapidly I must have changed, at least in my grasp of the world around me. In my late teens, I had loved the Beatnik writers but must have sensed that I could not travel alone like Jack Kerouac. After graduation, I married a young man, who "was going to be a writer" and went to live in Spain and Morocco with him. For the first time in my life, I smoked kif and glimpsed the lonely world of expatriates. Back in New York a year later, I found myself ill with a serious case of hepatitis. While I was in the indigent ward of the hospital, my Barnard friend brought me *The Mandarins*. That was the first book by you I actually ever read. Rereading it recently, I was astounded at how little of the political discussions which form the core of the book I could have understood then. Raised in the Midwest by refugee parents whose fears were aggravated by the cold war, my one childhood moment of political daring occurred when I told my schoolmates that my parents were voting for the Democratic candidate; and just as they had warned me, the schoolchildren taunted me for it. In college I read Marx's *Communist Manifesto* as part of a nineteenth-century philosophy course; but if there was any discussion of its political power or role, I don't remember it. Certainly, the discussions in *The Mandarins* about whether to expose Stalin's slave labor camps to a European public must have passed me completely by. What I do remember clearly from my first encounter with the novel, as I lay flat on my back in the hospital, is my erotic pleasure at the sections on Anne and Lewis in Chicago and my discomfort and fear at the idea of Anne's husband waiting for her to return home to Paris. In a Spanish seaside village, I had watched American and French writers and painters in their own little society of "free love," but had found it too disturbing to enter.

My marriage ended in the roughhousing, careless optimism of 1968. Although I didn't like the idea, I believed monogamy and the family were clearly dead; and being the obedient, serious woman I still was, I set out to adapt to the new sexual festival. If I had been told to live out my days strapped in a roller coaster I couldn't have been more baffled and unhappy. I sincerely thought I wanted to change, I worked hard at it, but I also knew that deep inside me lay a spiteful resistance and a longing for the old conservative ways.

In 1972, in a women's consciousness-raising group, I read *The Second Sex* for the first time. The flowering women's movement had already created enough of a new demand for the book that the paperback now sported a snappy white cover with sharp black and gold lettering. This copy, marked up then, as again over the years, stands in my bookshelf at my side as I write. There are pen notes indicating identification — "Yes," "Me too" — but also irritation — "Bah!" from this early reading. And on the empty back page are two old notes: "This is a very unsexy world," and a longer one expressing my annoyance that, given your relentless analysis of patriarchy throughout history, your final offer of socialism and a changed consciousness about women seemed unconvincing. Even at this early reading, a combination of recognition, fear, and anger characterized my responses to what you had written.

These days when I read *The Second Sex*, I feel the same frustration, though in different terms. It seems to me now that you depict a world where radical feminism is the only solution: a world where there really is no possible accord between women and men. At the same time, you clearly have little patience with what biology and society have made of women. In your despairing view, all those qualities that make women differ from men lead only to our demise. And so, while your picture of the world of patriarchy would lead women readers to feel that we must band together and go off on our own, your dislike of women (perhaps a kind of self-hatred) makes this completely unpalatable. It's a cul-de-sac that many women, including myself at times, have felt. But it makes your bid for men to take a different attitude toward women appear dubious and your proposal of socialism seem extraneous.

I understand your urge to offer a solution, even when none must have seemed clear. But there is an unhappy space I sense in general between the complexity of your description of the way things are and have been and the alternative visions you propose. I find this equally a problem in *The Coming of Age,* where your proposals for ending the plight of the aged seem unconvincing and almost silly given what has come before.

Perhaps the trouble lies at a deeper level. Even in your memoirs, you have a way of brushing aside the pain and ambiguity with which you have described an event or period and asserting the thing a success. I feel this, for example, when you assert that in your entire relationship with Sartre the two of you have "only once gone to sleep at night disunited."[2] Can the reader really be expected to believe this, after all your descriptions of bewildering, lost, or angry days? It is as if you must put a stamp of approval on your memories in order to go on. But the stamp simplifies the honest profusion of your life, and draws me to focus on your apparent dishonesty rather than on the brutal and wonderful honesty of the remaining passages. At times, writing this book, I have taken out such summary sentences, feeling a generosity toward you. For instance, when I quoted a section from *All Said and Done,* in which you spoke of not wanting to marry because Sartre did not — "I never should have been capable, even in thought, of forcing his hand in any serious matter" — I ended the matter there, since even that seemed to stretch your honesty. Yet there is an additional sentence that concludes the paragraph: "Supposing that for reasons I can scarcely imagine we had been obliged to marry," you say, "I know we should have managed to live our marriage in freedom."[3] Really! After what you've said about marriage in *The Second Sex* and elsewhere, how can one believe that you take that sentence seriously? Or do you see yourself so above all the traps life sets for others?

Perhaps a person as easily made testy about a writer should not write a book on her work. Certainly, I myself have often wondered about that over the past year or more. Yet there is another side to my reactions to you that comes out mainly in my sleep. About three or four years ago when I was deciding to leave the university and devote myself solely to my writing, you appeared in a dream to warmly wish me well. The dream was very important to me, the sternness with which I sense you in the day (so like my mother's) turning to kindness and support. And a few months ago, just after Sartre's death, when I was already deep in the writing of this book, I dreamed I had come to Paris to interview you. In the dream, you seemed so much softer than I had imagined you would be; and I made a note to myself to be sure to write this in the book. But I was also unsure about what to ask you. I seemed to have forgotten my notes, or else I had neglected to prepare. The house began to fill with other women. You went out and returned with a black tiara to indicate your mourning, and I thought I should offer my condolences. But then I let myself sit quietly in the room with the other women, feeling I was learning more about you by watching than if I had forced my way with a prepared interview. Waking from the dream, I felt peaceful and lighthearted. As in the earlier dream, my meeting with you had left me refreshed.

You must know that women my age and younger look to those of your generation as models, since our sense of what women can be has been so cramped by history (or its lack). Of course, this puts a pressure on your life and work which you only partially have asked for. At a deeper level, at least in my case, there is also the wish to repair the way we have been mothered by creating other relationships, even if only literary, intellectual, or in dreams, with other women. Unfortunately, you aren't that "good mother" I long for in my weakest moments. Although you have always taken young women under your wing, I sense your aloofness. Because of its echo in your memoirs, I take seriously the words you put into Anne's mouth in respect to her daughter, Nadine, in *The Mandarins*.* You have Anne say she feels "remorse because I didn't know how to make her obey me and because I didn't love her enough. It would have been more kind of me not to smother her with kindness. Perhaps I might have been able to comfort her if I simply took her in my arms and said,'My poor little daughter, forgive me for not loving you more.' "[5] Of course, Anne doesn't take Nadine in her arms, partly because Nadine has become a bristly young woman who couldn't bear it; just as my mother, too, long ago gave up trying to embrace me, because it seemed I couldn't bear it. You are brave for saying fictionally that Nadine's resistance to Anne's signs of affection is her knowledge of her mother's lack of deep acceptance. My mother has never been able to admit this in reality and is no writer of fiction. And who knows, in my case, where the first causes lies. I do know that in my waking life I am irritated by this and other traits that resemble my mother's, although in my dreams I have thankfully become able to give myself the warmth for which I long.

Why do I make you the mother in these fictional moments when your experience may as likely come from the side of the daughter? I wonder if you also tensed under your mother's embraces, feeling

---

*This is Anne speaking of Nadine:
> I hadn't wanted her; it was Robert who wanted to have a child right away. I've always held it against Nadine that she upset my life alone with Robert. I loved Robert too much and I wasn't interested enough in myself to be moved by the discovery of his features or mine on the face of that little intruder. Without feeling any particular affection, I took notice of her blue eyes, her hair, her nose.

And you in *The Prime of Life:*
> A child would not have strengthened the bonds that united Sartre and me; nor did I want Sartre's existence reflected and extended in some other being. He was sufficient both for himself and for me. I too was self-sufficient: I never once dreamed of rediscovering myself in the child I might bear. In any case, I felt such absence of affinity with my own parents that any sons or daughters I might have I regarded in advance as strangers.[4]

that she loved you insufficiently. Particularly after your loss of faith, you may have felt estranged. Or maybe, like me, you were tense because you knew you wished her harm in your competition for your father. And the images of Anne and Robert, or you and Sartre, as a unit alone are only resolutions of that wish to be a third no longer — to get rid of the third. But then why always crowd your life with him with "contingent" lovers? I can answer my own question: The symptom is an expression of, and a defense against, the unacceptable wish.

I don't believe in objectivity and I cannot pretend my attitude is neutral.

This June, it is exactly fifteen years since I first read *The Mandarins* and eight years since I first read *The Second Sex*. From time to time I have gone on to read your other books and now have read, I think, all of the books you have written and a number of Sartre's as well. I often do this, particularly with a woman writer: it is a way of getting beyond the work to the person. And just as I tend toward long friendships, I find myself drawing out my relationships with writers who interest me by returning again and again to the library for more of their books. With you, the relationship has always been ambivalent; perhaps that is its power. Certainly, it has never been strongly negative enough to push me away altogether. Yet, as with my mother, the anger seems ready, as if lying in wait for the least crime against me. And less accessible, but also there, is the longing for a deep warmth and acceptance.

It seems strange to me now that we know so little about how most biographers or writers of literary or philosophical criticism feel about the writers whose lives and works they are describing. I'm not talking just about whether the biographer liked or admired the person, although that interests me too. Over the past months, I, for example, have worried far less about whether my imperfect knowledge of French and France detract from my right to write about you than about whether my complicated feelings and needs take away this right. But I am also talking now about how the daily intense concern with another person — perhaps most similar to the attitude one takes when hovering over the sick — made the writer feel. Perhaps admissions on this score are too dangerous, given our prevailing demands for an objectivity born of distance. If a writer confessed to editing out angry, ironic, or pleading sentences, what would happen to the reader's trust in those nicely balanced, Olympian sentences left standing?

I know that, since one of the themes I find over and over in your writing is that of tension and confusion between the "I" and the "we," I can easily be accused of projecting my own difficulties in the world, in general, and in writing about you, in particular, onto you and your work. It's almost a joke, isn't it — too close for comfort — that we might share some of the same weaknesses? Possibly also some of the same strengths. My own sense of being an intellectual has certainly gotten stronger as I have studied your writings and experienced your own solidity in the area. But I am still talking of a "we" between us, where the boundary is unclear.

My first sense of distance slipping was, in fact, an eerie and continuing recognition of our similarities. I note that in early April I wrote in my journal, "These days as I read de Beauvoir I find myself less able to assert, 'I'm not like her.' I recognize the aloofness combined with the hysteria — and then wonder if I am distorting my own image of myself in order to be like her. In short, I'm losing the distance I had a year ago: liking her more, feeling more like her for better or worse." I was reading *The Mandarins* at the time.

A few days later, having just finished *A Woman Destroyed* [a slim volume containing three stories about older women], I noted, "Feel like de Beauvoir is making me experience death and aging as I've never experienced them — even though I've written about both for years." Both parts of the sentence are utterly true: You had just made me feel I had never before *really* experienced death and, in fact, most of my fiction is about death — including a novel on which I had worked for three years and had only recently completed. It seems, as I look at these notes, that a kind of annihilation of myself by you was threatening to occur.

Then, on April 16, while I was looking at early book reviews of your works, a young woman I didn't know glanced over my shoulder. "You know, Sartre just died," she said, concernedly. "It was in this morning's paper." Tears came to my eyes; I felt confused: a friend, a husband, a father? What was/is he? My own father had died fifteen years ago, and all deaths call up that time. Then, over the next days, I began to worry about what it meant to write about a woman who is part of a duo and then, suddenly, midstream, whose companion is dead. All my sentences about you and Sartre, once in a continuing present tense, had to be changed. Going over the text to make those changes made the death real to me. More important, his death seemed to bring a sacredness to your relationship; a superstition cautioned me: You can't attack anything connected to the dead.

When my father died, it seemed at first an enormous tension had drained away between my mother and me. I identified with her suffering. In my arrogance, I felt at times that I suffered more than she. Yet soon I began to focus with her on the ways in which she was better off without the domination and demands of my father.

But you see, for me the gestalt has a terrible way of reversing itself. These days, when I am with my mother I find myself ruthlessly attacking my father. My mother, who is protective toward him but also knows how I once loved him, is astonished — and so am I! Because when I am in New York and she is back in her city, I, in fact think longingly of my father and often wish he were alive — at the same time as the slightest provocation, whether through memory or a letter from her, sends me directly to irritation and anger at my mother.

It is no wonder then that I feel anxious about my changing reactions to you, and particularly about my attitudes toward your relationship with Sartre. Whenever you write that Sartre's ideas had changed, and yours with his, I hear a scream rising inside me. Even now, my mother maintains that she always felt in complete harmony with my father, who made several dramatic changes during their time together. I don't want to stretch the parallels. Yet your decision to remain with Sartre, to make him the center of your life, seems to have entailed a heavy sacrifice of body, emotions, and, yes, sometimes even mind. "I should never have been capable, even in thought . . ." Surely, he did nourish you intellectually; but to my generation, the emotions and the body are terribly important, offering truths and pleasures, a path to the self, which cannot be arrived at by a highly trained rational mind alone. At times, I have felt that you sacrificed some inner core in order to be a witness. Here is Anne in *The Mandarins* speaking:

> I've always been able to avoid being caught by the snare of mirrors. But the glances, the looks, the stares of other people, who can resist that dizzying pit? I dress in black, speak little, write not at all; together, all these things form a certain picture which others see. I'm no one. It's easy of course to say "I am I." But who am I? Where to find myself?[6]

I know that Anne is not you. Yet you speak similarly of Françoise in *She Came to Stay* and of yourself at times in your memoirs — who were you in relation to Zaza, you wondered. Writing itself does not seem to solve the problem of identity for you. Since at times I doubt your separateness from Sartre, or that of your female characters from their mates, the witness who is "no one" slides into being a surrogate witness for Sartre, Dubreuil, Pierre. I must say, I am suspicious of Sartre as well as you, when he also says that the two of you, in understanding each other perfectly, could evaluate each other's work "objectively," as if from the point of view of a witness who was "no one."[7]

I think that I must be terribly threatened by and weary of this level of merging, having fought so hard for separateness and still so often tempted to let my boundaries dissolve. It seems clear that my main difficulty in working on your writings is my fear or wish that the boundaries between us will simply disappear. That I will become a witness to you, who is "no one." I note a May entry: "Afraid of being swallowed up by her — afraid of losing the separateness I've struggled so hard for."

On the other side, just as I love my mother when she assumes her independence, I love your urge toward freedom, your sense of yourself continually creating your life through courage and imagination. Particularly the first two books of your memoirs are filled with this power. And while you are critical of the individualism of your early years, I find a tone of joyous exuberance that I miss in much of the descriptions of an older you who had become politically responsible and respectable. Perhaps that is the influence the 1960s still holds on me: I want a joyous political movement, one with fun and humor, no matter how grim our situation or how powerful our enemy.

Yet how grateful I was when, some years ago, I began to read Jean-François Steiner's *Treblinka*, the story of the daring rebellion by starving and exhausted Jewish inmates inside one of Hitler's extermination camps, and found that *you* had written the introduction. I had been among the millions of Jews who had been led to believe our relatives had "gone like sheep to slaughter." Treblinka had a more daring, hopeful message — which included the possibility for freedom inside the worst hell. As you say about the incredible rising of resistance at Treblinka, "If it takes only a few cowards to make the entire series become cowardly, it takes only a few heroes to make people recover confidence in each other and begin to dare."[8] Steiner had tried to re-create this shift from fear and deathly resignation to incredible courage; and you understood how crucial this message of freedom would be, perhaps particularly to Jews.

Oh, I sometimes find myself griping about your notion of freedom. Although you increasingly grounded it in the social world — to the point where in *A Woman Destroyed* or *The Coming of Age* one loses the sense of individual freedom and responsibility — I don't think you ever grasped sufficiently the way the unconscious can hold one back from grasping a freedom consciously chosen. Too often I see your sense of freedom being based on a rationalism that denies that murky inner world over which we have as little, or much, control as the world outside us. And, in fact, control would be your word, not mine. For I've come to believe that we have to love this deep inner self and try to be in harmony with it. We can't make our life a "continuous flight from the past," to paraphrase Sartre;[9] it often backfires when we try. I understand that your rationalism is a reaction to the Catholicism of your childhood and to the enormous leap you had to make to step out of the life that had been planned for you. It was a step into freedom, but it must have meant denying old longings for comforts you knew were poison. Music, even more than fiction (which you approach somewhat rationally), seems to be the one area where you allow that nonrational self to play in pleasure; and you have said that listening to music has become increasingly important to you in later years.[10] I think, though, that my generation, which didn't have to fight the irrational domination of religion, may be able to feel out some of the nonrational areas, including that of spirituality, which you so understandably shun, without losing our freedom, allowing us to become more whole.

Sometimes I fear that my arguments with you, however right they may be in content, are also a way of showing myself that we are separate. I hear in myself a tone that indicates a pulling away, an assertion of my own individuality. But, as my parents used to take pleasure in reminding me, I was always a rebellious child. Perhaps my temperament, in this sense reminiscent of your own, is not the best suited to that of a biographer or critic. Perhaps one needs either to be certain at all times of being separate, or to be comfortable with stretches of merging, to be able to offer the gift of empathy.

My trouble with working on my book about you reached a crisis about a month ago: it centered around a kind of mothering. Or around my unwillingness to mother. Like you, I am childless. Generous to my friends, I actually often feel stingy in my own eyes. And also easily drained. For years, I thought I wasn't having a child because I needed first to give to myself. Once, when unintentionally pregnant, I dreamed of being gnawed at by the fetus, as by a crow inside me. Later, when I began to give myself more of what I needed, that very self-feeding, since it came in the form of writing, seemed to take up all my time. I feel sad that I won't have a child: giving birth is an act of optimism about oneself and the world.

At moments, I have felt a rancor whose expression is: Why should I be devoting myself to you when you never did anything for me? Now, I know that through your books, you have done a lot for me. And the writing of this one is doing still more. But when I feel deprived and unacknowledged, I resent your righteous success and feel stingy about contributing toward the attention you already receive. Perhaps this resentment adds to my wish to be critical. In any case, one day I heard about a woman who wanted to give her pubescent children away; and, without understanding why, I felt compelled to turn her story into fiction. Putting aside your books, I stuck a new white sheet in the typewriter, wrote "Nothing for Nothing" as its title, and a short story poured out of me. For several days, I alternated between working on "your book" and writing my story. I find a note in my journal: "A feeling of congestion from working on de Beauvoir, as if I had a child who was home all the time and left me no space. No wonder I'm writing 'Nothing for Nothing.'"

I can assure you that this period, although highly productive, was quite miserable. By writing the story, I let my stinginess come out in full force. I contacted the feeling in me that I had nothing left to give another person, that I was fragmented, exhausted, worn to shreds by caring. For a few days, no one could give to me: all interaction was negative, stripping my depleted self further and further, until I felt the only rest was to lie on my bed quietly, out of reach of sound and light.

It seems to me now that this division into give and take, like the absolute division of subject and object, was at least part of the problem. I was "giving" by poring over your works, but I was holding myself back and trying desperately to keep you an object so that I would not be submerged. At a purely physical level, this posture can engender a severe backache — and it did. Is it possible that, if I could have let myself become more a part of you, at least temporarily, without the fear of losing myself, I could also have felt the rush of your giving, and mine wouldn't have seemed such an extraction?

This period is over, its culmination, at least in part, this letter to you. I wonder what other stages I will go through in the next months before I am done with my project. Yes, a lot of my anger has been relieved, some of my confusion and discomfort lessened. Certainly I can more easily send you affectionate respect now than three days ago when I began this letter; and I do send that to you. But I also know that I will remain me, and I suspect we may have some trouble again before the end of our mutual road.

June 4-7, 1980

Placed in the middle of my book, this letter tended to draw readers to it as immediately as a sexy centerfold and to create a stir with both its critics and its admirers. Including it within the pages of a book that, traditionally speaking, should have been about Simone de Beauvoir, *not* Carol Ascher (one in which Carol Ascher should have been invisible), was an act of bravery that warmed up the work to those who liked it and was both intrusive and proof that the rest of the book could be little more than projections and confusions of identity to those who didn't. Though one reviewer, expressing the positive end of the spectrum of reactions wrote that this "interesting interlude . . . does, in fact, clear the air and bring the reader, writer and subject closer together," the negative end was expressed most dramatically in an exceptionally large review headline: "de Beauvoir Biography Overshadowed by Its Author."

Granted that it was useful for me personally to "clear the air," why did I insert the chapter, in the center no less? At the time, what struck me as I looked through biographies and literary criticism was *exactly* the absence of such confessionals within their pages. Women and men had spent years — far more than I — thinking and writing about the lives and works of others. They must have come to impasses such as I was experiencing; I'm not that odd. Yet they had covered their tracks. *I,* I thought to myself, would leave for others a record of what might be entailed in a long, intense involvement with another woman on whom one was writing. The letter not only would describe the acts of regaining balance or objectivity and convey the quality of my experience, but it would also offer readers a clue about the perspective from which the remainder of the book was written.

What interests me now, nearly three years later, and with the insights engendered by the book's reception, are two issues. Put bluntly, they are *truth:* in what ways did my epistemological exercise help me regain my balance and aid my readers in gaining theirs? And *beauty:* what kind of an aesthetic experience was I offering?

To speak first to the issue of truth — as it concerns myself: I believe that, insofar as one sees things with any "objectivity," one does so only by clearing out those ignored and unresolved emotions that function like brambles, stinging one's eyes and blocking one's vision when one tries to look outward. Obviously, this "clearing out" is an ideal. Most of us know of that disinterested but ecstatic emptiness from which the world is seen "as it really is" only from tales of yogic and other mystic states. The more usual, "impartial" perspective of, say, scholarship or journalism is produced by a combination of psychological muffling and the obscuring (to the authors themselves, much of the time) of vested interest. Humbly acknowledging my incapacity for the former and my distaste for the latter, my supposition was still that, once I had "cleared the air," the remainder of the book would proceed with the same measure of evenhandedness which until then had satisfied me.

Emotionally, the letter was effective. Once I had written it, I continued working on the book with more fluidity and joy and an easier, warmer feeling toward Simone de Beauvoir. In a friendship, when one finally stops the flow of daily life to say exactly what has been driving one crazy, there is invariably an enormous relief and freeing up afterward. Just so with this book. Though a letter clearly couldn't resolve the deep issues that years of introspection still had left tangled, I *felt* back in balance. I had the distance I needed, I could see what was really there. At one level, I had simply given my "I" enough run to rectify the resented imbalance of attention.

Does all this mean that I judge truth by the way I feel? Partly. But not completely or necessarily. It seems an important aspect but one that demands constant tempering by self-reflection. Clearing the air may leave one even blinder, if one has gotten rid of discomforting emotions that act as warning signs. Moreover, two people's blind spots — the author's and her subject's mutually (but blindly) corroborated — don't create a reliable vision.

As I look back on my time studying Simone de Beauvoir's life and work, I am able to categorize my responses into several attitudes or kinds of feelings: (1) Coldness, utter disinterest, a sense that she was wrong, but I was insufficiently interested to sift through details and arguments. An endless volume on China, which she wrote rapidly after a visit in the 1950s and which quickly proved naive, didn't seem even worth treating in my book. (2) Neutrality, brief or minor flares into negative or positive responses, but in areas that were clearly central to de Beauvoir's life and thought, so that I felt obliged to give them play. Her ideas on aging and death are a good example: Where Elaine Marks's work on de Beauvoir focused entirely on de Beauvoir's vision of aging and death, I devoted merely a chapter to the subject. (3) Appreciation of an area of de Beauvoir's life or work where, although I might disagree or disapprove of points, it seemed easy to separate my own point of view and where I never felt caught. Her ideas of freedom and choice are good examples — perhaps the content itself helped here. Finally, (4) irritation, conflict! Areas where my own personal conflicts seemed to both contaminate and illuminate what I was seeing in her. Interestingly, the areas that provoked me most were those showing the underside of freedom and choice: In my book, I dealt with them in the two chapters of which I wrote in my letter that my conflicts overlapped with hers. In one I traced de Beauvoir's life according to the concepts of the "I" and the "we"; in the other, I followed her early novels as they worked out a similar struggle between what I called "the self and other."

As I read and reread Simone de Beauvoir's memoirs, I found myself wincing at the failures in freedom she herself so often noted: She's not separate in her relations with a friend! She wants to merge with Sartre! She is trying to dissolve her personal identity and problems in the world's atrocities! (This last, in reaction to a passage in which she slipped back and forth between rage at the torture of an Algerian boy and at her own aging.) The question that her life and work continually raised, but did not solve, was for me: How can one be an "I" at the same time as one is part of a "we"? How can one retain one's separate identity when one is a devoted lover, a loyal friend, a committed activist — or, for that matter, an engaged biographer?

A major category in Simone de Beauvoir's writings is that of "the Other." It is handled overtly in *The Second Sex* and in *The Coming of Age* to describe women and the aged, respectively. And, though more covert, it is key to understanding most of her novels, from *She Came to Stay* to *The Blood of Others*, *All Men Are Mortal*, and even *The Mandarins.* A Hegelian category that Sartre transformed for his own philosophical purposes, the notion of the Other was seen by both de Beauvoir and Sartre as directing attention to the most primitive aspect of human beings: our refusal (in their view) to accept finiteness and our wish to obliterate the frailty of our finite selves through either dominating or being dominated by others, thus creating illusions of infiniteness. Many of Sartre's plays explore the sado-masochism of human relationships as his characters seek omnipotence. With a slightly different emphasis, de Beauvoir stresses the wish to merge, and in a sense to accept domination, in her female characters. Moreover, in *The Second Sex* de Beauvoir uses the same concept for historical explanation, arguing that the oppression of women could not have occurred (neither social class nor penis envy nor biology is sufficient to explain it) "if the human consciousness had not included the original category of the Other and an original aspiration to dominate the Other."[11] That is, in men's domination of women throughout history, a psychological necessity has been played out in which both women and men give up their freedom through women's becoming the Other, the Object, of men's domination.

But all philosophies, as I asserted in my book and still believe, are both personal philosophies and systems intended to be universal. The desire to dominate or be dominated — to merge — that both de Beauvoir and Sartre saw as the failure of our mortality was also a failure that they themselves were aware of in their relationship. One might say, in fact, that their own conflicts illuminated this area of existence. Though existentialism both evolved out of de Beauvoir's and Sartre's difficulties and gave them a tool with which to see their problems with "the Other" in both life and art, it only partially helped them resolve or overcome these problems. That they gave to the problem of "the Other" an existential, necessary character may also be one reason it had such a continuing hold on them. Living without God meant for them an irrepressible wish to *be* a god, to be infinite by obliterating those awesome distinctions between oneself and another that are essential to our mortality.

It seems to me now that de Beauvoir's very preoccupation with the self's tendency to merge with the other was partly responsible for my increasing discomfort as the months progressed. That is, not only was I not projecting my problems onto her (as I feared in my letter) but her problems in this area — the very painful way they appeared in her novels and memoirs — evoked the same uncertainties in me. As a good writer is able to do, she made me feel what she had experienced as well as stirring up my own unresolved difficulties.

My invention of the "I" and the "we" was an attempt to incorporate but also transcend her terms and conflicts, which seemed to offer no resolution as stated. Philosophically, I simply did not accept the primal place of the Other. To me, the idea of the Other, as worked out in de Beauvoir's memoirs, sociology, and fiction, seemed, at best, a powerful image or insight and, at worst, a rather pompous inflation of jealousy or hatred to a world view. Whereas philosophically and personally the "we" for de Beauvoir was always either unstable or a merged unity that threatened the existence of one "I," I had a vision of a "we" that was both ongoing and made up of simultaneously autonomous "I"s. Reaching toward this ideal in my own life, I also used my belief in its possibility to cut through the scenes of de Beauvoir with Sartre, the fictional characters she created, and her basic term, the Other.

Did I achieve truth? About myself or Simone de Beauvoir? To avoid endless regression, I will answer the question as it relates to de Beauvoir. Certainly I did not re-create her "as she really is." Since I was writing, not creating clones, this couldn't even have been my goal. The portrait I painted, at best, would have related to the richness and complexity of her being as a good gesture drawing relates to a live person standing before the painter. This is particularly so in my case, since I had no intention of covering every aspect of de Beauvoir's life and character. The arms or the feet of my drawing, say, were deliberately only sketched in.

With or without the letter, was there a truth in my gesture drawing? And having written the letter, did I have a special line on truth? By whose judgment? I was thrilled when Simone de Beauvoir, upon seeing the completed manuscript, was satisfied by its truth and penetration. (It was a moment that gave me a much needed mothering.) Yet approval from the source, however comforting, might mean only that my distortions coincided with hers! Others — friends,

even critics — thought they saw de Beauvoir in my drawing. Shall I
then trust in the corroboration of numbers? How would Sartre, or
someone who knew her intimately, have judged it? Did Lanzmann,
the man with whom she lived for seven years while retaining her
relationship with Sartre, see her in the same way as Sartre did?
What if one of them had seen a side of de Beauvoir that was nowhere
else revealed? Would it throw off the outlines of my drawing or
simply fill in a hazy area with delicate detail? I imagine Simone de
Beauvoir sitting in the live-model drawing class I once took. People
sit or stand on all sides of her. Some see her from the right, others
from the left. One drawing focuses on a bent elbow; another captures the edge of a cheek. All the drawings are of Simone de
Beauvoir, but only the teacher, who moves godlike about the room
and rests momentarily beside each student, can begin to perceive
the whole. And even then . . .

The drawing class has brought me to the epistemological and
aesthetic question of including the letter in the book. In an interesting portrait, the painter Velázquez inserted himself at the edge of
the painting. Some find that this oddity enhances the painting.
Others think it an annoying intrusion: His other portraits, filled
solely by their subjects, are so much more powerful! Because it is a
painting, a form that has been accepted as subjective, and not a
biography or a work of literary criticism, the issue of truth is of little
concern to most viewers. Yet by putting himself in the painting
Velázquez tells his audience, 'Here are some characteristics of the
man who created the picture. You may be able to judge something
about the accuracy of the portrait by seeing my face and the similarities and differences I have chosen to portray between myself and
my subject.' This act of rectification and warning may well help
attentive viewers gain their "balance" or sighting in judging the
painting.

Through my verbal self-portrait, I hoped I was giving readers
information about myself that would help their capacity to judge my
portrait of Simone de Beauvoir. My letter made clear, for example,
that I was someone who valued personal honesty and attention to
one's feelings and who would therefore be more critical than most of
de Beauvoir in these areas. On the other hand, while another writer
might one day devote herself to an analysis of the shifts in de
Beauvoir's political positions and their relation to her activism, this
was only of peripheral interest to me.

The question of inserting oneself in the portrait is also an aesthetic
one. I imagine a different history of painting in which all pictures
show the eye of the artist within the frame. In fact, the last five

hundred years of painting offer us something like this, although we have come to read it so easily that we scarcely take notice. Until the Renaissance, paintings were executed as if from a universal point of view ("the eye of God"), which is not so different from our current objective voice in prose. However, starting in the fourteenth or fifteenth century, the institution of perspective in painting created for the first time a reference to the specific point from which the painter eyed the scene. Thus, houses receding in one way indicated that the painter had stood a little to the right, mountains falling away in another implied that the eye of the painter had been on a hill behind the viewer, looking down on the scene.

I suspect that those early painters who inserted perspective into their paintings worried that they were diminishing the grandeur and beauty of the art to insist on the truth of the specific human point of view. Certainly, they must have understood that they had given up representing the universal, God-like stance. On the other side, their new style also asserted the centrality of the "I" and its very specific perspective. It raised the eye of the individual creator to new importance.

The courageous step these painters took nearly five hundred years ago reminds me, in fact, of de Beauvoir's and Sartre's break with the world view of Catholicism to create a philosophical view, existentialism, in which human beings alone and together are the moral judge, the measure of all things. And the awkwardnesses and ugly moments in de Beauvoir's writings are the combined result of her being new at the enterprise and our being unused to seeing its expression.

Perhaps the insurgents of each generation must in their own way fight once again to "clear the air" of the conventions of the powerful solidified into universal truths. Increasingly during our century, the universal God-given standards have been replaced by those of science. And as God as judge and mediator had his prose style, so science has its. Yet the human interests that these truths protect remain the same: the interests of ruling white, Western men. As Simone de Beauvoir herself remarked in the opening pages of *The Second Sex*:

> But if I wish to define myself, I must first of all say: "I am a woman"; on this truth must be based all further discussion. A man never begins by presenting himself as an individual of a certain sex; it goes without saying that he is a man. The terms *masculine* and *feminine* are used symmetrically only as a matter of form, as on legal papers. In actuality the relation of the two sexes is not quite like that of two electrical poles,

for man represents both the positive and the neutral, as is indicated by the common use of *man* to designate human beings in general; whereas *woman* represents only the negative, defined by limiting criteria, without reciprocity.[12]

And if one must strike out again and again to assert the *humanness* of one's perspective, its specificity, then that movement into what seems uncharted space must necessarily seem awkward. Cranky. Even grandiose. Until it becomes a new convention, viewed as aesthetically satisfying by the current standards, and must again be broken down.

Days when I look at "Clearing the Air — A Personal Word" nestled as it is in the midst of a book dotted with "I"s, I wince at whatever aesthetic judgment allowed me to place it there, whatever I thought of its value as truth. Why couldn't I have written a book whose clean, sleek surface lay unbroken, invulnerable, unruffled by the squirms of a conflicted "I"? The "I" of a woman still seems so much more naked on the page than that of a man. The aesthetic almost has a moral component: A good girl wouldn't expose herself that way, and in public! But then I imagine a new aesthetic (and a new morality) in which people, including myself, are more at ease with closeness, with uncertainty about truth, and with the confusing mix of subject and object that constitutes what is finally there to be seen — and what the reader's eye and mind take in with her or his own predispositions. I suspect that if such an aesthetic were to develop it would be accompanied by an easing of the stranglehold of fact and science, which in our day so often makes us fear a world beyond our control. It would likely be a nicer, more egalitarian, safer world all around — perhaps more beautiful as well.

Notes

1. Carol Ascher, *Simone de Beauvoir: A Life of Freedom* (Boston: Beacon Press, 1981), 107-22.

2. Simone de Beauvoir, *Force of Circumstance*, trans. Richard Howard (Harmondsworth, Eng.: Penguin, 1968), 569.

3. Simone de Beauvoir, *All Said and Done*, trans. Patrick O'Brien (New York: Warner, 1975), 28.

4. Simone de Beauvoir, *The Mandarins*, trans. Leonard M. Friedman (Glasgow: Fontana, 1960), 81; and Simone de Beauvoir, *The Prime of Life*, trans. Peter Green (Harmondsworth, Eng.: Penguin, 1965), 77.

5. de Beauvoir, *Mandarins*, 78.

6. de Beauvoir, *Mandarins*, 48.

7. Michel Sicard, *"Interférences: Entretien avec Simone de Beauvoir et Jean-Paul Sartre,"* *Obliques, Numero Spécial sur Sartre, dirigé par Michel Sicard* 18-19 (1979), 325-39.

8. Simone de Beauvoir, preface to *Treblinka,* by Jean-Francois Steiner, trans. Helen Weaver (New York: Simon & Schuster, 1967), 10.

9. See Hazel E. Barnes, *Sartre* (Philadelphia: Lippincott, 1973), 22.

10. de Beauvoir, *All Said and Done*, 210.

11. Simone de Beauvoir, *The Second Sex*, trans. and ed. H. M. Parshley (New York: Vintage, 1974), 64.

12. de Beauvoir, *Second Sex*, xvii-xviii.

Alice Dunbar-Nelson

Gloria T. Hull

Gloria T. Hull

ALICE DUNBAR-NELSON:
A PERSONAL AND LITERARY
PERSPECTIVE

Soon after I began teaching one of my first Black American literature
courses a few years ago, a student in the class — a young Black
woman — came up to me after a session on Paul Laurence Dunbar
and told me that she knew a lady in the city who was his niece.
While I was digesting that information, she ran on, saying something about Dunbar, his wife Alice, the niece, the niece's collection
of materials about them, and ended by stressing that there was, as
she put it, "a *lot* of stuff." From that unlikely, chance beginning has
developed my single most significant research undertaking — one
which has led me into the farthest reaches of Black feminist criticism, and resulted in new literary scholarship and exhilarating
personal growth.

This essay is a description of that process of researching and
writing about Alice Dunbar-Nelson. It is only my own, one Black
woman's experience, but in a certain limited sense, it can also be
regarded as something of a "case study" of Black feminist scholarship. We need to uncover and (re)write our own multistoried
history, and talk to one another as we are doing so. I emerged from
(not to say survived) this particular experience with insights
relevant to myself, to Dunbar-Nelson as woman and writer, and to
the practice of Black women's literary criticism.

At the end of that first conversation, the student promised to
introduce me to Ms. Pauline A. Young — Dunbar's niece by virtue
of his marriage to her mother's sister — but somehow this never

happened. A year or so passed, and I finally met Ms. Young after she happened to see me discussing her "Aunt Alice" on a local television program and called the producer. By this time, I had begun a serious study of early-twentieth-century Black women poets, including Alice Dunbar-Nelson, and was convinced that she was an important and fascinating figure who warranted more than the passing attention which she had heretofore received.

A good deal of this attention focused upon her as the wife of Paul Laurence Dunbar (1872-1906), America's first nationally recognized Black poet. Nevertheless, on her own merits, Alice Dunbar-Nelson was an outstanding writer and public person. She was born in New Orleans in 1875, grew up in the city, taught school there, and was prominent in its Black society, especially in musical and literary circles. She moved North, finally settling in Wilmington, Delaware, in 1902, where she remained until shortly before her death in 1935. From this base, she achieved local and national renown as a platform speaker, clubwoman, and political activist. She associated with other leaders like W. E. B. Du Bois, Mary Church Terrell, and Leslie Pinckney Hill. In addition, she was a writer all through her life. She poured out newspaper columns, published many stories and poems, the bulk of which appeared in two books and in magazines like *Crisis* and *Collier's*, and edited two additional works.

Knowing what I had already learned about Dunbar-Nelson, I was more than eager to become acquainted with Ms. Young and her materials. When I did, I was astounded. There in the small cottage where she lived was a trove of precious information — manuscript boxes of letters, diaries, and journals; scrapbooks on tables; two unpublished novels and drafts of published works in file folders; clippings and pictures under beds and bookshelves. I looked at it and thought — ruefully and ironically — of how, first, word of mouth (our enduring oral tradition) and, then, sheer happenstance accounted for my being there. I also thought of how this illustrated — once more — the distressing fact that much valuable, unique, irreplaceable material on women writers, and especially minority women writers, is not bibliographed and/or publicized, is not easily accessible, and is moldering away in unusual places.

In order to use this collection, I had to impose myself and become a bit of a nuisance. Being a Black woman certainly helped me here; but, even so, Ms. Young was understandably careful and protective of her documents. She never told me exactly everything she had (indeed, she may not have remembered it all herself) and allowed me to see it a little at a time until gradually I gained her confidence, got the run of the house, learned what was there, and began to use it. As I did so, my good fortune became even more apparent. This one source was the only place where some of these materials existed. They will probably be willed to the Moorland-Spingarn Research Center at Howard University, and then scholars will have to wait some years before they are sorted, catalogued, and readied for public use.

Ms. Young herself is a retired librarian and Delaware historian — which partly accounts for her consciousness of the worth of her holdings. Her years of trained habit also, no doubt, put many of the dates and sources on what would otherwise have been tantalizingly anonymous pictures and pieces of newsprint. In general, Ms. Young proved to be one of the biggest resources of all. With her memories and knowledge, she could share family history, identify people and references, and give invaluable information about their relationship to her aunt which no one else could provide. Once I puzzled for two days over the name of a companion in Alice's diaries only to learn finally from Ms. Young that it was the family dog.

Our personal relationship was even more charged and catalytic in ways which benefited us as individuals and further enhanced the work which we were doing. Interacting, we moved from cordiality to closeness. Several factors could have hindered or even stopped this development — the most elemental being Ms. Young's instinctive protectiveness of her aunt and family. Although her feelings probably included some ambivalence (and possibly more difficult unresolved emotions), these had been softened by time until her most powerful motivations were admiration and the desire to see her aunt get her due. Other complicating factors could have been the generational differences of perspective between us, and whatever undercurrent of feeling could have resulted from the fact that my writing on her aunt fulfilled a wish which unpropitious external circumstances had made it harder for Ms. Young herself to realize.

What tied us together was our common bond of radical Blackness and shared womanhood. We were two Black women joined together by and for a third Black woman writer whose life and work we were committed to affirming. Our building of trust and rapport was crucial to this whole process. Despite some rough spots, it enabled us to relate to each other in a basically honest, usually up-front manner, and to devise means (both informal and legal) for apportioning the labor and the credit.

The episode which most challenged — but ultimately proved — our relationship was the question of how Dunbar-Nelson's sexuality should be handled. When I discovered while editing Dunbar-Nelson's diary that her woman-identification extended to romantic liaisons with at least two of her friends, I imparted this information to Ms. Young. Her genuinely surprised response was, "Oh, Aunt Alice," and then immediately, "Well, we don't have to leave this in!" The two of us talked and retalked the issue, with me saying over and over again that these relationships did not besmirch Dunbar-Nelson's character or reputation, that they did not harm anyone else, that there is nothing wrong with love between women, that her attraction to women was only one part of her total identity and did not wipe out the other aspects of her other selves, and that, finally, showing her and the diary as they in fact were was simply the right thing to do. I knew that everything was fine when at last Ms. Young quipped, "Maybe it will sell a few more books," and we both laughed. Inwardly, I rejoiced that at least this one time, this one Black woman writer would be presented without the lies and distortions which have marked far too many of us.

Studying Dunbar-Nelson brought many such surprises and insights. Their cumulative meaning can be stated in terms of her *marginality*, on the one hand, and her *power*, on the other — a dual concept which suggests a way of talking not only about her, but also about other Black women writers, singly or as a group. First of all, Dunbar-Nelson has usually been seen as the wife of America's first famous Black poet who incidentally "wrote a little" herself. This is a situation which those of us who research minority and/or women writers are familiar with — having to rescue these figures from some comfortable, circumscribed shadow and place them in their own light. Furthermore, Dunbar-Nelson's basic personal status as a Black woman in the world was precarious. On the economic level, for instance, she always had to struggle for survival and for psychic necessities. That this was so graphically illustrates how the notion of her as "genteel, bourgeoise" needs revision. Black women generally occupy an ambiguous relationship with regard to class. Even those who are educated, "middle-class," and professional, and who manage to become writers, almost always derive from and/or have first-hand knowledge of working- or "lower"-class situations. Also, being Black, they have no entrenched and comfortable security in even their achieved class status (gained via breeding, education, culture, looks, etc., and not so much by money). And, being women, their position is rendered doubly tangential and complex. Dunbar-Nelson herself revealed these contradictions in the dichotomy between her outward aristocratic bearing, and the intimate realities of her straitened finances and private fun.

Her determination to work in society as a writer also made her vulnerable. Things were not set up for her, a *Black woman*, to be able to make her living in this way. This had to do with the avenues of publication which were open to her and the circles of prestige from which she was automatically excluded. When she needed one most, she was not able to get a job with even the *Crisis* or the NAACP, or a Black newspaper press service — her excellent qualifications notwithstanding. She was compelled always to accept or to create low-paying employment for herself, and to work under the most trying conditions.

Only the power emanating from within herself and strengthened by certain external networks of support enabled Dunbar-Nelson to transcend these destructive forces. Her mother, sister, and nieces in their inseparable, female-centered household constituted a first line of resistance (sometimes in conjunction with her second husband). Then came other Black women of visible achievement, such as Edwina B. Kruse, Georgia Douglas Johnson, and Mary McLeod Bethune, with whom she associated. In varying ways, they assured each other of their sanity and worth, and collectively validated their individual efforts to make the possible real. Yet, in the end, Dunbar-Nelson had to rely on her own power — the power of her deep-seated and cosmic spirituality, and the power which came from the ultimately unshakable inner knowledge of her own value and talent.

Everything that I have been saying throughout this essay illustrates the Black feminist critical approach which I used in researching Dunbar-Nelson. Having said this much, I am tempted to let the statement stand without further elaboration since, for me at least, it is much easier to do this work than to talk about the methodological principles undergirding it. There is the danger of omitting some point which is so fundamental and/or so integrally a part of the process and oneself as to feel obvious. And, with so much feminist theory being published, there is the risk of sounding too simple or repetitive.

Very briefly, then, here are the fundamental tenets: (1) everything about the subject is important for a total understanding and analysis of her life and work; (2) the proper scholarly stance is engaged rather than "objective"; (3) the personal (both the subject's and the critic's) *is* political; (4) description must be accompanied by analysis; (5) consciously maintaining at all times the angle of vision of a person who is both Black and female is imperative, as is the necessity for a class-conscious, anticapitalist perspective; (6) being principled requires rigorous truthfulness and "telling it all"; (7) research/criticism is not an academic/intellectual game, but a pursuit with social meanings rooted in the "real world." I always proceed from the assumption that Dunbar-Nelson had much to say to us and, even more importantly, that dealing honestly with her could, in a more-than-metaphoric sense, "save" some Black woman's life — as being able to write in this manner about her had, in a very concrete way, "saved" my own.

It goes without saying that I approached her as an important writer and her work as genuine literature. Probably as an (over?) reaction to the condescending, witty but empty, British urbanity of tone which is the hallmark of traditional white male literary scholarship (and which I dislike intensely), I usually discuss Dunbar-Nelson with high-level seriousness — and always with caring. Related to this are my slowly evolving attempts at being so far unfettered by conventional style as to write creatively, even poetically, if that is the way the feeling flows. Here, the question of audience is key. Having painfully developed these convictions and a modicum of courage to buttress them, I now include/visualize everybody (my department chair, the promotion and tenure committee, my mother and brother, my Black feminist sisters, the chair of Afro-American Studies, lovers, colleagues, friends) for each organic article, rather than write sneaky, schizophrenic essays from under two or three different hats.

In the final analysis, I sometimes feel that I am as ruthlessly unsparing of Dunbar-Nelson as I am of myself. And the process of personal examination is very much the same. For a Black woman, being face-to-face with another Black woman makes the most cruel and beautiful mirror. This is as true in scholarly research as it is on the everyday plane. Once I was dissecting an attitude of Dunbar-Nelson's of which I disapproved to a dear friend who has known me all of our adult lives. He gave me a bemused look and said, "You can't stand her because you're too much like her." I had never thought of it in quite those exact terms. Then, I rose to her/my/our defense.

However, it is true that Dunbar-Nelson and I are locked in uneasy sisterhood. On the one hand, I feel identity, our similarities, and closeness. On the other, there are differences, ambivalence, and critical distance. Superficially, one can see such commonalities as the facts that we were both born in Louisiana, lived in Delaware, wrote poetry, engaged in social-political activism, put a lot of energy into our jobs, appreciated our own accomplishments, did needlework, liked cats, and so on down a rather long list. External differences are equally obvious.

On a deeper level (as my friend perceptively pointed out), our relationship becomes most strenuous when I am forced to confront in Dunbar-Nelson those things about myself which I do not relish — a tendency toward egoistic stubbornness and toward letting oneself get sidetracked by the desire for comfortably assimilated acceptance, to divulge but two examples. Seeing my faults in her and, beyond that, seeing how they relate to us as Black women, fuels my efforts at self-improvement: her most enduring role-model effect is positive, inspirational. I think of her existence from its beginnings to the eventual scattering of her ashes over the Delaware River, and know that she was a magnificent woman.

Now that most of my work on her has been completed, she is no longer as strong a presence in my life, though she remains a constant. Hanging in my hall is a painting which she owned (a small watercolor given to her by a woman who was her friend-lover); and two of her copper mint-and-nut plates sit among the dishes on a pantry shelf. Alice herself has not deigned to trouble me — which I take as a sign that all is well between us.

Lynda Koolish

Lynda Koolish

THIS IS WHO SHE IS TO ME: ON PHOTOGRAPHING WOMEN

In 1962 I studied painting at Chouinard Art Institute. I remember very little about Watson Cross, my teacher that summer, other than his mustache, which I think of in retrospect as resembling Lech Walesa's. I do remember with acute clarity the passionate, disturbing ink washes and red conte crayon drawings of my friend Anne. She is the daughter of Auschwitz survivors and is herself a survivor of incest. It was she who first taught me about anger and tenderness as an artist.

Most of the important things I have learned as an artist were taught to me by women friends, many of them not visual artists.[1] From Anne and from other women I learned about integrity, about paying attention, about vulnerability, and about power. From many of the women I photograph, I continue to learn about these same things.

Since the summer at Chouinard, I have seen myself as an artist in one form or another. I have been a painter, a poet, a sculptor, a collage maker, and a furniture designer. But I never felt fully at home in any medium until I began photographing in 1971, in the context of an evolving feminist community that I wanted both to celebrate and to document. In the early 1970s, when "women's music" first began and the first women's presses began publishing mimeographed and offset chapbooks of women's poems, there was no Olivia Records or Persephone Press, no big poetry readings or feminist concerts at Carnegie Hall. In the San Francisco Bay Area, women began coming to performances at places like the Bacchanal, Artemis, and the Full Moon Coffee House with inexpensive cassette recorders and tinny microphones. We didn't have technology and we didn't have money, but we wanted to surround ourselves with women's culture, to share it with one another. I was one of those women, eagerly taping those first women's concerts and poetry

Margie Adam

readings. I recorded J. J. Wilson talking about Virginia Woolf and
Tillie Olsen reading "I Stand Here Ironing"; I assisted in the production of several public radio programs of feminist poetry and music.
But when women's culture began to flourish, I wanted to do more
than simply document it. I wanted to be a part of shaping it, to
suggest in as original a way as I could what this new culture represented, what our dreams and sources of power were. The photograph of Margie Adam was one of my earliest music photographs.
Most of all I wanted to help define the ethical vision at the center of
our nascent culture. I had been writing poetry, or rather trying to
write it, for years. Suddenly, compelling new themes began to
emerge in my poems, and I began writing again with energy and
direction. At about this time a friend loaned me her camera, took me
photographing, and taught me the rudiments of darkroom proce-

dure. I was hooked. I bought a Nikkormat and spent the next year
doing nothing but writing poems and making photographs.

I took my camera to the first Country Women's Festival in Albion,
California, in 1972. I fell in love with the land and the women's
community there and stayed for seven weeks, photographing
women building barns and cabins, splitting wood, milking goats,
and teaching each other skills such as welding, chainsaw repair, and
sheep shearing. My first photographic series was of women using
carpentry and farming tools. This project continued for several
years and was the foremother of the work that is most important to
me now: photographing women writers.

At the end of that summer, I returned to the Bay Area because I
was beginning a Ph.D. program in modern thought and literature at
Stanford University, but I remained deeply attached to the Albion
women and their land. They represented to me the future of feminism. I became one of the main photographers for *Country Women*
magazine, and later I became its poetry editor. For five or six years I
returned to the Albion area almost every month to photograph and

Dobie Dolphin

sustain my sense of belonging to that community and to see the women I loved. I wanted to make alive for other women my reverence for the work of the Albion women and the visions they were spinning. I was looking as an observer and a commentator at women's friendships, work relations, and relations with the land; women's aesthetics in architecture and in traditional arts like weaving and quilt-making. While documenting other women's visions, I was making my own art, my own vision. The photograph of Dobie housebuilding is one of my earliest Albion work photographs. Its sensuality and joyousness still give me pleasure.

Increasingly, I became involved with feminist literature, as a poet and later as a teacher. I began to see that the feminist vision was more complex than I had recognized at first. What I wanted to explore didn't necessarily happen with tools you could see. The tools were in women's minds. I wanted to photograph women writers and artists whose work was to think, to imagine, to speak. Gradually, the tools themselves faded in the images I was making, as my definitions of the meaning of work began to expand. But this meant that I had to search as deeply as I could into the psyches of the women I was photographing in order to photograph what they did.

What I depict as beauty in women is a kind of responsiveness — forthrightness, expressiveness, internal strength. It took me some time to understand that a visual celebration of female strength did not necessarily require images of women swinging hammers or axes. Instead, women's strength could be a reserved, quiet presence, the willingness to challenge one another's ideas, the capacity for making choices that are compassionate, responsible, and loving.

During the summer of 1974, I photographed the Third Country Women's Festival in Mendocino, where 150 women gathered for five days to share skills and community. For five consecutive days I worked from 7:00 A.M. to 7:00 P.M. and was absolutely exhilarated. The next year, I brought the photographs back to the festival as an exhibit. For the entire week, women who had been at the previous year's festival came up to me saying, "I don't know how you did it, but you caught the one moment during last year's festival that was most important to me — the one conversation, the one moment lost in thought. How did you see it? How were you there?"

I really don't know how to explain those images. I felt as if I were meditating with my camera, waking up at dawn and photographing from early morning until there was no longer enough light to see. The Mendocino Woodlands provided more than a familiar, essential geography. Nestled in its isolation, women had created a temporary Herland, a Wanderground. I felt a part of a collective sense of

Susan Raphael

celebration and a participant in individual friendships and moments of solitude. That deep connectedness to other women enabled me to feel completely uninhibited about walking up to women in the midst of intimate conversations, setting up my tripod, and photographing them on the spot — something I would normally be apprehensive of doing at a feminist meeting or academic conference. And not once in the entire five days did anyone indicate the slightest uneasiness, the smallest indication of feeling interrupted or intruded on. It was a boldness I have never felt before or since — and one of the deepest spiritual experiences of my life.

Four of the photographs in this essay were taken at the festival. I find the portrait of Susan Raphael particularly poignant. Women at the festival slept outdoors in sleeping bags. Susan, a poet and a musician, awakened us each morning by playing Vivaldi and Mozart on her violin as she walked through the Mendocino Woodlands. By tradition, on the last day of the festival, women gather in a circle and pass a gourd rattle. As the rattle is passed, each woman is invited to speak. When Susan's turn came, she hesitated out of shyness. Many of us had been very moved by the beauty of

Slim (Nancy) Te Selle and Ruth Ann Crawford

her morning concerts, and out of nowhere, spontaneously, many woman's hands appeared on Susan's shoulders and arms, giving loving support to hear her forth out of silence.

Hands are also central to the photograph of Slim and Ruth Ann talking. Ruth Ann's hands, animated and curved into a circle, almost merge with Slim's. They echo the curve of Slim's collarbone, the curve of their two bodies, and the way the two women flow into each other's physical and psychic space.

The final portrait from the festival included here is of the poet Elsa Gidlow. I am drawn to the photograph partly because it violates the most basic photographic rules yet everything works. I used Tri-X film (a fast, grainy indoor film) in bright sunlight, and I photographed a seventy-six-year-old woman in harsh light. Because Western culture so fears aging, photographers are expected to hide indications of age by using soft focus and diffuse light when photographing older people, especially women. I refused to do either — yet there she is, so *lovely.*

I see my work as a celebration of women's culture, a celebration of us all as writers, poets, artists, musicians, dancers, craftspeople, farmers, carpenters, mothers, daughters, sisters, lovers, friends.

Elsa Gidlow

Most of all, my photographs celebrate intelligence, articulation. I see the writers I photograph as catalysts for change, and because I am part of making their work visible to the world, part of helping a writer's vision take seed, take hold, in other women's lives, I am also partly a catalyst for change. I still get a thrill when I walk into a bookstore or a friend's home and spy a book on the shelf that has my photograph, my vision of the writer, on the dust jacket.

During the first few years that I was photographing, I sometimes had to struggle to hold on to a sense of myself as an artist, not merely as a reflection of someone else's work. Portrait photographers (especially those who work with musicians or other artists) are often treated as publicists — employees or pawns, the ones who take the photographs of the *real* artists — whose work is not art. Such a feeling is reinforced when photographers' work is returned dog-eared, Scotch-taped, or with crop marks and other notations inked directly onto the print, an infuriating and hurtful experience that has happened repeatedly not only to me but to every photographer I know. The first time my photographs were exhibited and the first time a photo-essay of mine was published apart from an article or other form of publicity for the work of a writer — as an artistic accomplishment on its own terms — I felt acknowledged in a way that is still important to me.

Most of all, I feel awed to be able to make a portrait of a writer I care about, to be able to tell other women, "This is who she is to me." As a critic or scholar, I am accountable to some notion of objectivity. As an artist, I am asked to allow my most personal and subjective experiences to emerge.

A friend and academic mentor tells me that as a critic I write appreciations rather than criticism. Luckily, as a photographer I am free to make a statement that is sensual rather than analytic, emotional rather than intellectual — one that is formed by what the writer's work means to me.

Both teaching and photographing have shamanistic functions for me. Each is an activity in which I can listen, take someone in, lose my own ego, stop focusing on how I am being perceived or whether I am feeling insecure, and simply *pay attention*, really deeply *pay attention*, to another person.

Photography is both the most intimate and the most isolate work I have ever done. When I'm photographing someone, even at a public event, I usually feel that I am in the middle of an intense conversation. I think that's why I am often told that it feels like conversations were going on in many of my portraits, even when only one woman is visible. The conversations — spoken and unspoken — that I have with the women I photograph are absolutely essential to me. But they happen only sporadically, when someone I want to photograph happens to be in the Bay Area or if I am at a conference in another city or state. When I teach, I have the opportunity for more frequent conversations with colleagues and students. Feminist teaching also feeds the vision that makes possible the kinds of photographs I take. And photographing women I love, whose work nurtures and inspires my life, feeds the vision that makes me passionate about writers and ideas in the classroom.

For every hour I spend behind a viewfinder, I spend days alone, developing and printing in the darkroom; mounting, matting, and framing prints; and reading, thinking, and writing about the work of the women I photograph.

Everything comes together when I photograph. I am sure of myself. I feel contented and happy and clear. I know what I want to say. I'm not worried about how to say it. With writing, I have to struggle and struggle and struggle to come close to what I want to say. Maybe that's why I photograph writers: I'm as obsessed with words as I am with images, even if I have not yet developed the same sense of sureness in language.

When I was writing my dissertation on feminist poets, or now when I write about literature, I never have that feeling that my work is finished. As a writer, a critic, even when I am writing with inspiration, energy, and love, I usually feel that whatever I have written doesn't quite do justice to the work I'm talking about. As a photographer, I often feel the satisfaction and certainty that I've absolutely done justice to the person I've photographed.

"What does it mean to you," I recently wrote to a colleague and dear friend, "to see yourself, the integrity and vision of who you are, shining in my eyes?" I was referring to an extraordinary conversation, in which each of us felt deeply apprehended by one another. Rereading that letter, I suddenly understood how closely those words match my feelings when I send a writer for whom I care deeply a photograph I have taken of her. Years ago, a friend told me that I photograph women as one would photograph a lover. That statement has a startling metaphysical accuracy for me. For one apprehends a lover differently — not because you make love but because there is an openness that you see. You *delight* in who the other person is. When I am photographing a woman, I want to come to understand who she fully is, for me and in the world. Most of my photographs are portraits of individual women, but it is the light they hold within them for other women that I seek.

Although I rarely photograph people I don't know, sometimes, when I am photographing at a feminist conference, I may photograph women I haven't previously met but whose presence at that conference provides a psychic and visual context for me. They no longer feel like strangers. It's a very loving experience for me to photograph someone. I care about people in a different way once I've photographed them. I've chosen to know them, to experience them as deeply and fully as I can. That's a very intimate experience. In an odd way, it does almost have the intimacy that being lovers can confer on a relationship.

I don't think you can ever photograph somebody well if you haven't opened your heart to them. It just doesn't work. The portrait of Susan Leigh Star with Maude Elizabeth, an Abyssinian cat, is one of the most tender and sensuous photographs I have ever taken, and it gives me a special pleasure because women's sexuality is so often depicted as a reflection of male definitions of the erotic. Sensuality here is joyous, self-affirming, intensely private, and spiritual.

The way that I work demands a personal, mutual relationship with the women I photograph, yet if I have never photographed someone before it is presumptuous of me to expect her to bother to know who I am. But once I've made a photographic statement about who someone is, I have found that she also wants to know who I am.

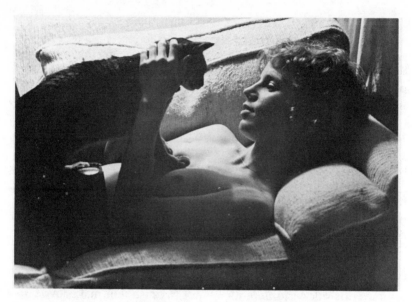

Susan Leigh Star and Maude Elizabeth

So my first photograph of someone is like a passport. It gets my foot in the door. Then I can deepen the relationship and take the photograph I really want to take. Because I usually learn a lot about a woman the first time I photograph her, in subsequent shootings I know more about what to listen and look for.

When I have photographed someone whose work I care about, I almost always send her a print. The relationship that may emerge from that transaction is important to my work as an artist because if a woman I've photographed feels that I've really caught some part of her, *seen* part of her, then she wants it to happen again and I get a chance to make deeper and richer photographs. I haven't actually photographed many writers — maybe forty. But many of them I have photographed repeatedly over a long period of time. For example, I have been photographing Judy Grahn for twelve years, Tillie Olsen and Adrienne Rich for nine years, and Audre Lorde for almost that long. I continue to photograph someone once I have a "good" portrait of her.

Certain things are necessary for a portrait to coalesce. First, I need to have a sense of what that person does in her life — what her life work is, not necessarily what she does for a living. Second, I need to care about her work. It might be political work, writing, painting, making ceramics, working with children, any number of things. Third, and most important, the person must care intensely about her work, and she must communicate this passion to others. I need to be able to find in her work a statement about the world because it is the relationship between the person and the world that I want to capture.

When I prepare to photograph a writer, an artist, or a musician, I immerse myself in her work. If I'm planning to photograph a musician, I play tapes of her music for several days before I go to photograph her. Before photographing a friend who is a painter and a calligrapher, I spent a lot of time in her studio and covered the walls of my own study with her calligraphy. Before photographing a writer, I read as intently as I can the parts of her work that are most moving to me. I try to listen to whatever is central to a poet so that when I go to photograph her I already have a sense of what to pay special attention to. I may be an observer as a photographer, but I don't feel at all passive about that process. I want to engage in part of a dialogue about women's collective work and about the individual work of the women I photograph.

My camera equipment virtually disappears for me when I am most emotionally and visually "on." Then, there is no mediation between the person I'm photographing and my eye. Sometimes I experience what Ruth Bernhard calls "pure seeing" even when I am not behind a camera lens. The first time I was aware of this was after I saw Marcel Marceau perform. I left the auditorium physically drained and needing a shower. I couldn't figure out why watching mime would be so exhausting, but I suddenly realized I had spent the preceding two hours unconsciously framing horizontal and vertical shots of Marceau transiting on the stage between being a hulking Goliath and a light-footed David.

I enjoy looking at contact sheets as well as individual prints because they document the flow of interaction between me and the person I photograph. Once, when I looked at the contact sheets of a morning spent photographing a famous novelist and poet, I realized that neither she nor I had moved during the entire session; her head and shoulders occupied about the same area of the negative in each successive frame. The elements that contribute to taking a good portrait were present; we had talked over a leisurely breakfast together before I set up my camera. I was familiar with and moved by this writer's work, and I was photographing in the Berkeley home of a friend of the writer's, an environment in which she felt comfortable. But I couldn't find a way to break through either her reserve or my own intimidation. So my self-consciousness is indelibly stamped on those contact sheets.

I have a deliberate way of photographing that I almost always utilize. I enjoy composing in the camera rather than in the darkroom, and I prefer to photograph from a conversational distance (about four feet with a 105-mm lens). So I tend to frame very tightly — that is, I almost always use one hundred percent of the negative area, and I rarely crop when I print. For this reason, my prints are usually 6½″ x 9½″ rather than the standard 8″ x 10″ format.

Other characteristics of my photographs have remained esentially unchanged since I began working in this medium. For instance, I still use a tripod and Tri-X film, even outdoors. In one sense, this is a holdover from so many years of photographing in the fog-shrouded Mendocino Woodlands, but it is also a deliberate and chosen method. By using a high-speed film, I opt for a technology that enables people to move around and be comfortable. Although a slower film can look more technically accomplished when it is printed because of its finer resolution, it also can produce portraits that look "studied" or posed, because slower films tend to make photographers discourage movement in their subjects. And I work with a tripod because, in spite of its apparent formality, it enables me to concentrate almost entirely on seeing and to forget at least consciously about technique. I can move to the side of the camera and look directly at someone as though I were behind the camera. I have photographed this way for so long that I no longer need to look through the viewfinder to know what the camera is seeing. I can be involved in conversation with the person I'm photographing and squeeze the shutter release without returning to the viewfinder.

The second reason I use a tripod is ethical rather than technical. When I use a tripod, I am not a "candid" photographer. I cannot sneak up on a subject, with my camera under my coat, and attempt to catch someone off guard. Instead, I want the person to be fully aware that I am photographing her. The photograph then becomes a portrait of what I am able to see when someone chooses to share herself with me, not an imposition of my mythologizing image of her.

In my approach to women as subjects — which is extremely direct, even spare — I want to convey their strength and vibrancy. I don't use tricky angles or complicated backgrounds or staged lighting. If I were to have photographed Bette Davis, for example, it would have been Bette Davis as herself, not Bette Davis as the Queen of Sheba. That's why I photograph people in their own spaces, even if the environment is not physically visible in the photograph.

One thing that distinguishes a photograph from a snapshot is how carefully the photographer has paid attention to background. Once I took a photograph of Cris Williamson singing. There was a vase on a bookshelf in the background that I had not noticed, and when Cris sang, her mouth opened *into* the vase. Since this exper-

Carolyn Kizer

ience, I have rarely been careless about distracting backgrounds. My backgrounds are characteristically plain, often a white wall, a dark curtain behind a speaker, the wooden siding of a house.

If what I choose invariably is the plainest possible background — a white wall, for instance — I still want to photograph a woman against a white wall of her own house. It is more important to me that someone feel comfortable in her own space than that I have the ease of working in a studio environment, where I could totally control the lighting, for instance.

In the photograph of Carolyn Kizer, the books in the background are visible not as props to make her look more distinguished, but because Carolyn felt comfortable being photographed in her study, a space that is essential to her sense of self. The architectural setting was not accidental, however. The elegance, formality, and massiveness of the bookshelves underscore one way that I see Carolyn — as a woman of substance, a woman to be contended with.

Sometimes the starkness of the backgrounds I choose contributes a sense of power and intensity to my photographs. In the portrait of

Tillie Olsen

Tillie Olsen, taken at the 1974 Virginia Woolf Symposium at the University of California at Santa Cruz, the diagonal black and white striped lines in the background were made by a graphic on the wall against which Tillie was standing. These lines draw the viewer into Tillie's stark, almost hawklike profile. They encourage an emotional and visual tension between the gentleness and compassion of Tillie's face and the angularity of the setting and her profile. The composition and juxtaposition are meant to suggest some of Tillie's determination, wisdom, and power.

When I am photographing at a conference, part of what I capture is the interaction between the audience and the speaker. If I am not careful about how I move or how much noise I make with my equipment, I might ruin the dynamic of that interaction, which is in many ways as delicate as a private conversation. But at a conference, I don't have to concentrate on keeping a conversation alive with the woman I'm photographing. And most people being photographed at an event are far less self-conscious than they are in a formal, prearranged sitting.

Photographing at someone's house is very private, very personal. The emphasis is on my relationship with the woman I am photographing, even when I am meeting her for the first time. When I photograph a writer in her own space, the intimacy we might share can spark a connection between us that creates a more vulnerable portrait, one that reveals more of both of us than a public conference setting would permit.

When a person looks at a portrait of mine, she often has the sense of being in the living room of the subject. Even when it is clear that the photograph was taken at a poetry reading or a conference, it still conveys a feeling of intimacy. There is eye contact between the woman being photographed and the viewer, although I may not make direct eye contact with the subject.

There is a certain patience in my portraits that I recognize as the same kind of patience a landscape photographer must have. A good landscape photographer watches the light. I place myself in relation to an individual or group and watch and watch and watch, just as I might watch a sunset, the lighting on a cathedral, or a tree or a river shrouded by fog to see some change that occurs in nature. I wait for an expression, a gesture, a tone, a form, or shadow.

When Ruth Bernhard does a still-life study of a nude or seashells, she doesn't take the *likeness* of the nude or the shells. She waits for the light to reveal a moment in time. That's the kind of attention — waiting for that moment — that I try to bring to my portraits. This is something I learned partly from Ruth, with whom I studied briefly several years ago.

I once brought to her class a photograph of the octagonal barn at T'ai Farm in Albion. I had shot it with a 6 x 7 camera (2¼" x 2¾" negatives), which made the print incredibly detailed. The women who built the barn loved the photograph and jokingly referred to it as "the barn portrait." The photograph was widely published. When Ruth saw it, she said it looked like a real estate ad because I had *shown* the barn rather than psychologically *entering* the barn. I had photographed the barn at a moment when I happened to have my camera handy. I had not paid attention. Ruth saw this instantly. She told me to go back to the barn and stay there for four days to watch the light change and change and change. Then I would know the moment in which to photograph.

One reason that it is so important for me to use natural light is that I want to know exactly what I am seeing. When you use a flash, you cannot know what you are seeing. How someone looks psychologically and visually is determined by how the light falls, the way the shadows form. When light falls on a person's face in a particular way, it makes her skin glow and sculpts her face, sometimes creating a sense of inner luminescence.

June Jordan

In my portrait of June Jordan, she looks almost lit from within. This effect is created by the actual light, yet it is also the light within June that illuminates the portrait. So much of June's radiance, her presence for other women, appears in this photograph. A photograph's luminescence is created by the interplay between how someone is lit from within by her own spirit and how the light falls.

The photograph of Paule Marshall catches her in a private, reflective moment, although it was taken while she was reading from her novel *Brown Girl, Brownstones* at the University of California at Berkeley. I think it has a similar quality of light to the Jordan portrait. Although the photograph suggests strength and determination, Marshall's face reflects a quality of sorrow that I find deeply moving.

Paule Marshall

The portrait of Adrienne Rich was taken at the 1978 WAVPM (Women Against Violence in Pornography and Media) Feminist Perspectives on Pornography Conference held in San Francisco. This photograph acknowledges for me how Adrienne's work is connected to my love for other women, my determination to be part of a struggle to transform our lives, my understanding of the meaning of integrity, and, most of all, my belief that women, in claiming new ways to love one another, are "reconstituting the world."

One snowy Vermont evening when I was teaching at Goddard College, I stayed up half the night talking and drinking Jack Daniels with a sculptor friend from Scotland. I wanted to name what was happening between us — two friends who would never be lovers, two friends who loved one another deeply, two women who came to understand ourselves and each other through talking about our work and about the passion that made our work both necessary and possible. I did not have sufficient words of my own to name this splitting open, this fracturing of old self-definitions — who we were to one another, who we were becoming, what each of us meant to the other's work.

I had brought a copy of Adrienne Rich's *The Dream of a Common Language* to Vermont. That night I read my friend the poem "Paula Becker to Clara Westhoff," about the extraordinary friendship between the painter Paula Modersohn Becker and the sculptor Clara Westhoff. I especially wanted to read these lines:

> How we used to work
> side by side! And how I've worked since then
> trying to create according to our plan
> that we'd bring, against all odds, our full power
> to every subject. Hold back nothing
> because we were women. Clara, our strength still lies
> in the things we used to talk about:
> how life and death take one another's hands,
> the struggle for truth, our old pledge against guilt
>
> Clara, I feel so full
> of work, the life I see ahead, and love
> for you, who of all people
> however badly I say this
> will hear all I say and cannot say.

Adrienne's poem says much of what I say and cannot say to Meg, just as the portrait of Adrienne says much of what I feel for Adrienne and have no words for.

In the photograph of Adrienne, much of the expressiveness lies in her hands. She was in the midst of an animated conversation with Audre Lorde. Usually I am careful not to invade anyone's privacy when I am photographing, but I couldn't resist slowly moving up the hallway with my camera and tripod when Adrienne and Audre were taking a break from the workshops. Their delight in each other, their engagement with each other's thoughts, is what I saw when I took this portrait.

Photography is the most acute listening I do in my life. When I am photographing someone, I "take her in," with a kind of active

Adrienne Rich

receptivity. If this process does not occur, then nothing meaningful appears on film. I value the quality of listening in other women and therefore I take a great deal of pleasure in photographing it. This is one reason that I loved photographing Audre Lorde. Her listening is one of the most active and aware experiences I have ever photographed. The portrait of Audre included here was taken at a workshop during the 1978 WAVPM pornography conference. There is so much energy, acuity, and presence; even in the act of listening, nothing about Audre Lorde is passive, unfocused. This quality of attention, which is so much a part of Audre's perceptiveness as a writer, comes alive in the portrait. In my best moments as a photographer, the activity of acute listening bleeds through to the activity of seeing.

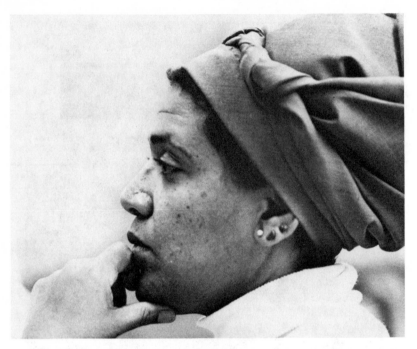

Audre Lorde

Judy Grahn is another poet whose work radiates intensity and clarity. One of Judy's many strengths is her ability to write about the lives of ordinary women, to convey their beauty and their power. Judy's example has helped to keep me honest, helped me resist the temptation to glamorize a woman when I photograph her. In the photo of Judy, taken almost ten years ago at a poetry reading, she is Druid-like, magical. What delights me in this photograph is that this small, almost frail woman, whose eyes are as enormous and com- pelling as Pablo Picasso's, possesses the power of a priestess.

In a review I wrote of Judy's most recent book, *The Queen of Wands,* I commented that the book "is charged with an awesome responsi- bility, one shared by all great poets: to seek and imagine meaning, to interpret, reveal; to be a spider webster, she who spins a web of words; to be a truth teller."[2] I believe this also describes my purpose in my work as a photographer, although it is a web of images, not words, that I spin. In this photograph of Judy I can vividly see the poet as shaman.

My portrait of Alice Walker is the most recent photographic por- trait in this essay. It was taken at a party celebrating the publication of *The Color Purple.* Like other women who have found themselves swept into the lives of Alice Walker's characters, I feel my own life

Judy Grahn

enlarged and transformed by characters like Celie, Nettie, and Shug. Gloria Steinem wrote that she "noticed that the readers of Alice Walker's work tend to speak about her as a friend: someone who has rescued them from passivity or anger; someone who has taught them sensuality or self-respect, humor or redemption."[3] Alice Walker's characters have assumed a life of their own, for the author as for all of us. In this photograph, her delight in them is mirrored in her face.

Printing has always been an important part of photography for me because the quality of the print transforms a completely private vision into a public image for other women to see. In a truly luminous print, the blacks are so deep that your eye seems to swim beneath the surface. Each photographic print is unique. Just as a woodcut may pick up ink differently from print to print, a photo-

Alice Walker

graphic print can also have a different "feel" because of variations in time spent in the developer or the method of drying, as well as more obvious differences like cropping or duration of exposure.

When I watch a print rise up from the developing solution, I sometimes feel an extraordinary thrill, as though what is happening is pure magic.* Sometimes typing up a draft of a poem that I've

*There is a painful irony in my discussing photographic printing in this essay. Because of an illness that makes exposure to any form of chemicals, including darkroom chemicals, extremely problematic, it has been almost two years since I last set foot in my darkroom. With increasing health, some protective equipment and the newly completed redesign of my darkroom, I may be able to start printing again within a year. But the frustration of having to have my work printed by someone else and not knowing when or if I'll be able to safely print again has eroded my sense of myself as a visual artist. I have taken fewer photographs during this period, and much of my new work is visible only in negatives or on contact sheets. This hiatus in my work is in the process of transformation. Writing this essay and a recent exhibit of my photographs — the first in two years — have helped to rekindle my determination to reclaim the work that is at the center of my life. Whether or not I am able to print my own photographs, I plan to keep my eye behind a viewfinder for a long, long time.

written out in longhand provides the same sort of excitement: the image actually leaps from the page. As an artist, sometimes I can make everything come out just the way I had envisioned it, and that's an occurence that rarely happens in other arenas of my life. My poem "The Photograph" was written about that:

The Photograph

The mirror image
is burned in shades
of black and white; reflected
through light the image fades

and is gone, dissolving
the emulsion into a kind
of permanence. Startled, I watch
your image rising up, the paper signed

indelibly by the sureness
which binds my eye to hand.
I make decisions in the darkroom;
this photograph is the one I planned.

Sometimes when I am deeply moved by a writer, by her work, I find myself unable to fully articulate in words my response. My camera then becomes a means for articulation. I try to photograph at the moment of spontaneous convergence of what is visually exciting and what moves me emotionally. Sometimes the photograph, like the poem, becomes a window filled with light.

Notes

1. This essay is informed by the generous spirits of several mothers in art, women with whom I have had generative and sustaining conversations. Susan Leigh Starhas celebrated, encouraged, and honored my work as an artist. Merline Williams, whose visions of feminism I hold dear, helped spark the spirit of this essay. Jinx Bridges, Wendy Cadden, Carmen Goodyear, and especially Meg Walker are all visual artists whose lives and work have been emotionally resonant for me. J. J. Wilson's knowledgeable and infectious enthusiasm for women's art continues to inspire and delight me. Leigh and Wendy helped me to focus the material in this essay by interviewing me on tape about my work as a photographer. Ruth Linden helped pare down the manuscript. And finally I would like to thank Claire Moses, who first suggested that I contribute a photo-essay to *Feminist Studies*, and Josephine Withers, who wrote an appreciation for that photo-essay. Excerpts from correspondence with Josephine, published in *Feminist Studies* 7:2 are included here.

2. Lynda Koolish, "Helen of Troy and Female Power: A Review of *The Queen of Wands*," San Francisco *Chronicle*, 20 February 1983, book review section, 3–6.

3. Gloria Steinem, "Do You Know This Woman? She Knows You: A Profile of Alice Walker," *Ms.* (June 1982), 36.

Virginia Woolf

Sara Ruddick

Sara Ruddick

NEW COMBINATIONS: LEARNING FROM VIRGINIA WOOLF

For Elizabeth Coleman, Dean of
the Seminar College, 1972–1984

*The aim of the new college, the cheap college should be not to segregate
and specialize, but to combine. It should explore the ways in which
mind and body can be made to cooperate; discover what new combinations make good wholes in human lives.*
— Virginia Woolf, *Three Guineas*

Virginia Woolf changed my life; the melodramatic hint of conversion seems appropriate. Yet it is difficult to credit, let alone share, a
change that was largely internal. I continue to live in the same city
with the same man and our children. I remain a cautious, wordy
person, quite unlike the activists I most admire. My conversion
involved rethinking, refeeling, rather than life changes. Yet the
division between before and after is, emotionally, a chasm.

Before my encounter with Woolf, I was fragmented and anxious.
Living on the edge of professional life, I depended on the smiles,
opinions, and invitations of Distinguished Thinkers. Along with
Hannah Arendt, I hoped that the thinking ego was "sexless" and
without a "life story." But like many women, I secretly believed that
Thought belonged to men, women being only its handmaidens and
interpreters. Strength too resided in men and power, for women, in
the male connection. Understandably, I resented and feared the
men in whose presence I felt inferior and powerless. Yet the idea
that my own life might offer a distinctive perspective on shared
human concerns did not occur to me. I was passionately involved in
the details of my children's lives and in the parental work I shared
with my husband and women friends. But in my eyes motherhood
meant self-denial and boring domesticity; the intensity and various
pleasures of mothering only made me feel more anxious that I was
losing my own direction. To be a *person* meant fitting child care into
the interstices of Interesting Work. Nonetheless, the rich texture of

my emotional life made the clever academic world, with its exhibi-
tionism, defensiveness, and self-preoccupation, seem like a flat-
tened version of elementary school. But maddeningly, once I was
present at the parties or meetings of Great Thinkers, the reality of
my emotional life faded. I became anxiously quiet or defensively
exhibitionist myself.

My encounter with Virginia Woolf began in 1971. Since then I
have radically transformed my ideas about mothers and being a
mother, about thinking and Great Thinkers, about the search for
authority in women, and ultimately about clearsighted, loving independence from any authority one trusts. I now live contentedly
on the margins of academic life with time for writing that seems
intimately connected to my work and politics. Though my story is
personal, it revolves around emotional changes familiar to many
women. What may seem eccentric in the story is the central place I
give to my work on Virginia Woolf. Of course there was more to my
life than Virginia Woolf; in particular, the sustaining force of
teaching, family and friends, and the challenging support of feminism. But Virginia Woolf was the personal, direct agent of change in
my life; it was she who freed me from dependence on men's
judgment, who made women real for me, who helped me recover
my own mind, eyes, and voice.

Many people find it difficult to hear about these "unreal" loves,
this "sucking off the life of another," as one friend put it. I too worry
about looking for rescue from a woman who sanctions your own
desires. But I think we may be scenting pathology in the wrong
place. The real danger lies in the romance of Great Thinkers and
Fascinating Men; it is under their spell that women lose initiative,
judgment and self-respect and, in the worst cases, comply with,
even thrill to, the violence of their states and professions. The desire
to be in, on top, included by Men of Power, is widespread in a
society as cruel and stratified as ours. Virginia Woolf taught me to
say "we" and mean women, to say "we" are different and to value
differences. She envisioned a "society of outsiders," a society of
people who are "shut out" or "shut up" because they are women, or
because they are "Jews, because [they] are democrats, because of
race, because of religion." She showed me a place outside of
charmed circles where I could stand.

Surrendering to Woolf's influence, I was not left at her mercy, not
enthralled by her Greatness. It is true that I had to work through
temptations to idealize her and also to suspect and discount her just
because she was a woman. This is part of my story. But she never
tempted me to self-loss and she tempered, rather than exaggerated,

the arrogance of class and profession. Why is it we are so skittish about learning from women, so afraid we'll lose our Politics, forget ourselves, or be trapped in the second-best sex? I'm asking these questions of myself as much as of my readers; I'm telling this story — and I helped put together this book — in the hope that another generation of women will not have to ask these questions because they can trust their love for the women they learn from, trust themselves.

★

As a freshman in college, I studied *To the Lighthouse*. I shared the Ramsay children's anger at their father's tyrannical whims; I don't remember loving Mrs. Ramsay. But when, in the space of brackets, Mr.Ramsay stumbles along a passage one dark morning with outstretched arms only to discover that Mrs. Ramsay had died rather suddenly the night before, I suffered a shock that only great writing can administer.

To the Lighthouse haunted my imagination, but my Great Teacher that year was Socrates and, more immediately, the philosophers, all men, who were teaching me to think. "My dear Crito," Socrates warned his student, "I appreciate your warm feelings very much — that is, assuming they have some justification; if not, the stronger they are, the harder they will be to deal with."[1] I took his warning. The summer before, the Rosenbergs had been executed; I understood nothing of the politics or history of this monstrous act, only that the executioners were filled with crazy, ignorant hate. Some of the teachers I knew best were studying the emotional origins of fascism; others were victims of McCarthyism, of stupidity, bigotry, and superstition. It was not a time to trust feeling.

Did I also suspect that power, good or bad, lay clearly with men? I remember my philosophy teacher — born the same year as my father, built like him, sounding like him. When my father visited, the two men admired each other and me. I can still see them talking away, well above my head, agreeing that philosophy was good "mental exercise," a wonderful activity for the young. Even — the teacher assured my father, as he would later assure his own students — very good training for a mother. I was taught *To the Lighthouse* in my mother's voice, by a woman I passionately but reluctantly adored. To her, I insisted vehemently that literature was not "serious," that I was going to do only the most difficult and abstract work.

Not long after, I became a wife, a good one. Putting my husband's career first, I landed in an academic community in which the subordination of women was as normal and unnoticed as the clean New

England air we breathed. The few "strident" complainers were dismissed with amusement or psychiatric labels. I was uncomplaining, an Interesting Woman writing a thesis on Wittgenstein while cooking gourmet dinners. Unfortunately, I was totally unable to work — to write, even to outline, even to read anything connected with my thesis.

In the college library I discovered a book on Virginia Woolf that described her first two novels as attempts to reconcile marriage with a sense of self. Intrigued, I read *The Writer's Diary*, in which Woolf writes about her intentions for *Mrs. Dalloway*: "I adumbrate here a study of insanity and suicide: the world seen by the insane and sane side by side." The diarist seemed so eminently alive, able to work, and sane, that I hoped her novel would be an antidote for my craziness. Turning to it, I read:

> And there is a dignity in people; a solitude; even between husband and wife a gulf; and that one must respect, thought Clarissa, watching him open the door; for one would not part with it oneself, or take it against his will, from one's husband, without losing one's independence, one's self-respect — something after all priceless.[2]

I was beginning to recover my mind.

Two years later I had conceived a child, written the thesis, borne the child, revised and defended the thesis. The two kinds of labor clearly enabled each other. But I was too content (or perhaps too disturbed) to try to understand. Through the New England winter I sat by the sleeping, fussing, playing baby rereading long familiar novels — *Middlemarch*, *The Portrait of a Lady*, *Anna Karenina*, and once again *To the Lighthouse*. I lived to the rhythms of an infant and to those of "unreal" worlds we seemed to share. Literary heroines lent their seriousness to my domestic life. I was "part of a literary community and a tradition of women who talk well about their lives and link them, by language, to a larger subject."[3] Unfortunately, as I insisted to others and to myself, I was only a visitor to the "community and tradition of women," taking "time out" from my *real* work. I acquired the habit of starting philosophy papers, writing with some interest — for a few hours, some days — then putting them aside. The clutter on my desk reassured me that I was not *merely* a mother.

★

By my mid-thirties, I lived in Manhattan with two small children and a child-care-sharing husband. I had a series of more or less satisfying part-time teaching jobs and managed to finish a few papers at the request of editor friends. I looked for the lucky break that would set me down on a familiar — that is, tenure — track but meanwhile was busily involved in a fragmented maternal life, trying without success to weave my passions and ambitions into some recognizable whole. Then the luck I waited for, the tenure track to run on, became a real possibility; I was asked to apply for two full-time jobs that I was encouraged to believe could be mine. Opportunity threw me into disarray. I suffered a near paralysis like the one I had had over my thesis. I hadn't yet heard of fear of success. I knew only that philosophy seemed without charm or purpose, professional life unbearable. I didn't apply for the jobs, and then I became demoralized, unable once again to write, kept afloat only by the teaching I continued to enjoy and to do well.

In retrospect, I understand why I refused the jobs. My part-time jobs were close to home; the new jobs were at some distance, the more attractive one requiring me to spend two nights away each week. I could reconcile my part-time jobs with domestic and social life and with occasional writing. Most important, philosophy had become exactly what my teacher and father predicted, a pleasurable mental exercise charged with nostalgia for the thrill of the abstract. Why would I want to spend hours away from home, among people whose manner and ambition were increasingly strange, worrying about the children I'd left behind? At the time, however, I was shamed by my failure to live up to my ideals of feminist independence. I berated myself for being unable to take advantage of opportunities other women didn't have and for depending on a husband, his money, and the choices they brought when most mothers worked at far more demanding and less rewarding jobs than the ones I was turning down.

In this restless, dissatisfied mood I read that the New York Public Library had acquired the manuscripts of Virginia Woolf's diaries. Trying to find ways to make use of the city since I was "good for nothing else," I decided to take a look at them. Very quickly, that look became an absorbing hobby. I began to go to the library on Fridays, after a week's teaching, for the first time choosing to do something unrelated to work, that kept me away from home after school hours. I called my children from the library, brought gifts from the library shop, even read my six-year-old daughter the whole of *Flush* and *Orlando*. Waiting for the bus home at closing time, I felt torn from a secret world, an illicit passion.

The library itself was oddly discomfiting. In a chilly room an imposing priestess and her anxious assistants presided over treasures that people off the streets and campuses could not appreciate. I was warned not to lean on the manuscripts, turn the pages too quickly, come near them with ink. I was sure I had dirty hands and a runny nose. The estate, which eventually wanted to publish the diaries, had decreed that no one could take notes from them. I read with the published, abridged version by my elbow, slipping in phrases from the manuscripts when no one was looking. For fear that one of the authorities might glance in my book, I used a code I can no longer decipher.

It was a regressive moment in the life of a middle-aged mother. Neither my childishness nor my absorption in Woolf's life made sense to me. No professional task or identity helped me to feel my self. In my childhood, a profession had legitimized my father's social ambitions and justified his domestic rule. I loved visiting his law office and chose his chair to read in at home. For a time I had planned to become a lawyer myself, and for some years I had believed that my own profession would give me a passport to his world. But my failures were forcing me, for self-respect, to deprofessionalize my imagination. My library visits, my childish absorption in the life of another woman, my disorientation were first steps in that direction.

Like most readers of Woolf, I began to keep a journal, its subject a mix of Woolf and me. For the first time since adolescence I attended to my days. I walked for hours, watching people watching each other and themselves; following Woolf, I imagined their inner life. In Woolfian rhythms, I heard the city's voices, personal conversations, and impersonal markers — subways, traffic, clocks. Woolf wrote, "There's no doubt in my mind that I have found out how to begin (at 40) to say something in my own voice . . . At forty I am beginning to learn the mechanism of my own brain — how to get the greatest amount of pleasure and work out of it."[4] I was discovering my eyes and ears, I was only thirty-six; there was time for my voice.

Often when I turn to women, I lose myself in their lives out of a sense of inferiority. Since I did not find Woolf a model of virtue or of worthy long-suffering, I was in less danger than usual of succumbing to heroinism. Reading while "on holiday" I delighted with Woolf in small pleasures, sympathized with her worries about time and money, and felt only relief that she showed openly an edginess, jealousy, and snobbery that others work hard to conceal. I could have felt drowned in Woolf's incredible energy and sheer brilliance. Yet surprisingly, Woolf inspired me to find, not lose, myself. I am not sure how she conferred this gift of self-recovery — the sense that my life, in its daily ordinariness, not in its labored cleverness, was worth attention. I may not understand, but I cannot doubt my memory. Time and again, students, writing with grateful astonishment of the ways Woolf enhances and deepens *their* lives, remind me of this mysterious gift of authenticity Woolf confers.

Authenticity was certainly helped along by my reading. Early on, Woolf gave me a political language to express what had seemed only my personal trouble in the professional world. To be sure, I had many memories, beginning in graduate school, of academic professionals who would let war continue, certainly let racism and poverty flourish, if to resist would require that they relinquish their cleverness, training, or pet preoccupations. Though distracted by my efforts not to be a "mere" mother, even I could see that worthy Great Thinkers lived off the labor of others, including those who took care of the children who meant so much to them when time allowed. But because I insisted on my right to do the work I had trained for and feared the judgment of the men who did it, any doubt about the institutions of work seemed only cowardice. Woolf began to give me the courage of my perceptions. "The professions," she said, "have a certain undeniable effect on the professors. They make the people who practice them possessive, jealous of any infringement on their rights, and highly combative if anyone dares dispute them. And do not such qualities lead to war?"[5]

As the hold of professionalism loosened, I began to imagine working without the ever-present curriculum vitae and my academic judges hovering over my shoulder. Woolf encouraged me to delight in female minds, to appreciate hers and my own. I had bought the going stereotype: minds were male, my mind and my father's. Now I could countenance the idea of a "thinking woman." But I had worked halfheartedly for so long that I needed to relearn skills of concentration and commitment. Woolf worked hard and regularly. As she set and missed deadlines, dealt with interruptions, had bad days and breakthroughs, I began to get a sense of the patience and dedication involved in writing, of the countless visions revised to achieve the gracefulness I had thought one of nature's gifts. The clutter on my desk no longer betokened effort, let alone discipline.

The very idea of discipline forced me to think about the place of writing in a life that included teaching and a lively family. Did I have space for even a minimal commitment to writing? If, a short time earlier, I had been asked to free-associate to the phrase "dedicated to his (as it would have been) work," something like this would have come out: "irritable, stingy with time, self-occupied, controlling, demanding of sympathetic service . . . " In short, a portrait not unlike that of Mr. Ramsay in *To the Lighthouse*, certainly not a figure to wish on students, colleagues, friends, or family. I would have made up this portrait partly from my acquaintance with professional men but also from my fears of the sacrifice work would require and my fantasies of the privilege that success might generate. Woolf, however, gave me a different sense of the human meaning of dedication. Her diaries record an almost obsessive conflict between the needs of others, writing, and social pleasures. It was important to me, as it was so often with Woolf, that she lived with the conflict rather than talking or acting it away. She never relinquished her myriad friendships and loves; nor her walks, parties, letter-writing, work for the Hogarth Press, projects for the cooperative women's guild, political polemics, needlework, or serendipitous reading. To be sure, Woolf sometimes rued the "lost" hours, and there are those who wish she had protected herself from variety. But in her public stands she was clear. Both her fictional portraits and her political essays declare that the professional model of demanding, self-absorbed work cripples those who succumb to it.

> Sight goes. They have no time to look at pictures. Sound goes. They have no time to listen to music. Speech goes. They have no time for conversation. They lose their sense of proportion — the relations between one thing and another. Humanity goes . . . What remains then of a human being that has lost sight, sound, and sense of proportion? Only a cripple in a cave.[6]

For two years I read Woolf's diaries, then her letters, then, with the most excitement, manuscripts of her novels. At home I read the published novels, A Room of One's Own, and Three Guineas. The spring of 1974, my husband's sabbatical year, we went to England. Absorbed by Woolf, I lived in a different England, not the anxious Oxford that had shadowed my former visits but the England I loved as an undergraduate studying Shakespeare, the England my mother had passed on to me when, many times over, she showed me the photographs of her one trip abroad before she married. England contained important Woolf papers and I was determined to see them. My husband and I had known for a long time that an equal division of family duties, besides being just, made for our happiness. But for many reasons, we had been unable to match our practice to theory. That spring, working out of pleasure and deep personal need, I was able to make the demands on my family that I believed in. While my husband cared for the apartment and children, I would get up at five in the morning, take the train to Cambridge or

Sussex, read all day, and return to London in the evening. I did this roughly every other day and sometimes for a few consecutive days. I still feel vividly those early morning departures, the morning and evening lights of the English countryside, the hours of intense reading, and the "off" days on which my children and I "haunted" (Woolf's word) the places Woolf lived.

When I returned from England I was given a chance to present my work on Woolf at a conference. To legitimate my presence among "real" critics, I wrote a philosophical introduction to my paper about life as a "text," called my work hermeneusis, cited Ricoeur, and alluded to Barthes. Fortunately, an early reader persuaded me that this package was both dreary and unnecessary. Woolf encouraged all women to speak in their own, not a borrowed voice. Yet without my clever introduction I felt exposed.

My paper was about Woolf's relation to her mother. I called it "Learning to Live with the Angel in the House." In her late fifties, Woolf wrote

> Until I was in the forties — I could settle the date by seeing when I wrote *To the Lighthouse,* but am too casual here to bother to do it — the presence of my mother obsesses me. I could hear her voice, see her, imagine what she would do or say as I went about my day's doings . . . It is perfectly true that she obsessed me, in spite of the fact that she died when I was thirteen, until I was forty-four . . . I wrote [*To the Lighthouse*] very quickly and when it was written, I ceased to be obsessed by my mother. I no longer hear her voice; I do not see her.[7]

Trying to understand how writing *To the Lighthouse* cured Woolf of her obsession, I looked first at her memories of the mother who haunted her. According to Woolf, her mother created and kept alive the "panoply of life." She was "the very centre of that great Cathedral space that was childhood"; "the word central gets closest to the general feeling I had of living so completely in her atmosphere." She was beautiful, a stern taskmaster, an almost driven philanthropist who wrote a book on nursing and publicly opposed women's suffrage. With three older children from her first marriage, four children from her second, and nearly full responsibility for her husband's schizophrenic daughter, she was incredibly busy. Woolf remembers her as almost always surrounded by others.[8]

From the then unpublished memoirs I chose two memories to capture the particularly unresolvable pain of Woolf's loss at her mother's death. The first, allegedly Woolf's earliest memory, was an impression of red and purple flowers which soon reveal themselves to be figures on a black background, her mother's lap in which the young Virginia sat, on a train or bus, traveling in London or to St. Ives. Deliberately vague about the details of traveling, Woolf conveys the sense of being surrounded by beauty, both safely held and effectively moving. I placed this memory next to Woolf's recollection of her last visit with her dying mother. As she leaves the bedroom, her mother admonishes, "Hold yourself straight my little goat." In this memory I saw the intense and self-conscious thirteen-year-old abandoned to judgment, to demands for female graciousness, to self-conscious shame, and then ultimately to anger and grief.

Turning to *To the Lighthouse,* I searched the manuscript, concurrent diaries, and finished text to discover how the forty-four-year-old writer freed herself from her obsession. Mrs. Ramsay, Woolf's created mother, is stunningly, lovingly competent with her youngest children, she empathically understands the adoring middle ones, but is often estranged from the oldest, especially the daughters, whom she finds critical and who dream of lives different from hers. She lovingly trains her children in the very ideology of womanliness that damages her and them, yet Woolf gives her an inner meditative life and a capacity for self-knowledge and change that win the reader's respect. Early on, blocked in her writing, Woolf transformed a minor character, a rosy-cheeked, spinster amateur painter in her fifties, into a deviant-artist-daughter whom we know as Lily Briscoe. I watched Lily confront the meaning of Mrs. Ramsay's life as she tries to shape a life of her own, moving through stages of attempted merging, idealization, anger, realistic perception, and painful mourning. In the end, Lily is able to live quite differently from Mrs. Ramsay and to take pride in their differences, without denying her indebtedness or her love.

Like Woolf, I wrote as a daughter, and when I presented my paper I felt that I was memorializing both Woolf's mother and her fictional counterpart. I shared the feeling of independence I attributed to Lily and took comfort that I was still younger than she was when she finished her painting. I did not think consciously of my own mother or of my relation to her.

Yet from the beginning my mother had been a barely concealed third presence in my encounter with Woolf. In 1968, when I was thirty-three and she was sixty, my mother nearly died from a stroke complicated by pneumonia. We had rejected life supports and had begun to make funeral arrangements when, astonishingly, she began to recover and then, by force of will, resumed a nearly normal life. Both anticipatory grief and joyous relief awakened in me an intense childlike love. My adult relation to my mother had been, and still is, a warm, affectionate triumph over adolescent ambivalence. But my new passionate love for her required, for balance, a new kind of knowledge.

The surprising intensity of my feelings for Woolf partly resulted from my unconscious search for ways in which she was like my mother. Indeed, in my eyes the two women share many traits: humor, capacity for pleasure, skill at fine needlework, delight in vigorous outdoor exercise, a courageous, determined cheerfulness that sometimes served them badly, a real appreciation of the costs of anger, and excessive doubts about its expression. Both are very smart, very thoughtful women. In her life, Woolf enjoyed many of the same activities my mother and I had enjoyed together — gossip, books, plays, dinners, travel. In the colors and rhythms of her prose, Woolf invokes the intensities of experience which, for me, were inseparable from the childhood world suffused with the sounds, smells, and tastes of my mother's house. When I peered into Woolf's diaries, letters, and manuscripts — into the private life behind published appearances — I was peering into, making sense of, my mother's life as well.

If Woolf was in some sense a mother, she was even more a daughter who expressed daughterly longings and confusions remarkably like my own. My relation to my mother, like Woolf's to hers, was part fantasy, a reconstruction of childhood perception and love that no actual woman could fulfill for another. Woolf seemed to know all about this: "divining, through her own past, some deep, some buried, some quite speechless feeling that one had for one's mother . . . quite out of proportion to anything she actually was." Both Woolf and I wanted to know the "secrets" of mothers' lives, a desire that for me became almost obsessive after my mother's recovery. Both of us were tempted to believe, as Lily believed of Mrs. Ramsay, that a mother "lock[ed] up within her some secret which . . . people must have for the world to go on at all." But Woolf rejected this fantasy as well as the lures of merging and idealization that go with it.[9]

The two memories I had chosen to convey the unresolved pain of Woolf's relation to her mother now seem as much about my own experience as about hers. With exquisite competence my mother had created for me a childhood in which I was both held and safely moving, both secure and enabled. Yet I remember, as an adolescent, often feeling abandoned to critical judgment and conventions of femininity. I had selected these particular memories from Woolf's then unpublished memoirs, relying on notes that were especially subject to autobiographical intensities. In working on my paper, I was doubly identifying with Woolf, who in her writing had "expressed some very long felt and deeply felt emotion. And in expressing it explained it and then laid it to rest."[10]

Woolf allowed me both to express my love for and to achieve some critical distance from my mother. As she insists in *To the Lighthouse*, it is not "irreverent" to appreciate a mother's eccentric foibles, to think coolly about the motives and conditions of maternal power, and to face up to maternal compliance in the sexual inequities of mastery and pleasure that damage both mothers and children. At the end of *To the Lighthouse*, Mrs. Ramsay becomes for Lily Briscoe a benign rather than obsessive presence, as Julia Stephen had for Woolf herself, as my mother had for me.

For four years, Virginia Woolf's life was nearly at the center of mine. During this time, partly under her inspiration, I tried to understand and overcome my vacillation and halfheartedness in work. Writing about Woolf, being responsible in public for the fruits of my private reading, was the final step in the loosening of professionalism. I knew now that "work" could satisfy deep personal need *and* be intellectually challenging *and* still mean something to attentive strangers. Woolf's witty portraits of combative or needy male egos under stress had defused the appeal of Great Thinkers, while the larger spiritual world she explored rekindled my human need for connection and significance that professional life would have buried.

But I do not want to idealize the rescuing angel. I did not experience Woolf's wit and wisdom in a vacuum. In 1972 I began to teach in what has since become the Seminar College at the New School, where I was required only to devise seminars addressing issues central to my intellectual life and worthy of public consideration. Here, in the absence of the traps, trappings, and rewards of professionalism, I worked through my desires for status and respectability — but not without considerable ambivalence and backsliding. It certainly helped that I had an "affiliation" to attach to my name, a library card, a schedule, and a small salary sufficient for self-respect. Even more enabling were the lively, quirky, gifted students the college attracts and the colleagues of original and genuine intellectual seriousness, many with equally eccentric relations to their own professions.

Nor was Woolf the only angel to whom I turned. Although I wanted to write, desire was not sufficient for action. Needing to develop the confidence and discipline required for independent work, I began to ask other women how they shaped their days to allow writing and what strategies they had for dealing with the blank mind or the empty page. From several women I heard how economic oppression, arrogant discrimination, or straightforward sexism had destroyed the conditions for work. Many women had developed inner prejudices against their own abilities or worthiness. I wanted women to tell their stories, to speak personally of the meaning of their chosen work and the struggle they had doing it. Along with Pamela Daniels, I began putting together *Working It Out,* a collection of personal essays about women's relation to their chosen work. Soon this project replaced my absorption in Woolf. Yet the book was never free from her influence. As one reviewer said, Woolf kept appearing in the essays, like a guiding spirit.

The very evening we toasted the publication of *Working It Out* with our editor, Jane Marcus phoned to ask me to write an essay for a collection of feminist essays on Woolf. By this time, I quite consciously took Woolf as a teacher who enabled me to resolve problems in a feminist understanding of women's lives. I decided to write about Woolf's relation to her brothers. The topic had little to do with me personally. (I have one much younger brother; our relationship is distant and unproblematic.) But I had become intrigued by the fascination and power of brothers in the lives of many women writers and friends. In *A Room of One's Own,* Woolf had created Shakespeare's now famous sister as a comment on the material oppression of women's lives. In *Three Guineas* she spoke as a sister to a brother, insisting on the distinctiveness of a sister's education and morality. Surely the brother-sister relation was resonant with literary, biographical, and political possibilities.

I wrote the essay without thinking about the anthology's space limitations or the attention span of readers. In eighty-odd pages, I traced Woolf's real and fictional relations to three kinds of brothers. Woolf's rivalry with a younger brother who stole her mother's attention seemed well accounted for in familiar psychoanalytic terms. Woolf's much older half-brothers apparently toyed with her sexually and certainly abused the power that age and family position gave them. Woolf later wrote of some of these painful episodes with either witty detachment or bewilderment. "What is the word for so dumb and mixed a feeling?" she asked on behalf of her younger self, who had remained silent, at a loss for the word that no one, except perhaps her sister, would have believed.[11] I wanted to give her the words to understand the effect of even "mild" sexual abuse when it occurs in a family that allows the strong to have their way with the younger and weaker while those who see what is happening will not name the violation. Many of her biographers have argued that Woolf's experience with her half-brothers largely accounts for her later inability to experience heterosexual pleasure. I did not deny these theories, but I emphasized the political meaning of Woolf's early experience of the sexualization of abusive power. Whatever its personal cost, this experience created a precocious political identity as an outsider to the "patriarchal circus," an identity that lay at the heart of Woolf's feminist-pacifist vision.[12]

Virginia Woolf's good brother — a year and a half older, beautiful, distant, and adored — died young. Woolf mourned and recovered him through fiction. This mourning was suffused with the allure of male power when embodied in good rather than evil brothers and mixed with envy and fear — political as much as psychological — of the arrogance of men. Woolf dealt with her hatred of arrogant, dangerous male power and her simultaneous love for her brother and other men by distinguishing the private brother, whom "many of us have reason to respect," from the public brother whom society creates, "a monstrous male, loud of voice, hard of fist." In her fiction, she created beautiful brothers without losing sight of the society in which their arrogance thrives or of the wars they make that kill them and us. In *The Waves*, Woolf invented a hero and subjected the very idea of heroism to witty criticism. Through writing this novel, I argued, she finally put to rest the ghost of her brother by expressing her love for him while renouncing masochistic or idealistic sisterly relations to brotherly power.

Beginning my essay on Woolf and her brothers, I noted with relief that I wasn't writing about myself. But of course this paper was about me, about the male heroes I'd longed for and the Great Thinkers I'd enviously, angrily adored; about arrogant brother academics; about my daughter and about her older brother, my son. Most of all the essay was about my son, the "private boy" I loved so intensely, whose adolescence now forced me to look at what it meant to be a man in America's public world.

After the paper was finished, Woolf once again receded into the background of my work. Yet it seems as if, during the many years I worked on her, my mind itself had changed. I play easily with abstractions, spontaneously searching out the general amidst particulars. Working on Woolf required relishing the particular for its own sake, moving to generality only by tracing increasingly complex webs of connection and layers of meaning. I was only looking at "texts," yet I seemed to learn new ways of attending to the natural world and to people, especially children. This kind of attending was intimately connected with caring; because I cared I reread slowly, then found myself watching more carefully, listening with patience, absorbed by gestures, moods and thoughts. The more I attended, the more deeply I cared. The domination of feeling by thought, which I had worked so hard to achieve, was breaking down. Instead of developing arguments that could bring my feelings to heel, I allowed feeling to inform my most abstract thinking, reversing the message of my Great Teacher, Socrates. "My dear Crito," I would warn *my* student, "I appreciate your clear, clever arguments very much — that is, assuming they are informed by honest feeling and attentive to need; if not, the stronger they are, the harder they will be to deal with."

None of this happened quickly. Both my process of work and its subject — caring attention to particular texts, children, lives — were "womanly" in the conventional sense. My well-educated head was steeped in conventional definitions, secretly thought of itself as male, and openly claimed to be genderless. Moreover, the style of public thinking in the feminist circles I frequented could be as abstract and competitive as in academic meetings. Given my training and delight in polemics, I am easily drawn to battle. But at least I have a new conception of minds and their uses. I now care about my thinking and think about what I care for — about lives and what endangers them, about women and our work.

Woolf continues to inspire my writing and teaching but she is only occasionally their subject. Yet living my life, I suddenly find her claiming my attention with her familiar power. Partly, there are many unresolved tensions in my relation to this woman who has meant so much to me. Also, I am drawn to defend Woolf when others attack her. Then again, Woolf opened up for me a world of women. And oddly enough, whenever my interest in another woman becomes particularly intense in the ways Woolf herself made possible, somehow Woolf gets mixed up in the relation too.

For several semesters, just after finishing *Working It Out*, I became intensely interested in Simone Weil. Weil writes about the moral centrality of work and the deep shame a society bears when it does not even attempt to provide its members with dignified labor. Her account of the damage that real or threatened violence exacts from both the violent and the violated is a major contribution to pacifist theory. And her analysis of violence as a force that turns a person into a thing gives us a way to identify violent threats, acts, and policies in a family, a classroom, a government position, or an assembly line as well as on a battlefield. When writing about Woolf and her brothers, I used Weil's account of affliction to express the pain Woolf suffered from her half-brothers' abuse. Later I called on Weil's portrait of the warrior, on her stunning analysis of a hero's intoxication with violence, to supplement Woolf's perceptions of male arrogance.

Personally, however, Weil challenged my sympathies, though not because of her mystical Christianity or intellectual and political beliefs. By that time I didn't need to accept all the beliefs of a teacher, even of a woman who was a major inspiration. My problems with Weil concerned her person, and mine. I was repelled by Weil's self-hatred and the anti-Semitism that was one expression of it. Her strenuous, unremitting moral seriousness depressed me. When I, who love to eat, read that in a hungry world a full meal is a kind of theft, I was defensively exasperated, and I remembered Weil's alleged anorexia. But ultimately I couldn't shake the challenge of her purity. I am affluent, white, and Gentile. If the world is divided between oppressors and oppressed, each adjective puts me among the oppressors. I could barely listen as Weil spoke eloquently of the pain of the oppressed, a pain to which the oppressor must not let herself contribute by so much as a gesture, accent, or tone of voice.

At one point my ambivalence about Weil — I might almost say the self-torture she induced — broke into the open in the midst of a seminar. I was talking about Weil's life to give students a background for the essays they would read. To my shock, I heard myself telling Weil's story in a tone of contemptuous pity, punctuated by giggles. I made all of her sufferings — from the exhaustion of factory work to excruciating headaches — into the "symptoms" of a masochist and a social isolate. The saga of her career as a soldier especially aroused my scorn. Despite her deep revulsion from violence, Weil volunteered to fight in the Spanish Civil War because she was unable to prevent herself "from participating morally in that war — in other words, from hoping all day and every day for the victory of one side and the defeat of the other." Although issued a gun, she did not engage directly in the fighting. Because of her nearsightedness, she stepped in a pot of boiling oil. With difficulty and in pain, she made her way to a hospital, where she was rescued by her parents. Back in France, she expressed her hatred of the violence even of a just war:

> As soon as men know that they can kill without fear of punishment or blame, they kill; or at least they encourage killers with approving smiles. If anyone happens to feel a slight distaste to begin with, he keeps quiet for fear of seeming unmanly. People get carried away by a sort of intoxication which is irresistible without a fortitude of soul

which I am bound to consider exceptional since I have met
with it nowhere . . . One sets out as a volunteer, with the
idea of sacrifice, and finds oneself in a war which resembles
a war of mercenaries, only with much more cruelty and with
less human respect for the enemy.[13]

I told this story *laughingly,* heartlessly, carelessly indicting Weil's
sacrifice, idealism, disillusion, and of course her physical clumsiness.
Finally, I shocked myself into silence and ended the class. By the
next meeting my fit had passed and, abashed, I apologized to my
students.

I have thought of this episode many times. I think I learned a lot
from it — for example, that moral heroism will find a limited response with hedonists like me and that guilt can lead with surprising speed to retaliatory anger. What upset me most at the time
(aside from the shame of my unteacherly hysteria) was the intensity
of my response to this woman. Why couldn't I just let Weil — and
myself — alone, like others who read her?

I needed to develop a rational relationship with Weil if I was going
to use her work wisely. Casting about for ways to do this, I suddenly
(I can remember the exact place and moment) had the idea of
teaching a seminar on her and Woolf together. This strange, nearly
unworkable coupling surely had extrapedagogical motives. I said I
would use Weil to "deepen" Woolf. Less consciously, I was using
Woolf to "rescue" Weil both from herself and from my contemptuous pity.

I began achieving this rescue in my essay about Woolf and her
brothers. Like Woolf, Weil had a good older brother. When his
exceptional gifts made her own "inferiority" apparent to her, she
fell into a pit of "bottomless despair" in which she seriously thought
of killing herself because of her "mediocrity." Weil says that she
pulled herself from this despair by a radical, spiritual vision of
equality. From that vision, in conjunction with an empathic participation in others' suffering, came the purity and moral strenuous-
ness that laid her (and me) low. I wanted Weil to have Woolf's
tolerance of weakness and ambivalence, to accept what Camus calls
"the holy innocence of those who forgive themselves."[14]

In her last diary entry, when she was dying of self-induced
starvation, Weil wrote:

From [the] alliance between matter and real feelings comes
the significance of meals on solemn occasions, at festivals
and family or friendly reunions, even between two friends
. . . And the significance of special dishes: Christmas turkey

and marrons glacé — Candlemas cakes at Marseilles —
Easter eggs . . . The joy and the spiritual significance of the
feast is situated *within* the special delicacy associated with
the feast.[15]

Is it such a long step from that London hospital bed to Mrs.
Ramsay's table with its candlelight, voices like those "of a service in
a cathedral," and the "still space that lies about the heart of things"?
Food is at the center of Mrs. Ramsay's festival: I wanted Weil, like
the other guests, to accept her gift.[16]

When I was teaching *To the Lighthouse* in the seminar on Weil and
Woolf, I had a dream of almost hallucinatory intensity.

> Weil stands on the shore of a lake looking across at a rolling
> range of mountains. I see her first from the back, knowing
> her immediately in her familiar cloak and beret; then I look
> into her sad eyes. Weil cannot get to the mountains. Though
> she could walk on water, she will not, for fear of blasphemy.
> And the only boat that would take her is already overfilled
> with fishermen (Weil was intensely drawn to fishermen)
> whose space she dare not usurp. She stands absolutely
> motionless. I wake up crying.

It was my fantasy, I think, that Woolf could fashion for Weil a boat in
which she could travel.

This was, of course, *my* dream. A friend asked me why I didn't let
Weil swim. Or, for that matter, walk. Partly, of course, I must have
wanted Weil to be stuck, a price for the pain she caused me. More
important, I would guess, is that at the time of the dream my
children were young adolescents who often seemed as stuck as Weil
in their own unhappiness. I was slowly learning to accept the fact
that they too could be rendered motionless because, like Weil, they
framed their dilemmas in ways I was powerless to change. In the
dream I was allowing Weil, as I was learning to allow my children,
the suffering they found necessary. That it is possible to accept an
irremediable sadness in ordinary lives, even in the lives you create,
lives, and sadness too, for which you are responsible; this also
seemed a Woolfian "secret . . . people must have for the world to go
on at all."

After the seminar, my relation with Weil became less obsessive
and self-destructive. Woolf too became again a benign but unnoticed presence, except for the occasional enchanted weekend. But
it was not long before she emerged again, this time heralded by a
critical clatter.

When I began working on Woolf in 1971, no one, so far as I knew, was talking about her. Soon, however, she became a kind of public event, an inspiration for many women, the subject of fierce and loving feminist appreciation, and then, inevitably, the object of attack. Some people resented the attention Woolf received when other women were yet to be heard. Others were discomfited by feminists who challenged not only the old ways of reading Woolf but also the critical, detached ranking and canonizing style of reading altogether. And some *feminist* critics took Woolf to be an antiheroine, the mother we must destroy, a prisoner of class and racial arrogance, a sexual conservative mired in a romantic account of womanly difference.

Needless to say, I was not indifferent to these attacks on the woman I loved. Sometimes I would hide my defensiveness — and love — in lit-crit babble. At other moments, I would fiercely fight off attackers' real misunderstandings and ignorance while masking the failures I was afraid to admit. Such protectiveness and idealization had their price. How could I trust a woman who needed my defense? How could I rely on the wit and intelligence of someone whose "faults" I'd hidden? It was as if I had to accept everything from her or relinquish her gifts altogether.

Around this time, I heard a distinguished critic say that she did not "accept" Woolf's suicide. Some friends and I affectionately mocked the critic's defensiveness and her silly idea that Woolf's suicide was up for acceptance. But this critic's fierce loyalty provoked me to examine my own. Hadn't I denied Woolf's despair and cloaked what she boldly called her "madness" in a feminist mist. Didn't I forget that Woolf only imagined Mrs. Ramsay's dinner? That she, like Weil, often refused to eat and suffered from excruciating headaches? On the other hand, wasn't I afraid, just like her critics, that Woolf was superficial or too womanly? Why had I needed Weil to "deepen" Woolf? Why, for that matter, did I always lard my seminars on Woolf with other writers as if she herself weren't worthy of students' full attention, not even for a few hours a week? I made little headway with my confused and defensive admiration until I encountered Woolf again, this time amidst three other women, Charlotte Brontë, Elizabeth Gaskell, and my daughter.

In 1981, an invitation to speak in Germany became the occasion for a trip with my fifteen-year-old daughter. She devised our itinerary, the emotional center of which was a visit to Charlotte Brontë's home in the north of England. My daughter loved *Jane Eyre* as a child, and during the past troubled year she had lived some weeks with *Villette*. I, on the other hand, had been only the most superficial of Brontë readers.

While traveling I read *Villette* along with an updated version of Elizabeth Gaskell's biography of Charlotte Brontë. Earlier, I had read Helene Moglen's literary and biographical portrayal of Brontë's life. I began to form a picture of Brontë as a struggling woman living in a small village, determined to write despite ill health, isolation, poverty, and incredible personal loss, desperately trying to come to a political understanding of her society and of the place of a woman's passion within it. This heroic figure was also working her way through an ordinary unrequited passion for a married man who had been her teacher (her "master") during one of her few attempts to live independently outside her village. But this is to put the matter far too trivially. First in her passion and then in her fictional reconstructions, Brontë expressed, then mastered, a deep conflict between sturdy, self-respecting independence and the desire to serve and adore a masterful man. This meant fighting off the demons of useless self-sacrifice, "madness," and the sweet allure of fantasy. Brontë's life story has the force of myth; even without my daughter's prodding I would have fallen under its spell. But I was with my daughter; I saw Brontë as a daughter, as young and in need of support. Like all daughters, she deserved respect for her struggles and a hearing for her passion.

My vehement loyalty to Brontë as a daughter was reinforced by an event on the trip. I asked my daughter to read *A Room of One's Own* when we were visiting the places where Woolf had lived in London. I hoped she could overcome her earlier jealousy of Woolf's claim on my attention, and in any case every young person should read *A Room of One's Own*. Although I know that any book I recommend to my daughter is somewhat tainted, I was nonetheless unprepared for her vigorous attack. She found the very idea of the "shapely feminine sentence" offensively sexist and inhibiting. She scorned the charge that "Charlotte Brontë, with all her splendid gift for prose, stumbled and fell with that weapon ["a man's sentence"] in her hands." The brunt of her attack, however, was reserved for Woolf's criticism of Brontë's anger. According to Woolf, Brontë's anger "deformed and twisted" her books so that she wrote in a rage when she should have been calm, wrote foolishly where she should have written wisely, wrote of herself where she should have written of her characters. My daughter accused Woolf of cold-hearted indifference to the real, material limits of Brontë's life. Moreover, Woolf was self-deceived. Wasn't she herself very angry? And she was cowardly, for unlike Charlotte (with whom my daughter has a first-name relation) she couldn't risk expressing her anger. Finally, Woolf failed as a critic by missing the *meaning* of Brontë's passion, both of Brontë's anger, which she scorned, and of her sexual longing and will to be strong which she ignored.[17]

At first I disciplined myself to look for the truths in these attacks. I reread *A Room of One's Own*, then admitted to my daughter Woolf's fear of anger and sexual passion, though not *so* great as my daughter imagined. Yet I too found it hard to accept the apparent heartlessness and cold arrogance of some of Woolf's phrases: "She [Brontë] is at war with her lot. How could she help but die young, cramped, and thwarted?"[18] (It is hard even to write these words here.) Up to this time, Woolf had been a rescuer and mentor. Now she was censoring and misreading my daughter's heroine. I, by contrast, was determined not to belittle Brontë's pain or her strength. It was the first time that I had competed with Woolf, trying to outmother her, as it were.

In the spring of 1982, I taught a seminar on Charlotte Brontë and her friend and biographer, the novelist Elizabeth Gaskell. The syllabus included *A Room of One's Own*; in the classroom we reenacted my daughter's debate with Woolf and me. But it was Elizabeth Gaskell who helped us think about how women should, in justice and love, represent their friends and heroines to the public. Gaskell brought to her friendship with Charlotte Brontë the same voracious interest in people and wide, unjudging sympathy that inspired her fiction. Immersed in her busy family and community life, Gaskell seemed blessed with wit, social skill, and a knack for happiness. Yet she never closed out or patronized her awkward, shy, eccentric friend. Brontë was always strengthened by visits with Gaskell. Gaskell heard Brontë's terrible life story, and the two shared their thoughts about writing and the gossip of the literary and political world. These two very different women responded to each other's books with tactful honesty and warm appreciation. Once, when they were publishing novels at nearly the same time, Brontë wrote movingly to insist that there was only friendship, not competition between them.

When her friend died at the age of thirty-nine, Gaskell decided to write Brontë's biography. A mother herself, Gaskell expresses wonderfully in her fiction both the values and limitations of maternal thinking. Turning to biography, she brought to her research a mother's attentive concern for the detail, the quality of Brontë's inner life. At the same time, with incredible energy and wit, she created for the reader a lively sense of Charlotte's village, family, and friends, both explaining and re-creating the sense of Charlotte's isolation. In her fiction, Gaskell firmly defended people others might cast out — for example, "fallen women" — and tried to translate domestic sympathy and fairness into claims for social justice. She brought the same compassion and respect to her vision of Charlotte Brontë.

Gaskell claimed that she wrote her biography to make the world "honour the woman as they have admired the writer." If Brontë was attacked for being too sexual or too angry, Gaskell would be ready with stories of Brontë's devotion to others' needs and her isolated, celibate struggle to write. Gaskell claimed that she "weighed every line" with her "whole power and heart" in the interests of Brontë's honor.[19] In the light of fuller evidence, we can see that in her weighing, Gaskell managed to avoid a lot. She is notorious for covering up Brontë's unrequited love. She also barely hinted at Brontë's obsessive exploration of heterosexual passion and certainly diluted the painfulness of her ambition and her sharp resisting anger.

This self-censoring does not make for dull reading. The biography reads like one of Gaskell's own novels; filled with the lively details of place and person, it is both a great nineteenth-century memorial and a passionate maternal plea for justice and sympathy. In its attentive love for her subject, Gaskell's biography provides a model for reflecting on women. But I also take from it a warning. In her aversion to anger, personal ambivalence, and unhappy sexuality, Gaskell reveals the limitations of too cautious and protective a love. She never minimizes Brontë's pain, or certainly her virtues. But in simplifying Brontë's psychic life, Gaskell keeps from us complicated, uncomfortable truths we need; truths we are able to ponder because Brontë mustered the courage to reveal them.

It would be nice to be able to end by saying that I now bring to Woolf not only Gaskell's attentive love but also the clear, truthful gaze of feminist inquiry. Certainly, I *try* to see Woolf's life whole. I take intense pleasure in her words and wisdom without forgetting her nervy egocentricity, malicious gossip, and long periods of despair. But the habits of twelve years may be indelible. Still looking for guidance, I alternately celebrate Woolf's pacifist theory and blame her for its shortcomings. Still looking for solace, I bask in Woolf's capacity for pleasure and self-renewal as she lived through her fifties, only to feel sharply once again the angry loss of her death. I am inspirited by Woolf's celebration of the small miracles of daily living until I look from our bellicose country across the sea and through the decades where I see Woolf fighting beautifully and bitterly and totally without effect against the cruelty, greed, and war that drowned her and the whole of Europe. Then I am afraid.

But I will not end this essay in a somber tone; for one thing, Woolf herself would have abominated such a heavy note. Twenty days before her death she wrote: "I insist upon spending this time to the best advantage. I will go down with my colors flying."[20] It is the flying colors I will look for in my changing encounters with this remarkable woman.

Notes

1. Plato, "Crito," in *Collected Dialogues*, edited by Edith Hamilton and Huntington Cairns (New York: Pantheon, 1961), 46b, 31.
2. Virginia Woolf, *Mrs. Dalloway* (New York: Harcourt Brace, 1925, 1953), 181.
3. Rachel M. Brownstein, *Becoming a Heroine: Reading about Women in Novels* (New York: Viking, 1982), 24. Brownstein's book was very helpful to me in writing this essay.
4. Virginia Woolf, *The Diary of Virginia Woolf*, vol. 2, edited by Anne Olivier Bell (London: Hogarth Press, 1978), 186.
5. Virginia Woolf, *Three Guineas* (New York: Harcourt Brace, 1938, 1966), 66.
6. Ibid, 72.
7. Virginia Woolf, "A Sketch of the Past," in *Moments of Being*, edited by Jeanne Schulkind (London: Chatto and Windus, 1976), 80. My paper was entitled "Learning to Live with the Angel in the House," in *Women's Studies*, special issue on Virginia Woolf, vol. 4, 181-200.
8. Woolf, "A Sketch of the Past", 81-82 and passim.
9. Both quotations from Virginia Woolf, *To the Lighthouse* (London: Harcourt Brace, 1927, 1955), 123, 78.
10. Woolf, "A Sketch of the Past," 82.
11. Ibid, 69. See also Virginia Woolf, "22 Hyde Park Gate," in Schulkind, *Moments of Being*. I published part of my paper on Woolf and her brothers under the title "Private Brother/Public World" in *New Feminist Essays on Virginia Woolf*, edited by Jane Marcus (London: Macmillan, 1981), 185-215.
12. "Patriarchal circus" and, more generally "Patriarchy" are Woolf's own terms, not anachronistic projections. See Woolf, "22 Hyde Park Gate" and *Three Guineas*.
13. Simone Weil, letter to George Bernanos, in *The Simone Weil Reader*, edited by George A. Panichas (New York: David McKay, 1977), 73-78.
14. Weil, "Spiritual Autobiography", *Weil Reader*. Albert Camus, *the Fall* (New York: Vintage, 1962), 145.
15. Simone Weil, *First and Last Notebooks*, edited by Richard Rees (London: Oxford University Press, 1970), 364.
16. Woolf, *To the Lighthouse*, 165, 158.
17. Virginia Woolf, *A Room of One's Own*, (New York: Harcourt Brace, 1929, 1957), chap.4, esp. 71-73, 80.
18. Woolf, *A Room of One's Own*, 73.
19. Elizabeth Gaskell, *Letters of Elizabeth Gaskell*, edited by J. A. V. Chapple and Arthur Pollard (Manchester, 1966). The first quote is from a letter to George Smith, Brontë's editor (365), the second from a letter to Ellen Nussey, Brontë's close friend (454). Both are quoted in the excellent introduction by Alan Shelston, editor, to Gaskell's *The Life of Charlotte Brontë*, (London: Penguin Books, 1975).
20. Virginia Woolf, *A Writer's Diary*, edited by Leonard Woolf (London: Harcourt Brace, 1953), 351.

Julia de Burgos

Myrtha Chabrán

Myrtha Chabrán

EXILES

Factor 1, Animas
Arecibo, Puerto Rico

Querida mami,*

I have been doing some work on Julia de Burgos and suddenly realized that you and she belong to the same generation. I was surprised. I always thought of Julia as my sister and fought with her the battles that we fight with our other halves. I fought with her the way Rosario Ferré (you know, the ex-governor's daughter, and

---

Mami is pronounced "mommie" and *papi* "poppie." I also owe you a cartography of my family and our region in Puerto Rico: My family consists of six members — my parents, my oldest brother Harry, Rafaelito (who died in 1942), my sister Mary, and myself. My parents and my brother and his family returned to Puerto Rico in 1968, after a twenty-one-year stay in California. My sister lives in Idaho with her family. I returned to Puerto Rico in 1976 and left in 1982. Of my three sons, one is in Japan, another in New York, the youngest in California.

Arecibo, the district where we come from, is on the northern coast of the island. Esperanza, my mother's ground, is one of Arecibo's oldest and largest rural barrios. It is now famous for the Ionospheric Laboratory, which houses the world's largest radio telescope. Factor, another rural barrio in Arecibo, is where my parents have lived since 1968.

There are three rivers: Río Grande de Loíza runs through the northeast part of the island; Río Patillo joins the Río Grande de Arecibo; Río Guamaní belongs to Guayama in the South, where I lived from 1977 to 1982.

the author of *Papeles de Pandora,* the book I've been translating) did in her "Open letter to Julia de Burgos," which was part of her book *Sitio a Eros.* But as it turns out, she is your sister as well, thus becoming the bridge across which I greet you: my mother, my sister. Do you know Julia? Julia is a great Puerto Rican poet, *the* Puerto Rican woman poet. I gave papi a book of her poetry a few years ago, and he lent it to Junior nextdoor, who didn't return it.

I first came across Julia de Burgos through Alida when we lived in California. I was in my early twenties then, a student of literature who knew nothing of our literature or anything else about our colony. Alida gave me a Puerto Rican cookbook because I was going to marry her brother, and in it I copied Julia's "Poema para mi muerte" (Poem for My Death). Not long ago, in one of my sad moments, I wrote Mary and told her that I wanted a stanza from that poem as my epitaph:

> Que nadie me profane la muerte con sollozos,
> ni me arropen por siempre con inocente tierra:
> que en el libre momento me dejen libremente
> disponer de la única libertad del planeta.

> (Let nobody profane my death with sobs
> nor cover me forever with the innocent ground:
> Let me in the moment of freedom freely enjoy
> the only freedom permitted on this planet.)

Julia's death coincided with my discovery of her poetry. She was only thirty-seven. She died alcoholic and anonymous at Harlem Hospital. She called herself a teacher and a poet when she was admitted to the hospital, but in the admission form they wrote "amnesiac." Her body lay unclaimed for three days. When family and friends finally found her, they collected money to send her body back to Puerto Rico to be buried. It was not possible to let her lie in what she herself has called "un trágico horizonte de piedra" (a tragic horizon of stone):

> Morir conmigo misma, abandonada y sola,
> en las más densa roca de una isla desierta.
> En el instante un ansia suprema de claveles,
> y en el paisaje un trágico horizonte de piedra.

> (To die with myself only, abandoned and alone,
> in the densest rock of a deserted island.
> At that moment a fierce longing for carnations,
> and in the landscape, a tragic horizon of stone.)

In your last letter, mami, you warned me of my vices. Julia's mother must also have worried about her vices. There are some parallels between our family and Julia's. Both her father and my father were rural schoolteachers who loved literature and liked to drink. Julia's and my passion for the life in books must have come from our fathers. Also our loneliness, which seeks refuge in rum.

But Julia's life was more difficult than mine. She was the oldest of thirteen children; I was the youngest of four. Our family was poor, but hers infinitely poorer. She was an orphan while still a young woman. I'm lucky to be forty-eight and still have the two of you. Don't worry, mami, I shall not die like Julia; her death was sacrificial. Now that I see myself as a Puerto Rican woman writer in exile, Julia becomes my roots, not my example.

The four of us — Julia, her mother, you, and I — are river women. Julia learned from her mother about the Río Grande de Loíza, about the spirits who live in the river. She also grew up, like you, with the river as a presence, an entity in her life:

Río Grande de Loíza . . . Azul. Moreno. Rojo.
Espejo azul, caído pedazo azul de cielo;
desnuda carne blanca que se te vuelve negra
cade vez que la noche se te mete en el lecho;
roja franja de sangre, cuando bajo la lluvia
a torrentes su barro vomitan los cerros.

(Río Grande de Loíza . . . Blue. Dark. Red.
Blue mirror, blue piece of fallen sky;
naked white flesh which becomes black
each time the night steals into your bed;
red strip of blood, when under pouring rain
the hills vomit their mud.)

Your river, mami, was the Río Patillo, and I can hear you telling me stories about crossing the river to go to school and how when it flooded you had a holiday. You graduated from the eighth grade and my father, blue-eyed teacher from the city and nine years your senior, asked for your hand in marriage. Your school days ended; your river went underground in you.

My river came late into my life. You know how much I hated the country when I was growing up in Arecibo on the northern coast of our island. It was only during my second stay in Puerto Rico that I discovered my river — el río Guamaní. I lived in intimacy with my río for four years. It was my teacher, and to it I wrote:

Enséñame a desafiar mi sangre
como tú tu gravedad.
(Conozco tu secreto:
Eres espejo de celestiales espejos
y de noche te levantas

dejando solo el murmullo
acostado en tu lecho.)

(Teach me to defy my blood
as you defy your gravity.
(I know your secret:
you are a mirror of celestial mirrors
and at night you arise
leaving only your murmur in your bed.))

I begin to understand Julia the woman better when I see her as your sister. And perhaps I understand you as a woman a little better when I see you as her sister. Yet you chose different lives. Julia married young, like you. Like you, she worked in a government program that gave milk to hungry children. But she went to the university, divorced, wrote three books of poetry before she was thirty, and left Puerto Rico to follow her lover.

She was a revolutionary, a member of Albizu Campos' Nationalist Party.

Río Grande de Loíza . . . Río grande, llanto grande
el más grande de todos nuestros llantos isleños,
si no fuera más grande el que de mí se sale
por los ojos del alma para mi esclavo pueblo.

(Río Grande de Loíza . . . long river, long lament,
the longest of all of our island's laments
except for mine, which escapes
through the eyes of my soul for my enslaved people.)

She rebelled against the role of women in our society:

Yo quise ser como los hombres quisieron que yo fuera:
un intento de vida;
un juego al escondite con mi ser.
Pero yo estaba hecha de presentes
y mis pies planos sobre la tierra promisora
no resistían caminar hacia atrás.

(I wanted to be what men wanted to be:
an attempt at a life;
a game of hide-and-seek with my own self.
But I was made of the stuff of present time,
and my flat feet walking on promised land
refused to travel backward.)

I am no longer angry with her for throwing her life after a man who left her. I am no longer angry with her for her self-destruction. I no longer pontificate over her having returned to Puerto Rico only in death. "Pero no quiero ir a Puerto Rico. Cada día me aleja más de su superficie para encontrarme en su entraña, en lo más hondo de su corazón" (But I don't want to go to Puerto Rico. Each day takes me farther away from its surface and finds me in its gut, in the depths of its heart). I understand Julia now.

Julia rebelled and, woman of her history and circumstance, she felt she had to be punished. It was her dignity that made her the instrument of her own punishment.

You, mami, chose to be the good woman. My father's wife for almost sixty years. The mother of four children, grandmother and great-grandmother of several. You've worked twice as hard as any man. You matched Julia's eleven years as an exile with twenty-one years as an immigrant in California. You loved being an immigrant, you felt free. And that's how I know that Julia's passion and rebellion were also yours. That's how I know that your river went underground in you.

But how you and I fought! I refused to be like you. (And yet I looked like you.) I didn't want to serve a man, society, or children. I didn't want to accept, adjust, adapt. You were scared of me and so you punished me. I realized much later that you were scared *for* me. I was your dreams lying restless in the marrow of your bones.

I am so happy we fought! In some way you let me see that your arguments with me were arguments with yourself, that I was your other you just as you were my other I. I owe my life to you in more ways than one. And when you had your last operation I could announce to you, "Now I am your mother." We both laughed.

Lately, mami, I've been considering myself an exile. This change in definition of myself puzzled me; that's why I have been reading Julia. Though I've lived most of my life outside of Puerto Rico I had not considered myself a foreigner, not an exile, and certainly not an immigrant. When we made our exodus in 1947 — I was thirteen then — I remember being excited by new possibilities: learning English, being able to work and save money to go to school. But I had a dream the other night that showed me the other face of leaving. I dreamed that Harry (the oldest of the four of us), treating me as if I were a suitcase, had taken me to Miami when all I needed was to go to San Juan. The dream shocked me. The fury and the impotence I must have felt when I was taken from Puerto Rico had been buried for thirty-five years! Yet it is now, when I have made a self-conscious decision to leave, that I feel like an exile.

The decision to leave Puerto Rico in 1947 was not a bad one. California was good to Mary, Harry, you, and me. But for my father

it was an unspeakable place called Loneliness which he could survive only with the help of his "medicina." Your return to Puerto
Rico in 1968 was also right.

All my life, as you know, has been lived with books. As a child I
read fairy tales; as a teenager I transformed myself through comic
books, romances, and mysteries. I — lazy, useless child — gave you
many headaches. I went to college because I was too young to work.
There I discovered Medea. Medea was a foreigner, a barbarian. She
was exiled from her country for her deeds on behalf of Jason and
went to live with him in his country. They had children. After a
while, Jason decided to marry the king's daughter and banish
Medea with her children. She chose to kill her children rather than
subject them to exile. It was also revenge: She knew that the way to
make Jason pay was to destroy his seed. I loved Medea. I loved her
passion, the passion of a foreign woman spurned.

We were living in Monterey then, remember? Robinson Jeffers, a
poet who lived in a stone house in Carmel, had written the modern
version of this ancient Greek play. Medea for me became part of the
landscape — I found her in the pines, cypresses, and redwoods of
the Monterey Peninsula. She was part of the California coastline.
She was a tree that would not bend to the winds.

I went to the University of California to continue my education
and found a phonograph recording of Medea. Whenever I felt that
my violence was turning inward, threatening to destroy me, I listened to Medea growl and snarl as she killed her children and laugh
in triumph as the cloak she made for Jason's bride enveloped her in
fire. Twenty-eight years later and as many moves — you know what
a gypsy I've been all my life — I still have that recording. Medea was
my secret self. As Santa Teresa said, God can be found even in the
stew.

One evening in 1971 when I was living in Santa Barbara after my
divorce, a group of us sat in Rose's Mexican resturant and discussed
our secret images of ourselves. I brought my Medea out and she was
chillingly received. (Perhaps my friends feared for my three
children!) I became ashamed of her and disowned her. But she
would not let me be. She would show up in poems and in dreams,
until I had to acknowledge our comradeship as sisters and
barbarians.

I realize now that I first understood my condition in the world
through Medea: Being a woman, becoming a mother, being a
foreigner, becoming an exile are all inextricably tied up for me. And,
unconsciously, I began to look for those pieces in other writers.

When I moved to New York in May 1971 I read a collection of
essays by an English writer named Doris Lessing. One of the essays

is about Olive Schreiner. (Did you know that Cousin Olive was named after her?) My acquaintance with Lessing and Schreiner is old. Though I had known that Lessing had been born and raised in Africa, and both had traveled to the metropolis (England in their case), this time I began to sense a pattern. A pattern — voyage from the colonial world to the metropolis — that included Julia de Burgos and Jean Rhys. (Rhys was an English novelist born and raised in the West Indies who went to Europe.)

There is another essay in that collection in which Lessing writes about her father. It touched something in me, but I put all that aside while I found an apartment, got sick and got well, found a job and quit it.

"Mad! Mad! Everyone! Everywhere! Mad!" — Doris Lessing remembering her father in his African farm as he shakes his fist at the sky. She remembers him on another occasion looking still at the same sky and saying that if we were foolish enough to blow ourselves up, there was plenty more where we came from. Still another recollection has him accusing her of having no imagination because she was not interested in his scientific ideas.

Doris' father was a man looking for the right soil for his roots, and when he did not find it on this thin crust (he tried England, Persia, and Africa), he was willing to look for it in the stars or in the molten center of the earth. His daughter is writing space fiction now, continuing her father's search for rooting soil.

Doesn't he sound like my father? Except that my father is happy with his physical roots in Puerto Rico, though his soul is rooted elsewhere.

"I came into contact with the English very early in life, because as it turns out, my father was an Englishman . . . it was not until I had been in England for some time that I understood my father," Doris wrote about her father. But I always understood my father's *genio*, his character. It was you, mami, I did not understand until I came to terms with my being a woman.

Roots. Nature. Landscape. I love to hear you talk about your childhood in Esperanza, where our ancestors' land has now been impregnated by a gigantic telescope. It represents the most advanced technology — a huge disk of mirrors meant to communicate with outside worlds. The first time you took me to see it you were so happy pointing out to me the hills that as a child you slid down, sitting on a palm frond, the spot where Cousin Arturo had his store, the little school your father founded, the cement steps which were all that was left of the house in which you celebrated your wedding, the cemetery where your mother was buried when you were eleven.

The towers and cables of the giant telescope look over all this now, like masts of a ship marooned in that sacred bowl.

The writers I have been telling you about, mami, carry similar memories of the wild places where they grew up. Those memories are like fossils or petroglyphs imprinted on their brain. Jean Rhys, for example, who wrote mostly about lonely women in European cities, goes back to memories of her childhood in Guadeloupe to write a beautiful novel called *Wide Sargasso Sea*. It is a memory built out of sensations — smells, sounds, tastes, pictures, textures — sensations that are the main filters through which, as children, we structure the world.

After Doris Lessing lived in London for seven years, she went back to Africa for a visit. It was "going home" to her, which is what she called the book she wrote about that trip. From the airplane she looks at the landscape and knows it, much as a woman knows her house. She could have been at our *parcela* in Factor when she describes the sun:

> The red deepened and pulsed, radiating streaks of fire. There hung the sun, like a luminous spider's egg, or a white pearl, just below the rim of the mountains. Suddenly it swelled, turned red, roared over the horizon and drove up the sky like a train engine.[1]

She compares living in London to living in Africa, and she sounds like a Puerto Rican contrasting New York with home:

> On that morning . . . I learned that I had turned myself inwards, had become a curtain-drawer, a fire-hugger, the inhabitant of a cocoon. Easy enough to turn outwards again: I felt I had never left at all. This was my air, my landscape, and above all, my sun.[2]

In that same book, *Going Home,* she tells of her efforts to recreate her African house in her mind while she was living in London:

> It was urgently necessary to recover every detail of that house . . . I had to remember everything, every strand of thatch and curve of wall or heave in the floor, and every tree and bush and patch of grass around it, and how the fields and slopes of country looked at different times of the day, in different strengths and tones of light . . . I used to set myself to sleep, saying, "Now you dream of that room, or that tree, or that turn in the road" . . . Over months, I recovered the memory of it all. And so, what was lost and buried in my mind, I recovered from my mind.[3]

Maybe because for these women writers a change from one country to another coincides with a shift from rural to urban settings, memories of childhood landscapes merge with our desires for home, for paradise. The topography of our country becomes our skin.

Destierro. Julia's word. Uprootedness. As an exile I gave up those childhood landscapes to gain — what? Why did I leave them? I left them to find education, refinement, fortune, bigger spaces for myself as a woman. My *destierro* taught me to be an observer, to be an outsider, to have a double vision, to sleep with my eyes open, and to see with my eyes closed. And never to feel at home anywhere except for brief moments.

Doris Lessing offers yet another geography for our exile: to be exiles on a cosmic level. She tells us through her space fiction that the broader our consciousness, the more we are aware that we are travelers. Everywhere is home, nothing is home. We have fallen from grace and are exiles in the kingdom of God. I used to debate Lessing's novels with her — in my mind, of course — and now I discuss my life with her.

But I know that at my cellular level being an exile is being an orphan. It was again Doris who gave me this clue by writing about her father. I remembered you and my father telling me stories of those shadowy figures from the past: my grandparents, called "mama y papa" by you, and "papito y mamita" by my father. Like every child, the child in me is afraid of being an orphan.

All journeys end at the beginning. I have taken you from the point of exile, to women in literature, to women, and back to exile. Thank you, mami, for allowing me to write this letter to you.

Julia wrote of her mother what I would like to write of you:

Ella me alzó de un salto con su mano de estrella.

(She took a jump and lifted me with her hand to a star.)

Te quiere,

Myrtha

Notes

1. Doris Lessing, *Going Home* (London: Michael Joseph Limited, 1957), 11.
2. Lessing, 12.
3. Lessing, 50.

Hannah Arendt

Elizabeth Kamarck Minnich

Elizabeth Kamarck Minnich

HANNAH ARENDT:
THINKING AS WE ARE

I studied with Hannah Arendt formally and informally for more than ten years, taking classes with her at the Graduate Faculty of the New School, serving as her teaching assistant, talking with her over all kinds of food, corresponding and then visiting with her when I could after I left New York City. I loved her, admired her, and was terrified of her. This essay has been very hard for me to write: It has forced me to pick out some of the strains of her thought that seem revealing of who she was, while trying not to disappear myself. I want to think about her, but I can't do so without thinking *with* her. Hannah Arendt made sense to me even when I couldn't claim to understand her — there was and is something about the way she thought that speaks to me on more levels than I can comprehend. I know it sounds melodramatic, but I can only say that she affected my existence.

One of the oddities I run into when I try to explain the depth of her meaning for me is that during my time with her I learned very little about the facts and events of her life, and she knew very little about mine. Yet, as I learn more about her life, I discover that I am not at all surprised. I did know her; it is harder for me to say that she knew me, but I think it's true. So I am left with the need to talk about someone whose thinking *was* who she was, in a way that uncovers, also, how and what *I* think, and so, who I am. Anecdotes, personal facts — all the things that usually help a person become real and vivid are, in this case, distractions. At least they are for me in talking about her, and also in talking about myself. There are all kinds of things I could say about myself, who and what I am, but I honestly do not think I could say much that is as revealing of myself, of my passions, as what I am about to say. Whatever that means about me, it has something to do with the heart of my relation with Hannah Arendt. Our most intimate conversations were about thoughts. That thinking is not merely intellectual, that it is intensely personal, that it is profoundly relevant to the world, that clarity and sanity depend on each other — all that, Hannah Arendt helped me realize.

What that also means is that she helped me become a feminist. Hannah Arendt was never anyone but herself, but she didn't make the error of thinking that she could be free from the world-imposed *what* of her identity. She was a thinker. She was also a Jew and a woman. No identity is merely a private matter when what we are (as *what* is defined by the political realities of our historical era) takes precedence in the world over *who* we are. I will return to this idea later, but first I have to say that Hannah Arendt was not a self-proclaimed feminist. Her noninvolvement does not matter, however, unless we refuse to listen to people unless they claim the same labels we do. I would take such a refusal to be contrary to my understanding of feminism: a turn of mind that accepts nothing inherited as given and inviolate, and a turn of heart toward the kind of friendship that is possible only between equals.

Let me start, then, with some tenets of feminist thought I first found in Hannah Arendt. She held that thinking must take precedence over knowing because it is thinking that frees us to make judgments, the essential bridge between principle and individual case; that we can therefore no longer follow the Great Minds of the past, however much respect and friendship we have for them; that there is no real thinking that is not thinking for yourself any more than there is thinking that is entirely private; that thinking depends for its possibility on a world in which political freedom guarantees the public space for conversation; that although the "thinking ego" is utterly free from attributes, including gender, the thinker never is and cannot afford to deny attributes in the world; that if we would understand the human condition, we must be able to think about our kind in our plurality, ridding ourselves of the hypnotic hold of the singular, partial "Man"; that we must learn about what is private as well as what is public if we wish to understand human life and its meaning; and that among the strongest thinkers are poets, storytellers, and rebels.

Those are tenets of thought I take to be feminist, or, to put it the other way around, I am a feminist now largely because it is only among feminist thinkers that I have found a consistent commitment to tell the truth about the real world of humankind.

Hannah Arendt was a radical: She always went after the root of things as they are. She engaged in heated political debates and worked for causes in which she believed — Zionism, freedom of speech, opposition to the Vietnam War among them. Admitting that she had more need to understand than to act, she did her political work as a thinker who spoke out. The courage she showed in speaking and in withstanding the sometimes intense reaction to her thought gave me a picture of courage to hang on to; she was living proof that genuine thinkers cannot retreat from the real work, the real action of politics. Her passion to understand is precisely what kept her political.

In being a thinker, she was different not only from those who lead their lives thoughtlessly but also from those whose desire to know draws them toward truth "even if the world be damned," as she would say. Hannah Arendt preferred the world and sought meaning — which she distinguished from truth — in it. Because I met her when I was a young graduate student in philosophy, it was her difference from other academics that first struck — and de-lighted — me. Despite her own immense erudition, it was not a lack of knowledge that appalled her (much as our American lack of familiarity with the classics sometimes defied her hopes for us as students). It was thoughtlessness that was her enemy, and she took it on in blunt comments that made her a terror not only in class but in her relations with her colleagues. Displays of knowledge disguised as questions ("Dr. Arendt, don't you think that . . .") usually elicited an abrupt "No." I loved it . She was just as fierce with people who tried to emulate her style. She did not want parrots or performers; she wanted thoughtfulness. The requirement that we be simul-taneously precise, careful, and independently thoughtful created problems for us, of course. There were no games to play, no rules to follow. While I loved it, I retreated at first into silence in class. But the silence was not passive. Usually, whoever shuts me up also loses my attention — I make a very poor audience. Hannah Arendt, though, enlivened me. Following her was not alien, or passive, or submissive. She made sense. Even in silence, I breathed a great sigh of relief. Doing philosophy with Hannah Arendt did not mean suspending all disbelief.

She often used stories in lectures, seminars and private conversa-tions to make her points. Stories help uncover meaning, whereas rational argument can be used to force agreement. Her stories freed, and invited, an effort to understand their internal meaning and an equal effort to understand what they meant to us. One of her favorite stories concerned God and a thinker: God appeared to a scholar one day and offered what most scholars want — final, conclusive knowledge. But this scholar proved to be a thinker: the gift was refused because such knowledge would mean silence falling on the world.

If we had final knowledge, what would we have to discuss? And if we were silent, we would soon find ourselves unable to think and unable to act. The voices of others in us enable us to think. The voices of others, in public, demand and create a public space in which we can appear and be with others as equals. We may need solitude in order to think, but that is so we can hear our own inner dialogue, so that we can actualize in ourselves our own differences. Agreement, which matters deeply among friends, is also dangerous both personally and politically if it becomes an overpowering goal. It is *difference* that maintains the separateness essential to equality. Sameness is an opposite of equality.

Vagueness, stupidity (which she most often seemed to equate with a kind of willful obtuseness about reality), lack of imagination, all kinds of thoughtlessness upset Arendt on every level. While she was young, a student and then a friend of the great teachers and philosophers of Germany, she was forced to see that "the life of the mind" was no protection against personal and political failings. It was then that her life-long crusade began. As Hitler came to power, many of those she had admired crumbled before her eyes. Even Heidegger, her teacher, inspiration, friend, and first passionate love, joined the Nazi party (however briefly). Many others fell silent or, worse, actively cooperated in the silencing of others. She learned that neither knowledge nor brilliance brings courage or political wisdom. I believe she never forgot that lesson — it drove her work throughout her life.

At the same time, she saw, throughout her lasting relationship with Karl Jaspers, a model of clarity of thought that seemed expressive, as well as creative, of extraordinary courage and political morality. She also learned something else: She always said, when she spoke of Jaspers, that he was was married "to a woman in every way his equal." Heidegger, in stark contrast, remained in a marriage to a woman unequal to him and a bane to his friends. In addition to learning about the political failings possible for scholars, Hannah Arendt learned something lasting about the congruence — or incongruence — of the personal, the intellectual, and the political.

Those early experiences, which led her to articulate and present to the world an understanding of thinking that prepares us to make judgments "when the chips are down," nevertheless did not turn her against all scholarship or all scholars. She engaged in conversation with anyone she found to be both honest and interesting, and that included great philosophers, poets, friends, students, taxi drivers, writers.

What she never did again was to take anything on authority, nor ask anyone else to. She lectured as if she were talking with the thinkers on the reading list (and whoever else occurred to her). She also taught philosophy using texts no one else would have considered at all proper. We read Kafka, Broch, Brecht, Faulkner, Heller, Auden. We were supposed to think about the questions posed in the classes rather than master texts. She clearly thought "poetic rebels" had as much to teach budding philosophers as did philosophical works. She used to say that English philosophy is best represented by the great poets.

I know that the soul-deep relief I felt in her courses (together with the continuing terror and awe) is one reason I still have trouble teaching "straight" philosophy courses. I have, in fact, taught mostly as an administrator, which has meant that I could offer any course any department would agree to list — without being subject to a department's definition of propriety and necessity. I have taught "Philosophical Reflections on Courage," "Politics and the Problem of Meaninglessness," "Thought, Action, and Morality," and my courses have been listed through political science and German departments. I now teach for the Union Graduate School of the Union for Experimenting Colleges and Universities, a non-traditional graduate school in which programs are developed for each student, starting with her or his deepest question, with what she or he wants to know, and why. In this work as in my teaching, lecturing, and writing on feminist scholarship and pedagogy, I am trying to work through what it means to learn to think with others in a way that does not create dangerous chasms between who we are and what we know — chasms that Hannah Arendt helped me recognize. She gave me a vision of thinking that *is* political, that can help us act right "when the chips are down" (a phrase she used often).

I have to admit, though, that she wasn't always a model for my effort to find a way of teaching that develops that vision and is consonant with it. I want to work in a way that is as radical in its intent as Hannah Arendt's but a whole lot less frightening. Hannah Arendt believed in and practiced the art of conversation, but she was not very good at helping discussions happen among people who are not and may never be friends. She was abrupt and impatient, and I was by no means the only one who fell silent in her classes. Silence was not what she wanted from us, she of all people, but her utter lack of a model for the kind of class I am quite sure she would have preferred (she was educated in Germany, remember), and her own force, did tend to leave us gasping.

Her manner, though, was always contradicted by what she thought about in front of us and the way she thought. She not only told stories, she personalized the philosophers she did include on her reading list. When I think of Spinoza now, for example, I think of Hannah Arendt's characterization of him as the lens grinder who refused prestigious teaching posts because they might interfere with his thinking. Spinoza, with Socrates, was to her someone who *"was* a philosopher," as distinct from someone who teaches philosophy (or writes it). Both Socrates and Spinoza were persecuted for their thinking, and both refused to stop despite excommunication and mob threats in Spinoza's case and a death sentence he refused to avoid in Socrates'. Hannah Arendt always also added that Spinoza had "the luxury" of continuing to believe that the one freedom that cannot be taken away is the life of the mind. "He was wrong," she said. "He did not know totalitarianism. Thinking may actually be one of the most fragile of our abilities." Thinkers, she was quite clear, cannot be removed from the messy world of politics, *not if they would remain thinkers.* They may even be among those who have the highest stake in preserving political freedom.

That was heavy stuff to a graduate student in the middle of the Vietnam War era, struggling to understand why thinking mattered at all when there was so much to be *done.* At the same time I knew, with a sense of some shame and a great deal of concern, that I would really rather think. There I was, suddenly faced with a woman who had made herself an entirely independent creature by thinking and speaking her thoughts in public. What an inspiration, relief, challenge! She wrote once, "it may even be nice that we" who have lost both authority and tradition have also lost "the monopoly of what Kant once very ironically called the professional thinkers. We can start worrying about what thinking means for the activity of acting." And then she, who was so clearly anything but cowardly, otherworldly, or Ivory Tower-bound, proceeded to say, "I will admit that I am, of course, primarily interested in understanding. This is absolutely true. And I will admit that there are other people who are primarily interested in doing something. I am not. I can very well live without doing anything. But I cannot live without trying at least to understand whatever happens." As she spoke her understanding, she reaped the consequences of appearing in public. It was through her public experience as well as her thinking about politics that she learned how political speech can be, and how much courage is required to appear in public.

Anyone who wanted an ally or a disinterested teacher or a parent figure rather than a friend had trouble with Hannah Arendt. Maybe one of the reasons she could be so frightening was that she was uncompromisingly independent, and she demanded the same from her friends. Since I was then considerably younger, less educated, and most assuredly less tested in the business of being seen for who I am, I found it hard to be uncompromisingly independent with her. I just did my best to be thoughtful and to be as honest and as clear as I could be, heart beating all the while. Actually having to deal with what you want and need and believe in is hard. So little prepares us for it.

Once, when Hannah Arendt took me along to hear her speak on a panel of political people, writers, and activists, I watched her correct, offend, and inspire a roomful of people who did not take lightly to being corrected, offended, OR inspired. The all-male panelists were America's "arrogance of power" as exemplified by our actions in Vietnam. Hannah Arendt opened her remarks by saying, in her typical abrupt style, "The problem is not our arrogance, of which we have a great deal. The problem is that we have lost power." For her, power is something that springs up among people, that only increases with being shared, and that is the mark of politics, the public life, as distinct from society, which she took to be home and community life writ large. When violence must be employed, she said, power has been lost. Power depends on speech, not weapons; on persuasion, not violence. Those who must use guns demonstrate by that very act that no one follows them, that no one is with them anymore. They need violence *because* they are powerless — a strikingly different formulation from the pervasive one that equates power with a legal right to use force, or sees power as springing from the barrel of a gun.

She was alone in her insistence that we keep trying to understand what we are saying, how we are thinking, in the middle of a tense political situation. However much she might otherwise have agreed with some of the panelists' positions, she was not going to let them pass around the phrase "the arrogance of power," as if it were adequate. I think she did not like it as much because it was a bemusing slogan as because she thought it implied a faulty analysis.

She also argued with members of the Jewish community with whom she shared in debate and analysis of Zionism, Israeli politics and actions, and what it meant to be Jewish after Hitler and with the existence of Israel. She wrote a response to a letter from an eminent Jewish scholar that expresses and exemplifies her way of thinking. He was sorrowfully angry with her for what he took to be a lack of loyalty and "love" for the Jewish people, as he interpreted her position. She wrote, "Whatever objections you may have to the results [of my thinking], you won't understand them unless you realize they are really my own and nobody else's . . . I have never in my life 'loved' any people or collective — neither the German people, nor the French, nor the American, nor the working class or anything of that sort. I indeed 'love' only my friends and the kind of love I know of and believe in is the love of persons."

She did not in any way deny her Jewishness. Quite the contrary. Because she was a thinker, a Jew, a woman, she was through no choice of her own (except the crucial choice never to deny what she was) an outsider. Accepting that she was an outsider, she chose to be independent. She taught me that being independent is something we can and do choose in the face of our world, as a way of both living with and not succumbing to our reality.

Being independent is also a way of refusing to be an exception, an odd creature who belongs to no group. Hannah Arendt wrote about the "Exception Jews," and her analysis remains useful for anyone who can be tempted — as we all can — by acceptance into a world that simultaneously brands and, apparently graciously but not consistently and never, never reliably, overlooks the brand.

She wrote and spoke more often about what it meant for her to be a Jew than about what it meant for her to be a woman. Being a Jew in her times overwhelmed all other issues. It was a life and death matter and, when no longer that, a matter of sanity, of never losing touch with reality. The fact that my grandfather was a Russian Jew who did not practice, but never denied, his religion made me respond thirstily to Hannah Arendt's thinking about what it means to be Jewish. I am and will be Jewish in the face of anti-Semitism, whatever I make of my heritage in other ways. She helped me see with great clarity that *what* one is must be part of *who* one is.

I have drawn on Hannah Arendt's thoughts about being Jewish in an effort to understand what it means to be a woman. What she says can be extended to illuminate living as any prefixed person: a woman philosopher, a Black poet, a Native American politician, even though I believe she misunderstood feminism to be efforts on the part of women to be the same as men. Equality is political, sameness is personal or social, and she felt feminists needed to direct their attention primarily toward specific *public* issues. She sometimes seems to have missed the connections she herself helped me understand.

It means a great deal to me that the greatest thinker I studied with, and undeniably one of the greatest of our age, is a woman. I now have no doubt but that part of the depth and range of my feeling for her springs from that fact. From the very beginning I felt a kind of closeness to her for which I had no grounds but that moved from being terrifying (because it was both so strong and so unexplained) to being healing as I have struggled to understand what she meant to me.

She would think it odd of me to care so much that she was a woman. She never doubted it, never fought it, never took particular pride in it — and yet refused as stubbornly to be an Exception Woman as she refused to be an Exception Jew. She would not assimilate in either case, since it was never, in fact, irrelevant to the world or to her deepest sense of herself that she was both Jewish and a woman. But she took not only her womanhood but her femininity calmly. Without exerting much effort, she took some care to be attractive, and she could be very charming indeed. I had the sense that she accepted some social aspects of a gender-divided world with humor and tolerance for individual men's need to be charmed, while maintaining utter disregard for the standing expectation that women would make themselves less than they could be personally, intellectually, politically.

When she felt the world made an issue of gender, she claimed her own sex with pride, but otherwise she tried to go about her own business. On the personal level, for herself and, I felt, for her students and friends, she did not mind "la petite différence." We could make little bows in the direction of femininity so long as we did not take them too seriously — and, I think she preferred them to signs that we might think women ought to be the same as men.

In fact, I think Hannah Arendt did not want to be bothered much with "the woman question." Being a Jew pressed much harder on her, and being a thinker took precedence over all. What she knew and taught was that what we are must not be denied, even though *how* we live out what we are may indeed vary with the world and with time. She wrote, "I cannot gloss over the fact that for many years I considered the only adequate reply to the question, Who are you? to be: a Jew. That answer alone took into account the reality of persecution."

As Hannah Arendt put it, in speaking of those who refuse repressive identifications simply by denial, "Those who reject such identifications on the part of a hostile world may feel wonderfully superior to the world, but their superiority is then truly no longer of this world; it is the superiority of a more or less well-equipped cloud-cuckoo land." Somewhere between "*I* have never been oppressed because I am a woman" and "I *am* my oppression as a woman" we can get on with living, and thinking, and fighting. When I once again lose clarity, one of the things I remember is Hannah Arendt's notion of "the conscious pariah," something one can be in the world with enemies as well as with friends; something that all women may indeed be in this white man's world that we can neither deny nor join without losing not only reality but our greatest source of strength.

Before I began to understand that, my own successes as a student in schools that passed on a culture and a body of knowledge in which women are invisible and cannot be made visible left me with a strong sense of personal hypocrisy. What did good grades mean, except that I had played a game well? I didn't then understand why I felt so uninvolved in the game, but I did know that praise did not speak to who I was. Hannah Arendt, however, offered me acceptance on terms that neither patronized nor inflated — nor required any kind of assimilation. I have begun to understand that my own fear of success was not neurotic, a nice, safe way of defining away politically accurate responses as 'merely' personal. Success for a woman when I was in school carried with it, at best, the status of Exception. I did not want that. I just wanted to do my work and know that it had been understood, and judged, as it deserved. I wanted, and want my work and who I am to be *seen*. But like others who are not of the privileged few who define "mankind" in their own image, being seen is for me a rare and very special experience. I have had it from friends; from Hannah Arendt I received it for the first time from a teacher.

Still, acceptance for myself, truly seen, is not easy to accept. False pride is in some ways easier to live with, because one can then say, "Oh well. My success just means I can play that game." And, in saying that, avoid not only self-discovery but the challenge to change the rules. One vivid memory: When Hannah Arendt returned the first paper I wrote for her (and the first paper I had ever rewritten; I usually wrote and handed papers in as they emerged from the typewriter) with an A+ and "Congratulations!" written on it, I went into a state of shock. I had left myself no excuses "I didn't work hard on it," my usual, is a good excuse for success as well as for failure but I *had* worked on this paper. I talked to an older woman about my feelings of pleasure and, even more, fear. After listening to me carry on about how the paper wasn't very good, she said, "Whose judgment of it is best, yours or Hannah Arendt's?" I was suddenly confronted with the fact that I could not write off my success without writing off Hannah Arendt, and my respect and love for her went far too deep for that to be possible.

From then on, I lived in terror that I would fail her. Of course, she ruined that game too. My next paper, which I wrote in such a numb state that I still can't say what it was about, she returned saying, "A fine and spirited attack on my position." I hadn't realized that I was attacking her position. It became, slowly, clear even to my be-numbed psyche that I was going to have to live with the fact that she was not going to change her view of me. I was going to have to take my own possibilities seriously.

Hannah Arendt had an extraordinary gift for friendship, which I was forced not only to see but to accept. She saw people and liked them for their unusual qualities, not for their exemplification of characteristics she found comfortable or safe. Her friends and select-ed students were all Characters — well-defined people very differ-ent from each other. I can see the special qualities clearly in the others but only sometimes on good days in myself.

One of the most fascinating of Hannah Arendt's books, drafted when she was very young, is a biography of a strikingly singular person. It is, I think, a model of friendship. *Rahel Varnhagen* shows the necessity of understanding women who came before us, the ones we need and the ones with whom we must make a peace that the world has often denied us. Rahel Varnhagen was an eighteenth-century Jewish woman who ran a salon that was, for a time, at the center of a culture that accepted her only as an exception. Hannah Arendt wrote about Rahel not to praise or judge or explain her, but to understand her. The biography was an effort to "narrate the story of Rahel's life as she herself might have told it." It is not our explanations or justifications or heroine-making that we or the women who preceded us need: It is their voice, precisely what they — and we — have always been denied.

Rahel's life, as Hannah Arendt believed Rahel herself would have seen it, was "the history of a bankruptcy and a rebellious spirit." Rahel lacked everything (social standing, wealth, beauty) that would have made her world accept her on its terms, and she suffered from her Jewishness. Yet, although she desired acceptance and never gave up looking for a love that eluded her, she fought BOTH her exclusion and her exceptionality. She wanted to fit, but would not assimilate. She railed against her Jewishness and her lack of beauty and wealth as if she would change her condition, and yet she never became what the world wanted and would have accepted. She chose to suffer because she was not allowed to act, and to remain aware of her suffering. She was not just an exception; she was not wholly a pariah. She was a *conscious* pariah, an outsider who lived what she was given.

In this biography, as in her essay on Rosa Luxemburg, Hannah Arendt makes it evident that Rahel's being a woman *mattered*. She wrote of Rahel's times, "The Woman Problem, that is the discrepancy between what men expected of women 'in general' and what women could give or wanted in their turn . . . was already established by the conditions of the era and represented a gap that virtually could not be closed." Furthermore, Rahel was not beautiful and so lacked a source of power that was granted to women. Hannah Arendt did not make the political fact of womanhood a central issue, but here she did recognize the personal reality of political givens. It has always impressed me that she did not say Rahel's lack of beauty was either irrelevant or only a personal issue: She noted that it meant a lack of power in the terms of Rahel's world.

In the course of thinking through what Rahel's life meant to Rahel herself, Hannah Arendt brings out her own hard-won understanding of what it means to live in the world, denying neither it (however much one might be tempted to) nor oneself. She writes, "It may well be difficult for us to understand our own history when we are born in 1771 in Berlin and that history has already begun seventeen hundred years earlier in Jerusalem. But if we do not understand it, and if we are not outright opportunists who always accept the here-and-now, who circumvent unpleasantness by lies and forget the good, our history will take its revenge, will exert its superiority and become our personal destiny." It is in these terms that I first understood that "the personal is political"; it is in these terms too that I recently wrote a paper on the critical importance of feminist scholarship, entitled "From Fate to Inheritance." We must understand the stories of the women before us who were only rarely given the gift of being seen as they were.

It seems to me that Rahel showed Hannah what it is to live in a world that does not accept us and yet tempts us with promises of inclusion — if only we will agree to trivialize ourselves, except ourselves from our own kind, disappear. Both Hannah Arendt and Rahel Varnhagen decided that real life cannot be lived in the recognized victories and losses in such a world; those victories and losses will always be on someone else's terms. It is only in living an independent life, in feeling and acting and thinking and speaking and seeing as clearly as possible, with a rebellious spirit, that we can live our own lives.

At the close of *Rahel Varnhagen,* Hannah Arendt quotes a letter Rahel wrote to a brilliant young friend as Rahel approached her death: "No philanthropic list, no cheers, no condescension, no mixed society, no new human book, no bourgeois star, nothing, nothing could ever placate me . . . YOU will say this gloriously, elegiacally, fantastically, incisively, extremely jestingly, always musically, provokingly, often charmingly; you will say it all very soon. But as you do, the text from my old offended heart will still have to remain yours."

Hannah Arendt, as well as all the Rahels of our inheritance, was and is misunderstood; no one seems quite to trust her, not even those to whom she most belongs. Our world may be different from Rahel's and Arendt's, but the "offended hearts" of such women are a source of truth as well as strength. Both these women rejected comforts, even preferred the conscious suffering and rebelliousness necessary to preserve both self and world. They were and are difficult women.

I do not know whether Hannah Arendt would have approved of the work I do now in a nontraditional graduate school and as a feminist philosopher trying to understand and to speak about the implications of feminist scholarship. But I have never doubted that she would approve of the effort to understand that has brought me where I am. I believe that it is in her spirit that I work, and the very fact that she might not approve of some choices in which I persist is itself entirely appropriate for a student of hers.

An eminent male philosopher said to me recently that it was odd that Hannah Arendt left no students behind, given her stature and accomplishments. I asked him why he thought this oddity had occurred, and he said it was because she didn't "play the game right." She was supposed to "train" students, to place them in important positions in academia, to promote those who would carry on her work.

Hannah Arendt's students were not, for the most part, those registered for her courses. They were people she selected from wherever they came, people she regarded highly enough to be willing to converse with yet to let go, often even refusing to teach them in the usual sense. Guests wandered in and out of her classes, and she held no particular stake in tying any of us to the academic life. I did not have to write my second paper. She told me I should do whatever I wanted — she already knew what mark I should get. Performance as defined by academic rules simply did not interest her very much. But she had no qualms about playing a caretaking role when it expressed real care and not a role. She fed me, she worried about whether my coat was warm enough, she was bluntly honest with me, she expected excellence. She had a huge stake in what I — what we — chose to do: She cared about the world.

In the spring of 1982, I did a workshop with some faculty members at a respected small college. We worked together on trying to understand what feminist scholarship means for all of us and specifically what it means for the courses we teach in our traditionally defined disciplines. After the workshop I talked with a very bright woman whose field is political science. She was having a terrible time accepting and thinking through the fact that her teaching materials took no account of the realities of women's lives, actions, contributions. As she became more aware of the anomaly of being a woman teaching as if women did not exist politically and not questioning the canon she taught, she became more and more uncomfortable. Finally, she burst out, "What we're talking about is father-killing, isn't it? I always thought I had done all I had to do for women by making it in a field where there are very few women. Now I find out I have to question the whole field. I don't know if I want to do it. It was HARD getting here." To want and need the approval — and the jobs — offered by the very world that sees us as "women in general" first and individuals a poor second, the very world that accepts us only as long as we are willing to be exceptions or to assimilate, is twisty, painful, and familiar to us all. I cannot begin to say all I learned from Hannah Arendt because I think with her all the time and will always do so. But Hannah Arendt, simply by being there and accepting me, freed me from The Fathers who do not want us to ask our own questions or to take ourselves seriously enough to refuse both exceptionality and assimilation, yet whose approval can still seem to be the only kind that really matters.

As Hannah Arendt, speaking of the modern world, said, we have lost tradition and, with it, authority. This is cause for great confusion and a sense of irremediable loss. It is also an invitation to think, more freely than ever before. The possibility that we might be able to do so, and not as women students of men whose whole way of thought excludes us, exists. Hannah Arendt, who knew that in order to think as ourselves we must think through what we are in the real world, is one of those who can help us.

Hannah Arendt clearly knew that trying to be like a man in a man's world was as dangerous as being a woman on man's terms. Between these shoals, she took her own course, being always "only myself," realistically, in ways that turned out to be rebellious (even against prescribed forms of rebellion for women). Her lack of self-conscious feminism (in the terms we are forging for ourselves with such difficulty and excitement) may have left her somewhat more alone than she might have been, but I am not sure. Her thinking was not hampered, as is often the case with women who reject feminism: She did indeed think about "the human condition" and not only about "man's fate." I remain awed by her ability to think through the tradition that excluded the majority of humankind and to emerge with wholly new thoughts. She wrote, for example, about *natality* — she even coined the term for the human condition for action. Humans may die alone, but they are not born alone, and *that* fact matters, not just to our species or to our individual development but to our shared, public world. I have recently been struck again with the power of that realization: It means that relatedness, interdependence, sameness, *and* difference are givens for humans. What happens when we start *there*, and not with the historic obsession with mortality, with our given ultimate aloneness?

Hannah Arendt always had women as friends, again not misunderstanding the friendship of women as a private matter but realizing that friendship itself is "political, and preserves reference to the world."

For us all, I still mourn that she died and left us; at the same time, I am increasingly aware of how much she is still here as a demanding friend through her thinking. For her, I am deeply satisfied that she died well, among friends, and with her most fundamental manuscript almost — but not quite — finished. It seems right that she would not tie things up, finish them, leave at the end of a conversation with the last word having been uttered.

For myself, I am more grateful than I can possibly say that she was in the world and that I have her with me, always, whenever I find the courage to think.

Mary Wilkins Freeman

Leah Glasser

Leah Blatt Glasser

"SHE IS THE ONE YOU CALL SISTER": DISCOVERING MARY WILKINS FREEMAN

She is the one you call sister
you blaze like lightening about the room
flicker around her like fire
dazzle yourself in her wide eyes
listing her unfelt needs
thrusting the tenets of your life
into her hands

> — From Adrienne Rich,
> "The Mirror in Which Two Are Seen as One"
> (in *Diving into the Wreck*, 1971)

When I first began to write a critical biography of Mary Wilkins Freeman, I thought I had a mission. Here was my chance to set the record straight, to redefine and reevaluate a New England woman who had been overlooked and misinterpreted. Freeman had been traditionally categorized as merely a local colorist, a "minor" American writer of the post-Civil War period whose primary talent lay in depicting the peculiarities of her New England region. I saw, however, that Freeman's work demanded feminist analysis, and I recognized that her subject in fact had little to do with regionalism. With her focus almost entirely on women's struggles and concerns, their intricate forms of repression and rebellion, Mary Wilkins Freeman explored the psychology of women's conflicts as she knew them. By giving voice to her silent, "shy old maiden," Freeman opened a door to what the "spinster" of her time generally kept "in a closet hidden, like a skeleton."[1] I felt an obligation, a deep connection to a woman whose work had been so misunderstood.

At the start, I looked at Freeman's life and work as though looking in the mirror Adrienne Rich beckons us toward, "the mirror in which two are seen." I understood Rich's line "She is the one you call sister." But my relationship with this "sister" has been turbulent, the "mirror" a mirror of distortions. The process of working on Freeman has been far more complex than I had imagined. It has involved discoveries about my subject that I have tried hard to evade and it has consequently become a process of self-discovery.

My first impulse was to admire Freeman's exposure and criticism of a restrictive society that demanded both female submission and sexual suppression. I so wanted to identify with her as the strong, independent woman writing alone, able to support herself through the work she loved, that I strategically evaded the dual nature of her work. When I had to confront the Freeman whose weaker stories were sometimes apologetic and submissive in both tone and message, I felt afraid, appalled, and defensive. Although I was dismayed by her frequent method of framing powerful psychological portraits with safe, sentimental beginnings and endings, I still tried to write out of a sense of loyalty to the Freeman I loved and selected stories to analyze accordingly. I found myself longing to rewrite beginnings and reshape endings of her stories or to manipulate details to fit my notion of a feminist model. At the time, I could not confront the complexity of Freeman's work. In my fantasy, Freeman was wholly a rebel; but in reality, like Brontë's governess Jane Eyre, she was both "rebel" and "slave," a "divided self."[2]

Freeman wanted to rebel openly, but at the same time she sought shelter and acceptability even at the price of enslavement to standards that she knew to be oppressive and unjust. Initially unable to acknowledge Freeman's ambivalence, I became distressed whenever the energies of both "rebel" and "slave" would appear in the same work and disturbed by inconsistent characterizations. As long as I was impelled to remake her fiction through my interpretation of her work, I avoided confronting the significant questions of why, how, and where Freeman's work became an uneven expression of self-division and conflict. It has taken me time to recognize all of this, to embark on an honest journey into Freeman's world.

By facing Freeman's "slavery" as well as her "rebellion," I am now able to appreciate her paradoxical characterizations of women and the fascinating contradictions buried in her work. My journey has helped me understand the process of evasion and idealization that often occurs when we look for our heritage in fiction by women. Perhaps these temptations are especially marked for women working on "minor" writers; but I suspect that many who work on "major" writers succumb to them also. I hope that retracing my own process of discovery may help other feminist critics to recognize the necessity of analyzing women artists in truthful ways.

As I look back on my journey, I see that I have moved gradually through several stages of discovery. What first attracted me to Freeman, a writer whose work seems, on the surface, so distant from the concerns of women today? Surely one could identify more easily with writers such as Virginia Woolf or George Eliot. Yet my first discovery was that Freeman's world was not as remote as some critics assume. This became clear when I went beyond the limited information available in the biographies to explore Freeman's sense of the role of work in a woman's life. While she observed women in her community whose work was rarely self-directed and whose lives centered around the needs of others, Freeman saw her own work as the center of her life. In an autobiographical sketch, she gave herself "the tardy credit of being perfectly conscious, whether or not I have succeeded, in caring more in my heart for the art of my work than for anything else."[3] In many of her stories, women struggle alone to define their lives in terms of their work.

I was drawn to the complexity of Freeman's comments on writing in her essay "The Girl Who Wants to Write: Things to Do and Avoid." She speaks of writing as something a woman may do not out of "some seething of the central fire of genius" but "for money with which to buy a French hat." On the surface, the comment seems to show Freeman's acceptance of a view of her work that has little to do with rebellion or assertiveness. She flippantly presents a "female" perspective on writing as a way of buying a stylish hat, as though her work were merely a means toward greater femininity and therefore acceptability. Yet, as with many of Freeman's statements, I sensed an underlying double message. The French hat itself reflects the very "seething fire" that her own statement satirically rejects and has nothing to do with the woman's concern for style. In her village community, the appearance of the foreign hat would have been associated with freedom, extravagance, even rebellion. The mention of the foreign hat, instead of the typical cap or bonnet of the village spinsters she depicted in her work, suggests Freeman's desire to rebel and suggests, as well, that she associated her work with the possibility of attaining all that the hat represented — something strange, free, exotic, outside the village norm. In "The

Girl Who Wants to Write," Freeman speaks with a kind of urgency
and defiance of her profession: "If a woman be at liberty to write, let
her write as if she were running a race in the sight of the world . . .
She must write above all things the truth as far as she can see the
truth."[4] Expressing the truth about her need to rebel was something
Freeman knew she would have to do as though "running a race in
the sight of the world." She stresses the goal of writing as a woman's
"liberty," perhaps a liberty from all of the limitations of which
Freeman was so acutely aware, a liberty that women must aggressively seek.

    Freeman's comments on her profession inspired me because of
their stress on self-discovery and self-possession. She advised
young women writers to trust their own intuitions and observations
of life, to be independent:

> A young writer should follow the safe course of writing only
> about those subjects she knows thoroughly, and con-
> cerning which she trusts her own convictions. Above all,
> she must write in her own way, with no dependence upon
> the work of another for aid and suggestion. She should
> make her own patterns and found her own school . . . The
> keynote of the whole is, as in every undertaking in this
> world, faithful, hopeful and independent work.[5]

As I was just beginning to discover and define what work meant to
me, I was struck by the way in which these comments showed
Freeman's commitment to "independent work."

    Freeman's commitment, however, was full of complexities and
necessitated a considerable struggle against social expectations. Devotion to her work seemed to carry with it the price of isolation.
What did it mean to be a woman alone? What were the psychological
effects of living with the stigma of spinsterhood, of wanting acceptance in her small New England community yet enjoying her autonomy? For Freeman, the effect was twofold. She associated married
life with happiness, security, and acceptable sexuality, and part of
her longed for this. But she also saw marriage as a threat to her
hard-won independence, to her sense of herself as a woman writer
whose work satisfied her own need to create.

    The pressure to marry began early in Freeman's life. The only
option her parents could see for their daughters was to marry "early
and well."[6] But Freeman would not satisfy their expectations. While
her younger sister was out attending parties, Mary Wilkins was
withdrawn, "curled up on the sofa with a book or gazing out the
window."[7] She lasted only a year at Mount Holyoke Female

Seminary (1870), where she says her "young morals" were looked after but where she "did not behave at all well."[8] Her love for Hanson Tyler, a young ensign, was never returned, although she continued to cling to his memory until the end of her life. In this sense, unrequited love became Freeman's form of self-protection, an excuse not to marry. It was clear from the start that Tyler was unattainable, but by worshiping him long after his departure, Freeman was able to avoid entering relationships with others.

I began to read Freeman's letters and unpublished work with great interest, for they reveal a little of what the biographies only hint at. Her letters reflect that she both enjoyed unmarried life and was ashamed of this pleasure. In an unfinished, unpublished short story, Freeman expressed what spinsterhood had come to mean for her. The voice of the spinster narrator, Jane Lennox, is full of rage, fear, disillusionment, and yet pleasure:

> I am a rebel and what is worse a rebel against the Over-government of all creation . . . I even dare to think that, infinitesimal as I am, . . . I, through my rebellion, have power. All negation has power. I, Jane Lennox, spinster, . . . am a power.[9]

I was intrigued by this voice, by its assertion of power. I could not dismiss it as a passing "tormented mood" of a "troubled woman," as one of her biographers had.[10] What became increasingly interesting to me — and a little unsettling — was Freeman's analysis of the spinster's dilemma. While Jane feels "pride which intoxicates like forbidden stimulants," pride in her autonomy, she also expresses ambivalence: "I often wonder if I might not have been very decent, very decent indeed, if I had laid hold on the life so many of my friends lead. If I had only a real home of my own and a husband and children in it." Seeing husband and children as her "deprived birthright," Jane internalizes the very view that has ostracized her. She sees herself as incomplete: "I am a graft on the tree of human womanhood. I am a hybrid." Through Jane, Freeman expressed the need for isolation and rebellion as well as the desire to be "very decent." At this early stage of my work, I celebrated Freeman's struggle to maintain her independence. Not surprisingly, I chose to focus only on Jane's sense of "glory" in her power, even though I detected her fear of such forbidden power as well. I sympathized with the conflict, though I also avoided its implications by dwelling on Jane's pleasure. I smiled when I read her words: "Sometimes I think I am a *monster*, and the worst of it is, I certainly take pleasure in it."[11]

Submitting to the need for a "decent" life, Freeman did marry when she reached fifty. But her long engagement reflects her hesitation. Although she met Charles Freeman in 1892, she did not marry him until 1902, and the marriage was announced and denied many times in that interim. After six years of unhappy marriage, Freeman wrote a chapter entitled "Old Maid Aunt" in the novel *The Whole Family: A Novel by Twelve Authors*. Her character, Lily Talbert, finds a "powerful tonic" for having "missed" marriage in her "womanly pride," her sense of control over her own life.[12] This was a control Freeman began to lose. Marriage required a complete change in her lifestyle. She had to leave Randolph, Massachusetts, the locale for so much of her work, for Metuchen, New Jersey, where she found "I have not a blessed thing to write about."[13] Her husband demanded that she give up the sleeping sedatives she had used for years and she would "walk the floor at all hours of the morning."[14] Finally, her husband slipped into a desperate alcoholism and the marriage dissolved.

While I continued to read her letters and papers, searching for clues to what seemed such a hidden life, I found the most revealing material to be Freeman's short stories portraying women alone. At this stage, I discovered that for most of Freeman's heroines, to live alone is to bury the sexual self; to marry is to bury the creative, independent self. When I taught "A New England Nun" as part of a fiction course at Smith College, I saw Freeman's power to convey this conflict. Students were surprised and saddened by this icily precise portrait of self-imposed, seemingly neurotic spinsterhood. The heroine, Louisa Ellis, waits fourteen years for her sailor fiancé, Joe, to return from sea; when Joe does return, the thought of marriage terrifies Louisa and she brings the relationship to an end. In many ways, the defensive isolation of Louisa Ellis reflects Freeman's. Her years of waiting for Tyler far exceeded Louisa's, and his failure to return was an unspoken source of relief; it enabled her to pursue her craft without interruption. Freeman's world allowed no room for disorderly male conduct. A male contemporary of Freeman's, Hamlin Garland, recalls a visit to Freeman's home:

Her home might have been used as a typical illustration of her characters. Its cakes and pies, its hot biscuits and jams were exactly right. I felt large and rude like that man in one of her tales, "A New England Nun," who came into the well-ordered sitting room of his sweetheart with such clumsy haste that he overturned her work-basket and sat down on the cat.[15]

Freeman, like her heroine, passionately protected her self-made territory of order. The tipped work basket suggests the danger Freeman's heroine associates with the entry of a man into her life.

In "A New England Nun," I saw Freeman's sense of the price a woman pays if she is to maintain selfhood. Louisa looks at her "solitary home" with "almost the enthusiasm of an artist."[16] For Louisa, her home and her capacity to care for it provide her with a clear identity: "She had throbs of genuine triumph at the sight of the window-panes which she had polished until they shone like jewels" (9-10). As narrow as her world may appear, it is Louisa's creation. Just as Freeman saw marriage as a threat to her writing, Louisa watches Joe track in "a good deal of dust"; she sees his power to erase what she has constructed. For self-protection, Louisa builds cloistered walls behind which she buries her sexuality. Her hobby is to distill the essences from rose petals, and she stores the oils in vials for no apparent use. This small detail indicates Louisa's stored-up though ultimately unrealized and useless sexuality. Similarly, bird-like Louisa locks up the wild flutterings of her canary in a tight little cage. When Joe enters the room, the canary "fluttered wildly beating his little yellow wings against the wires" (3). Although she may inwardly "flutter wildly," Louisa is careful to keep the wires of her cage firmly shut whenever Joe visits. The one thing she fears most in marrying Joe is that her dog will be unchained. Ever since the dog had playfully sunk its teeth into a neighbor's hand fourteen years ago (the time span of Joe's absence), Louisa has locked the dog away. Indeed, the hermit dog becomes Louisa's double. When she feeds him, directly after her own dinner, we hear the "clank of a chain." Louisa denies the dog "innocent canine joys," as she denies herself sexual joys. By avoiding marriage, she never need release the passions her imprisoned animals represent.

In Louisa, we see a contradictory set of fears. On the one hand, Louisa fears the inevitable loss of independence in her required service to Joe. Simultaneously, she fears the release of sexual energies that she has learned to suppress after years of living alone. Like Jane Lennox, Louisa has "power"; she maintains her self-defined identity. The victory, however, brings with it a different form of imprisonment. Louisa's passionate self, the sexual "monster," will remain locked within her nunnery. Her canary will turn itself "into a peaceful yellow ball night after night and have no need to wake and flutter" because of a disturbing male presence; her dog's little "hermit hut," like Louisa's, will be safe as "the snow might fall on its roof year in and year out, but he never would go on a rampage through the unguarded village"(16).

In "A Symphony in Lavender," Freeman explored even more deeply a woman's fear of and longing for sexual fulfillment. The heroine, Caroline, has an unsettling dream. She is carrying a basket of flowers when she meets a young man:

> When he reached me he stopped and looked down into my face and then at my basket of flowers. I stopped too — I could not seem to help it in my dream — and gazed down at the ground. I was afraid to look at him, and I trembled so that the lilies and roses in my basket quivered.[17]

At first the dreamer's response reveals all of the passion she has learned to hide in her conscious existence. Caroline's basket of flowers embodies her conflict, for it contains the lilies we associate with purity and virginity as well as the rich red roses of heightened sensuality. The quivering flowers suggest the intensity of Caroline's desires, yet her trembling also suggests the fear of what society forbids a woman to feel. When the young man requests a flower, the dreamer gathers courage: "When his eyes met mine it did seem to me that I wanted to give him one of those flowers more than anything else in the world" (44). Guilt and fear, however, interfere with the sensual flower-giving. Caroline "wanted at once to give him the lily and would have died rather than give it to him" (44). This is a remarkable description of the conflict between socially unacceptable fulfillment and acceptable self-denial.

Caroline struggles against her own sensuality. As she gazes at her young man's face, it suddenly begins to transform to mirror Caroline's painful conflict: "As I gazed, his face changed more and more to me till finally . . . it looked at once beautiful and repulsive" (45). In the face of her possible freedom, horror mixes with longing. While Caroline craves sexual pleasure, she has internalized her society's equation of female sexuality with evil. Accordingly, her vision of the man's face reflects her fear of "ugly" sexuality. She flees, firmly gripping her basket of flowers and feeling "a great horror of something, I did not know what, in my heart" (45). Caroline acts out, in her dream, the drama of a conflict that ultimately causes her to suppress her desire for passion. The conflict between her inner compulsion and her fear of the external social definition of its ugliness shapes her destiny. When a young man does appear in her life, one year after the dream, the dreamlike horror returns; she sees the same transforming visage and she runs again. Freeman's portrayal of the cloistered worlds of these "New England nuns" made me feel both compassion for the heroines and anger at the choices allowed them.

After reading of such confinement, such thwarted desire, I longed to see Freeman's characters rebel. Her portrayal of the spinster's conflict and consequent repression was brilliant, but I was determined to discover some solution to the dilemma in her work. I wanted to see other women characters breaking through the barriers Louisa and Caroline faced. Surely if Freeman had the capacity to understand the bottled sexuality of her repressed characters, she could, to satisfy my feminist inclinations, release their hidden energies in other stories.

What I found instead was something much more complicated. I saw rebellion in various forms in much of her work, but I also detected Freeman's hesitation, her fear. Certainly, in her perception of the unmarried woman as victim, Freeman offered feminist analysis. But she would not move on to the feminist conclusions I was seeking. I wanted the hidden sexuality of her characters to be released; I wanted them to crush their fears, to assert and rebel. Instead, I found her rebels paradoxically submissive.They were often quick to withdraw after momentary assertiveness; they would fight within narrow and acceptable arenas rather than risk being labeled "monster." The effect of this discovery on my approach to Freeman was devastating.

I wonder now if this search for feminist rebellion was not a projection of my unfulfilled need to rebel. In so many ways, my life had followed a pattern of complacent conventionality. Being the youngest child in the family and having parents who were already wise and accepting of adolescent behavior, I had no clear or genuine target for rebellion. I was a "good girl" even when I wanted to be "bad." Unlike so many other feminists of my generation, I am comfortably married. Furthermore, I got married in the early 1970s when many women had decided to live alone, just as Freeman's heroines had done, but without their sexual repression. Yet somehow I managed to feel free and unexploited even within this traditional pattern. Unexpressed energies to rebel, even against my own contentment, must, however, have lurked beneath the surface. In looking back, it is not surprising to me now that I originally intended to write my dissertation on the use of the psychological double, the "madwoman in the attic" in *Jane Eyre* and in other works by women.

My need for finding rebellion in Freeman had another dimension. When I began working on Freeman, I knew that I was doing more than just discovering a woman writer of the past. I was fulfilling an established requirement that I had begun to resent — a dissertation that would earn me a Ph.D. I knew that completing the dissertation would give me the freedom to do what I love: I desperately wanted to teach without experiencing the kind of exploitation part-time ABD (all-but-dissertation) instructors are subjected to. Yet I saw no connection between the act of writing a scholarly dissertation and the work I would subsequently be free to enjoy. Actively rebelling against writing the thesis could only hurt me; however, if I could find an outlet for the urge to defy the requirement by finding fictional rebellion in Freeman, then I might rebel indirectly. I confess that I still read of rebellion in fiction with great satisfaction, feeling somehow that a heroine has won *me* some sort of freedom by way of her aggression.

Recently, as I entered my study to write, my beautiful but distracting toddler crawled up the stairs calling, "Mama? Mama?" Even now that I passionately defend the need for work in "a room of one's own," I could feel the urgency of my need to respond to Rachel's call. The study door swung open and there she stood, her large brown eyes pleading that I leave the work that beckoned me. My husband had been unable to keep her from me and went back downstairs. I sat at my desk, gazing at my daughter and feeling the pressure of the conflict between my desire to work and my daughter's need for my attention. Finally, my rage at the sheer difficulty of the situation rose to the surface. I brought my daughter to her father, asserted my right to some time to myself to work in peace, closed the study door, and sat down at my desk in a state of confused anger. Oddly enough, I found myself riding on the energies of this anger. I was suddenly able to think more clearly about my connection to Freeman and to write with greater ease than before the anger struck.

Perhaps at those moments when I close the study door for my time alone with my work, I am releasing my hidden rebel. When Rachel naps, I will turn away (not without a touch of this anger I am describing) from the sink full of dishes, the floor full of the remnants of her lunch, the unmade bed; I will then enter my work with a passionate, new sense of connection, heightened by the fact that I am taking this time for *me*, not the house chores or the baby. It seems strange to some when I confess that having a baby, despite all of the new demands it has placed upon me, has actually freed me from work paralysis, enhanced my capacity to become engaged with my work, made me a better teacher. I view the time I put into my writing differently now. It is time I have had to fight for, to win. Perhaps when this fight first began, I wanted Freeman to sanction what I was doing. I remember vividly, a year ago, sitting at my desk, savoring my work time alone and visualizing Freeman in the seclusion of her room on the second floor, the room she needed for writing. One of

her biographers described it as a room full of windows that overlooked the "elms of Main Street and beyond . . . the coastal hills." I
looked out my own windows and imagined Freeman sitting in this
room at her "low table and amid the plainest things,"[18] writing, just
as I was writing.

Given my recent struggles to balance writing and mothering, I
wanted Freeman to satisfy my definition of writing as a form of
self-affirmation for women. I remember clearly my early reaction to
the tone of submission in Freeman's introduction to her volume of
short stories, A Humble Romance and Other Stories. Not surprisingly, I
was extremely impatient. Freeman referred to "these little stories"
about the "village people of New England" as studies of "features of
will and conscience" characteristic of their New England ancestors.
Her reference to her stories as "little" disturbed me instantly. But I
was even more upset when she said, "It has been done with the best
results by other American authors."[19] I thought I detected the
insecurity of an unknown woman writer; but I also recognized her
urge to undermine the power of her own form of rebellion, however
tame it may have been, by shadowing it with a submissive apology
for her "little stories." As one observer put it, Freeman's "succinct,
low-voiced comment was often lost in the . . . clamor of less
important voices."[20] I knew how worthy the stories were and how
often they surpassed similar works by "other American authors." I
was defensively loyal to Freeman — I defended her even against
herself and her own indirect attacks on her work.

I can see now that my rage at Freeman's apologetic tone must
have been partly connected to my own apologetic feelings about
working on a woman writer nobody seemed to have read. At a
cocktail party for English department colleagues, I would await the
dreaded question "What is your dissertation topic?" I would carefully hold back the word "minor" and say "a turn-of-the-century
New England writer, Mary Wilkins Freeman," but "minor" would
inevitably slip out. Why did it always sound apologetic? Hadn't her
"minor" works contributed in "major" ways to my understanding
of women? And if her work had contributed to my understanding of
women, was it really minor? I wanted to shout this out, but in
Freeman-like passivity, I would generally retreat to a corner of the
room.

At this stage of my work, I was hunting for rebels. I could not read
objectively. I first came upon Sally, a simple kitchen maid. On the
surface, "A Humble Romance" is just what the title indicates, a
humble love story: peddler meets maid. But couched within the

conventional framework, I saw a lurking rebel, Sally, whose "finger joints and bones were knotty" and who "from head to foot . . . was a little discordant note." Her expression "was at once passive and eager."[21] Passivity and assertiveness are exactly the conflicting qualities that appear in most of Freeman's rebels. The story speaks to the issue of women and work. Jake convinces Sally to leave her exploitative job as maid to marry him: "I owns a cart and horse and disposes of the rags and sells the tin all on my own hook" (5). Clearly his work is independent, unlike Sally's jobs as maid or prospective wife. He asks Sally to leave her dishes, to "ride like a queen and see the countryside," but her new "job" would essentially match the old one in terms of her dependence. While I read the story, I struggled to define *my* work. I was writing to fulfill an institutional requirement, and my only immediate rewards were the pleasures of reading and discovering my subject. Not receiving any paycheck for my work, I was like Sally in that I was almost a "wife" to the dissertation: I served it without expecting any monetary reward.

As I read of Sally's romance with Jake, I was skeptical and uneasy. Where was my rebel? Then Jake suddenly abandons Sally and disappears, leaving her his cart and a note asking her to "bear up." She takes over the role of peddler, which was considered a man's job. Now I began to feel relieved. This is what I was looking for! Sally takes pride in her work for the first time. She becomes active, assertive, independent. As Freeman reminds us, "a woman running a tin-cart was an unprecedented spectacle." Having never run my own "tin-cart," I embraced my first rebel eagerly. But as I read on, the ambiguities became unavoidable. This was my first encounter with Freeman's passive rebel, the "rebel slave." The rebel Sally carries a pistol to protect her property. But the passive Sally explains her role to the public carefully, with "meek dignity," an odd pairing of words. The dignity reflects an active, assertive pride; the meekness, her apologetic passivity. My own instinct to evade this duality rose to the surface as my pen itched to blot out the word *meek*.

Sally trades well, gives good bargains, and proves to be an exceptional peddler. In fact, she improves Jake's business in her bold trading with town dealers. It was good to read of the woman peddler's success. But when I realized that it was her innovation of adding "pins, needles, and notions" to the stock that improved the trade, my heart sank. Sally simply would not conform to my notion of or my longing for the rebel. What made her better at the business was her method of feeding traditional female expectations. At the time, I failed to see this as shrewd business sense. All I could see was defeat. I had to face that Freeman would let her rebel go only so far. And Freeman reminds the reader that all Sally's peddling was done in the interest of her "bearing up" for the sake of her prospective husband until his return.

In an almost unbearably sentimental conclusion, Jake does return. My heart sank even lower. He tells "little un" the complicated circumstances that motivated his departure and I felt defeated by Sally's response: "Jake, I did bear up . . . Oh Jake, my blue silk dress an' the white bonnet is in the trunk of the cart . . . an' I can git 'em out an' put 'em on under the trees . . . an' wear em to be married in." I can remember my sense of utter disillusionment. I wanted Sally to turn Jake away and drive off as a new and independent woman peddler, an "unprecedented" model of feminist assertiveness. At the very least, I longed to end the story several pages earlier, before Jake's return. Why, I asked myself, does Freeman snatch away the freedom that she granted Sally of taking pride in her work — not the work of a wife for her husband, but the work of a woman for herself? Why does she push her character back to the role of "little un," of little wife? I looked back to my earlier unqualified admiration for Freeman's comments on writing and work. Now I was discovering that she continuously struggled with what she called "the uncomfortable feeling I have that I am not telling things exactly as they are."[22] In fact, her own need for acceptability made her willing to compromise for her public, made her willing to add "sentiments and uplifting ones," as she promised in a letter to an editor.[23] At her weakest, she was, as one critic put it, "willing to add sentiment and morality to her stories like sugar to a cake recipe."[24] Not accepting the complexity of Freeman's motive for taming Sally's assertiveness, I felt only disappointment and paralysis. At this stage of my work, I found it impossible to approach Freeman with any degree of objectivity.

I stopped writing and turned to "The Revolt of 'Mother,'" a better known story of rebellion, to satisfy my thirst for Freeman's "revolt." After her husband builds a new barn for the animals, refusing to build a much needed new home, Sarah defiantly moves into the barn and creatively redesigns it. By the end of her intensive labor, the barn is virtually a work of art — a new, comfortable residence for Sarah Penn and her family. I delighted in the spirit and determination of the heroine's decision not to allow her husband to place the needs of animals above hers.

As I view Sarah now, I think of the stanza in Adrienne Rich's poem "The Mirror in Which Two Are Seen as One":

She is the one you call sister
Her simplest act has glamor,
as when she scales a fish the knife
flashes in her long fingers
no motion wasted or when
rapidly talking of love
she steel-wool burnishes
the battered kettle[25]

Unfortunately, in my initial approach to the story, I failed to see the "glamor," the skill, the worth in those womanly tasks that would not fit my notion of freedom. In my own marriage, I had been careful to create a sense of equality with my husband in relation to the chores that Sarah took upon herself automatically. Nothing could have appealed to me less than the idea of working hard at creating a home in which I could be an expert servant. Rather than appreciating the value of Sarah's "steel-wool" work of setting up a new home, I itched to lift her out of the domestic context in which Freeman had set Sarah's rebellion and to channel those energies elsewhere. I failed to accept (although I had to acknowledge) that the home was the one sphere in which it was acceptable or even feasible for a woman to exert Sarah Penn's sort of power. The home is, after all, Sarah's "work," and she is expert at it. But Freeman's precision in demonstrating this fact escaped me.

Sarah's bold defense of her action is worth studying:

"I think it's right jest as much as I think it was right for our forefathers to come over from the old country cause they didn't have what belonged to 'em . . . I've got my own mind an' my own feet an' I'm goin' to think my own thoughts an' go my own ways, an' nobody but the Lord is goin' to dictate to me unless I've a mind to have him."[26]

Reading this, anyone can imagine a rebel-hunter's glee; it might be taken as a humble form of feminist manifesto. Yet I was troubled by what Sarah fights for. For forty years, Sarah has placed the needs of others ahead of her own needs, as any "agreeable wife" should. Like Eva in Tillie Olsen's *Tell Me a Riddle*, she has "moved to the rhythms of others" without objection. But unlike Eva, Sarah "revolts" only to return immediately to the role of serving her husband's needs. Having won the victory of creating a new home,

Sarah is overcome by her triumph. Yet to my mind, she had won only the victory of providing her husband and family with a place in which to serve them better.

Once again, I longed to rewrite when I noticed that odd mixture of rebellion and submission. After disobeying wifely codes of behavior by moving into the barn, Sarah gets to work on her husband's dinner: "However deep a resentment she might be forced to hold against her husband, she would never fail in sedulous attention to his wants" (122). I saw Sarah as a rebel within an ultimately safe arena. Freeman found a way, through Sarah's ambivalent defiance, to express her own suppressed rebellion without losing the security of society's approval. Surely no one could object to the "revolt" of a woman in the interest of establishing a better home for her family. The energy of the "revolt" emerges in Sarah's creative and independent action and in the forcefulness of language, but the plot and frame of the story undercut the rebellion. This story exemplifies Freeman's need to feel safe in the roots of New England morality and her conflicting urge to spurt out Sarah's anger.

Freeman later rejected "The Revolt of 'Mother' " in an article in the *Saturday Evening Post:*

> In the first place all fiction ought to be true and "The Revolt of 'Mother' "is not true. . . . There never was in New England a woman like Mother. If there had been she certainly would have lacked the nerve. She would also have lacked the imagination. New England women of the period coincided with their husbands in thinking that the sources of wealth should be better housed than the consumers.[27]

My reaction to her statement was like my rage at her apologetic preface, for I believed that Freeman renounced the finest aspects of her own art. I wanted to shout back, "Fool, you have rejected the essence of your work." Her statement was an apology to her public, and I was angry. She was conceding that if a woman rebels as Sarah does, she must be insane; such a woman could not exist.

At this point, I almost put my work away. But fortunately I was beginning to recognize that my inclination to recreate my own model of what a feminist writer should be was mistaken. I realized that I now needed to know more about Freeman's life. Although I had explored her life at an earlier stage in my work, I had done so selectively, looking only for those details that would feed my expectations. New questions now came to mind. What, for instance, were Freeman's feelings about her mother when she wrote "The Revolt of 'Mother' '"? Was it appropriate for her to stage this revolt in the domestic sphere? But then why did she feel a need to apologize for the story later? Was it possible to see Freeman in a larger social context, to see her work more meaningfully in the context of her life? To stop projecting? How much more useful it now seemed to openly explore the conflicts that Freeman's art embodied.

Soon after Freeman's sister Nan died in 1876, her parents were forced to give up their little cottage because her father's financial position worsened. In 1877, the family moved into the home of Reverend Tyler, the father of Hanson Tyler, Freeman's unrequited love. Freeman's mother, Eleanor, was hired to serve as housekeeper for the invalid reverend and his wife. I could easily imagine Freeman's response to her mother's suddenly subservient position. As Michele Clark explains in her afterword to *The Revolt of "Mother" and Other Stories*, "Eleanor, the wife, the mother, was now deprived of the very things which made a woman proud, her own kitchen, furniture, family china; and she had lost the one place in which it was acceptable for her to be powerful: her home.''[28] Certainly Sarah's desperate determination to win a decent work environment in the form of a fine kitchen reflects the need Freeman must have sensed in her own mother. I could see connections, a context that I hadn't seen before. Warren Wilkins, like Adirondam in "The Revolt of 'Mother,' '" had long ago given up his original plan of building the house that Eleanor had wanted for her family on a site they had purchased when they first moved to Brattleboro.[29] Perhaps "The Revolt of 'Mother' '" offered Freeman the delight of transforming that harsh experience into something positive. She transformed her mother's subservience into revolt and created the home her mother never had.

Now I returned to passages in the story that I had avoided, the ones in which Freeman expresses her respect for Sarah's domesticity:

> She was a masterly keeper of her box of a house. Her one living room never seemed to have in it any of the dust which the friction of life with inanimate matter produces. She swept, and there seemed to be no dirt to go before the broom; she cleaned and one could see no difference. She was like an artist so perfect that he has apparently no art. (121)

The passage stresses the seriousness with which Sarah approaches her job. She has created an art out of daily chores. Freeman's respect for Sarah's "art" was, I thought, yet another response to her mother's life story. As an adolescent, Freeman had struggled against becoming her mother and subsiding into her mother's forms of passivity. She had fought against her mother's world of domesticity and resisted domestic work throughout her life. This was always a source of friction between mother and daughter. In this story, Freeman writes a tribute to her mother's work, a form of work she never valued. In a rare moment of candid self-expression, Freeman mentioned that she wished her parents "might have been spared" to her, that she "longed to make some return to them for their love and care, but that now as they were gone" she would have "to pass it on to someone else."[30] I could see now that this story was, in some sense, Freeman's vehicle for "passing it on." It was interesting to see that the story allowed Freeman to invest her fictional mother with the spirit, the self-determination, and the self-knowledge that her own mother never exhibited. Perhaps the mother she created is the mother she wished she could have had.

The more I looked at Freeman's life, the more connections emerged between her life and her art. Wasn't Freeman's depiction of Sarah as a kind of artist a clue to understanding Freeman's artistic struggles? As a woman writer in a tiny New England village, Freeman shared Sarah's battle. Just as Sarah struggles to have her work recognized, Freeman fought to be taken seriously as a writer. For decades, critics categorized her subject matter as small, insignificant. Yet like Sarah Penn's vision of great possibility in the simplest things — a barn, for example — Freeman's work always moves to some other level of possibility, always explores the largest question in the smallest incidents.

As I analyzed my difficulties with Freeman, I tried to stop thinking and writing defensively and began to think and write analytically, searching only to understand and to gain from that understanding — no more imaginary rewriting of her stories, no more remaking of her characters. I realized now that I had been avoiding Freeman's ambivalence. Pushing Sally back to the level of obedient wife in "A Humble Romance" helped Freeman tame her own rebellion, make it acceptable. And acceptability meant survival. But at the same time, allowing Sally and Sarah their forms of rebellion enabled Freeman to express her hidden need to defy the "gentility" required of her by the "young girls'" magazine in which she published.[31]

It was a new experience to analyze without anger or disappointment. My response to yet another inconsistent rebel, Hetty Fifield in

"A Church Mouse," made me realize how my approach had
changed. Hetty battles against a hostile community for the right to
choose her own form of work. I realized now that whenever Freeman wrote stories that drifted away from acceptable standards for
"lady readers," she herself was engaged in a similar battle. In "A
Church Mouse" the heroine rejects her community's assertion that
the job of tending the local church can be held only by a man. The
male authorities in the village present Hetty with their objections:
she has lost the room she had kept as a domestic. Where will she
live? How can she do the jobs that require men's strength such as
tending the fires or working to ring the bell? Hetty's revolt is energetic, aggressive. She creates a room for herself in the church gallery.
When a boy comes to ring the bell, she sends him away with pride
and vigor: "I'm goin' to ring the bell; I'm sexton." She is proud of her
new identity as sexton and refuses to give up this role. Finally, with
community rage intensifying, Hetty barricades herself inside the
church, making "her sacred castle impregnable except to violence."[32]
She peers out the window and confronts the now growing crowd
below with the "magnitude of her last act of defiance." In her
"small, lofty room," Hetty finally wins the battle. Yet despite this
final victory, Hetty still manifests Freeman's ambivalence. In her
fight for the right to personal fulfillment through work, Hetty faces
the danger of losing the acceptance and love of her community.
Perhaps this explains why Freeman subtly deflates Hetty's heroism
and has her shift from aggressive confrontation to timid pleading.
After she successfully bars masculine intrusion into her self-claimed
territory, Hetty appears meek and begins to plead to receive permission to remain in the church from the very authorities that she
had earlier dismissed. It is only after such pleading that she can win
the battle. She never asks to earn a salary equal to her less competent
predecessor, nor does she ask for the right to a decent room inside
the church instead of in the gallery. In the last scene, she appears
timidly at the window to beg for " 'nothin' any better.' " She covers
her face with her hands so that "her words end in a weak wail"
(159). But then Freeman offers another mixed message. Beside this
new image of Hetty — "small and trembling and helpless before
them . . . like a little animal driven from its cover" — Freeman places
the *women* in the village, who now demand that the men submit to
Hetty's will (159). In this way, Freeman shows that Hetty's war is
every woman's war.

The change in Hetty's tone is radical. The change in my response
to this reversal in tone and character was also radical. Instead of
feeling disappointment, I recognized clues to a richer understanding

of Mary Wilkins Freeman. Clearly Hetty's shift in strategy was a matter of survival. At this point, I was able to see Freeman and her heroine in a larger social context. What enrages the male villagers most about Hetty's behavior is her self-sufficiency and independence, her satisfaction in living and working alone in the church. The deacon tells her "it ain't fit for an old woman like you to be alone in the church" (153). To the male eye, as Charlotte Wolff explains, "women by themselves appear to be incomplete, as if a limb were missing."[33] Freeman surely sensed this attitude as she looked out at Main Street from the room in which she worked. The deacon's response to Hetty's actions is to assume that she has lost her senses, that she is mad, an assumption that Freeman must also have faced because of her devotion to her work rather than to a husband.

Freeman's choice of the title "A Church Mouse" and her frequent reference to Hetty as a "little animal" made me think of Freeman's reference to her "little stories," her underestimation of her own worth as a writer. But now I was not angry. I could see new parallels. Freeman describes Hetty as a "fierce little animal with claws and teeth bared"; her littleness, in fact, is deceiving: the "little animal" rebel has "claws and teeth." Freeman's self-deprecation when she claimed that her type of story had been done "with the best results by other American authors" had deeper roots than I had realized initially. Her self-conception was a direct response to her perception of the attitudes of those who judged her. Like Hetty, she faced an attitude in her society that continually reduced her size and power. In an autobiographical piece she contributed to *My Maiden Effort*, Freeman described the reaction she sensed when she received her first prize for a short story: "The story won a prize of $50 and when I went with a friend to claim it, the Prize Committee thought the friend must have written the story because I did not look as if I knew enough."[34] Although she was aware that they misjudged her, she couldn't help but allow their judgment to influence her vision of herself. Perhaps I was doing exactly this when I faced the reaction of colleagues in my department to my "little" project on an "insignificant" writer. Seeing my work through their eyes, I would often put it aside for more "important" matters — such as teaching Henry James.

In *My Maiden Effort*, Freeman described the initial reaction to her fine story "Two Old Lovers": "It was accepted after being nearly turned down because the editor at first glance at my handwriting thought it was the infantile effort of a child not worth reading."[35] Again, she was reduced to the child's size (a size she interestingly

attributes to almost all of her rebel heroines) and was considered
unworthy of serious attention. The effect on Freeman is clear in the
conflicting messages she gave to young women writers: She warned
that the young author is "in danger if she places much stress upon
the opinions of others" but at the same time "even the truth must be
held back unless it is of a nature to benefit and not poison."[36]
Following her own advice, Freeman created the lively heroine Hetty
and allowed her to break rules, to ignore "the opinions of others."
Freeman then "held back" the "poison" and had Hetty shrink from
monster to mouse so that she can win her battle and acceptance at
the same time. For Freeman, bound by the double need to rebel and
to belong, it was crucial that even a determined rebel like Hetty not
stray too far from the boundaries of community acceptance. Freeman needed and loved the village culture as much as she rejected its
narrowness; she was "disdainful of and dependent upon its restricted horizons."[37] Something of this double bind comes across in
her placement of Hetty in the corner of the church gallery behind a
"sunflower quilt" she has made. Freeman locates her character in
the writer's own predicament; Hetty is both trapped within the
boundaries of the narrow congregation (ultimately answerable to its
rules) and set apart by the quilt she hangs, her art, to announce the
significance of her separateness, her individuality, her ability to
fight back.

In her response in the *New York Times* to winning the American
Academy Medal, Freeman described her sense of victory on receiving her first acceptance and a check for the story: "I felt my wings
spring from my shoulders capable of flight and I flew home."[38]
Recognition of her work gave her the feeling of liberty (like Hetty's
feeling when she rings the church bell), but the "flight" had to be a
flight "home," and this reality, this need to fly home, also grounded
her.

My response to another story, "Sister Liddy," best shows my new
ability to accept Freeman realistically. Here Freeman offers a fictionalized exploration of the artistic process that might have been at
work when she wrote her most sentimental stories or added the
sentimental conclusion to "A Humble Romance." Reading "Sister
Liddy" helped me understand these intrusions of sentimentality in
a new way. "Sister Liddy" is a powerful story depicting the desper-
ation of a woman for whom "the world had seemed simply standing
ground; she had gotten little more out of it."[39] Here Freeman avoids
the trap of sentimentality as she paints the portrait of Polly, a
woman who spends her life within the narrow corridors of an insane

asylum for the poor. Given how often Freeman's villagers label as insane heroines who refuse to conform, it is interesting that in this story the heroine is in fact locked away. To compensate for what is essentially an unlived life, Polly creates an imaginary "Sister Liddy." She tells the other women patients the "story" of her imaginary sister's life in a "flood" of rich details. She equips her fictive sister with all that she lacks: happy marriage, baby, silk-lined cradle. For Sister Liddy, all things end well: she is conventionally "pretty" while Polly is not; she has the love of the husband and child Polly has never had; she is accepted, free from the corridors of Polly's asylum. Polly's story becomes appallingly flowery, a parody of Freeman's sentimental prose at its worst.

When I read this story and became aware of my response to it, I knew that I had arrived at a clearer understanding of Freeman's work. Now I saw ambivalence in Freeman rather than weakness. Whenever Polly begins to drift into her dreams of conventional bliss, Sally, a figure of rebellion and violence, flies down the hallway in a rage. Sally rips the sheets on her bed to shreds every day, an act of desperate violence. She acts out the repressed violence that is in Polly and, I have come to believe, in Freeman as well. She is, in this sense, the other sister, the other Freeman. Sister Liddy is the self that society encourages, the one who marries, who belongs, who conforms. Sister Sally is the "madwoman" that society rejects; she can only fly down the hallway with all the anger that must remain trapped within the asylum.

The story concludes with Polly's confession on her deathbed. But as she confesses to the "sin" of having lied to create Sister Liddy, Freeman describes Sally's wild actions:

> Sally trotted past. . . she had just torn her bed to pieces. As soon as she got her breath enough, Polly Moss finished what she had to say. "I s'pose I was dretful wicked," she whispered, "but I never had any Sister Liddy." (98)

The connection between the rebel Sally and the passive Polly is implicit. Polly must gather her breath for the confession almost as though she herself had just finished tearing her bed apart. Perhaps it is not "never having had a Sister Liddy" but never having *been* a Sister Liddy that has made Polly think of herself as "dretful wicked." Women like Freeman who would not completely conform to the model of a Sister Liddy were left with exactly this conflict. Even as

Freeman expressed her anger through Sally, her longing to be the acceptable Liddy remained. In studying this story, I discovered what the real center of my work on Freeman would be, what my contribution to our understanding of Freeman could be. I now see Freeman's work as a fascinating interweaving of Liddys and Sallys, an often brilliant expression of a conflict that is still with us today.

In my early approach to Freeman, I was trying to make of Freeman a *sister*. Initially I adopted the role of a patronizing "big sister." Perhaps being the youngest in my family influenced this urge to be the oldest in my relation to Freeman — to have control over my subject in the way that an older sister can sometimes have control over a younger one. When I think of my relationship with my oldest sister, I realize how many stages it has gone through. We have now reached a level of mutual acceptance, but I think of all the times that my sister must have wished that I were different. I could see that when I married, she had wished I would have stayed single, lived more independently, experimented in more radical ways. Knowing this always made me feel a bit of a victim — a victim of someone else's vision of *my* life. And yet this is precisely what I was doing when I tried to manipulate Freeman, to turn her into the woman of my own creation. Thinking of how I treated Freeman as "little sister," I feel a strange sympathy for her, as though she had been shortchanged somehow by her "big sister" who could not accept her on her own terms.

Writing this essay has been invaluable for me. It helped me overcome a work paralysis that was directly connected to my initial inability to approach Freeman with honesty. Before I began to write this essay, whenever I found myself disliking a characterization, a conclusion, one of Freeman's apologies, my hands would freeze at the typewriter. As I faced the ways in which I had resisted the reality of Mary Wilkins Freeman, I felt my fingers ease.

In exploring the process of my evasion and discovery, I began to realize that the heart of my interest in Freeman had much to do with my own sense of womanhood. My roles as teacher, writer, wife and mother had brought with them conflicts that were there for Freeman in different ways, but unexpressed, locked within that closet she describes in her poem "A Maiden Lady." For Freeman, the process of writing worked to both open and close the door to that closet. For me, the door has opened.

As we look to the history of women writers for an understanding of our roots, we must avoid creating imaginary "sisters" to satisfy our longings for an unambiguous feminist heritage. I had wanted to create a Sister Freeman who could satisfy *my* need for clear, unambiguous roots in a feminist past. "Listing her *unfelt* needs," as Adrienne Rich put it, I was really listing my own needs.[40] I now can look at Freeman with honesty and truly say "she is the one you call sister." And the sister I see is not the creature of my own imagination. She is the real, conflicted, and struggling sister of our past.

Notes

1. Mary Wilkins Freeman, "A Maiden Lady," *Century* 30 (August 1885), 654.

2. Jane refers to herself as a "rebel slave" when she is being locked in the red room. As she sits a prisoner in the room (the punishment for her rebellion), she begins to internalize her opponents' sense of the wickedness of her rebel self and becomes, in fact, a "slave" to their judgment of her actions. Throughout the novel she wavers between "rebel" and "slave," just as so many of Freeman's heroines do. Charlotte Brontë, *Jane Eyre* (New York: Norton, 1971), 9.

3. Mary Wilkins Freeman, "Mary E. Wilkins," in *My Maiden Effort: The Personal Confessions of Well-Known Authors,* ed. Gelett Burgess (New York: Doubleday, Page, 1921), 267.

4. Mary Wilkins Freeman, "The Girl Who Wants to Write: Things to Do and Avoid," *Harper's Bazaar* (June 1913). All references to this article are to page 272.

5. Mary Wilkins Freeman, "Good Wits, Pen and Paper " in *What Women Can Earn,* ed. G. H. Dodge et al, (New York, 1899), 28-29.

6. Edward Foster, *Mary E. Wilkins Freeman* (New York: Hendricks House, 1956),32.

7. Ibid.

8. Mary Wilkins Freeman, letter to Miss Helena Todd, 6 March 1907, from the collection of Miss Todd. Quoted by Foster, *Freeman* , 31.

9. Mary Wilkins Freeman, undated, untitled manuscript given to Foster by Mrs. A. B. Mann, Randolph, Mass. See Foster, *Freeman,* 142-44. All references to this manuscript are to these pages in Foster.

10. Foster, *Freeman*, 143.

11. Ibid.

12. Mary Wilkins Freeman, "The Old Maid Aunt," in *The Whole Family: A Novel by Twelve Authors* (including William Dean Howells, Henry James) (New York: Harper and Brothers, 1908), 34.

13. Mary Wilkins Freeman, letter to Carolyn Wells, undated, from Metuchen, N. J., Mary Wilkins Freeman Collection (#7407), Clifton Waller Barrett Library, University of Virginia Library.

14. Foster, *Freeman*, 158.

15. Hamlin Garland, *Roadside Meetings* (New York: Macmillan, 1930), 33.

16. Mary Wilkins Freeman, "A New England Nun," in *A New England Nun and Other Stories* (Ridgewood, N. J.: Gregg Press, 1891; reprint, New York: Harper & Row, 1967), 1. All references are to the 1967 reprint; page numbers are cited parenthetically in the text.

17. Mary Wilkins Freeman, "A Symphony in Lavender," in *A Humble Romance and Other Stories* (New York: Harper and Brothers, 1887), 44. All references are to this edition; page numbers are cited parenthetically in the text.

18. Foster, *Freeman*, 87.

19. Mary Wilkins Freeman, Preface, *A Humble Romance and Other Stories* (Edinburgh, 1890).

20. Garland, *Roadside Meetings*, 33.

21. Mary Wilkins Freeman, "A Humble Romance," in *A Humble Romance and Other Stories*, 2. All references to this story are cited parenthetically in the text.

22. Mary Wilkins Freeman, letter to Mary L. Booth, 17 February 1885, Mary Wilkins Freeman Collection (#7407), Clifton Waller Barrett Library, University of Virginia Library.

23. Mary Wilkins Freeman, letter to Elizabeth Jordan, 12 July 1904, Elizabeth Jordan Papers, New York Public Library, Manuscripts and Archives Division.

24. Thomas R. Knipp, "The Quest for Form: The Fiction of Mary E. Wilkins Freeman" (Ph.D diss., Michigan State University, 1966), 310.

25. Adrienne Rich, *Poems Selected and New, 1950-1974* (New York: Norton, 1975), 193-95.

26. Mary Wilkins Freeman, "The Revolt of 'Mother,' " in *The Revolt of 'Mother' and Other Stories* (New York: Feminist Press, 1974), 134. References are to this edition; page numbers are cited parenthetically in the text.

27. Untitled article, *Saturday Evening Post* , 8 December 1917, 25.

28. Michele Clark, Afterword, in Freeman, *The Revolt of 'Mother,'* 177.

29. Perry Westbrook, *Mary Wilkins Freeman* (New York: Twayne, 1967), 28. The family had moved from Randolph, Mass. in 1867 to Brattleboro, Vt., with the hope of bettering their financial situation. Warren Wilkins had purchased a large plot of land in Brattleboro, but then could not afford to build on the property. The family had to take a small cottage instead and eventually move in with the Tylers. Years later, Mary Wilkins returned to live in Randolph.

30. Anna L. Hufford recounts Mrs. Helen French Gulliver's recollections of Mary Wilkins as a student at Mount Holyoke Female Seminary, MS undated, Mount Holyoke College Library/Archives. These are reported to be the words Freeman wrote to Gulliver.

31. Foster, *Freeman*, 58. The pages of *Harper's* contained "nothing which could not be read aloud by the entire family."

32. Mary Wilkins Freeman, "A Church Mouse," in *"The Revolt of 'Mother,' "* 150. References are to this edition; page numbers are cited parenthetically in the text.

33. Charlotte Wolff, *Love Between Women* (New York: Harper & Row, 1971), 211.

34. Freeman, "Mary E. Wilkins," 266.
35. Ibid.
36. Freeman, "The Girl Who Wants to Write," 272.
37. Clark, Afterword, 167.
38. *New York Times*, 24 April 1926, sec. 1, 7.
39. Mary Wilkins Freeman, "Sister Liddy," in *A New England Nun and Other Stories*, 93. All references are to this edition; page numbers are cited parenthetically in the text.
40. Rich, *Poems*, 194.

Isak Dinesen

Janet Sternburg

© 1983 Thomas Victor

Janet Sternburg

FAREWELL TO THE FARM

Mid-January, two weeks before the performance of Isak Dinesen's writings, which I'm adapting and directing for the Manhattan Theatre Club. We've rented St. Peter's Church, a space large enough to hold a big audience and also one that is evocative of Dinesen, an austere, elegant, bare-bones sanctuary of light oak and high white walls. Now at five o'clock, I'm dashing from my job, onto the Madison Avenue bus, to get to St. Peter's and meet the stage manager, the technical director, the rest of the crew. In the half hour between daytime services and evening vespers, we will find out whether an idea of mine is going to work. I want to project photographs of Dinesen onto those high white walls, each image dissolving into the next, as counterpoint to Zoe Caldwell's performance. Now the slides are in boxes, in the hands of my colleagues, just a few blocks away as the bus inches up the avenue in the winter early dark.

I'm running late, hoping the stage manager will begin projecting the slides, trying out the effect without me. I jump off the bus and race to the door of the church. All the lights are on — good. But the door is locked, okary, Janet, use the side entrance. The sanctuary is one story below ground, with enormous street-level windows. As I go by the windows, suddenly the space below becomes totally black. I stop in my tracks.

★

There rising in the dark, twenty feet high, is Dinesen, her image projected large. The photograph is one taken toward the end of her life. Close-up, in three-quarter view, wearing a turtleneck fisherman's sweater, she is luminous. Her large black eyes dominate; her hair is frizzily pinned back, revealing the structure of her bones; her face tapers from brow to chin in an expression of concentrated intelligence and sensibility.

It is night on the avenue. This image has loomed up so quickly that I gasp. At the same time, I sense someone else walking up to the windows, standing nearby. I turn to see who has been drawn to this. . . she also turns. By the kind of coincidence that feels like a sign, it is the woman who had been my therapist for many years. We exclaim, we embrace, we both recognize some meaning in this encounter. As Dinesen writes, "If I looked in the right place. . . the coherence of things might become clear to me."

My interest in Dinesen began several years ago, in very particular circumstances. A friend gave me Dinesen's memoir, *Out of Africa*, at a time when my husband and I had separated and I was living alone, away from the apartment we had shared for more than ten years. My sublet was highly temporary and highly inadequate; the neighborhood (Manhattan's Upper East Side) was deeply alien to me. I felt like an exile in the city where I had lived for more than half my life.

One day I picked up *Out of Africa* and read its opening sentence:

I had a farm in Africa, at the foot of the Ngong Hills.

A simple declarative sentence. But the word *had* triggered in me an intense sense of loss. In that sentence, I heard Dinesen say, "A whole part of my life, one in which I invested deeply, is over. I mourn it." I wasn't able to go on reading.

From my journal of that time: "Three months after the separation. Just made myself an egg and coffe for the first time in this 'kitchen' so tiny that two pots on the hot plate is a major challenge. On the first sip, the most wonderful pleasure floods me, then, a second later, tears. With that familiar taste comes all the years of marriage. I used to carry that cup of coffee to the livingroom wing chair, sip, read, exchange a companionable smile with my husband. For months, I've been looking forward to the return of feeling. I didn't know that with it would come such pain. I run to this journal, snatching moments from the morning. I'm writing for relief."

Later: "My therapist suggests I adopt a 'picaresque' attitude toward life . . . if I let go of the past, I can move forward and greet whatever the present offers. She mentions Colette as an example — Colette, with her three marriages, a lifetime of writing, and an appetite for experience which constantly fed her work. I know she is right, but her advice is so far from possible that I am angry at my old heroines. All my homes are disappearing."

★

In 1929, Isak Dinesen lost her home in Africa. After sixteen years of managing the coffee plantation in Kenya and struggling to hold on to the profound connection she felt to the place and people of the Ngong Hills, she had to give up: the farm had failed. So too had her marriage to Bror Blixen — entered partially as a way to escape her intrusive family — and leaving her with the permanently damaging consequences of the syphilis she had contracted from him. So too had her later intense love affair with Denys Finch Hatton, who was only intermittently present in her life and was killed in a plane crash shortly before her final departure from Africa. She was forty; she had lost everything that mattered to her. It took seven years after her return to her mother's house in Denmark to sit down and write the memoir that portrays her life in Africa. In the meantime, she had transformed herself: Karen, her given name, she changed to Isak ("the one who laughs"). Isak Dinesen the storyteller came into being.

It was only Dinesen the storyteller of *Seven Gothic Tales* and *Winter's Tales* that I knew two years after closing *Out of Africa* at its opening sentence. Now as I sit down to write the adaptation, my table with its stacks of books and Xeroxes has begun to resemble a cluster of chimneys on the verge of toppling — a landscape that is familiar and oddly comfortable. It is here that I've sat with other stacks as I've worked on other women's lives — H. D., Colette, Louise Bogan, Virginia Woolf; here, too, the manuscripts piled up for the collection of essays that became *The Writer on Her Work*. The aspect of a woman's experience that has most concerned me is the process by which she becomes an artist. I have focused on the ways in which a woman finds, claims, and expresses her voice and on the ways in which her life and work intersect. But my involvement has never been simply a professional sphere of interest. Instead, I know that much of this work has been done as part of an effort to extricate myself from the blocks that stand in the way of claiming my own vision. I continue to fight daily my fear of revealing myself, of being taken over, of the childhood twin terrors of being emotionally engulfed and abandoned. I fight, too, against the legacy of various lacks — money, education, position — that were part and parcel of my background. There is every reason to believe that these terrors can be laid to rest, that I should now possess the essential sense that I am entitled to create. The evidence of achieved work is there, and for years I have stood in strong and emotionally rich relation to my parents, my friends, and to the family that includes relatives and the community that one makes for oneself. But without wishing to deny these very real advances, I know too that the struggle, while less potent, remains. My abiding interest in women artists is a kind of recruitment of the past to join in that struggle, an enlistment of their voices on the side of my own victories. I travel into the lives of other women and evoke them so as to find what I need to make my words whole.

But working on Dinesen has been hard. I am haunted at first by the sense that here is a life that is not exemplary. Instead it feels to be, in the title of one of Dinesen's own stories, a "cautionary tale." This shattered, syphilitic woman, forced to return to her mother's house — is this not a story to avoid, if one can?

I could not avoid it, as I found myself increasingly engaged in her writing. During the several months I spent working on the script, the events of the last years of my own life came back to haunt me. The failed attempt at reconciling my marriage, which was, even as I wrote, playing out its last awful throes; the death of a young friend; the loss of a small piece of property in Maine that I had fiercely loved. Inevitably, I felt drawn to this woman I had chosen to adapt; inevitably, also, I pulled away, troubled by aspects of her circumstances and temperament that felt too close.

As I read on, marking passages, cutting and pasting bits to form a script, I began to enter into a changing relationship with her. I saw how she was visited by difficulties that were, in her case, extraordinary; I saw also how she was very much the architect of her own choices. She was telling me not what life could be, but what it exacts. She was offering a sense of *cost*, in the way that one comes to understand it as one gets older: the *experience* of the consequences of one's actions. And she was offering something more — a stance, a self-fashioned set of personal, moral, and artistic imperatives that sustain in the teeth of pain.

She survived her losses. In the shaping and distilling of those years in Africa, she gives happiness its full due; so too does she fully claim suffering. Accept the paradoxes of one's own nature, she implies, and of all nature. Be true to the story: *tell it.*

★

Now I must tell what happened as I tried to finish the adaptation. At first I had wanted to create an evening that would give the full range of her work: tales, memoirs, essays, letters, and the great arc of her life as well. The task defeated me. Dinesen was too big a figure, too complex a writer, to be encompassed fully within the confines of a single evening. Instead, I was drawn to *Out of Africa* as the centerpiece of the play. I worried: By choosing that strand, was I trivializing her, telling only the part of her story that would fit into *my* themes? With opening night fast approaching, I made a decision. I would use *Out of Africa*, framing it with her essay "Mottoes of My Life" and weaving in portions of her letters.

Then something strange happened. I had chosen most of the selections; I had even found the connective tissue that would link the dramatic line to a poetic resonance of images and metaphors. But I couldn't finish the script — because I couldn't finish *Out of Africa*. Oh, I intended to. I had to! Each night I would get into bed, start to read the last chapter, and fall asleep. Once this tendency started, I tried to safeguard myself by setting the alarm for 5:00 A.M.; *then* I would finish it, in early morning clarity. But 8:00 A.M. would find me barely opening my eyes, struggling to get dressed and to my office in time. After a week or so of this, I panicked. Very cautiously, as though I were about to walk on glass, I said, "Okay, Janet, think this through." The answer was clear, and painful.

The last unread chapter is called "Farewell to the Farm." Its opening sentence intimates disaster.

My farm was a little too high up for growing coffee.

At the beginning of the book Dinesen wrote of her early encounter with the freedom and grace she found in Africa: "Here I breathe easily. . . . I wake up each morning saying 'here I am, where I ought to be.' " And I knew, after losing parts of my life that had once felt as essential as breath to me, I was faced with the task of reading and of finally saying farewell.

Early the next morning I finished the book. All my own memories and rawnesses poured into and out of Dinesen's losses. It was a bad morning. But it was over. I had let go.

I remember words that Dinesen had written in connection with one of her mottoes, *Je Répondrai* ("I will answer"): "In the long valleys of the African plains, I have been surrounded and followed by sweet echoes. . . I feel very sure that to a woman at least, the presence of echoes in her life is a condition for happiness, or is in itself a consciousness of rich resources."

As of this writing, I am working in an apartment filled with cartons. The house of marriage is finally being dismantled. No longer an interior created by two, not yet a bare space to be filled again by one, the apartment is a no-man's-land. I reach, expecting to find a book in its familiar place, but it is not there.

Dinesen, though, has remained with me, months after the performance is successfully past; her words from the last chapter: "Other things were sold out of the house, packed and sent off, so that the house, in the course of these months, became noble like a skull, a cool and roomy place to dwell in, with an echo to it."

I reach for my own words and hear my voice sent back, returning across a distance, reverberating with the lives of other women. The length it has traveled has transformed it, necessarily. Old friend and stranger: I will answer you.

Charlotte Brontë
National Portrait Gallery, London

Jane Lazarre

Jane Lazarre

"CHARLOTTE'S WEB": READING *JANE EYRE* OVER TIME

Having been obliged to experience themselves as objects, women understand both their need and their capacity for awakening from a living death; they know it is necromancy, not image magic — a resurrecting confessional art, not a crucifying confessional penance, which can do this without entangling yet another Other in what they have escaped.
Sandra Gilbert and Susan Gubar, *The Madwoman in the Attic*

Women's art seeks meaning. All the splits — between content and form, between the search for self and symbol, between the good girl and the bad girl — represent false directions. Charlotte Brontë was considered a bad girl for writing inappropriate truths, and her fictional heroines always speak out as well. They understand that silence can be a catalyst of madness and loss of self. Charlotte must have known this too, and so she translated the passions of her life into women like Jane Eyre. Where Charlotte ends and Jane begins is in some ways beside the point, and at the same time is the crucial point for me.

It can no longer matter to Charlotte Brontë what connections are drawn by biographers or literary gossips between Jane's passions and her own. During her lifetime, she protected herself with a male pseudonym. But today, when the lines between fiction and autobiography have been so blurred, at times obliterated entirely, it is a scary business to write the sort of fiction that draws its power from the passions of one's own life. I have written both autobiography and fiction of this kind, and the initial ecstasy of self-revelation, the sense of power and of doors opening in an infinite line into my deepest heart has been replaced by wariness, at times the inability to reveal myself: by fear. And yet I believe as much as ever that the most powerful and beautiful fiction, however translated into the language of dreams or the variations of fantasy, grows out of a real experience that reverberates with sufficient depth to force a many-layered story into the world. *"Writers down of what happens"*, Doris Lessing calls fiction writers — *chroniclers* — and that at our best is what we are.

It is not merely the fear of exposure that keeps me silent at times, but the fear of criticism that slides nastily over the work and becomes a moral damnation of myself or a condescending and reductive parlor psychoanalysis of my life. "Obviously she is still hung up on her father," one reviewer said about my autobiographical work. As for my novella *Some Kind of Innocence*, people in my life who recognized characters or parts of characters continually assumed I had simply sat down at my desk and, as if I were keeping a journal, translated literally my experience onto the blank page. This could not be further from the truth, of course, since fiction is above all else a choosing of connections; a vision of the connections between experiences; a stream of associations given concrete form. Still, it is disturbing to stand in the supermarket line and have to answer the question How could you write that? Isn't your husband embarrassed? (Because the main female character who bears an obvious relation to myself has sex that is carefully described.)

After the publication of three books that were seen as being either "courageous" or "immoral," I was unable to write at all for some time. And yet the ability to write was the only possible reparation for a spirit that was ragged, shredded almost to bits. But there was no way to write without the willingness to reveal myself again, to go even deeper than before, at least if I wanted to write fiction that was true to ordinary life. Cornered by overlapping contradictions, I nevertheless understood that I could not write because I had accepted the world's definitions of myself as a bad girl. Writers expose their most personal feelings over a lifetime of work because, whatever their self-doubts, they consider themselves to be the soul of virtue — virtue in the Greek sense of performing the task one is suited for — a revelation of the underside of things beginning with the underside of the self. But I had come to believe, as a result of being criticized and misunderstood, in the ugliness and wrongness of that self. I had no urge to express, only to hide, an urge so great that for many months the insights and connections I discovered had no curative effect on my inability to write. I desired silence.

I set about on a system of reparation, each aspect of which involved the increase of self-control — dieting, exercise, forcing myself to read every day instead of retreating into the deadly depressive stare that always leads me like a fish on a hook to the refrigerator. Helene Moglen's biography of Charlotte Brontë, *The Self Conceived*, had great medicinal properties for me. It led me back to that adored book of my childhood, *Jane Eyre*, which I had not read in twenty years, and through her story to a new perspective on the nature of my fears.

I was fifteen years old in 1958 when I read *Jane Eyre* for the first time, and she hit me right between the eyes, spotlighting a truth that I had always known and that was at the same time brand new. An enlightenment. Like Jane, I was a rebel, a chronic bad girl by social definition, and Jane exploded my life into reality. Bad girls were nongirls in a way — unfeminine, tomboys, *what kind of girl would do that?*, nonexistent little devils, female bodysnatchers. I was a non-being in a way; I had looked into the mirror of fiction for so long and seen at best distorted reflections, at worst emptiness. And for a reader, that can be a frightening experience. I was looking for connection, the opposite of escape (though adventure in exotic lands or in the world of the heart were always welcome). I was looking for company in the real world, validation of what I sensed to be true.

When I first read *Jane Eyre*, it was as if I had found a sister, or more precisely an aunt, who, however dead she might be to others, assumed flesh for me. I knew she was alive because I clearly heard her voice. And it was right to think of her as an aunt because although, like Charlotte Brontë's and Jane Eyre's, my mother was dead, aunts were numerous.

But no one like this suddenly discovered aunt with enough love to leave me the legacy of her story: a portrait of a rebel-girl. She shouted and fought for her rights. She believed in the absolute necessity for moral behavior that often defied conventional notions of propriety. She angered many people with this quality, but she didn't shrink from conviction or righteousness. She knew her excesses and the ways in which her excesses came from the same source as her strengths. She thought she had a premium on morality, and she would shout down anyone to prove it.

Even when Jane succumbs to the adoration of Helen Burns, who is a portrait of Charlotte's dead, older sister, I had the sense that Brontë had a bit of her tongue in her cheek. Helen is the stoical, virtuous girl who is as bad as Jane inside but who accepts the social definition of her badness and is willing to redeem herself in others' terms, welcoming self-punishment to the point of death. Since the terms are externally defined and assume Helen's inherent, sinfulness, redemption becomes humiliation. I saw this important connection, but I did not perceive until much later the implications for my own silence. The old, adored rebel-girl had become for me truly bad, robbing me of confidence in my perceptions and stripping away the bad girl's only defense against extinction — defiance.

The bad girl may try, as Jane often does, to curb her temper, show more gratitude to those who deserve it, subdue her passions (which are always getting the best of her), and even, when it is not a threat to the core of her being, obey the rules. All my life I had tried to temper my endless capacities as a troublemaker with obedience and moderation because I did not want to hurt people I admired or those who had been good to me. I didn't want to relinquish my passions, only to bring them under my control. I was a bad girl who secretly thought she was good, which is what enabled me to become a writer.

But there is a part of the bad girl who believes she is rotten to the core. Charlotte Brontë struggled all her life with a sense of unentitlement, with survivor guilt after the deaths of her mother and sisters, with the debilitating self-doubt that came from a lack of confidence in her own essential virtue. That lack of confidence was intensified by her passionate nature, which did not allow her to accept contemporary illusions of female purity, and by her ambivalent position as the daughter of an intellectual father, a girl with great strengths that at the same time were the core of her social "badness." Her self-doubt was increased when she was criticized for writing "unseemly" novels full of inappropriate emotion.

My core of self-hatred got its start with my early guilt for rage at my dead mother. That death, like an explosive bullet that tears through the muscle and tissue of the body, not lodging in one finite place, left me with a few nearly suicidal convictions: that my rage had caused my mother's death; that therefore my power was murderous and corrupt; and that I had to exert this murderous power, even in distorted ways, or succumb like Helen Burns to just retribution in the form of my own destruction.

My self-hatred, in other words, became connected, thanks to the ironic twists and paradoxical turns of interior life, to my need to insist, through temper and rebellion, that I was good, that I knew all the answers, and that I would die proving them. I understood completely Jane's tantrum in Mrs. Reed's house, her uncompromising moralism at the Lowood School, even her priggish self-righteousness toward Rochester when he begs her to stay with him. If she didn't prove beyond the shadow of a doubt that she was right, she would be devoured by her capitulation to the accusation of badness.

Perhaps it is the need to survive the threat of such absolute extinction that gives rise to the rebel-girl. She is split, but her splitness is her salvation: When the rebel is a girl, and not a boy, in a society that generally defines heroism and nobility in male terms and that specifically identifies female sex and anger with madness, then the rebel-girl (who like the rebel-boy needs guidance and respect so that her passion can mature into vision) can easily become reduced to the bad girl who believes in her own badness.

Most of us believe on some level that if girls and women speak too truthfully we will encounter something grotesque. The boy, or the male writer, does not have to question his right to self-revelation because by shared belief he is a metaphor for the human condition, his own life a symbol of life. Therefore, when he reveals himself, we comfortably expect to encounter a recognizable, human soul. The lives of male writers in history are not constantly analyzed as the "secret" source of their art. Kafka's tyrannical father and James Joyce's Irish boyhood are assumed as the background of works that are nevertheless accepted on their own. Living male writers are rarely badgered into explanations of the relationship between their lives and their novels. Women are asked to account for their revelations, and we are assumed to be at best naughty, at worst whores, when we write about sexual life. Celebrated women writers are usually those who describe life at a distance from their personal selves. When a boy in a writing class reveals his own experience, he invokes Kerouac and Hemingway. Girls apologize for being "merely autobiographical." Clearly, it's the female life that threatens, that we want to hide, translate, and clean up.

It's a dangerous business to believe in your own badness. It's a bottomless swamp of misguided effort, bitterness, the worst self-pity, and, finally (since it is so awfully lonely in the swamp), the desire to pull others down with you. Jane Eyre knows she must fight to believe in her own goodness, that her salvation lies in an insistence on her own point of view. That is the creative heart of what can sometimes be expressed as self-righteousness. Masochism is in part a love of passivity because one's own power has come to seem dangerous. It implies a willingness to be defined by, ultimately used for, the purposes of another person whose power is at once superior to your own and also, paradoxically, bequeathed by you. Jane fights that sort of masochism as the fire-breathing dragon it is. Later when the dragon has retreated, the hurricane died down, she can bend in the breeze again. Charlotte too must have been convinced of some worthy, noble core, even though she lived her life with "a sense of unworthiness never to be erased." People who are thoroughly convinced of their own unworthiness don't become and remain writers.

The recognition of this contradiction in Charlotte's life was a part of my own healing process. I felt for all the world as if silence was my only option. But somewhere there must be a part of me who was filled with pride, or how could I have written in the past? I continued looking in Jane's story, and in Charlotte's, for more information on the geography of the rotten core.

A rebel-girl can come to accept her own badness when she is cut off from her own mother. That alienation is the condition for her interior split. Charlotte Brontë lost her mother when she was a child. Jane Eyre is motherless. So are Lucy Snowe and Shirley. Many feminist writers have written about the generic situation of motherlessness in patriarchal society — the absence of true maternal power, not the power to control others but the power of naming, of interpreting reality, or of recognition in the world. Either she can identify with the weakened mother who teaches her daughter how to survive as a slave — the foot-binder — or she can identify with her father, as so many rebel-girls who became writers did, and thus be doomed to an interior splitting of her sense of power from her female being, a split that is perpetuated by guilt for abandoning her mother. The actual motherlessness of Charlotte or Jane can be seen as a symbol of the situation of motherlessness in patriarchal society.

But when I first read *Jane Eyre* and saw myself in that lonely girl-woman who is constantly on the lookout for a woman to imitate, a mother to claim, a home to which she might belong, I saw her as a literal motherless daughter and in that most central aspect of my identity as a young girl I found a reflection.

At several crucial points in the novel, Jane looks around for mothers to adopt. In a sense she is looking for lessons in how to be a woman because that identification, which ought to be effortless, has by necessity of her loss become a conscious lack in her. She closely observes Miss Temple, the teacher at Lowood who befriends Helen Burns, and says of her, "she stood for me in stead of mother." She describes Miss Temple in passionate terms: "I was well contented to stand [at her side], for I derived a child's pleasure from the contemplation of her face, her dress, her one or two ornaments, her white forehead, her clustered and shining curls, and beaming dark eyes."

Later, Jane sees Mrs. Fairfax, the housekeeper at Thornfield, in maternal terms of another sort — the older woman whose presence provides serenity born of complete acceptance, her simple *liking* of the younger woman. And, finally, she finds mothers in her friends and cousins at Marsh End.

I too was always on the lookout for a mother, continually choosing new women to use in my effort to create a fully imagined maternal presence in my head, a woman who, like Mrs. Fairfax and Miss Temple, would like me, notice my goodness, for whom I would not have to be extraordinary, from whom I might learn the simple things a "woman does." As the daughter of a powerful father, I was sure I was human, but being a woman was something I had to learn. Some of the richest images I ever found were in the person of a good friend named Leona. She was small and dark, as my own mother had been. But the aspect of her character that drew me into a spiral of ecstatic copying was the graceful way she had of ordering the physical world. I watched the way she cleaned the kitchen, ordered the shelves, wiped an iron pan dry, the way she straightened and arranged her children's room, the way she dressed herself in matching undershirts and tights on a cold day, and in every case I set about to do things the way she did until her patterns had become my own. I was twenty-five when I met Leona, and I no longer follow her around hoping she won't notice the relentlessness of my observation of her every move. (The way she wipes her hands with a paper towel after the dishes are done, slowly drying the spaces between her fingers, the soap line gathered under her ring.) Now, whenever I see her, I am warmed by the recognition of gestures in her that have long become my own.

It may seem like a brutally self-conscious search for wholeness, but my healing had to be brutally conscious since the rending had been so pervasive and extreme. When, at thirty-eight, I was reading *Jane Eyre* again and discovered the biography by Moglen, the very title brought chills down my spine, promised to turn on that occasional and powerful spotlight and enlighten me. The "self conceived" was what women did through their fiction — what I had done and would continue to do — and that process, wonderfully familiar to me, was just another translation of copying Leona. Also, an aspect of my silence became very clear. As long as a woman writer revealed experience that could be seen as *human*, it was okay. But I had written about motherhood and sexuality, tried to reveal the female self, one of the most threatening subjects known to man.

During the period of reading biographies and novels of women writers, I began to feel the early signs of reparation of my voice, to experience at least occasionally the desire to write. As a feminist, I wanted to continue to try to reveal the female self. As a mother, I had learned that increased self-control, as much as self-expression, was an aspect of growth. And as a writer I had come to believe that each new book, besides possessing its own separate integrity, represented a mending of torn parts, a new healing of old wounds. I began a novel that in its earliest draft was called *A Reliable Witness*, because in addition to telling a story I was doing battle with my doubts about my right to tell it. The artistic problem of this early stage was an uncomfortable split between the story itself and the voice of the narrator. The title, it turned out, was not so much an appropriate title for the novel I was writing as it was a precise description of the mending I was after in my personal life.

My experience as a mother provided other lessons for managing this split. Although it had taken me almost ten years to integrate the sense of myself as a mother into the old, familiar me, although the early years of motherhood had constituted one of the most dramatic crises of my life, being a mother in the past few years had come to include the tantalizing suggestion of some as yet unimagined transformation of the rebel-girl. For what sort of woman would the rebel-girl grow up to be? What would the rebel-mother look like?

Jane Eyre's description of mothering was altogether unsatisfactory, a short paragraph set in romantic terms and tied to an idealistic vision of marriage. But Charlotte had given some initial clues about the nature of the transition, if not the transformation, from rebel-girl to rebel-woman. I began to see my cornered, silent position as in part a problem of being an overgrown rebel-girl, understanding the significance of anger and sex but in some crucial way not yet in charge of either. It was certainly neither my anger nor my sex that I wished to relinquish, but rather the sense of my own badness that could transform my anger into monstrous rage and my sexual desire into slavery. How, then, to become a self-possessed woman and still not lose the passion, determination, and courage of the rebel-girl? For the injunction to relinquish her was manifest not only in the voices of the proponents of socially defined womanhood who constantly tell us to calm down and shut up. It was a voice in my own head, the prison guard of my writing voice. How would I answer in tones of the rebel-woman, the rebel-mother?

In accompanying Jane on her journey once again, I now found the last part of the book to be the most compelling. When I read the novel as a girl, I hardly noticed the last section, except for the very last page when Jane returns to Rochester and announces, "Reader, I married him." I recalled only the disastrously foiled marriage, the image of bloodthirsty, animalistic Bertha, and the eventual reunion of Jane and her "master," this time brought down to size. Mad Bertha was only a monster to me then, conveniently killed off by her own hand and thus leaving no trail of guilt behind. But more of Bertha later.

Jane determines to leave Rochester after the revelation of the existence of his mad wife. And his attempts to keep her are as seductive as they are smart. He plays just the tune most likely to hypnotize. He would never have been her soul mate if he didn't possess this knowledge, and he uses it like a champion. He throws himself on her mercy. He plays on her powerful guilt for abandoning him, knowing that no one feels the guilt for abandoning as much as one who lives in fear of abandonment. He assures her that without her he will suffer inconsolably, perhaps even die. He calls her his rescuer, his hope, his life. Only she can save him, he cries. But she says, I am going. Reading this scene in my late thirties, I recalled how angry I had been when I read it in my teens. Oh, why doesn't she stay, I had moaned, craving the only happy ending I had been taught to expect, wanting whatever happened after they got married and lived happily ever after to be as unclear and veiled in illusion as it was in my favorite fairy tales. But Jane Eyre suffered no such illusions.

She was certainly tempted by love. But she could resist the temptation because instinctively she understood the price. She may have been moralistic in this scene. She may have been self-righteous. Uncompromising. Even arrogant. But not because she was afraid of the unconventional, of man's interpretation of God's will. As a child, she had not been intimidated by the cruel Brocklehurst, so why would she be a coward in the face of convention now, as a young woman, when everything she wanted was about to be lost? Jane's (and Charlotte's) adherence to a foundation of Victorian morality, the sanctity of monogamous marriage, is of course an issue in the parting of Jane and Rochester. But, as motivation, it rests on a deeper perception, a more individual and female sense of truth.

"Sir," says Jane to Rochester after the traumatic interruption of their marriage ceremony, "you are inexorable for that unfortunate lady: you speak of her with hate — with vindictive antipathy. It is cruel — she cannot help being mad."

And Rochester answers, "Jane, my little darling . . . you don't know what you are talking about; you misjudge me again: it is not because she is mad that I hate her. If you were mad, do you think I should hate you?"

"I do indeed, sir," answers Jane. For if she were mad she would not be the lovely, intelligent, firm, and decisive little angel in the house. She would be a wild woman, roaming her cell, all her passions unleashed, a bad girl who was convinced that she was worse than a bad girl — an evil woman. Jane's understanding of the reality of the situation is remarkable. If she goes with Rochester, she will lose herself in his distorted image of her, a distortion that becomes obvious to her when she is confronted with Bertha. For Jane is to be cast as the angel, the good girl, the one who is inevitably unseen, unknown. This is just the environment that encourages the growth of the bad girl who believes in her own badness. She will not be tempted by Rochester's lie, the lie by which so many of her descendants have been tempted: You are so different; I will treat you differently than I treat my wife. She knows he is out to possess her completely, and that that very possession, when time has drained it of its erotic need, will look like any other ordinary slavery. Charlotte Brontë makes Jane's refusal of Rochester so rigid because as a rebel-girl caught between her own power and her sense of corruption, Brontë knew very well the attraction of the Byronic hero, the man whose own outsidedness permits hers; to whom one is all too anxious to submit, wishing only to melt one's boundaries and relinquish one's will. She confronted this deadly attraction and the struggle to gain power over it in everything she wrote.

If victimization is in part a crisis of will, a rigid self-defense is a last-ditch effort to preserve one's will from extinction. It is self-control Jane is after, and not only because she is in love with liberty. When one feels in control of oneself there is no danger of unsuccessfully repressed demons taking over. In fact, self-control implies an acknowledgment of one's (ordinary) badness as well as the capacity for real virtue. Broken as she nearly is, Jane clings desperately to her own point of view. She needs love intensely, is in terror of separation and loss. She craves the blurring of boundaries in sexual ecstasy, which might redeem the loss of that early love she had so briefly known. Still, "I am going, sir," she says. And she leaves. In the moment of exercising her will, she strengthens it and perceives the direction for remedy. She must withdraw behind inflexible boundaries for a time.

Years before writing *Jane Eyre,* Charlotte Brontë had written "Farewell to Angria" — a formal leave-taking of the fictional world she had conceived with her siblings from the time they were young adolescents. In this "Farewell" she speaks of her need to leave familiar surroundings, which have promised security and love, to be true to herself and thus generate the possibility of further discovery.

> When I depart from these [old, familiar characters and scenes she had been writing for years] I feel almost as if I stood on the threshhold of a home and were bidding farewell to its inmates. When I try to conjure up new inmates I feel as if I had gotten into a distant country where every face was unknown and the character of all the population was an enigma which it would take much study to comprehend and much talent to expound. Still, I long to quit for a while that burning clime where we have sojourned too long too long — its skies flame — the glow of sunset is always upon it — the mind would cease from excitement and turn now to a cooler region where the dawn breaks grey and sober, and the coming day for a time at least is subdued by clouds.

Jane uses the same remedy to save herself from the temptation of a possessive love as Charlotte used earlier to wrench herself from a passionate but ultimately infantilizing involvement in a collaborative fantasy work with her brother. In both cases, Charlotte Brontë knew that a painful but restorative distancing of the heart was the temporary direction of reparation. Whether figuratively wandering (in the case of Charlotte looking for new material for her fiction) or literally lost (Jane on the road to Marsh End) reparation involved an isolation that included hiding her past, engaging in useful if dull work, activity rather than self-indulgence, and the fierce rebuilding of boundaries that had crumbled before the dream of a perfect love. The old longing for perfect merging can be expressed toward a person or an idea. In either case, the force of the eventual disappointment comes from the fear that home — passion and primal love, which include self-revelation and acceptance on the deepest level — may never be discovered again. Acceptance of this real possibility is a path away from suicide. The courage to take it is born of necessity.

The need to write is as close to the soul as the need for love. The immersion in each is oceanic and therefore at some point uncontrollable. In both cases, a woman must be willing, or temperamentally destined, to experience periods of enormous passion and, just as inevitably, periods of lonely wandering, homeless again and again while boundaries are rebuilt, the self, as Helene Moglen puts it, conceived again in the cooler region where new controls are practiced and learned. Without the periods of passion there would be no content for feminist art. Without the period of lonely wandering there would be no artist, for she would long ago have drowned in one ocean or another.

At the point of understanding the everchanging balance between knowledge and passion on the one hand and reparation and choice on the other, I stopped fearing my silence. It was a way of relearning self-revelation, not an escape from it. I had gone through a very similar process in trying to become, in my own terms, a good mother. Not that I had been a bad mother before, I had just been a little-girl mother who didn't know how to manage her panic. My strength with my children had always been my ability to be honest with them, to let them know me. My weakness (dull repetitions of themes have the advantage of hitting you over the head with the undeniable) had to do with lack of self-control, which could express itself in temper tantrums, in overwhelming anxiety about the children's safety, or in a sense of total powerlessness in managing the physical chaos that family life includes. These are crises of a merely domestic nature, perhaps, but the struggle with them points to a deeper truth.

The rebel-mother must be able to claim the reality of her own power over human life and to assume the responsibility for that power. In the process, she will have to face down the fear and hatred of female power rooted as deep in her spirit as in her brother's. Charlotte Brontë, having established the conditions for Jane's reparation, began to imagine the character of the rebel-woman whose power equals Rochester's in the end. She is a character whose depth and dimension is still in the midst of conception today.

I have found suggestions of her in Doris Lessing's Al-Ith, the powerful and nurturing queen of the balanced and peaceful Zone Three who is fated by the gods to marry the king of Zone Four, an insensitive and domineering man who nevertheless has something to teach the proud and wise queen. Having learned the lesson that even perfectly crafted boundaries must repeatedly be broken if new growth is to take place, Al-Ith, like her foremother Jane, becomes a wanderer on an unplaceable road between zones. She is no longer able to rule with her husband in the warlike Zone Four where she has given all she has to give, but neither can she go back to her peaceful Zone Three. And before she can begin to envision something new, she must be rootless, without direction, friendless, without words and without hope.

Women of our time are wanderers; our transformations are only beginning to be imagined. In discovering ourselves we are trying to give birth to an image of powerful womanhood, to draw the portrait of the rebel-girl grown up, the mother whose daughters (and sons as well) will not have to split themselves into warring, energy-draining parts in order to create.

I found the rebel-woman again in Alice Walker's *The Color Purple*, in Celie, who grows from ultimate victim to proud survivor, the cornerstone of her survival being her love for the passionate, sexually vital, and clearminded Shug. Shug is a bad girl only by conventional definition. She never complies with that denigrating claim. Gilbert and Gubar, in *The Madwoman in the Attic*, revealed the Bertha Mason in us all by articulating the tradition in women's literature that narrates the centuries-old split betweeen the good girl and the madwoman. Walker's *The Color Purple* is a part of that tradition, only now Bertha has developed into the wonderful Shug, and Celie, victim of racism, poverty, and brutal sexism, is saved by falling in love with Shug, who, it turns out, is not crazy at all, just crystal clear about her anger and proud of her sexuality wherever it leads her. There are other parallels as well. As a survivor, Celie makes beautiful and comfortable clothing for women. Al-Ith wears only clothing that is suited to the body's need for movement and grace. Jane too wore clothing chosen for comfort and dignity. Rochester's arrogance is brought down to size by external catastrophe — he loses the use of one hand and is blinded. Albert in *The Color Purple*, who only achieves the dignity of being named at the end of the book, relinquishes his claim to patriarchal manhood, including its brutal misogyny, is nursed back to health from a breakdown by his son, and, having grown into a real man in woman's terms, becomes Celie's friend. As a strong survivor, Celie welcomes her children home, is witness to their strength and eternal tie to her, and yet to their inevitable separateness, for they have led different lives. Al–Ith, nurtured by the very kinship structures she has helped create, is a loving mother who is always defined separately from her children, and "her children" include many more than her biological offspring.

Mothers, at their best, are careful orderers of life. When not split, harassed, guilt-ridden, and enraged by our inability to provide for our children at the same time as we provide for ourselves, we order physical space in which people can live comfortably. We order children's clothing after the wash into convenient drawers. We order their meals into nutritional balance. We order their toys and books into boxes and shelves. We order their confusing emotions as they move through the changes of the life cycle. You seem so wild and angry lately, we say, what is bothering you? Here are some new clothes for the spring, we say, as we drag out the packing box at the bottom of the closet. Mothers order family life because we take it seriously, and anything taken seriously must be done with discipline or fall into chaos. Eventually, children learn of the many forms of women's powerlessness in the world. But we are powerful to them. We exert the power of naming and judging forever in their lives. Their hardest task is to envision us as merely human. In the process of becoming an orderly mother, I had to confront the bad mother in myself who was the bad girl convinced of her own badness. No wonder I didn't want to face her. She had grown too big for safety. Like the bad girl, she was not my private creation. The conventional good mother, of course, is not her opposite but her twin. I like to believe that if Charlotte Brontë had been a mother and by some miracle continued to write fiction, she would have written, by the necessity of her temperament and the truth of her art, the portrait of a rebel-girl grown up into a rebel-mother.

After wandering between zones, frightened of death by exposure, stopped by numerous, long silences, I finally finished the novel which in its final form repaired my most recent split. But just like the reader looking for company in books, when I write my experience as the story of some fictional woman I am hoping to do more than simply describe a life to you. I am hoping that in this life you will see yourself and thus I will feel less alone. Of course, it never works in the final sense, and so I must write another story, sometimes the very same story over again in another way, as if I were saying, What? You didn't like that one? Well, here's what I really meant. You'll really see yourself in this one.

The rebel-girl meets the accusation of her badness with defiance or, like Helen Burns, she is destroyed. But, especially if she has no woman to acknowledge her simple human virtue, her worth, she always carries around with her a secret that can sabotage her clarity, her energy, and her endurance: the powerful wish to be accepted as a good girl. Only after a period of reaching for all the conventional virtues was I able to embrace the rebel-girl again. The desire to become a good girl and the belief in my own badness had of course been the coordinates of my silence.

Now I am writing a new novel about a rebel-girl, a born survivor who must choose the proper medium for the expression of her powers. Her name of course is Charlotte.

Georgia Douglas Johnson

Quetta, Erlene, and Nissy Stetson

Erlene Stetson

SILENCE:
ACCESS AND ASPIRATION

To be a woman in this age carries with it a privilege and an opportunity never implied before . . . To be a woman of the Negro race in America . . . is to have a heritage unique in the ages.
— Anna Julia Cooper

I find it difficult to write an essay that considers the personal joys and frustrations about my work on Black women. I am too much like an earlier sister, Mary Edmonia Lewis (1846-1890), who as a Black sculptor and lesbian was nonconforming in her lifestyle and dress because she could no more find a skin to be comfortable in than a dress to be comfortable with. She was disagreeable and uncoopera- tive — a recalcitrant dandelionlike weed among flowers. For a long time I have had to admit that it is the dandelion, a tenacious (obnoxious, some say), resilient, willful, unwanted "flower" that metaphorically explains my situation (unladylike and unprofes- sional) as a Black woman activist, teacher, and researcher. Mary Edmonia Lewis was judged by *her* detractors (who included Lydia Maria Child and Frederick Douglass) as "too wild" — possibly a dandelion too.

Yet, given the chance, I will and do opt to preach here against what I consider to be the foremost problem — the silence and invisibility of Black women — that hampers me in my research. It is a problem of which even the publishing company that pays for this essay is guilty. There is a symbolic silence that surrounds Black women's public identities. The status of Black *women* repressed even in the language of civil rights and equal opportunity legislation is inaccessible to the marketplace of visibility, dissemination, and public critical acclaim. "Woman" means "white" implicitly, and "Black" means "male" implicitly. The very language we speak lapses into a cul-de-sac as we approach Black women, in terms somewhat analogous to a cosmic/galactic phenomenon: Immense black holes in space swallow light, simply to absorb it. Science apparently is just getting around to spotting these pockets of density, while little else beyond their mere mind-boggling presence is known. For these reasons, if for no others, students, teachers, and scholars deserve to be informed about what is happening to Black women if we are to fashion strategies for changing the business-as-usual state of things. On pain of the pragmatic whip, I will continue to preach to this end, prompted as much by professional sanity as personal need.

Although it is still difficult to write personally about my joys and sorrows when I am actually studying, researching, and teaching about Black women's history and literature, I know that I cannot be engaged in a more worthwhile struggle. In a sense, the purpose of our struggle is to reclaim our history. Black women's studies allow me to bring to consciousness several generations of women, Black like me, who survived the harrowing experience of being women of color in America. I have much to learn from their individual and collective history. More important, their lives, their incredible survival in an indifferent-to-hostile world, teach me to understand my own personal experiences. I am able to place my experiences on a par and in a continuum with women's experiences across the centuries. They empower me to speak. I am no longer merely content to feel sheer bafflement and frustration when I think that I have suffered or that I am oppressed. It is precisely that Black women's history — from servitude and slavery to freedom — tells me how to live, how to survive, and how to be. To survive, Black women had to invent themselves and did. They defined the terms of their existence and much more. Alice Walker's poem "Women"[1] captures their inimitable spirit:

> They were women then
> My mama's generation
> Husky of voice — stout of
> step
> With fists as well as

Hands
How they battered down
Doors
And ironed
Starched white
Shirts
How they led
Armies
Headragged Generals
Across mined
Fields
Booby-trapped
Kitchens
To discover
Desks
A place for us
How they knew what we
Must know
Without knowing a page
of it
Themselves.

Adrienne Rich, in her poem "For Memory,"[2] defines the terms of
the existence of these women:

freedom.
It isn't once, to walk out
under the Milky Way, feeling the river
of light, the fields of dark —
freedom is daily, prose-bound, routine
remembering. Putting together, inch by inch
the starry worlds. From all the lost collections.

I cannot remember precisely when it occurred to me that white
America had some strange ideas about Black women. It is too
convenient to date it as having occurred when I was twelve and
seventeen. But I know that at both ages I had experiences that I'd
like to share.

Like most Black women in the South, I cannot ever remember not
working. At any age I was a worker in the fields, in the homes of
others, and in our home where the work included at least ten hours
of child care, some cooking, and cleaning. At the age of twelve, I
worked for the wife of a Coca-Cola bottling executive. As a maid's
helper I did whatever chores the all-purpose maid ordered me to do.
In the maid's absence, I assumed her general responsibilities as well
as my own.

One day, owing to circumstances I can no longer remember, I took my youngest sister to work with me. Since she was only a year old, I carried her in a red wagon. I discreetly placed the wagon in a corner of the porch nearest the kitchen since my first chore was dishwashing. Conveniently, the baby was asleep.

I had almost finished cleaning the kitchen when I was interrupted by the arrival of my employer's eight-year-old niece. I was told that she would be staying for two weeks and that I should show her to the guest room and give her a tour of the house. After the tour, I suggested she come to the kitchen for a sandwich. This would allow me to finish my kitchen chores as well as be near my sister, who had begun to cry. My employer's niece came over and when she looked at the baby her expression was one of surprise and shock: "Auntie, come quick and look, it's a baby maid!"

Certainly, I had always accepted work as a permanent feature of my life. All the women I knew worked. Those who were lucky had sons or daughters who stayed home and did their housework. But until the encounter with an eight-year-old white, I had thought that it was as right for me, a Black girl, to be a maid as it was for white girls of my age to play with dolls and have pajama parties. I knew that my job was not a particularly demanding one and in many ways was a great deal better than the jobs held by my friends. My employer was reasonable, tolerant, and fair. Most important, she paid me promptly.

But suddenly — without warning — I had to consider my identity. Was I born a maid? Did this public label meet with my private knowledge of who I was or thought I was? Was my baby sister a maid, albeit a baby one? Does my race define my role? As a twelve-year-old I had easily accepted the fact that I was a Black and a Baptist ("Stay Black and die!") as the unchanging circumstances of my life, but nothing else. Long after this encounter I remained in a confused state. I considered the subject of what I could be, and the possibilities were not endless. In fact, by my calculations they were limited to two — I could be a preacher or a teacher. And what could my baby sister be?

I did not suddenly stop being a maid. For a few years more I continued to be a maid, but I also had a vague, uncomfortable feeling that something was wrong. I did not want to be a maid for reasons that had less to do with my private desires than with the fact that I rejected the someone who had predetermined what I should be.

This was at twelve. When I was seventeen my grandmother died. Among the few possessions she left me were two 1937 issues of *Life* magazine. Because she could not read and could barely print her name, I wondered why she would bequeath to me two outdated (well over twenty years old) unspectacular-looking "white" magazines that could have nothing to do with me. Not knowing the answer to these questions but wanting to connect myself to her, now that she was no longer alive, I decided that I would read each issue from cover to cover. I would read what she could not and see the pictures she saw.

Both covers featured Blacks in stereotypical summer scenes. The *Life* cover of July 19, 1937, revealed a summer city scene of Black children enjoying an open fire hydrant. I wondered about the scene's meaning for my grandmother, a country woman who loved children. The experience of happy faces she must have accepted as familiar, while the urban scene was foreign to her own. The second issue, dated August 9, 1937, featured on its cover a Black man driving a load of watermelons to market. This rural experience she knew well, for her sons were farmers who took their own melons to market. But how did she regard what she saw on page 52 of this issue? I deeply resented the insult to herself and, as I was now seeing it, to me. A photograph of a Black woman eating watermelon while nursing her child carried this cutline:

> Nothing makes a Negro mouth water like a luscious fresh-picked melon. Any colored "mammy" can hold a huge slice in one hand while holding her offspring in the other. Since the watermelon is 92% water, tremendous quantities can be eaten . . . what melon the Negroes do not consume will find favor with the pigs.

I felt anger. I wanted to strike someone or something. I knew that the photograph carried an insidious message. I had more than a feeling that the world did not like Black women. I felt the conscious pain of knowing. Both incidents helped me to see that I belonged to a group — Black women — and that what happened and was happening to me could not be separated from what happened and was happening to them. I belonged to an outcast race, sex, and class, and as such my experiences were not merely personal.

I am firmly convinced that both these episodes pointed me in the direction of Black women's history. The questions raised for me were quite modest: Who were these women? Where were they? How did they live? What is their connection (meaning and relevance) to me? Would the history of Black women determine my present and future in ways that would limit me? Certainly there was enough mythology promulgated in that one photograph to suggest an answer. Would Black women's history help me to expand and grow as I instinctively felt that it would? The paucity of books on Black women helped me to think that I was not meant to know about them except as *Life* and eight-year-old white females conceived them. Far from being dismayed by what I was not able to find, I became intrigued by another question: What is it about Black women that I am kept from knowing? Because the women in my community gave the lie to the mammy and maid image, I trusted my experience and so it was easy to remain skeptical about the images of black women that the media (radio and print mostly) foisted upon the public.

Though the idea that all Black women were maids or mammies who preferred watermelon was instinctively unacceptable, the larger, more subtle idea that made such an assault possible was also intolerable. I had little knowledge of Black women beyond those in the rural, southern, depressed community of which I was part. They were undertakers, hairdressers, practical nurses, teachers, maids, ministers, sharecroppers, field hands, and managers of drycleaning establishments. And there was the notorious threebreasted Mrs. Linnie, who rode a bicycle. The range of their work and personalities was a telling enough indictment of their public image as mammy or maid. But the truth was that my historical knowledge of women was abysmal. It is one thing to know in your heart that a lie is a lie, but it is an exquisite feeling to have public recognition of the same.

There was Harriet Ross Tubman (1821-1913) and Phillis Wheatley (1754-1785), whose lives coincided for me in the truncated history of a dramatic production. The occasion was Black History Week, a yearly celebration held at Holsey Cobb Institute, the private school that once a year acknowledged that Blacks were part of American history. I knew both women well because I, shy and high achieving, was invariably cast as Wheatley, who was described as a "frail," "shy," "genius poetess." A particularly loud, bold, and gregarious classmate who frequently was in trouble of some sort invariably played the aggressively headragged Tubman to my scholarly eye-glass-clad (borrowed for the occasion) Wheatley. I found Wheatley hopelessly dull, and, unpopular as I was, I desperately hoped to die every year before Black History Week.

The dramatic production opened with an auction scene, a loud auctioneer, and bound and manacled classmates-turned-slaves. I had the unexciting task of interrupting the auctioneer with a rendition of Wheatley's poem "On Being Brought from Africa to America": "Twas mercy brought me / From my pagan land, / Taught my benighted soul / To understand . . . "[3] At the end of my recitation, bold Harriet, gun in hand, stepped forward, motioned the auctioneer aside, and led the slaves-turned-chorus in a rousing rendition of "Lift Every Voice and Sing," the Black national anthem.

It was not the unfamiliar language of Wheatley's poem that I resented so much as having to *be* Phillis Wheatley. I could tolerate being "darkened" to look "African," given glasses to look "gifted," but it was painful to be chosen precisely because I was as unattractive as I was high achieving — and this after all was the point of being a "lady poet."

The production always ended with an abrupt transition to some august male administrator who lectured on Blacks' contributions to America. Invariably the speech was a memorable litany of Black men whose names in horizontal progression suggested that Black History Week was, in the end, the retrieval of anonymous Black male heroes. If there were any women who made contributions, I didn't know them and the speaker failed to mention any. Harriet Tubman and Phillis Wheatley as they were presented to us were not "real," since they represented extremes and therefore none took them seriously, myself least of all.

At best the public and my private image of Black women was widely divergent. This was unsettling and remained so until I began to seriously study the lives of Black women. To study Black women of any period and in any area is not easy. No one has ever insisted on the importance of the words of Black women. Working against those Black women who have managed to get their thoughts and visions in print are condescending gatekeepers everywhere. So much misinformation, even mythology about early Black women writers, gets repeated without question from source to source that it is particularly important and often quite revealing to check on even the most commonplace information. In any textbook in any discipline Black women rarely appear as agents of change but as passive, helpless victims. Rarely do historical societies, libraries, and archival collections list their holdings on individual Black women separately or under their own names. The researcher is most often referred to broad subject headings such as "Negro women."

This problem reaches alarming proportions as earlier periods are studied. Much of the information on slave women is to be found in the family papers of their owners. Moreover, many white record keepers were not in the habit of according the courtesy of listing last names for Black women even when a rare few deigned to do as much in the case of Black men. In these same records one learns more about the size and coloring of Black women than about the Black families of which they were part. In these collections, most of the material on Black women has yet to be assembled, compiled, and cataloged. For me, and I suspect for many other Black women researchers, the slavery period is personally the most painful and difficult to explore. The omissions, the neglect, and the deliberate distortions found in Black history in general are repeated a thousandfold in slave women's history. Moreover, this period reminds us of our traumas, insecurities, and wounds that never make sense and are difficult to convey. Inevitably concerned with what went wrong, some of us cannot see beyond this and take courage in the examples of those women who did.

In the eighteenth and nineteenth centuries, the absence of any significant numbers of Black women in critical analyses and biographical studies suggests that the literary history of Black women rests on the shoulders of Phillis Wheatley at one end of one century and Frances E. W. Harper at one end of the other. Neither writer's work is available in paperback reprint for classroom use. Both are portrayed as unique, as exceptions; no mention is made of the numerous women that bridge the gap between the two. The public is kept in ignorance of Black women — in the plural — and is led to think that Black women in general are incapable of literary creation.

Added to the absence of data and the distortion in the records of Black women's work and creativity is the readiness of others (white men and women, Black men) to interpret and to claim Black women's voices. Some white women "wrote" their slave narratives, while still others along with black and white men "edited" the same. In every sphere Black women's voices are usurped by these "others" who think they know better than Black women how they feel and what they ought to feel. The following letter from the *Crisis* provides one of numerous examples of this kind of usurpation. It is by a self-proclaimed "southern white woman." She claims to be "deeply interested" in the "Negro race in America" and has worked for its "advancement."

> For several months I have been a subscriber to your magazine, have looked it over carefully each issue, and put it into the hands of my maid as an interesting thing. Perhaps, for her to read in a leisure hour. And I have watched its effect, which has not been a good one.
>
> Now I want to say this, and from the bottom of my heart; you are making a grave mistake in pointing out the woes of the Negro race which are no greater — if as great — as the woes of the white man. Besides, to point them out is not the way to remedy the evil that exists, if evil there does exist.
>
> A Southern White Woman[4]

The need to rediscover and bring to consciousness the rich literary tradition of Black women writers is known to be urgent by teachers and scholars who understand the costs of effacing the fact that Black women, working against extraordinary odds, have indeed been capable of literary creation. In the twentieth century, along with a growing interest in Black women's literature, there is a new awareness of the extent of Black women's invisibility: their exclusion from critical studies and literary histories and their virtual disenfranchisement by the publishing establishment. In my current research in the area of Black women's studies, I am forcibly reminded that the issues of access — that is, whether or not Black women were to be published — and aspiration — that is, whether Black women, even if given access, were encouraged to proceed in their intellectual development — are crucial to an understanding of their literary silence.

Silence is imposed and maintained by a self-serving, aristocratic, patriarchal canon that has always preferred to believe that writing is a divine gift bestowed on the seismographically sensitive and worthy white male. Writing is mystified into "art," sacred and inviolable object, immortal beyond its creator. The canon refuses to acknowledge that the impulse to write is varied and occurs without respect to an individual's race or sex. The literary histories of numerous Black women suggest that whether a voice speaks or remains silent is determined largely by external conditions.

It is fascinating, for example, to look at the years 1926 to 1929, during the Harlem Renaissance, an especially rich period for considering Black women's literary relationships because its politics were expressed in an interlocking network of racial/sexual prejudice, patronage and reward, personal stance and audition, public gesture and spokesmanship. Blacks constituted at that time and place an identifiable, visible, recognized writing community in which Black women writers might be expected to take courage. Moreover, between 1921 and 1931, popular and literary magazines were full of fiction by women, and no less than seven Pulitzer Prizes were held by women. There was no lack of critical acclaim for such writers as Ellen Glasgow, Pearl Buck, Willa Cather, and Edith Wharton.

Recently, I have studied the correspondence of Walter F. White, one of the Harlem literary patrons, with numerous well-known and unknown Black women writers.[5] White was a popular Black NAACP leader, activist, writer, and mentor. Like his close friend James Weldon Johnson,[6] he enjoyed close relationships with important white publishers and the Black reading public. Typically kind,

White nonetheless was frequently discouraging. In his own complacent, paternalistic way, he ended up patronizing and excluding
Black women. Just two examples from his voluminous correspondence will point this out.

In 1929, a young poet, Lucia M. Pitts (b. 1907),[7] asked Walter
White for help in seeking a publisher for her poetry manuscript
"Dream Dusting." She wrote:

> For a few years now, I have been doing some things in the
> line of poetry with a fair amount of success. Some of my
> scribblings have enjoyed publication in newspapers and
> other periodicals. Several people have recently suggested
> that I get a volume and I have been trying to find out lately if
> such a thing is possible for me. Of course I have no faith in
> my poems, but I make no superior claims for them — that is
> to say, that I'd appreciate your candid comments and won't
> feel too badly if you find they aren't exactly up to par. Then,
> I understand that it isn't a cinch getting publishers to accept
> poetry, so I'm prepared for a fight.

White was unimpressed. In a lukewarm reply, he suggested a
vanity press, observing that her poems were "not sufficiently strong
to interest a real publisher." In a subsequent letter he refused to
write a letter of introduction on her behalf, and he added that James
Weldon Johnson concurred.

White's correspondence does not rest entirely with "lost" women
writers. It reads like a Who's Who that includes Black women
writers on the order of Nella Larsen (1893-1963) and Georgia
Douglas Johnson (1886-1966). Johnson became one of the most
popularly acclaimed women poets since Phillis Wheatley and
Frances Ellen Watkins Harper. She wrote under several pseu-
donyms, most consistently using the name John Temple. She had
already published two books when she wrote White with offers to
pay him to publish a third poetry manuscript. White refused but in
his characteristic fashion was encouraging:

> There are certain poems such as "I Want to Die While You
> Love Me," "Song of the Sinner," "I Closed My Shutters
> Fast Last Night," and one or two others which are very good
> lyrics. The only fault that can be found is that they follow a
> much traveled path — so many others have written of the
> selfsame experiences and emotions. It is not that many of
> these are not well done, but that this style of lyric has been
> done so often before.

But he was not hopeful:

> Publishers and the poetry-buying public have become rather fed up on this particular style of poetry no matter how well it may be done . . . Publishers today demand freshness of viewpoint and novelty of expression.

But Johnson, already experienced by having to single-handedly promote her first two books, saw to it that *An Autumn Love Cycle* (1928) was published two years later. Her fourth book now extant was privately published.

Johnson was an experienced, surviving woman. Do her poems tell us something of the sufferings of even successful Black women who tried to make their voices heard?

> I'm folding up my little dreams
> Within my heart tonight,
> And praying I may soon forget
> The torture of their sight.
>
> For time's deft fingers scroll my brown
> With full relentless art —
> I'm folding up my little dreams
> Tonight, within my heart.[8]

The literary histories of Black women continue to remain as footnotes in various archival collections throughout the United States. The uncomfortable truth is that creative but unpublished Black women writers are the rule rather than the exception. Of course the attitudes of publishers, patrons, and men combine with other factors — work and children in their lives and the emotional sustenance and support they are expected to give men — to inhibit the creativity of Black women. Yet to a large extent the silence of these women seems externally imposed, a response to the indifference, neglect, and sometimes active hostility of a cynical literary public. This "lost" tradition is maintained by indifferent publishers like the James Weldon Johnsons and the Walter F. Whites who, despite their support, their cautiously worded and well-considered responses, exercise an awesome power as to who will be and who will not be encouraged. As would-be mediators they have much to atone for. It is not that male Black writers are more gifted than the women — gifted they all are and were. It is the complacent, paternalistic gatekeeping of these Black/white males with their chauvinist camaraderie that excludes Black women. Publishers and patrons in varying proportions create the symbolic silence that continues to surround Black women's literary identities since the time of the first

Black writer, Lucy Terry (1730-1821). Such patrons advise authors to produce made-to-order books, submitting to buyers' desires rather than to what they believe to be the intrinsic merit of the works themselves.

Arguing for women's suffrage, Mary Church Terrell (1863-1954) comments on male bias to explain the truly hidden nature of materials about Black women:

> The founders of this republic called heaven and earth to witness that it should be called a government of the people, for the people and by the people; and yet the elective franchise is withheld from one-half of its citizens, many of whom are intelligent, virtuous and cultured, and unstintingly bestowed upon the other half, many of whom are illiterate, degraded and vicious, because by an unparalleled exhibition of lexicographical acrobatics the word "people" has been turned to mean all who were shrewd and wise enough to have themselves born boys instead of girls, and white instead of black.[9]

In any area of Black women's studies one has to become not so much the surgeon but the surgeon's knife to cut away the myths, the deliberate distortions, and the half-truths that surround Black women's public identities. It is the surgeon's knife that cuts right to the diseased heart of the matter, demolishing fundamental assumptions, tearing them apart, in order to rechart and regain history with ourselves in it.

When a time arrives that I am comfortably able to concentrate on the intrinsic merit of the literary productions by Black women without first having to duel with a hostile — when not indifferent — establishment that seeks to canonize certain writers and therefore erase Black women from the literary marketplace, then perhaps I will with a clear conscience write of my love affair and share my joys and frustrations of women, Black like me, in an atmosphere of toleration, trust, and sensitivity. At such a time I will have cause to celebrate. But for now, the reader will have to take my word for what I believe to be a religious, mystical, social, literary, cosmic event — the study of Black women. Denied the knowledge of their existence for so long, I feel that my finding them is like the celebratory occasion of a company of women and their coming together, across centuries, as a family: Phillis Wheatley meet Ella Baker meet Margaret Walker meet Sojourner meet Lucy Terry meet Harriet Tubman meet Charlotte Forten meet Kelly meet Anonymous meet Elleanor Eldridge meet Frances Harper meet "a woman of color" meet Ida B. Wells. In bringing together through research and writing Black women who only a short time ago were prohibited assemblage, literacy, and certain modes of dress,[10] I am connected to a community of women in which our commonalities are more important than our differences because they define and join us as women living in various periods of American history. This joy of discovery is tempered by the knowledge that an indifferent society makes the lives and literary histories of Black women and their writings tantamount to a mystery. The critic and historian must become a detective. The search is made both necessary and necessarily difficult.

> A woman with a burning flame
>   Deep covered through the years
>   With ashes — ah! she hid it deep
>   And smothered it with tears.
>
> Sometimes a baleful light would rise
>   From out the dusky bed,
>   And then the woman hushed it quick
>   To slumber on as dead.
>
> At last the weary war was done,
>   The tapers were alight,
>   And with a sigh of victory
>   She breathed a soft — goodnight!
>
> Georgia Johnson, "Smothered Fires"

Notes

1. Alice Walker, *Revolutionary Petunias* (New York: Harcourt Brace Jovanovich, 1972).

2. Adrienne Rich, *A Wild Patience Has Taken Me This Far: Poems 1978–1981* (New York: W.W. Norton, 1981).

3. Phillis Wheatley, *Poems on Various Subjects, Religions and Moral* (London, 1773; first American edition, Philadelphia, 1786). *Memoir and Poems of Phillis Wheatley, a Native African and a Slave*, facs. ed. (Salem, N.Y.: Ayer Co., 1977).

4. Letter to the Editor, *Crisis* 4 (September 1912): 250.

250 BETWEEN WOMEN

5. Erlene Stetson, "Silence: Access and Aspiration," gives a fuller treatment and complete documentation. Unpublished; available from author.

6. Like Walter White, James Weldon Johnson was vigorously sought after by fledgling writers. He encouraged poet Annie Bethel Scales Spencer (1882-1975) to submit her poetry to *Opportunity* and *Crisis* magazines. He kindly suggested that she change her name to Anne Spencer. Her poems appear in Johnson's anthology *The Book of American Negro Poetry* (1922). Knowing of his reputation, a seventeen-year-old poet was led to submit individual poems from her manuscript "Songs After Sunset 1935-1936" for his reactions. He suggested several changes. That poet was Gwendolyn Elizabeth Brooks (b. 1917) who years later was to win a Pulitzer Prize for *Annie Allen* (1949), a sonnet collection, and continues to enjoy popular and critical acclaim today. The poems that Brooks submitted to Johnson were never published. The entire unpublished poetry manuscript is at Lilly Library, Indiana University, Bloomington, Indiana. For other references to poems in this collection, see Gwendolyn Brooks, *Report from Part One* (Detroit: Broadside Press, 1972).

7. Pitt's poems are found in various magazines of the period, such as the *Messenger*, *Opportunity* (November 1942), *Crisis*, *Challenge* (March 1934, May 1935), and a short-lived magazine, the *New Challenge* (1937), edited by Dorothy West. Her poems also appear in *Ebony Rhythm*, ed. Beatrice Murphy (New York: Exposition Press, 1948), *Negro Voices: An Anthology of Contemporary Verse*, ed. Beatrice Murphy (New York: Harrison, 1938), and a self-published volume with Tomi Carolyn Tinsley and Helen C. Harris called TRIAD, December 1945. Pitt's "Urns of Fate" is an unpublished sonnet sequence. A play "Let Me Dream" was written for and performed by Co. B, 6888th CPD, WAC, in Rouen, France.

8. "My Little Dreams," from *The Heart of a Woman and Other Poems* (Boston: Cornhill Publishing Co., 1918). Johnson's volumes include *Heart of a Woman* (1918), *Bronze* (Boston: B. V. Brimmer, 1922), *An Autumn Love Cycle* (New York: Vinal, 1926), and *And Share My World* (Washington, D.C., privately printed, 1962). See Erlene Stetson, "Rediscovering the Harlem Renaissance: Georgia Douglas Johnson, 'The Negro Poet,'" *Obsidian* 5 (Spring 1979): 26-34. Johnson's *Bronze* was reviewed by Alice Dunbar Nelson in the *Messenger* (April 1923): 698, 719; see also a review of *Bronze* by Zona Gale in *Opportunity* 1, no. 7 (1923): 211-13. Johnson personally distributed her two earlier volumes at southern colleges and libraries where she occasionally read her poems.

9. Mary Church Terrell, "The Justice of Woman Suffrage," *Crisis* 4 (September 1912): 250.

10. In the state of Louisiana it is still a punishable crime for mulatto women to appear in public wearing a headress other than the bandanna. This is to show their race because their complexion does not. The states of Alabama and Mississippi make it a punishable crime for Black women to appear in public without their aprons. The film *The Member of the Wedding*, based on Carson McCuller's book, has the Black woman attending a wedding wearing an apron. Thus art imitates life. In Creole New Orleans the tignon de Madras, worn by mulattos on their heads, was considered a badge of servitude; the expression "a tignon in the family" was an accusation of colored blood.

Bibliography

Black Sister: Poetry by Black American Women, 1746-1980. Bloomington: Indiana University Press, 1981.

Christian, Barbara. *Black Women Novelists: The Development of a Tradition.* Westport, Conn: Greenwood Press, 1980.

Morrison, Toni. "A Slow Walk of Trees (As Grandmother Would Say), Hopeless (As Grandfather Would Say)." *New York Times Magazine,* 4 July 1976, 152.

Murray, Daniel, comp. *Preliminary Lists of Books and Pamphlets by Negro Authors for Paris Exposition and Library of Congress.* Washington, D.C.: Library of Congress, 1900.

Stetson, Erlene. "Black Women in and out of Print." In *Women in Print,* ed. Joan Hartman and Ellen Messer-Davidow. New York: Modern Language Association, 1982, 87-107.

"Studying Slavery: Some Literary and Pedagogical Considerations on the Black Female Slave." In *But Some of Us Are Brave,* ed. Hull, Scott, and Smith. Old Westbury, N.Y.: Feminist Press, 1982.

Bertha Pappenheim
Leo Baeck Institute, New York, N.Y.

Ann Jackowitz

Ann H. Jackowitz

ANNA O./BERTHA PAPPENHEIM
AND ME

I, a native German girl, am now totaly [sic] *deprived of the faculty to speak, to understand or to read German. This symptom lasted during the time of a heavy nervous illness I had to go through in permanence longer than a year; since about four months it only returns regularly every evening. The physicians point it out as something very strange and but rarely to be observed; therefore, I will try to give, as well as a person who has never made any medical studies can do, a short account of my own observations and experiences considering this terrible estate.*

— Anna O., September 1882

She was a patient whose life became known to me to an extent to which one person's life is seldom known to another. She had never been in love. She never mentioned her sexuality despite childishly seductive behavior. She was astonishingly quick, extraordinarily intelligent. She had a thirst for knowledge, a penetrating intuition, but nothing beyond a high school education. She suffered from convulsions and hallucinations; yet in her lucid moments gave remarkable descriptions of her insane fantasies.

— Dr. Joseph Breuer, 1895

I first learned of the fascinating and unique medical case history of Anna O. while taking a psychology course at Simmons College.

Whether it was because she was the first female to be psychoanalyzed or whether it was that a woman could create a fantasy which in
turn could cause a physiological change as dramatic as a hysterical
pregnancy; whether it was that she named her own cure (the
"talking cure") or that both my grandmother's name and my own
were Anna — whatever the reason or reasons, I was thunderstruck.
An indelible impression was made, but it lay dormant for nearly
fifteen years.

Graduating with a B.A. in history and a minor in psychology, I
earned a master's degree in history at New York University. My first
career, as a humanities teacher on the high school level, had not felt
right and I left the field after I received my tenure. Floundering for a
couple of months and unsure about my future, I took a job running a
cigar stand in the lobby of a commercial building on Forty-ninth
Street and Madison Avenue. I began writing; my first short story,
"The Cigar Stand Episode or How to Meet Men over the Counter,"
was never completed. Although it was clever and funny, it was
laced with anger and ambivalence about both myself and my newly
acquired rather lowly professional status. I knew I had potential —
but potential for what?

Six months later, when the stand was about to be sold and I would
be forced to leave, I was rescued by a customer, a commercial film
producer who was setting up his own business. I ran his production
company for five years, learning and absorbing all the while. Ultimately, I earned a corporate title and became a film producer, but I
left the company when there was no further place I could go. One
area in film that offered opportunity and growth was sales. Consequently, for the next three years I was a sales rep for one production
company and then a director of development for another. I began
writing again, film treatments this time. Still, I wasn't satisfied.

In March 1978, I decided to take a year off. On my agenda were
items such as quit smoking, learn Hebrew, start jogging, find
meaning to my life. One evening I was invited by a friend to attend a
lecture at the New School. After class, over coffee with a group of
people, I met a woman who was working on a film project about
Anna O. Her background was neither film nor history nor psychology, but she was determined, and I admired that. This chance
encounter with a total stranger changed my life.

We exchanged telephone numbers and agreed to meet again soon
to discuss my potential involvement in her project. That night I
barely slept, and the next few days I spent in the library reac-
quainting myself with Anna O.

As the first documented case of psychoanalysis, Anna O. (a
pseudonym) is the infamous hysteric introduced in *Studies on*

Hysteria by Sigmund Freud and Joseph Breuer, Freud's mentor, in 1895. According to Breuer's account — he was her doctor, not Freud, which is often incorrectly assumed — at age twenty-one while nursing her dying father, Anna O. suffered from periodic loss of hearing, blindness and muteness, paralysis in the extremities on the right side of her body, less frequent but similar paralysis on the left side, a neuralgic tic in her face, an aversion to food and liquids (resulting in an anorectic condition), and a loss of the ability to speak in her native tongue, German. In a final phase of her illness, she relived her previous year day by day.

Coexisting with her physical dysfunctions were suicidal impulses and traits of a split personality, which she called her "good" and "bad" selves. These varied states of consciousness were compounded by memory loss and morbid, tormenting hallucinations. At times she hit the doctor, threw objects across the room, and verbally abused those around her. On other occasions, she was kind, charitable, caring, and amusing.

Breuer's treatment was unusual and unorthodox. Never had a doctor encouraged a patient to describe what was troubling her or him. And never had a doctor spent such an inordinate amount of time treating a patient. Beginning in December 1880, he visited her twice and sometimes three times a day for eighteen months. Since both Breuer and Anna O. were fluent in a number of languages, and Anna O. could not speak German, the treatment was conducted in English. Using hypnosis in the evening sessions, he repeated to her the frightened words she had spoken during her daytime "absences" (a French term meaning states of confused delirium), of which she had no memory. Through these sessions, which lasted for several hours, she was able to recall images and pictures of death heads, snakes, and other forgotten details of her terrifying hallucinations. Once she had talked these episodes through, she became calm and relieved of her fears and anxieties regarding specific events that had taken place. For example, her loss of hearing was traced in reverse chronological order to more than three hundred different occurences until she finally remembered the first instance in which she could not hear: once she had not heard her father entering the room. Although Breuer felt that the sexual factor played a primary role in causing hysteria, he felt that fright, anxiety, and anger were the specific causes of Anna O.'s hysteria. Once she talked out each instance in which she could not hear because she had been frightened, anxious, or angry, she released the pent-up emotion, and the symptom, deafness, disappeared.

From Breuer's account, one gathers that the content of Anna O.'s hallucinations and the source of her many physical incapacities stemmed primarily from situations relating to her father, as when she sat at her father's bedside and her arm suddenly became paralyzed.

In April 1881, her father, of whom Breuer says she was "passionately fond," died. Her mother did not tell her the news, so consequently Anna O. did not attend the funeral. When she found out about her father's death, a terrible relapse occurred, and although many of her physical symptoms had begun to be alleviated, she was institutionalized in June of that year for a short time. (What did this mean about the role her mother played in her illness? I had little to go on.)

Upon her return home, the last of her symptoms, paralysis of the right arm, finally disappeared. She recalled that her arm had become numb for the first time when she had had an hallucination of a large black snake trying to bite her father. This had occurred while she sat at her father's bedside. In an attempt to ward off the snake, she had uttered a prayer in English. After reporting this to Breuer, she was cured of her paralysis, and her native German was restored.

One also learns from Breuer's account how utterly dependent she became on him. Only he could feed her. Experiencing periodic loss of eyesight, as a consequence of her tears and grief (this is assuming, and I do, that the illness was psychosomatic), she could recognize only Breuer and then only by touching his face. The more I read, the more questions I had. For example, to what extent had Breuer encouraged this dependency and to what extent did he go beyond the boundaries usually established between doctor and patient? Nothing seemed to make sense. The doctor had called the treatment "catharsis." Anna O. had named it the "talking cure." But was she cured? What kind of illness was it really? Has anyone ever recovered from what she had? Was she perhaps, as some recent theories suggest, feigning this exotic array of symptoms? What happened to her after the treatment?

Then there was the question of the circumstances surrounding the end of the treatment. According to Breuer, both he and his patient had agreed that treatment would be terminated in June 1882, the anniversary marking her admission to the sanatorium the previous year. Although relapses occurred, in the 1895 edition of *Studies on Hysteria,* he detailed the treatment and stated that she was cured. (Breuer's 1882 unpublished account makes no mention of a cure.) Many years later, however, Freud took issue with Breuer's conclusion. Although Breuer never mentioned it publicly, he allegedly reported to Freud that Anna O. had experienced a hysterical pregnancy. According to the Freud-Jones version,[1] on the evening of June 7, 1882, when both doctor and patient had said farewell to one another, Breuer was called back to Anna O.'s house for an emergency. Under hypnosis, Anna O supposedly said, "Now, Dr. B.'s baby is coming."[2] The doctor, frightened by the consequences of such an irrational accusation, abandoned his patient, and went off on a second honeymoon with his wife, during which time they conceived a fifth child. Breuer, it appeared, gave up treating neurotics and hysterics, returning to his more general private practice and essentially retreating into history.[3]

Freud commented in 1925, the year Breuer died, that indeed the patient had not been completely cured by the cathartic method. Subsequently, he added that hypnosis had failed and that the doctor had experienced a countertransference, a situation in which the therapist projects intense sexual feelings such as love and rage toward the patient.

One day, examining unpublished material from the diaries of Marie Bonaparte,[4] I found that Freud had told Marie of a suicide attempt by Breuer's wife as a result of his relationship with Anna O. Puzzled, I wondered where all the pieces fit.

There was no doubt in my mind that I wanted to work on the film project presented to me by my new acquaintance. The possibilities of the subject matter were not only intellectually challenging but also extraordinarily rich for dramatic translation onto the motion picture screen. The relationship between the doctor and the patient, I decided, would be the paramount issue. The film would pose the question: Was it love that was healing Anna O?

Jogging near the East River, my friend and I talked more about Anna O. and what had become of her after Breuer's treatment.

Anna O., whose true identity was revealed only in 1953 with the publication of Ernest Jones's biography of Freud, was in fact Bertha Pappenheim, a woman as famous in her day as Elizabeth Cady Stanton or Jane Addams — a pioneer feminist. As one of the first social workers in the world, she defended the rights of prostitutes, unwed mothers, and illegitimate children. Ultimately, she was recognized by the German government in 1954 in a stamp commemorating her contributions in the field of social work.

After several more weeks of discussions, my New School acquaintance and I became partners with the understanding that a great deal of research had to be done at the same time as we had to package the property with an appropriate writer, director, and cast. Although

we had more than moderate success in attracting members of the
film community, we became stuck. My film treatment was well
received, but we still needed a screenplay. After a while we dis-
banded, and I decided to pursue the project on my own.

What had begun as a fantasy of mine — to produce my first
theatrical feature film — had become an obsession with Anna O./
Bertha Pappenheim. I understood neither why nor in what direction
it would lead me.

You can hope for everything, even for the most beautiful
things we may experience. But for me, work and you children
are my entire life, a life which I had to conquer.
— Bertha Pappenheim, letter, 21 November 1906

Aside from scattered fragments of information such as one recently gleaned from the guest list of a fashionable spa, Bad Ischl,
where Bertha Pappenheim and her family vacationed in the
summers of 1871-1874, little is known regarding her childhood or
youth. Born in Vienna on February 27, 1859, the daughter of
wealthy Orthodox Jewish parents, she was one of four children. An
older sister, Henriette, died at age eighteen when Bertha was only
ten. Another sister, Flora, died two years before Bertha was born.
Her only surviving sibling was a brother, Wilhelm, born in 1860 (he
died in 1937). Some stories claim the children did not get along.
Wilhelm became a lawyer, married a widow when he was forty, and
maintained one of the world's largest private libraries on socialism.

Raised in a very strict puritanical fashion, Bertha had a governess
and was educated in a Catholic girls' school until she was sixteen.
Years later, she described her upbringing as one typical of the
Jewish middle class, in which being born a daughter meant being
excluded from an independent or professional life. Attendance at
the university was forbidden.

Breuer described her home life as one of monotonous boredom.
Retreating into daydreams and fantasies, which she called her
"private theater," she spent her life tatting lace, riding horses,
attending concerts and theater, and embroidering — waiting to get
married. According to Breuer, until she took ill there seemed to be
no indication that pent-up psychic energies were at work. But this
was only conjecture.

Pappenheim remained totally silent about her illness during her entire life. While her family knew of it, she never spoke about it to either her co-workers or staff members. Consequently, and unfortunately, we have only Breuer's case histories of 1882 and 1895 and the medical records from one of the institutions in which she sought or, in a number of instances, was forced to seek aid between 1882 and 1887.

We know from medical reports that she became addicted to morphine and chloral, both of which relieved pain and allowed sleep. When and how she withdrew from these drugs is unknown. We also know that as late as 1887 she was still hallucinating in the evenings but that she was feeling much better. (These reports are from Martha Bernays Freud, a close friend, after a visit from Pappenheim.) Also, during this period, encouraged by relatives and her mother, she attended a nursing course, which was primarily for unmarried girls of the educated class. At the same time, she pursued writing, the content of which carried over from her storytelling days with Breuer. In 1888 she moved to Frankfurt with her mother. In 1899, she published a play entitled *Women's Rights* and a translation of the great eighteenth-century polemic by Mary Wollstonecraft, *Vindication of the Rights of Women.*

Traditionally, Jewish women of the upper classes felt it their duty to be involved in charity work. Rarely, however, would one get involved on a practical level. Not so for Bertha Pappenheim. Pappenheim began her work in Jewish charities by dishing out soup to the hordes of needy immigrants from Eastern Europe. (Breuer had commented on her sympathetic kindness toward the poor and helpless. Presumably she told him stories about her work during her sessions.)

In the late 1880s, Pappenheim began a career combining her crusade against injustices to women with her social consciousness. Her interests centered on women and children and to that end she organized a nursery school, sewing classes, and a girls' club. In 1895 she became a housemother in an orphanage, gaining experience as an administrator and educator. In 1902 she founded Care by Women, a Jewish women's society. Jewish women were allowed to minister to the dead or to work on relatively ineffective philanthropic activities. Pappenheim would change that. Her vision was to establish a Jewish social service network applying the goals of the German feminist movement through Jewish social work. In 1904 she founded the German Jewish feminist movement under the name the League of Jewish Women. At its apex in 1929, the organization numbered 50,000 women.

The league's main campaign was to deter the white slave trade. Two issues predominated — Jewish prostitution and illegitimacy. With the seemingly endless numbers of poor Eastern European Jews entering Germany, Pappenheim saw a clear connection between prostitution and illegitimacy. Under Jewish civil law, unmarried women had no real part in the life of the community and were not protected by Russian or Turkish authorities. Likewise, the Agunah (abandoned wife) who couldn't prove her husband's death or who hadn't received a valid divorce could not remarry and was consequently thrown out of the community. (This is still a problematic practice in Orthodox communities.) The double standard infuriated Pappenheim: Men could do as they pleased, and the women must be held in their place. Analyzing statistics gathered at international conferences as well as reporting on her own fact-finding missions, Pappenheim found that both men and women were involved. Duping poor, hungry Jewish parents with false marriage certificates and money for their daughters' dowries, pimps and traffickers arranged phony marriages only to turn their "wives" over to procurers who would ship them from Frankfurt to Constantinople, Buenos Aires, or New York. "The merchants and the merchandise are Jewish," proclaimed Pappenheim, who implored rabbis and the Jewish community to help her cause; for the most part she found the men hostile, ignorant, or full of denial. When she discovered that some synagogues catered to the religious needs of these prostitutes and their rings (they were called Synagogues of the Traffickers in Constantinople, New York, and Buenos Aires), she accused the rabbis of "letting the Jews rot."

I had never heard of Jewish prostitution. Here, I knew, was extremely volatile information that many Jews would not want exposed even today.[5] How was I going to deal with it?

Two other, related issues drove Pappenheim. First was the pursuit of women's equality with men in Jewish community life. Men and religious leaders were often discouraging and hostile, but Pappenheim was relentless in her effort to improve the status and self-image of women. Her organization offered strength in numbers. Also, she emphasized career training. Although the training was confined to household tasks, she urged Jewish families to educate their daughters for careers as teachers, social workers, and baby nurses. In 1907 she founded Isenburg, a Jewish Home for Wayward Girls — for unwed mothers, their children, and "morally sick" girls.

I amassed a great deal of information about Pappenheim, but nothing clicked. Like a sleuth, I was in hot pursuit of the elusive Anna O./Bertha Pappenheim for two years. If Anna O. absorbed and piqued my interest, Bertha Pappenheim was an enigma. How could they be one and the same? Such a gap existed between the two.

I desperately wanted to write my screenplay, but what was going to be the focus? While I knew that Anna O.'s story was romantic, Bertha Pappenheim's seemed dramatic without having a clear story line. How would I be able to reconcile the passive aggression of the young sick woman, subdued by a world of inner torment and substantial physical pain, with the outspoken courageous activism that led Pappenheim to establish the first Home for Wayward Girls in Germany, to travel extensively in Poland, Russia, and the Middle East trying to save Jewish women from the horrors of prostitution and white slavery, and to speak at the League of Nations in Geneva imploring the members' aid in combating prostitution? Of course, I could tell the story of Anna O. (which I still hadn't completely sorted out) and leave Bertha Pappenheim out, but that seemed irresponsible.

Repeatedly, I had been told by those with whom I shared my information that there were in fact *two* stories: the relationship between doctor and patient and what Pappenheim did with the rest of her life. While my job, as I saw it, was to connect the two, the problems seemed insurmountable. I narrowed my themes to three: madness within a Viennese world that was beginning to crumble, love between a married doctor and his paralyzed patient, and a young woman's struggle to live in a man's world, in which the patriarchal society and religion dictated her behavior. But still I had to resolve the question of how I would deal with the issues of Judaism, feminism, and psychoanalysis.

During Anna O.'s treatment, Breuer had noted that she was irreligious and rebellious, resenting the privileged position of Jewish men. Years later, she became a devout Jew while still attacking the exalted position of men. Although I could trace the seeds of her vehement feminism to after her treatment with Breuer, I saw no element of it in her crippled state — unless I equated her breakdown with escape and withdrawal. (Other early feminists, such as Jane Addams, Josephine Butler, and Elizabeth Cady Stanton suffered from headaches and other neurotic ailments.) And psychoanalysis? Pappenheim called it "a double-edged sword. It depends on the user and how it is used." Many years after her own treatment, one of her charges was emotionally disturbed; she refused psychoanalytical treatment for her. Why?

The more I knew, the more bewildered I became. Every time I came across new information, it changed my view of Pappenheim. Every time I wrote a note to myself or decided on a scene I would use, I would ask myself: Am I being fair to her? Am I being fair to Breuer?

Breuer, too, created a problem for me. Whereas information on Bertha Pappenheim's later life was extensive,[6] her publications were available, and the innumerable papers and discussions on Anna O. were provocative, there was scanty information on Breuer. I finally discovered a book on Breuer written in German by Albrecht Hirschmüller, titled *Physiologie und Psychoanalyse in Leben und Werk Josef Breuer* (Physiology and Psychoanalysis in the Life and Work of Joseph Breuer). So impressed with the book, I am looking for a U.S. publisher to translate and publish it.

Joseph Breuer, fourteen years older than Freud, was an accomplished physiologist. Prior to his meeting Freud, he made two important physiological discoveries. While still a medical student at the University of Vienna, he discovered the self-regulating mechanism of breathing. Several years later, he successfully demonstrated that the semicircular canals of the ear regulate posture, equilibrium, and movement. According to Frank Sulloway, author of *Freud, Biologist of the Mind*,[7] "Breuer's physiological researches provided a conceptual foundation for the pioneering theory of hysteria that he and Freud later proposed." As Freud's mentor and collaborator, Breuer not only shared his medical knowledge and elucidating research but also paid the rent on Freud's apartment for a considerable period of time. The cause of the estrangement between the two is not clear. In 1925, according to Freud, the issue had to do with Breuer's refusal to believe Freud's theory that sexuality was the prime pathogenic factor in hysteria and other neuroses. In 1895 both men felt that Anna O.'s case was nonsexual. Breuer continued to believe this although he never denied the role that sexuality played in neuroses. Freud, however, reversed his position regarding Anna O. in 1914, recalling the alleged phantom pregnancy and the developing countertransference between Breuer and Anna O. But Freud's account is a reconstruction, a reinterpretation of Breuer's case histories and does not adequately explain why the two men parted ways. Henri Ellenberger in a 1972 paper goes so far as to suggest that the hysterical pregnancy does not fit into the etiology of the case.[8] Hirschmüller further shows that Breuer did not retreat from Anna O.'s case as Freud had suggested. Nor did Breuer run off on a second honeymoon with his wife in June 1882 and their fifth child was in fact born the previous March. Also, Breuer continued to treat mental patients until 1912. Apparently the issues were more personal, but never surmountable. Their wives kept in touch but the two men did not. Interestingly, Anna Freud and Breuer's two grand-daughters remained close until Anna's recent death.

What was clear to me — though not supported by Hirschmüller, Kaplan, or anyone else — was that Breuer was a man in love with two women. Rather than acknowledge Pappenheim's effect on his family life or his feelings for his patient, which Freud considered merely natural and a part of the therapeutic process through coun-tertransference, Breuer's sense of moral responsibility and need to avoid scandal held sway. In other words, Breuer lost his objectivity, and, as Freud put it to Marie Bonaparte, bourgeois ethics replaced scientific truth. Breuer never confirmed or denied these charges. In Bonaparte's journal Freud also alluded to Mathilde Breuer's suicide attempt and the hysterical pregnancy. According to Freud in a letter to Stefan Zweig on June 2, 1932, one of Breuer's daughters sup-posedly confronted her father, and he confirmed the events. Breuer then went to Freud saying, "What have you done to me!"[9] On the other hand, there was a reported meeting between the two men where Breuer held out his arms to Freud. Freud kept his head down and continued walking.[10]

Did Breuer tell Freud that he had fallen in love with Anna O.? If he had, would Freud still have arrived at a rational explanation like countertransference? How much more effective could Breuer have been if he had continued seeing his patient? In June 1882, treatment was over. The daily visits were over, but Breuer did see Anna O. in 1883, wishing that she might die so "that the poor thing could be released from her misery." In early 1884 Breuer wrote, "I saw little Pappenheim today. She is perfectly healthy, without pains or any-thing else." Why, I continued to wonder, did Freud say Breuer abandoned his patient? Was there a pregnancy — hysterical or real?

Finally, I wrote to Anna Freud requesting two letters of her father dated October 31 and November 11, 1883, which, according to Ernest Jones, were proof positive of the phantom pregnancy.

She sent me the October 31 letter, which mentioned nothing about it. The only new information it contained was that Bertha's hair had turned gray (but when that happened is only speculation). The other, she said, was "personal," and Breuer's name was not even mentioned within the contents of the letter.[11]

I was becoming more and more frustrated with the information I was gathering. Still, I was determined to write my screenplay.

The film, as I wrote it, opens with Bertie (a nickname I created for her) attempting suicide by walking through a window of glass. Her mother sends for Breuer. Glimpses of Pappenheim's family life are seen. Breuer and Bertie begin the arduous task of treatment by hypnosis. A developing love relationship emerges between the two. Not accepting the theory that she had a hysterical pregnancy but not willing to believe that they had a physical affair, I had Bertie hallucinate their making love to one another. Since Breuer did give body massages to Pappenheim, I created a scene where they are physical with one another. I also included a scene in which Breuer's wife, suspecting their relationship, attempts suicide. Although Bertha experienced gradual improvement, she continued to have relapses, particularly after her father's death. On a hunch (a correct one, I have since discovered), I had her placed in an institution. Breuer, as a result of his wife's protest and out of guilt, sees her in the sanatorium but turns her care over to other doctors. Since no one knows how she recovered (and it's doubtful we ever will) or where her great concern about the plight of women, particularly Jewish women, originated, I invented a character named Fannie, who becomes Bertie's close friend at the sanatorium. Fannie is pregnant, deserted by her lover, and has been placed there by her parents to avoid scandal. Fannie is supposed to give her child up for adoption but wants to keep it. Bertie is drawn to her and is empathtic. They help one another. Bertie recovers and leaves for Mainz to visit her relatives. Fannie remains. Louise, Bertie's cousin, introduces her to charity work. There she meets a Jewish prostitute, Maimie, who takes Bertha out into the streets and into the underground world of prostitution, crime, and poverty. Soon thereafter, Bertie becomes totally immersed — professionally, intellectually, emotionally — in the needs of Jewish women. Her attraction to other women is suggested. Her mother moves her to Frankfurt, and she begins her career in social work. Looking for Fannie, she discovers that both mother and child are dead, having been abandoned by Fannie's parents. In a scene of dramatic reversal, Bertie sees Breuer once more at her brother's wedding in Vienna. While he is overcome with emotion, Bertie controls herself. Tirelessly, she continues her ardent battle on behalf of helpless women, those who have been victimized by the exploitation and domination of men. By establishing a network of contacts, she finally finds Maimie, who comes to Bertha's home to stay with her. The story ironically ends when ninety-three women at one of Pappenheim's affiliate schools commit a mass suicide rather than be taken by the Nazis as prostitutes. (The real Pappenheim continued to lead Eastern European Jews into Germany through the 1930s. She realized her mistake too late. A tragic flaw. The mass suicide is a true story.)

I tried selling my screenplay. "Fascinating" was always the general response, with the additional comments "too depressing," "too cerebral," "try PBS." I did try PBS. I met with every East Coast story editor at the major studios as well as at independent production companies. In all cases, they were women who were really interested in seeing Anna O. get off the ground. They tried, but romantic comedies were in vogue. I tried Hollywood, but my first commitment from a Hollywood actress resulted in her trying to steal the property from me. Two major Hollywood directors were interested. One offered little money, and, on the advice of my agent, I turned it down. (Today, I wonder if that was a mistake.) The other director was impressed, and we met, but he was on his way to Vienna to shoot *Amadeus* and would be gone for two years.

I tried shelving the project and decided to work on a novel. I became seriously interested in theater and conceived an idea for a play. I began working on both. As writing was somewhat new to me and I was still uneasy about it, I took writing courses, subscribed to *The Writer, Writer's Digest,* and *Publishers Weekly.*

But, Anna O./Bertha Pappenheim and I weren't finished. She continued to gnaw at me. I knew that it was no longer the drive to sell the screenplay, but rather some kind of identification with her, her experiences, her struggle to maintain her sanity. Encouraged initially by friends, relatives, film studio executives, editors, and agents, now I was being told to let her go, get on with my life. I couldn't. She was my inspiration and my albatross, and I felt that somehow I had failed her if I could not understand (and relate that understanding to others) how she recovered and how she was able to say she had a life that "she had to conquer." Also, I was determined to know what role Breuer really played in her life. What was the breakthrough that enabled Pappenheim to take charge of her life and to become a charismatic leader full of will and determination? How did she move from a state of mental and physical collapse, recurring relapses, and inertia to one in which she not only faced reality but strove to change it? Yes, of course, she had the financial means to do so, but there were few in her position who did more than donate their money. And why did she turn exclusively to women? What was it? Why was it so important for me to know her?

We had nothing in common, Bertha Pappenheim and I. We were a century apart, and our roots and heritage were profoundly different. She was a Viennese-German and a devout Jew; I was a second-generation American. All of my grandparents were Russian, ethnic Jews. She grew up with a younger brother; I, an older sister. She was raised Orthodox in a wealthy family; I, a holiday Jew, was the daughter of a milkman. She turned her life around and found satisfaction in her work and her "children." I, at thirty-eight, felt isolated and alienated, already on my third career.

Then there was an epiphany: I didn't identify with Bertha Pappenheim at all, but rather with Anna O., the helpless, dependent girl (not woman), full of ambiguities, fused by rage, trapped by her own despair and guilt, torn by her "good" and "bad" selves, and, as in quicksand, stuck in a fantasy world of her own making.

A childhood memory came into focus. In our small two-family house, we had a cellar in which I took refuge. I would sit there for hours at a time and cry, but I never knew why. From the ground-level window in the tiny, relatively dark room, I would stare out at all the cars going by, wishing I were in them going far away. It wasn't a bad world, the one I created there, but it was a womb. There, the two of us (or were we three, or four?) understood one another. I promised myself that life would improve, but I didn't know how or when.

As a child and a teenager, I was not unaware of mental illness. A married aunt, a trained nurse (the only one in my mother's or father's family to have any education beyond high school) and the kindest person I knew, was diagnosed a manic depressive. I visited her often when she was home. Institutionalized many times, she was never cured. In 1957, when I was twelve, I saw the film *The Three Faces of Eve*. I was devastated. For reasons I couldn't fathom, I convinced myself I would become either like my aunt or like the character Eve.

Many years later, I tried "the talking cure," not once but several times. It didn't seem to work. Oddly enough, I didn't have an inkling of the selves inside me until I was confronted by the splits within Anna O. Once I understood our commonality, the idea of knowing Bertha Pappenheim, knowing myself, and separating myself from her began to take place.

Pappenheim destroyed Anna O. through a means we will probably never know. Perhaps that is best, for each of us must find our own way. On the other hand, her extraordinary recovery and her determination to let go of the past set an example that I and others can learn from: It is possible to change one's life. Hirschmüller describes the transition and transformation of Pappenheim's character as a "twist in her lifeline," both unexplainable and unpredictable. The process of recovery, I believe, includes the act of separation.

Having suffered desperately for the first thirty years of her life, Bertha Pappenheim miraculously recharged her life. Is that what she's telling me? The world? That it is time to stop being helpless, that life is a struggle, and if one wants to battle hypocrisy and injustices there is no need for self-inflicted pain or despair, but that one can convert those self-destructive forces into positive action? I think so.

But I had another process that I had to work through. If symbolically I had become Anna O., my mother was Bertha Pappenheim. Although I admired and respected Pappenheim, she, like my mother, was tough, disapproving, and unaffectionate — caring but distant. As I told my mother once, "Charity begins at home, not in the synagogue." Was I jealous that Pappenheim and my mother were able to find happiness and strength by caring for others? Or was it, perhaps, that I saw myself as weak and insecure while Pappenheim and my mother were strong, independent women?

On the other hand, was I being too analytical? Yes, but I saw my questions as necessary. Only after the psychological blocks had become clear to me could I be clear about what provided the impetus for Bertha Pappenheim to transform herself.

What I learned is this: My attraction to Anna O. is not to the fragile victim but to the source from which Pappenheim evolved. Pappenheim denied, discarded, and separated herself from her past. She threw away the "invalid" and focused on her strengths. I, who felt chained by my past, and others who felt similarly, could draw from her experience.

Although it is unlikely that we will ever know precisely how Bertha recovered, I believe there are several possibilities: her change of environment when she moved from Vienna to Frankfurt; her beginning a literary career that served a cathartic function by releasing the expressions of a disturbed, troubled mind; and her increased responsibility in her position at the orphanage in which she eventually became head administrator. She began to trust her own instincts and to act on them. She was willing to battle hostility and rejection. She became independent. In understanding the life she "had to conquer," she cured herself.

I am filled with indignant anger! I will hold on to it, and let
it burn within — as long as conditions justify. I will not
become blind to infamous and harmful acts; I will not excuse
things which are dishonorable and inexcusable.

May I but retain the strength to protest, again and again,
in angry indignation against every injustice! (Bertha
Pappenheim, undated)

I have often thought if one has nothing to love, to hate
something is a good substitute. (Bertha Pappenheim, letter,
10 May 1912)

Cora Berliner, a vice-president of the League of Jewish Women,
wrote of Pappenheim:

A volcano lived within this woman; it erupted when she
was angered . . . But . . . she only fought about things that
were directly involved in her goals . . . She felt . . . the
tragedy of these battles . . . Her fight against the abuse of
women was almost a physical pain for her . . . Thus the
passionate nature of her battle against white slavery.

Anger, it would seem, was an intense driving force within
Pappenheim's personality. It was all-consuming and persistent.
What was sadly missing, in my estimation, was intimacy, love, and
a sexual life.

I admired her ability to arouse the emotions and energies of
thousands of women, to call attention to the Jewish involvement in
the white slave trade, to battle for the rights (although she preferred
the word *duties*) of women within the Jewish community, and to
dramatically alter the course that her illness seemed to suggest. But
do I like her? Would I in any way want to emulate her?

Bertha Pappenheim's personality was contradictory. While she
could be combative, unbending, and strict, she could melt in relationships with children and reveal a completely different woman,
one full of warmth, kindness, and love. Once, on her birthday,
when a number of women presented her with gifts, she was overcome with tears. "Forgive me, I am so little used to love that it easily
overwhelms me," she explained.

And so I continued my search to try to understand Pappenheim's
character. I placed author's queries in the *New York Times*, the

Aufbau, and the *Jerusalem Post*. I followed all leads. Finally, I sought relatives of Breuer and of Pappenheim. I was amazed by the contrasts between the two families. Breuer's family was assimilated, very proper, very private. Pappenheim's was very Orthodox, very outgoing, very cooperative.

I wasn't prepared, however, for the comment of one of Pappenheim's relatives. In a heavy Eastern European accent, she said, "Why are you interested in Pappenheim? She was nothing but a nut and a lesbian." I was painfully stunned by what she said. Was that all she could see? It was as if someone had stabbed me in the chest.

In interviewing former associates of Pappenheim and children of staff members who were raised at Isenburg, Pappenheim's Home for Wayward Girls, I found a variety of opinions. They ranged from reverence for her austere methods for dealing with people to bitter criticism. One woman who used to participate in Pappenheim's salons with unmarried women reminded me of Pappenheim's humor, her dry wit, in a statement that had initially inspired my interest in her: "If there be any justice in the next life, women will make the laws and men will bear the children" (8 April 1922).

Freud had this to say in a letter to Marie Bonaparte (October 1925):

> She never married. And she has found great joy in life. Can you guess how? What she does? . . . She is active in societies for the protection of white women. Against prostitution! She speaks out against everything sexual.

It is true that Pappenheim took it upon herself with a strong religious zeal to combat the political, economic, and sexual exploitation of women. But to state that she spoke out against everything sexual is to misunderstand and distort what Pappenheim represented. Love, she sadly commented (and I assume she meant sexual love), had passed her by. Once, when experiencing a tremendous bout of loneliness, she said, "I am not necessary. For nothing." She considered her state of being alone a "defect." Her attitudes about sex were for her time empathic: "It is not the worst thing in the world to have made love with a boyfriend in adolescent passion." And she exhibited a rather enlightened attitude about the kind of women who should run Isenburg. Married women who knew a sex life, she felt, would be better able to meet the needs of the delinquent girls at the Home. They would be neither too strict not too lenient, as an unmarried woman might.

The question that I still need to examine is whether her repressed sexuality was at the basis of her drive to correct the inequalities that existed between men and women or whether it was her anger, which was so focused and targeted toward men. Why didn't, couldn't, wouldn't she marry? If I can answer these questions for her, then perhaps I can answer them for myself. I, too, have never married.

Frustrated that I couldn't get any of Pappenheim's thoughts on these issues (the summer before she died she went to Vienna and burned all the letters and documents of the first thirty years of her life), disillusioned by Freud's misconstructions regarding Anna O., and totally confused by Breuer's personal involvement — without denying the aid he provided in helping Anna O. on the road to recovery — I have sought more contemporary analyses.

To me there seem to be two schools of thought: the psychological and the historical. The psychological is male dominated and male oriented, constantly intent on viewing Pappenheim as a patient and never asking the question of how she recovered. There is still disagreement as to the nature of her illness. (If, as I suggested earlier, Pappenheim largely cured herself, then it would diminish the importance of the role of the therapist.) Aside from one lone analyst, Alexandra Symonds, who suggests that Anna O. was suffering from repressed rage, *not* repressed sexual desire, and that the nineteenth-century taboos against rage among women were far stronger than the taboos against sex, a sea of psychobabble engulfs such questions as the nature of her hallucinations. One lecture I attended examined whether the black snakes that Pappenheim "saw" were penises or feces!

The historical school of thought seems strident, anti-individualistic, feminist, and almost apologetic, without, however, providing any insight about who Pappenheim really was. Even Marion Kaplan's book avoids Pappenheim's emotional life by focusing on her later years within a sociological framework — the German-Jewish community.

No one has dealt with Pappenheim's emotional life. I still must. Now, after almost five years of research, the confrontation is between Pappenheim and me. I no longer can hide behind the cloak of history, psychology, or drama.

My relationship with Anna O./Bertha Pappenheim has been rocky and ambivalent. Walking through her life has been like traveling through a maze. I identify with Anna O., but I want the strength and courage of Bertha Pappenheim. Will it take my getting angry to harness my energies?

My confusion and struggle with Pappenheim is connected to my fears. At times I see her as a bitter, lonely, cranky old woman who turns exclusively to women for comfort and solace, and the inability to sustain a love relationship with a man or a woman seems to me a severe if not tragic flaw.

Pappenheim distrusted men who, unlike women, put their selfish interests first. She allowed no men on her board of directors and felt compelled to maintain a separatist attitude. She insisted that her attack on men was not individual; yet intimacy with men was beyond her. Her ever-increasing rage, which had crippled her during her illness, became externalized, and she viewed men as sexual abusers. Is the lack of intimacy with men or women what we share?

Bertha Pappenheim no doubt died a virgin. She longed for motherhood and considered it the highest career a woman could have. She resolved her conflict with this issue by describing "spiritual motherhood" and as such was the "mother" of her orphans. How will I resolve my angst at my childlessness?

Bertha Pappenheim was a remarkable woman. She led, I believe, an ironically fulfilling yet tragic life. First, a debilitating illness, then a miraculous recovery, followed by a career in which she institutionalized her anger at men and her concept of motherhood. She was horrified when her articles on the Jewish involvement in the white slave trade were reprinted in the Nazi pornographic newspaper *Der Stürmer*. There had been warnings, but she continued to lead Jews into Germany through the 1930s. Her concern about the spread of anti-Semitism was real, but she did not foresee the power of Hitler. She was called to appear before the SS and, although released, she understood. She took to bed, her spirit failing, and died soon after.

Let Pappenheim speak as she did in the mock obituaries that she wrote for herself (1 May 1934):

> She was a woman who for decades stubbornly fought for her ideas. Ideas of her times. But she did this by ways and means which tried to anticipate developments and were not to everybody's taste. What a pity! (*Family News*)

> She was by descent and training an Orthodox woman, she believed herself separated from her roots — obviously under revolutionary feminist influence — She was often hostile — but did not defy her origins. With her descent she

should have done more for Orthodoxy — let us remember that her father was a co-founder of the Schiffschul at Vienna. What a pity! (*Israelite*, an Orthodox publication)

. . . a woman of real gifts, indebted both to Jewish essence and German civilization yet she remained consciously outside our ranks because she sternly rejected ideas she did not like. What a pity! (*C. V. Journal*, patriotic German-Jewish)

An old and active enemy of our movement, though one cannot deny that she had Jewish consciousness, and strength. She believed herself a German, but she was an assimilationist. What a pity! (*Jewish Review*, Zionistic)

In 1904 she founded the Jewish Women's Federation — its importance is not yet fully understood. The Jews of the entire world — men and women — owe her thanks for this social achievement. But they withhold it. What a pity! (*Blatter des Judischen Frauenbundes*)

Through what has been a period of self-discovery and self-appraisal, Bertha Pappenheim has been a source of hope, triumph, and strength, providing for me a *raison d'être*. It is hard even now to let go. She wants to be heard and remembered.

Notes

1. Ernest Jones, *The Life and Work of Sigmund Freud*, vol. 1 (New York: Basic Books, 1953), 223-26.
2. Freud to Stefan Zweig, June 2, 1932, in Sigmund Freud, *The Freud/Jung Letters*, ed. William McGuire (Princeton: Princeton University Press, 1974), 413.
3. Jones, *Life and Work*, 223-26.
4. All references to Marie Bonaparte's *The Journal of My Analysis, 1925-26*, are courtesy of Dr. Frank R. Hartman, New York City.
5. First published in London, Ed Bristow's *Prostitution and Prejudice: The Jewish Fight Against White Slavery* was published by Schocken in 1983.

6. The best historical treatment of Pappenheim is Marion Kaplan's *The Jewish Feminist Movement in Germany* (Westport, Conn.: Greenwood Press, 1979).

7. Frank Sulloway, *Freud: Biologist of the Mind* (New York: Basic Books, 1979), 51.

8. Henri Ellenberger, "The Story of 'Anna O.': A Critical Review with New Data," *Journal of the History of the Behavioral Sciences* (1972): 279.

9. Bonaparte, *Journal*.

10. Sulloway, *Freud*, 99.

11. Only recently — after Anna Freud's death — did I discover that she had mistakenly referred to my request for the November 11, 1883, letter of her father's as November 10, 1883. It is extremely difficult to gain access to unpublished letters in the Sigmund Freud Archives, as evidenced by *New York Times's* articles on August 18, August 21, and November 9, 1981; *Newsweek*, November 30, 1981; and *New York Review of Books*, December 16, 1982. I was most pleased when Anna Freud honored my one request. I hope her heirs and the directors of the Sigmund Freud Archives will do the same. I intend to continue my quest for what really happened between the doctor and the patient.

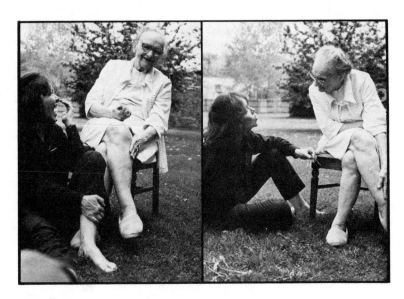

May Stevens and Alice Stevens

May Stevens

ORDINARY. EXTRAORDINARY.

In the mid-seventies class was a major divider of the women's movement. As a daughter of the working class I chose to place a working-class woman crippled by poverty, illness, and ignorance — in a word, crippled by class — next to the long shadow of a great political leader, a woman who was not a feminist although she was conscious of women's issues, not a Jewish nationalist although she was conscious of anti-Semitism, a woman who turned a superior education, relative affluence, and a successful familial background into the sublime chutzpah by which to go out to change the world.

Simone de Beauvoir said no woman ever thought she could change the world. Rosa Luxemburg knew we could and did. She knew there was only one way to stop her, the way they had to use — murder. Alice Stevens could not defend her own life. But she persevered and lives today in her eighty-ninth year, not worse off than her peers, equal at last.

Ingeborg Bachmann spoke of writing with the *burned hand on the nature of fire*. I write in this chain, in this triad of my mother, my political/spiritual inspirer, and myself who is flayed by their pain and set on fire by their triumphs. As I write and make these images, I and she and she, we are speaking. With my voice, I make us heard.

Luce Irigaray: *And what I wanted from you, Mother, was this: that in giving me life, you still remain alive.*

Rosa Luxemburg, zwölfjährig

Rosa Luxemburg [signature]

Rosa Luxemburg

Im Eden-Hotel: Der Mann mit hängendem Schnurrbart am Tisch ist Husar Rung
Jäger zu Pferde Krause bestätigt auf Befragen des Gerichtsvorsitzenden, daß am Tage nach dem Vorfall ein Photograph der
Gesellschaft im Eden-Hotel, um einen Tisch gruppiert, photographiert hat. Eine Kellnerin war auch dabei, und eine Wein-
flasche hat auf dem Tisch gestanden. Vorsitzender: „Das Ganze soll den Eindruck eines Zechgelages gemacht haben

Alia Dick aged 12, with her sister...
sister. Clinton, Mass...

Alia Dick Stevens with her first child
Barre, Mass. 1924

...Luxemburg, politician, revolutionary, theoretic...
...leader, murder victim. (1871 - 1919).
...e Stevens, mother, housewife, ironer and...
...r, inmate of hospitals and nursing...
...es (born 1895). Ordinary. Extraordinary.

Mais aussi pardonnez, si, plein d... beau zèle,
De tous vos pas fam...
Quelquefois du bon...
Et des auteurs...
Censeur un peu fâch...
Plus chelin à blâmer...

des auteurs ... j'attaque...
...seur un peu fâcheux, mais souvent nécessai...
...mer que savant à bien faire...

letter from Rosa Luxemburg to Fanny...

Mais aussi pardonnez, si, plein de ... beau zèle,
De tous vos pas fameux
Quelquefois du bon ...
Et des auteurs ...
Censeur un peu fâcheux,
Plus ... à blâmer que...

is aussi pardonnez, si, plein de...beau...
tous vos pas fameux obse...teur fidèle fid...
...je sépare le faux...fau...
...j'attaque...de...de
...x, mais souvent isent
...savant à bien faire...

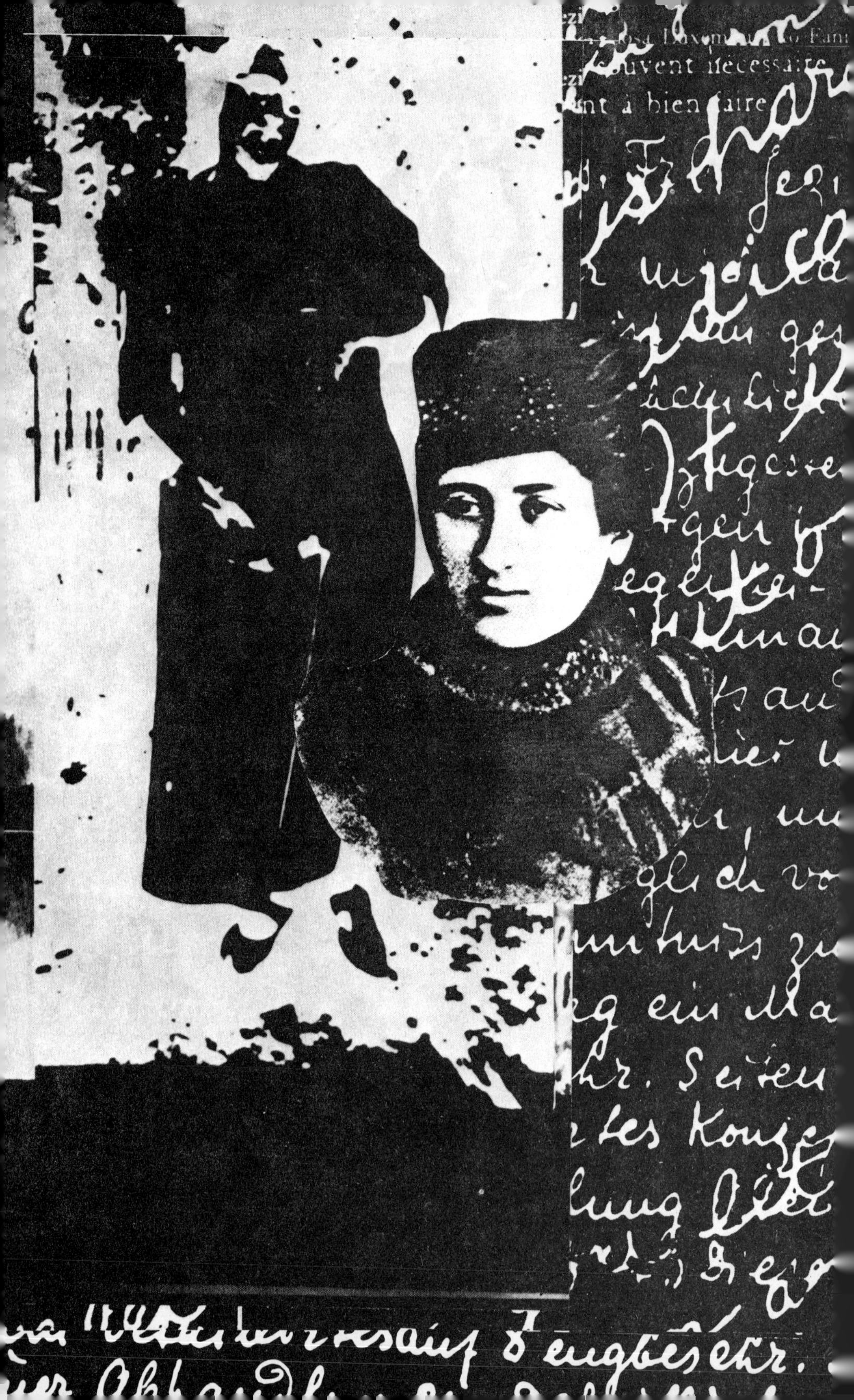
souvent nécessaire
à bien faire

This is Sunday, the deadliest of days
for prisoners and solitaries.

Wronke February 18, 1917

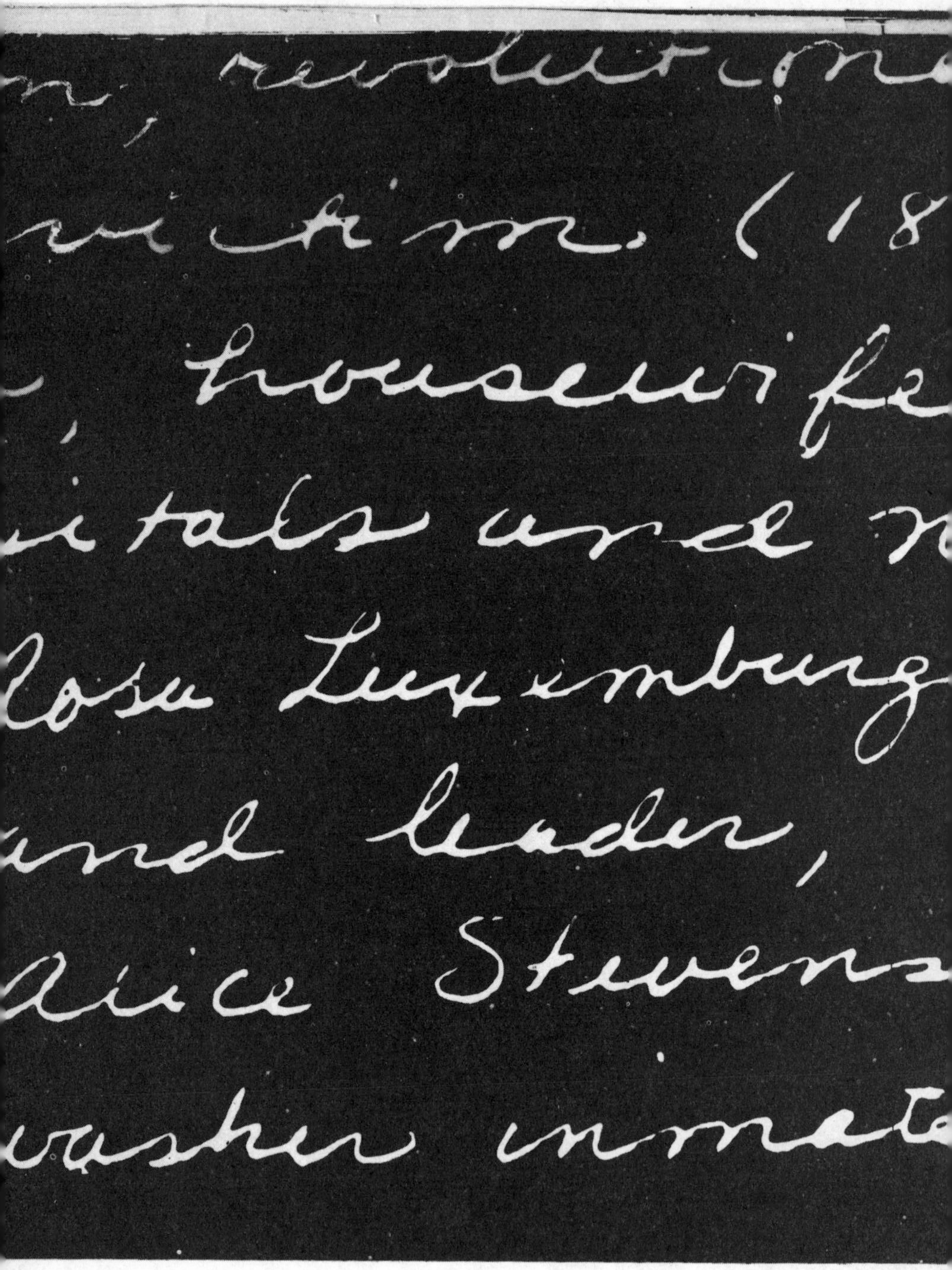

, revolutiona

victim. (18

, housewife

pitals and n

Rose Luxemburg

and leader,

Alice Stevens

washer inmate

ny , theoretica

r to you, let me once get out of prison and I shall
desperse your company of singing toads with trum
bloodhounds   see to it that you remain
   To be human is the main thing, and that m
strong and clear and of good cheer in spite

ned the red sunset over the corn   The wo
tiful in spite of all the misery and would
beautiful if there were no half-wits and cow
ke, 28 December 1916   Rosa Lu

of hospital.

ORDINARY. EXTRAORDINARY. A COLLAGE OF
WORDS AND IMAGES OF ROSA LUXEMBURG,
POLISH/GERMAN REVOLUTIONARY LEADER
AND THEORETICIAN, MURDER VICTIM (1871 –
1919) JUXTAPOSED WITH IMAGES AND WORDS
OF ALICE STEVENS (BORN 1895 –) HOUSE –
WIFE, MOTHER, WASHER AND IRONER, IN-
MATE OF HOSPITALS AND NURSING HOMES.
A FILMIC SEQUENCE OF DARKS AND LIGHTS
MOVING THROUGH CLOSE-UP TO LONG-VIEW
AND BACK. OBLIQUE. DIRECT. FRAGMENTS OF
ROSA'S THOUGHT FROM INTIMATE NOTES SENT
TO HER COMRADE AND LOVER, LEO JOGICHES,
AND TO HER FRIENDS; FROM AGIT-PROP PUB-
LISHED IN DIE ROTE FAHNE; AND FROM HER
SERIOUS SCIENTIFIC WRITINGS. IMAGES
FROM HER GIRLHOOD, HER MIDDLE LIFE,
AND THE FINAL PHOTOGRAPH OF HER MUR-
DERED HEAD. ALICE'S WORDS FROM THE
MEMORY OF AND LETTERS TO HER DAUGH-
TER. AN ARTIST'S BOOK EXAMINING AND
DOCUMENTING THE MARK OF A POLITICAL
WOMAN AND MARKING THE LIFE OF A
WOMAN WHOSE LIFE WOULD OTHERWISE
BE UNMARKED. ORDINARY. EXTRAORDINARY

THE WORDS OF ROSA LUXEMBURG

ON WRITING THE ACCUMULATION OF CAPITAL, HER MAJOR CONTRIBUTION TO POLITICAL AND ECONOMIC THEORY. TO HANS DIEFENBACH FROM PRISON, WRONKE, MAY 12, 1917:

THE PERIOD WHEN I WAS WRITING ACCUMULATION BELONGS TO THE HAPPIEST IN MY LIFE. I REALLY LIVED AS IF IN A STATE OF INTOXICATION, DAY AND NIGHT SEEING NOTHING BUT THIS ONE PROBLEM THAT WAS UNFOLDING ITSELF SO BEAUTIFULLY IN FRONT OF ME, AND I DON'T KNOW WHICH AFFORDED ME GREATER PLEASURE: THE THINKING PROCESS WHEREBY I PONDERED A COMPLICATED QUESTION WHILE SLOWLY WALKING UP AND DOWN THE ROOM...! OR THE SHAPING OF RESULTS INTO LITERARY FORM ON PAPER. DO YOU KNOW I WROTE THE ENTIRE 30 GALLEYS IN ONE GO WITHIN 4 MONTHS — SOMETHING UNHEARD OF! — AND THAT I SENT OFF THE ROUGH DRAFT TO THE PRINTER WITHOUT EVEN ONCE READING IT OVER?

NATURALLY, THE READER MUST, IN ORDER TO APPRECIATE MY "ANTI-CRITIQUE" BE A MASTER OF NATIONAL ECONOMY IN GENERAL AND MARXISM IN PARTICULAR, AND THAT TO THE NTH DEGREE. AND HOW MANY SUCH MORTALS ARE THERE TODAY? NOT A HALF-DOZEN. MY WORK IS FROM THIS STANDPOINT TRULY A LUXURY PRODUCT AND MIGHT JUST AS WELL BE

PRINTED ON HANDMADE PAPER.

IT IS ABOVE ALL NOW THE TENDENCY OF MY TASTE, IN SCIENTIFIC WORK AS WELL AS IN ART, TO TREASURE ONLY THE SIMPLE, THE CALM AND THE NOBLE: I NOW FIND THE MUCH-PRAISED FIRST VOLUME OF MARX'S CAPITAL WITH ITS SUPERABUNDANCE OF ROCOCO ORNAMENTATION IN THE HEGELIAN STYLE, AN ATROCITY (FOR WHICH FROM THE PARTY STANDPOINT I SHOULD BE PLACED IN A HOUSE OF CORRECTION FOR 5 YEARS AND DISGRACED FOR 10).

ON THE ROLE OF ORGANIZATION IN REVOLUTIONARY ACTIVITY (FIRST PUBLISHED IN ISKRA, JULY 10, 1904):

[LENIN] DECLARES THAT IT IS NO LONGER THE PROLETARIANS BUT CERTAIN INTELLECTUALS IN OUR PARTY WHO NEED TO BE EDUCATED IN THE MATTERS OF ORGANIZATION AND DISCIPLINE. HE GLORIFIES THE EDUCATIVE INFLUENCE OF THE FACTORY, WHICH, HE SAYS, ACCUSTOMS THE PROLETARIAT TO DISCIPLINE AND ORGANIZATION.

SAYING ALL THIS LENIN SEEMS TO DEMONSTRATE AGAIN THAT HIS CONCEPTION OF SOCIALIST ORGANIZATION IS QUITE MECHANISTIC. THE DISCIPLINE LENIN HAS IN MIND IS BEING IMPLANTED IN THE WORKING CLASS NOT ONLY BY THE FAC-

TORY BUT ALSO BY THE MILITARY AND THE EXISTING STATE BUREAUCRACY — BY THE ENTIRE MECHANISM OF THE CENTRALIZED STATE.

WE MISUSE WORDS AND WE PRACTICE SELF-DECEPTION WHEN WE APPLY THE SAME TERM — DISCIPLINE — TO SUCH DIS-SIMILAR NOTIONS AS: 1.) THE ABSENCE OF THOUGHT AND WILL IN A BODY WITH A THOUSAND AUTOMATICALLY MOVING HANDS AND LEGS, AND 2.) THE SPONTANEOUS COOR-DINATION OF THE CONSCIOUS POLITICAL ACTS OF A BODY OF MEN. WHAT IS THERE IN COMMON BETWEEN THE REGULATED DO-CILITY OF AN OPPRESSED CLASS AND THE SELF-DISCIPLINE AND ORGANIZATION OF A CLASS STRUGGLING FOR ITS EMANCIPATION?

TO LEO JOGICHES FROM BERLIN, 1898:

I WAKE UP AT 8, RUN INTO THE HALL, GRAB THE PAPERS AND LETTERS AND THEN DIVE BACK UNDER THE BEDCLOTHES AND GO THROUGH THE MOST IMPORTANT THINGS. THEN I HAVE A RUBDOWN WITH COLD WATER (REGULARLY EVERY DAY); I DRESS, DRINK A GLASS OF HOT MILK WITH BREAD AND BUTTER (THEY BRING ME MILK AND BREAD EVERY DAY) SITTING ON THE BALCONY. THEN I DRESS MYSELF RES-PECTABLY AND GO FOR AN HOUR'S WALK IN THE TIERGARTEN DAILY AND IN ANY WEATHER. NEXT I RETURN HOME, CHANGE, WRITE MY NOTES OR LETTERS.

I HAVE LUNCH AT 12:30 IN MY ROOM — MARVELOUS LUNCHEONS AND VERY HEALTHY! AFTER LUNCH EVERY DAY BANG ON THE SOFA TO SLEEP! AROUND 3 I GET UP, DRINK TEA AND SIT DOWN TO WRITE MORE NOTES OR LETTERS (DEPENDING ON HOW I GET ON IN THE MORNING) OR I WRITE BOOKS . . . . . AT 5 OR 6 I HAVE A CUP OF COCOA, CARRY ON WITH MY WORK OR MORE USUALLY GO TO THE POST OFFICE TO COLLECT AND SEND LETTERS (THIS IS THE HIGH SPOT OF MY DAY). AT 8 I HAVE DINNER — DO NOT BE SHOCKED — 3 SOFT-BOILED EGGS, BREAD AND BUTTER WITH CHEESE AND HAM AND SOME MORE HOT MILK. AROUND 10 I DRINK ANOTHER GLASS OF MILK (IT MAKES FULLY A LITER DAILY). I VERY MUCH LIKE WORKING IN THE EVENINGS. I HAVE MADE MYSELF A RED LAMPSHADE FOR MY LAMP AND SIT AT MY DESK JUST BY THE OPEN BALCONY, THE ROOM LOOKS LOVELY IN THE PINK DIMNESS AND I GET ALL THE FRESH AIR FROM THE GARDEN. AROUND 12 I WIND MY ALARM CLOCK, WHISTLE SOMETHING TO MYSELF AND THEN UNDRESS AND DIVE UNDER THE BEDCLOTHES . . .

TO LEO   MARCH 6, 1899:
NO COUPLE ON EARTH HAS THE CHANCE WE HAVE . . . .
WE WILL BOTH WORK AND OUR LIFE WILL BE PERFECT. WE WILL BE HAPPY, WE MUST.

WHEN I OPEN YOUR LETTERS AND SEE 6 SHEETS COVERED WITH DEBATES ABOUT THE POLISH SOCIALIST PARTY AND NOT A SINGLE WORD ABOUT ORDINARY LIFE, I FEEL FAINT.

DESPITE EVERYTHING YOU'VE TOLD ME ... I KEEP HARPING ON THE WORN-OUT TUNE, MAKING CLAIMS ON PERSONAL HAPPINESS. YES, I DO HAVE AN ACCURSED LONGING FOR HAPPINESS AND AM READY TO HAGGLE FOR MY DAILY PORTION WITH THE STUBBORNESS OF A MULE.

IF I'M INDEPENDENT ENOUGH TO PERFORM SINGLE-HANDED ON THE POLITICAL SCENE, THAT INDEPENDENCE MUST EXTEND TO BUYING A JACKET.

SEPT. 14, 1899

MY DEAR, DO ME A FAVOR AND STOP UN-DERLINING WORDS IN YOUR LETTERS; IT SETS MY TEETH ON EDGE. THE WORLD IS NOT FULL OF IDIOTS WHO, AS YOU THINK UNDERSTAND ONLY WHEN BASHED OVER THE HEAD WITH A CLUB-

JULY 16, 1897   ZURICH

IT MIGHT SEEM IRRATIONAL TO YOU, EVEN ABSURD, THAT I'M WRITING THIS LETTER — WE LIVE ONLY 10 STEPS APART AND MEET 3 TIMES A DAY.... WHY AM I WRITING INSTEAD OF TALKING TO YOU?

BECAUSE I'M UNEASY, HESITANT TO TALK ABOUT CERTAIN THINGS . . . . I CAN BE OPEN WITH YOU ONLY IN A WARM TRUSTING ATMOSPHERE, WHICH IS SO RARE WITH US NOWADAYS! YOU SEE, TODAY I WAS FILLED WITH A STRANGE FEELING THAT THE LAST FEW DAYS OF LONELINESS AND THINKING HAVE EVOKED IN ME. I HAD SO MANY THOUGHTS TO SHARE WITH YOU, BUT YOU WERE IN A CHEERFUL MOOD, DISTRACTED, YOU DIDN'T CARE FOR THE "PHYSICAL" WHICH WAS ALL I WANTED, YOU THOUGHT. IT HURT TERRIBLY, BUT AGAIN YOU THOUGHT I WAS CROSS MERELY BECAUSE YOU WERE LEAVING SO SOON.

LEO TO ROSA:

THERE ARE NO OTHER HANDS LIKE YOUR HANDS, DELICATE HANDS.

ROSA TO LEO: BERLIN, FEB. 11, 1902

FOR A CHANGE, AFTER THE MEETING IN MEERANE I WAS STRINGENTLY QUESTIONED ABOUT WOMEN'S RIGHTS AND MARRIAGE. A SPLENDID YOUNG WEAVER NAMED HOFFMAN HAS BEEN EAGERLY PURSUING THE QUESTION, READING BEBEL, LILI BRAUN, AND [THE] GLEICHHEIT. HE'S BEEN ARGUING TOOTH AND NAIL WITH THE OLDER COMRADES, WHO INSIST WOMEN BELONG IN THE HOME AND WANT US TO FIGHT FOR THE ABOLITION OF FACTORY

WORK FOR WOMEN. WHEN I AGREED WITH
HIM, HOFFMAN WAS TRIUMPHANT! "YOU
SEE," HE SHOUTED, "AUTHORITY SUPPORTS
ME!" WHEN ONE OF THE OLDER MEN
SAID IT WAS A SHAME FOR A PREGNANT
WOMAN TO WORK AMONG YOUNG MEN IN
A FACTORY, HOFFMAN CRIED, "THESE ARE
PERVERSE MORAL CONCEPTS! MIND YOU,
IF OUR LUXEMBURG WERE PREGNANT
DELIVERING HER SPEECH TODAY, I'D HAVE
LIKED HER EVEN BETTER!" I FELT LIKE
LAUGHING AT THIS UNEXPECTED DICTUM
BUT THEY ALL TOOK IT SO SERIOUSLY THAT
I HAD TO BITE MY LIP.

TO SONYA WHOSE HUSBAND KARL LIEB-
KNECHT, ROSA'S PARTNER IN REVOLUTION-
ARY LEADERSHIP, WAS ALSO IN PRISON:
BRESLAU, MID-DECEMBER 1917

THIS IS MY THIRD CHRISTMAS UNDER
LOCK AND KEY, BUT YOU NEEDN'T TAKE
IT TO HEART. I AM AS TRANQUIL AND
CHEERFUL AS EVER. LAST NIGHT I LAY
AWAKE FOR A LONG TIME. I HAVE TO GO
TO BED AT 10, BUT I CAN NEVER GET TO
SLEEP BEFORE ONE IN THE MORNING,
SO I LIE IN THE DARK PONDERING MANY
THINGS. LAST NIGHT MY THOUGHTS RAN
LIKE THIS: "HOW STRANGE IT IS THAT I
AM ALWAYS IN A SORT OF JOYFUL INTOX-
ICATION, THOUGH WITHOUT SUFFICIENT
CAUSE. HERE I AM LYING IN A DARK
CELL UPON A MATTRESS HARD AS STONE;

THE BUILDING HAS ITS USUAL CHURCHYARD QUIET, SO THAT ONE MIGHT AS WELL BE AL- READY ENTOMBED; THROUGH THE WINDOW THERE FALLS ACROSS THE BED A GLINT OF LIGHT FROM THE LAMP WHICH BURNS ALL NIGHT IN FRONT OF THE PRISON. AT INTERVALS I CAN HEAR FAINTLY IN THE DISTANCE THE NOISE OF A PASSING TRAIN OR CLOSE AT HAND THE DRY COUGH OF THE PRISON GUARD AS IN HIS HEAVY BOOTS, HE TAKES A FEW SLOW STRIDES TO STRETCH HIS LIMBS. THE GRATING OF THE GRAVEL BENEATH HIS FEET HAS SO HELPLESS A SOUND THAT ALL THE WEARINESS AND FUTILITY OF EX- ISTENCE SEEMS TO BE RADIATED THERE- BY INTO THE DAMP AND GLOOMY NIGHT. I LIE HERE ALONE AND IN SILENCE, ENVELOPED IN THE MANIFOLD BLACK WRAPPINGS OF DARKNESS, TEDIUM, UNFREEDOM AND WINTER — AND YET MY HEART BEATS WITH AN IMMEASUREABLE AND INCOMPRE- HENSIBLE INNER JOY. . . . DO NOT THINK I AM OFFERING YOU IMAGINARY JOYS, OR THAT I AM PREACHING ASCETICISM. I WANT YOU TO TASTE ALL THE REAL PLEASURES OF THE SENSES. MY ONE DESIRE IS TO GIVE YOU IN ADDITION MY INEXHAUSTIBLE SENSE OF INNER BLISS. COULD I DO SO, I SHOULD BE AT EASE ABOUT YOU, KNOWING THAT IN YOUR PASSAGE THROUGH LIFE YOU WERE CLAD IN A STAR-BESPANGLED CLOAK WHICH WOULD PROTECT YOU FROM EVERYTHING PETTY, TRIVIAL, OR HARASSING.

BRESLAU MARCH 24, 1918

MY DEAREST SONICHKA ——

IT IS SUCH A TERRIBLY LONG TIME SINCE
I LAST WROTE, BUT YOU HAVE BEEN OFTEN
IN MY MIND. ONE THING AFTER ANOTHER
SEEMS TO TAKE AWAY MY WISH TO WRITE
. . . . IF ONLY WE COULD BE TOGETHER,
STROLLING THROUGH THE COUNTRYSIDE
AND TALKING OF WHATEVER MIGHT COME
INTO OUR HEADS . . .

SHE WAS RELEASED IN NOVEMBER 1918 AFTER
THE ARMISTICE. SHE PLUNGED INTO REVOLU-
TIONARY WORK.

ON THE RUSSIAN REVOLUTION SHE WROTE:
THE DANGER BEGINS ONLY WHEN THEY
MAKE A VIRTUE OF NECESSITY AND WANT
TO FREEZE INTO A COMPLETE THEORETICAL
SYSTEM ALL THE TACTICS FORCED ON THEM
BY THESE FATAL CIRCUMSTANCES, AND WANT
TO RECOMMEND THEM TO THE INTERNATIONAL
PROLETARIAT AS A MODEL OF SOCIALIST TACTICS.

SHE REMEMBERED HER FELLOW INMATES
IN PRISON:

IN LEAVING THE HOSPITABLE ROOMS WHERE
WE RECENTLY RESIDED, LIEBKNECHT AND
I, —HE TAKING LEAVE OF HIS SHORN PRISON
COMRADES AND I OF MY POOR DEAR PROS-
TITUTE AND THIEF WITH WHOM I SPENT 3
AND A HALF YEARS UNDER THE SAME ROOF—

WE PROMISED THEM FAITHFULLY, AS THEIR
MOROSE GLANCES FOLLOWED US, THAT WE
WOULD NOT FORGET THEM.

HER TONGUE AND PEN WERE SHARP.
SHE WAS CALLED CANTANKEROUS. SHE
WROTE ON THE PROBLEM OF DICTATOR-
SHIP IN CHAPTER VI OF THE RUSSIAN
REVOLUTION:

THE PUBLIC LIFE OF COUNTRIES WITH
LIMITED FREEDOM IS SO POVERTY-STRIC-
KEN, SO MISERABLE, SO UNFRUITFUL, PRE-
CISELY BECAUSE, THROUGH THE EXCLUSION
OF DEMOCRACY, IT CUTS OFF THE LIVING
SOURCES OF ALL SPIRITUAL RICHES AND
PROGRESS.

SHE QUOTED REVELATIONS, CH iii, 15-16:

I KNOW THY WORKS, THAT THOU ART NEITHER
COLD NOR HOT; I WOULD THOU WERT COLD
OR HOT.

SO THEN BECAUSE THOU ART LUKEWARM,
AND NEITHER COLD NOR HOT, I WILL SPUE
THEE OUT OF MY MOUTH.

FIVE DAYS BEFORE SHE WAS MURDERED,
SHE WROTE:

'ORDER' REIGNS IN WARSAW! 'ORDER'
REIGNS IN PARIS! 'ORDER' REIGNS IN BER-
LIN! THIS IS HOW REPORTS OF THE GUARDIANS

OF 'ORDER' READ, EVERY HALF CENTURY, FROM ONE CENTER OF THE WORLD HISTO- RICAL STRUGGLE TO THE OTHER. AND THE EXULTING 'VICTORS' FAIL TO NOTICE THAT AN 'ORDER' THAT MUST BE MAINTAINED WITH PERIODIC BLOODY SLAUGHTERS IS IRRESISTABLY APPROACHING ITS HIS- TORICAL DESTINY, ITS DOWNFALL.

TOMORROW THE REVOLUTION WILL REAR ITS HEAD ONCE MORE, AND . . . WILL PROCLAIM, WITH TRUMPETS BLAZING:

I WAS, I AM, I WILL BE!

THE WORDS OF ALICE STEVENS

SHE LIVED IN A 4-ROOM HOUSE ON A WORK-
ING CLASS STREET FOR 20 YEARS. OVER
THE YEARS SHE SPOKE LESS AND LESS.
SHE DREW IN; LOST YEAR BY YEAR THE
HABIT OF SPEAKING. SHE SMILED. SHE NOD-
DED. I COULD MAKE HER LAUGH, OR BLUSH.
SOMETIMES SHE HELD ME, ROCKED ME.
BUT SHE HAD NO WORDS TO GIVE. WHAT
SHE WANTED TO SAY BECAME TOO BIG
TO BE SAYABLE, AND THE HABIT OF NOT
SPEAKING TOO FIXED. OR, AS SHE SAID
MUCH LATER: TOO BIG TO PUT YOUR TONGUE
AROUND.

SOME DAYS THE RESTRAINTS BROKE AND
WORDS CAME. WORDS ABOUT CARS THAT
DROVE BY IN THE NIGHT, BUT SHE KNEW
WHO THEY WERE. WORDS ABOUT VOICES
THAT CAME OVER THE RADIO, BUT SHE WAS
NOT FOOLED, SHE KNEW WHO THEY WERE.
WORDS ABOUT TURNING PICTURES TO THE
WALL: IT WASN'T SAFE TO LOOK AT THEM.

SHE NEVER ASKED WHY DO I RIDE IN
THE BACK OF THE CAR WITH THE CHIL-
DREN WHILE ANOTHER WOMAN RIDES UP
FRONT WITH MY HUSBAND? SHE NEVER
ASKED WHY IS A MOTHER NEVER A
WIFE NEVER A LOVER? SHE NEVER
ASKED WHY DOES MY HUSBAND CALL ME

BERTHA WHEN MY NAME IS ALICE?

THEY PUT HER AWAY IN A PLACE FOR
PEOPLE WHO CAN'T SPEAK, OR SPEAK IN
TONGUES. AFTER MANY YEARS SHE STOP-
PED BEING ANGRY. THEN SHE WAS CALM,
DISTRACTED, UTTERLY AMIABLE. BUT HER
FOOT MOVED CONSTANTLY, INVOLUNTARILY.
AND SHE HAD GAINED THE ABILITY TO
SPEAK, BUT LOST A LIFE TO SPEAK OF.

WHEN I WAS MAKING PAINTINGS BASED
ON MY FATHER'S IMAGE, SHE SAID: CAN'T
GET THAT BUILD OUT OF YOUR MIND, CAN YOU.

ON RECEIVING A LETTER FROM HER GRANDSON
IN HIS EARLY THIRTIES, SHE SAID: JUST A
BOY TALKING.

WHEN I CAME TO SEE HER, AFTER YEARS,
SHE SAID: WELL, I DECLARE · · ·

SHE WROTE FROM THE NURSING HOME,
FRAMINGHAM, MASS.:
MRS. MOORE HAS A SON BURIED ABROAD.
THEY HAD FLAG-WAVING ON THE LAWN.
ALL THE OLD CRIPPLES SAT AROUND. SHE
ENJOYED THE AFTERNOON. . . . PRETTY
QUIET FOURTH OF JULY.

· · · I'M GLAD YOU ARRIVED O.K. THE

DOUGHNUTS SOUND GOOD. YOU MAKE ME
HUNGRY. I'M GLAD YOU FEEL WELL AND
HAPPY. THE SUN IS SHINING, LOOKS BEAU-
TIFUL, GOOD. I WASHED MY BLOUSE THIS
MORNING. MRS. MOORE IS SOME BETTER.
YOUR LETTER WAS NICE AND LONG.

I WON AT BINGO, A BANANA. I DIDN'T
GET ANY MAIL TODAY.

DEAR MAY: YOUR LETTER ARRIVED TO-
DAY. SO GLAD TO HEAR FROM YOU. I SHOW-
ED TO MY NURSE. SHE SAID YOU MUST BE
QUITE AN ARTIST. I HAVEN'T GOT MUCH
NEWS. PLAYED BINGO YESTERDAY, WON
A CUPCAKE. MRS. MOORE ISN'T MUCH BETTER,
SHE SUFFERS WITH PAIN IN HER TOES. I
HAVEN'T HEARD FROM MARY NOR ANYBODY.
I COULD USE SOME IVORY SOAP. I HAVE-
N'T ANY CARDS. I HOPE YOU LIKE THIS
PAPER. I DO. MOTHER

WHEN SHE READ THE NEWSPAPER SHE
SAID: SOME PEOPLE DIED WHO NEVER
DIED BEFORE. THEY DIED JUST NOW, SHE
SAID.

ONCE SHE SAID, 80 YEARS OLD, LIVING IN A
NURSING HOME, EATING THE FOOD, WAIT-
ING FOR CHANGE, FORGETTING MORE EACH
DAY, SLIDING TOWARDS A SLIMMER CON-
SCIOUSNESS, SLIPPING SOFTLY AWAY:

EVERYBODY KNOWS ME.

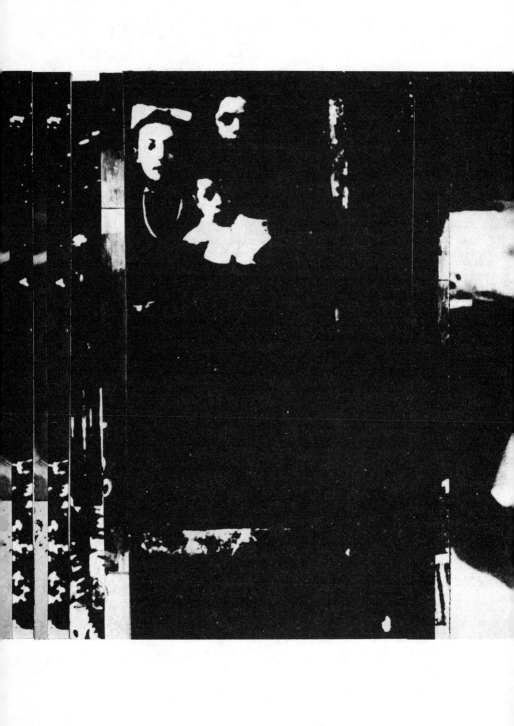

Mais aussi pardonnez, si, plein de ce beau zèle,
De tous vos pas fameux observateur fidèle,
Quelquefois du bon or je sépare le faux,
Et des auteurs grossiers j'attaque les défauts ;
Censeur un peu fâcheux, mais souvent nécessaire,
Plus enclin à blâmer que savant à bien faire.

du bon et je sépare le faux
peu fâcheux, mais souvent nécessaire
blâmer que savant à bien faire
Brief lag ein

Simone Weil

Michelle Cliff

Michelle Cliff

SISTER/OUTSIDER:
SOME THOUGHTS ON
SIMONE WEIL

I was an isolated child. I thought of myself as an outsider — and I hated to have attention drawn to me.

I tended to stay indoors. Partly because my parents were strict and saw America as a foreign country in which they didn't care for me to wander. "Stay close," they said. And I adjusted myself to their restrictions rather than rebel against them. The paths created by their restrictions, those I was permitted outside the home — to the library and back, to school and back — were well worn and suited me. I was for the most part an obedient child.

When I was older, I took to wearing an old khaki-colored raincoat once owned by a great-aunt of mine; an "old maid," she was a live-in housekeeper to a rich man in Oyster Bay and took me to Manhattan on her days off. She was in her late seventies and early eighties when I knew her, the sister of my great-grandmother, still working because she had nothing else to do, nowhere else to go. No children. The family complained she was "crotchety" and suffered from selective deafness. She died when I was sixteen, a week after she retired from her job. And I began to wear her raincoat. Walking around the block and to the library in it, telling myself I was a writer, carrying a pack of unsmoked cigarettes in the pocket.

Around the time of her death — I expect there was a connection — I began to stay in my room more than usual; rather, in the room carefully divided in half that I shared with my younger sister. My side of the room had a map of France on the wall and a jar into which

I put quarters and dimes, saving for the time when I would be able to get away. My great-aunt had stressed to me the necessity of independence and of "having your own money if you decide not to marry."

When the family went to dinner in a restaurant, on Sundays after church or on the evening following payday, I would often refuse to order a meal. I watched my father and mother and sister eat and sometimes accepted bits from their plates. I told myself my parents couldn't afford to buy another dinner; but I remember wanting to disappear, to merge with the leatherette of the booth or the heavy maple of the chair. My parents went along with my behavior, perhaps knowing, or thinking, that I would grow out of this self-denial — but probably naming it perversity. As they did when I wanted to attend a demonstration following the bombing which ended the lives of four Black girlchildren in Birmingham, Alabama.

We went to church. We girls attended Sunday school; our parents taught Sunday school. If nothing else — if for no other reason — shouldn't we mourn, protest the deaths of other children in Sunday school. Other children of color.

No. Stay close . . . Don't make waves . . . This is not our country.

But many members of our church, whose country it was, stayed clear of the demonstration. The exceptions were the white minister, who had suggested everyone join the protest, and a large number of the Black members of the congregation. For ours was the only integrated church in the vicinity — in New York in the sixties. Integrated in the sense that people of two races attended, sang and prayed together, but sat in defined areas, separated by the wide center aisle.

This daughter who did not date, who had high grades, who was a recluse from time to time, was also one of the most popular girls in school, making the other kids laugh and taking chances in the face of nonfamilial authority. I learned very early how to hide anything I didn't want others to see behind jokes. I split myself into parts — my mother and father would not have recognized me in school.

In my sophomore year in high school, in a class taught by an extremely elegant woman who looked somewhat like Lena Horne, I gave a report which I entitled "The Natural Superiority of Women," because in my travels I had found the book by Ashley Montagu. The other kids listened, maybe waiting for the punch line. I was deadly serious, although enjoying myself as I observed their reactions. The teacher was vaguely amused, perhaps remembering that my last report had been on Anita Loos's *Gentlemen Prefer Blondes*.

After reading Montagu's book, I turned to look for heroines — Amelia Earhart, Harriet Tubman, Susan B. Anthony. But I never talked with other girls about this, these discoveries I was making. I held on to a description of Amelia Earhart I read in a biography: "the girl in brown who walks alone."

It was not until several years later that I began to read the work of Simone Weil, but I think it necessary to tell you I was someone who managed to be unsettled by certain things I saw around me: that my aunt was working as a housekeeper in a pink-and-white starched uniform when most women her age I knew were resting from their life's work; that Black children were being murdered in America — blown to bits on Sunday mornings; that my mother and father were unable or unwilling to protest what they also saw; that in my high-school history classes no one mentioned Amelia Earhart or Harriet Tubman or Susan B. Anthony; that the center aisle of the church I belonged to seemed powered by a field of force. I realized that I was growing up, was becoming a woman, and I began to realize what some of these things would mean.

By 1970 I had finished college — not a very good college — with a B.A. in European history. The first member of my family to graduate from college, or even to attend one. I had been to Europe twice, on student fares and hitching around. And I had decided, along with a Black man I knew and a white homosexual man I knew, that to go to Europe forever was far easier than living in America. We thought "they" understood "us." I had also been through a serious illness, and at twenty-one I had to understand the fact that I was not immortal. Life was a very delicate gift and could easily be taken away. The Vietnam War had also taught me this: A boy I had known since childhood died when he stepped on an American land mine; his mother committed suicide. By 1970 I had bought my parents' philosophy in some way: This was not my country.

I was working in a publishing house in New York, in the production department. A colleague of mine, with whom I talked about books, gave me a copy of Simone Weil's *Selected Essays* to read. This man and I had a comfortable relationship that extended to having lunch, taking walks, and talking across the glass partitions of our tiny cubbies.

For me this relationship was not sexual — I had fallen in love with a woman — for the first time. I kept this fact to myself. Alternately frightened by it, alternately wondering if this extraordinary excitement I felt, this amazing warmth, would pass. I realized almost at once that I had never felt this way about anyone ever — or about myself. I had found a well, concealed within me, that I did not know existed. I could not believe I was "queer," as queer as the lesbians my parents used to point at on our annual two-week vacations in Provincetown. Men/women, they called them.

I never thought being queer could be joyful. I was afraid, yet I knew very well that I would be crazy to deny what I felt. I protected myself, keeping these feelings private, telling myself they were my business. As I sometimes felt my racial identity was my own business — only to be shared with others like me, or to shock into shame some white person, colleague or acquaintance, who made a stupid comment. My secret weapon. But how few of them were shamed; most often they expressed "sympathy" for my state, and I simply stopped speaking to them.

I did not admit my new knowledge to anyone — not even to the woman I loved — for a time. I never considered this new piece of identity political.

Because of my not-very-good college; because I couldn't afford to attend Mount Holyoke; because I am a mulatto from Jamaica, a colored immigrant to America, the child of a colonized society; because I am a female — all those pieces that fit together to form a pattern of difference, of outsiderhood, made me insecure about my mind. I am not of the class or race or sex or place of national origin that "thinkers" were from. I didn't feel able to carry on an intellectual conversation, to argue with any sense at all or without losing my temper, to win a game of chess. I felt dumb — in both senses of the word — much of the time.

Once I left college, my belief in the natural superiority of women had faded; I had come to know that such ideas had little viability in the real world, and I felt unable to defend them.

But I read Simone Weil and talked with my colleague about Weil's essays on the Romanesque, on poetry, socialism, the Great Beast, the human personality, the power of words, finding in her a mind which, though judged "brilliant," seemed to wander, to contradict itself, as did mine. Her writing seemed to travel in circles, wide arcs, not straight lines.

At that time I did not think about Simone Weil herself very much or exactly why her ideas appealed to me. Her complicated and idiosyncratic use of language, her insistence on the abstract, on "larger" questions, on disembodied forms and forces, on the perfect nature of the anonymous and the necessary erasure of the individual — all these aspects of her work made my knowledge of Simone herself very limited. Even her notebooks reveal little about her except that she was in thrall to the *idea* of Jesus Christ, in front of whom she saw herself as worthless. Unworthy.

I had been brought up under the idea of Jesus Christ; but I was breaking away. An adolescence in the church divided by the force field helped me turn from religion; I had lost my faith. In confirmation class the elders of the church taught us about the Elect, in which we had to profess belief. The Elect was formulated by John Calvin and consisted of that group of human beings God had already — before time, as the elders said — allowed into the ranks of the "saved." Those whose names were not compiled in God's heavenly roll would live and die as unreclaimed sinners. These men expected us to believe this without hesitation, rather than teaching us to question a belief which could sanction racism, classism, anti-Semitism, and could put them into practice in the very building in which we took our lessons. But the concept, of course, supported their world view, and people such as they — white and male and middle class — were its living proof.

There were other points of departure for me from church dogma, but the Elect stands out in my memory, apart from the others.

I think I might have been disturbed by Weil's excess of Christian belief, but my main quarrel then was with organized Christian religion; she had expressed her opposition to the Church (which she called the Great Beast baptized) absolutely. I understood Weil to be acting in imitation of Christ, and I did not take issue with that choice when I first read her work. While I did not choose to imitate Christ, and knew that it was beyond me, I did not condemn her choice — I may have admired it more than I am able to admit. I admired St. Teresa, whose ecstasies of faith were not unlike Weil's own. And she was also a brilliant woman. I did not ask myself why a Jew, Weil, would take this on, or what it would mean for a Jew to take it on.

And there are so many distractions in Weil's work, that the Christian piece can be overlooked for a time. The reader can dismiss books like *Waiting on God,* and turn instead to Weil's thoughts about Plato and Pythagoras, the Bhagavad Gita, Greek tragedy, Corneille and Racine (her Platonism is in fact as devout as her Christianity). And that is what I did. There are single sentences in Weil's notebooks, fragments even, which are able to nurture hours of speculation — about time, space, motion, the past. All the things which seem to be beyond us. Those things which I had been taught in my philosophy classes in college were the things of value. These things, removed from the mundane and day-to-day, were the things "brilliant" people contemplated. It never occurred to me to think about such contemplations as escape, intellectualizing, diversions — removing oneself from the real world.

And hadn't I also been taught that it is the *idea,* and not the person expressing the idea, that is most important? That ideas have a life of their own — are in fact immortal. (Weil did not think so; she thought ideas could be killed.) That the truth exists to be discovered and is not invented, constructed. That we and what we may perceive are the shadows of the things and not the things themselves. I think that for me Simone Weil at first consisted of her ideas. It was not until much later that I began to question what it was about her — to try to find out who she was, this lonely woman — and ask what had led her to write these things and to believe so absolutely in them.

I had found a woman with an exceptional mind and I thought I understood what she said. And that she spoke to me. Her words, although difficult, were accessible to me; perhaps I recognized her own sense of outsiderhood without even knowing it.

Weil dwelt often and consistently on the subject of oppression — oppression and its effects as she perceived them.

One has to state the facts, and not hide from anyone that millions of people are crushed by the social machine; one has to find out the causes, not only of oppression in general, but of such and such oppression in particular, then find out ways of making it less if one can. (*Lectures on Philosophy*)

This quotation is one of the most straightforward expressions of Weil's thought. Her vision of oppression was a radical one, in the sense that she emphasized over and again the extremity in which oppressed people live. She named the hopelessness, the damage done to those who are ground down day after day — like the workers she observed in her job at a factory in Paris. "If you think, you work more slowly," she wrote, describing one of the conditions of factory labor — to not be able to think, or be expected to think, in the noise and speed of the line. Weil compounded the oppression of factory work for herself. She never ate during her hours of work, for example; while the workers around her tempered their routine with food and conversation, Weil kept herself apart and turned her experience of the factory into one of extremity. When she could bear it no longer, she left. Of course the workers had no such choice.

Hopelessness ends with hopelessness. Weil believed that Western culture was absolutely irredeemable and that those of us who are outsiders according to the norms of that culture, those of us not included in the power structure, will forever labor under the effects of our oppression and what it has done to us. She states this in the passage quoted above; people are crushed by the social machine, and, once crushed, they are lost. Weil seemed unable to understand any form of survival within the system, any small act which might make the worker's situation less dismal and might be an act of revolt in itself, carried out by the worker for his or her own sake. The oppressed are lost and, she seems to suggest, without the imagination (because oppression has crushed their imaginations) to transform their situation in any real way. She describes this loss again and again:

> To lose more than a slave does is impossible, for he loses his whole inner life. A fragment of it he may get back if he sees the possibility of changing his fate, but this is his only hope. (*The Iliad, or the Poem of Force*)

Yes, slavery does damage people. But no, the slaves under the American slavocracy did not lose their inner lives. Envisioning freedom was an important aspect of their survival within the system, but I disagree that this vision was seen only with a fragment of their souls. It is more complicated than Weil is making it here.

Affliction was the name Weil gave to the state of oppressed people. Affliction being an internalized powerlessness, characterized by speechlessness, the inability of the oppressed to articulate in any real way. The oppressed, according to Weil, speak only in tongues, in what she called a "dull and ceaseless lamentation." When I first read her words about affliction, they made sense to me. Never including myself in the category of oppressed, because at that time I could not, I somehow understood what she said about speechlessness. I wanted to write, but I had no idea how or where to begin. I was tongue-tied for the most part. Something was wrong with me — I had an education, I read books — but I could not articulate in any real way. Even after I read Weil's words, I remained convinced that I was at fault; i.e., I was stupid. But I was still judging myself according to the standards of the dominant culture. I had rejected the theological concept of the Elect but not the secular Elect which defines culture and intellect. That is why I did not question her words "dull and ceaseless lamentation" until much later, when I understood more about expressions of resistance within oppression and when I recognized that the oppressors are determined to convince us that such resistance has not taken place: for example, Lincoln freed the slaves, Harriet Tubman (and others) did not organize and carry out a campaign which helped overthrow the slavocracy.

Who are the oppressed? For Weil they are the workers, under capitalism and socialism and communism. The colonized under imperialism. Those people, millions as she said, who have no power in the world and who live and die at the intentional whim of the managers, the dominators. These dominators are inspired and controlled by what Weil named the Great Beast — which for her was nationalism, statism, expansionism, warfare, fascism, totalitarianism.

In her truly extraordinary essay on Homer's *Iliad*, Weil observed that violence — named as might, force — was a primary means used by the state to carry out its program of oppression.

> The true hero of the *Iliad* is might. That might which is wielded by men, rules over them and before which man's flesh cringes.

> Due to might there where someone stood now stands no one. (*The Iliad, or the Poem of Force*)

But it is not just those who have violence done to them who are oppressed; it is every one of us who may become the chance victim of a violence at once deliberate and random in a system based on violence and oppression — governed by "the force that does not kill just yet." Force, might, violence keep us in our places, the places the state has decided will be ours. This violence ranges from the primitive combat of the Trojan War to the antiheretical campaigns of the Albigensian Crusade, the expansionism of imperial Rome, the organized genocide of what Weil called Hitlerism.

Like the American writer Lillian Smith, who stated that racism diminishes the racist as well as the person who is the object of his hatred, Weil observed that violence affects the violators also:

> . . . the conquering soldier is the scourge of nature. Possessed by war he, like the slave, becomes a thing, though his manner of doing so is different — over him too, words are powerless as over matter itself. (*The Iliad, or the Poem of Force*)

I am trying to remember what examples came into my mind when I first read Weil's essay on the *Iliad*. I know I thought about the war in Vietnam because I had been active in the antiwar movement in college, and I had known, for example, the boy who stepped on an American land mine. I probably thought about the murders of students at Jackson State and Kent State; perhaps I thought back to the bombings in Birmingham and the murders of Chaney, Goodman, and Schwerner. I would have remembered the murder of Martin Luther King, Jr., because his death had a deep effect on me. I wonder now if I thought about having lived my entire life during what people began calling the atomic age? I don't recall. It would have seemed to me then, as now, that postwar America was a true inheritor of the spirit of the Great Beast. It was not until later that I was equipped to examine more closely the character of the Great Beast and what sustains it. I would not have used the word *patriarchy*, for example, when I first read Weil. I would not have thought of myself as a victim of the Great Beast, even after I had been raped, because the rape had been committed by a man I had been dating, a white graduate of Oxford University, even though the bruises on my breasts, neck, and thighs took weeks to diminish. I didn't think of myself — a woman, a woman of color — as living under the state of siege Weil describes. As with my own speechlessness, I blamed myself. Now, having considered myself a lesbian, a woman of color, someone who is learning more and more to embrace her difference, I know well that I live in a state of siege.

While I have forgotten or dismissed many of Weil's ideas, I hold to her analysis of actual violence and potential violence more than before. I believe that living under the threat of violence compares to having actual violence done to you. Each is different in its effects, but they are related. Both act to modify behavior, to control the person who is threatened. Both act to damage one — because the person who is threatened must ask himself or herself what it is about him or her that makes violence possible, desirable. Both act to limit and perhaps obliterate freedom. And we may extend the definition of force and violence to include the violence committed when social programs are suddenly or gradually withdrawn, when access to housing or education is cut off, when a woman is denied control of her body. There is a violence involved in the consequences of poverty. A violence also that circles the life of a Black child in Atlanta, or elsewhere, who has *not* been murdered.

The violence committed against the self of one human being can travel through generations. When I read Helen Epstein's book *Children of the Holocaust,* which contains testimonies of the children of survivors of Nazi death camps, I thought again about Weil's idea. These children suffer from the violence of genocide differently than their elders, but they suffer just the same.

This violence breeds more than fear; there is a dulling in those of us who are oppressed which may preclude any action against oppression. May make the oppressed want only to pass into the dominant culture, rather than oppose it. What Weil gave me was the analysis; what a political movement — a feminist movement — gave me was the context in which to place the analysis.

And I also believe that the oppressor is damaged by his commitment to force and violence — else why would I feel such despair that the oppressor will ever turn his own course around. But I also know that it is up to us, those of us who are "other," to make the changes, or at least begin the changes which must happen in order to reconstruct society.

In the years when I was first reading Weil, working in publishing, later going to graduate school, even though I had doubts about my abilities, I convinced myself that I had to pass into the dominant culture — to "make it" on their terms. This belief was not absolute on my part, I felt some ambiguity about it, but I thought it would be the only way to survive. It was only when I rejected this ambition, and in rejecting came to terms with who I am, that I was able to understand Weil herself more clearly and how she herself was oppressed, afflicted.

I need to ask myself now why I ignored the fact that Simone Weil was a Jew. One who turned to mortification of the flesh and acted as if she were a martyr of the early Church. A Jew who starved herself to death during the years of the Holocaust. A Jewish woman who created her own death one year beyond the magical number of 33. And she seemed fully conscious of her self-sacrifice. How much was she conscious of? What drove her to it?

Weil wrote that when she read of the crucifixion she committed the sin of envy. What are we to understand when we read this:

> The human being can only escape from the collective by raising himself above the personal and entering into the impersonal.
>
> Perfection is impersonal. Our personality is the part of us which belongs to error and sin. The whole effort of the mystic has always been to become such that there is not a part left in his soul to say "I."
>
> . . . what is sacred in a human being is the impersonal in him. ("Human Personality," in *Selected Essays*)

When I first read Weil's essay on the human personality I did not examine how her belief in the perfect nature of the anonymous, the impersonal, might be connected to the obliteration of identity, the denial of the self, which accompanies, is necessary to, assimilation. Cannot the desire to erase the "I" also be the desire to deny the difference within us which the dominant culture has taught us is other, alien, wrong?

In these passages Weil is speaking of a high-level form of assimilation, to be sure, that in which the "sacred" part of a human being is joined with the larger oversoul, where the individual perceives her person as corrupt and her individuality, that which makes her different, to be denied. I wonder what "collective" Weil thought she was escaping. How had she erred and sinned? Maybe my use of the word *assimilation* is not quite right, meaning as it does a melding with the dominant earthly *collective*. But I do think that Weil's intellectual rejection of the individual, here and elsewhere, came from something deep within her. Perhaps joined to it was her lifelong difficulty with eating and her terror of being touched. She seemed to want to blend into the universe, not to be set apart. To erase herself. Not to be a Jew? A woman? I am not sure. I can only speculate from what I know about her life, and what I know about myself.

It is interesting to me that two women with extraordinary minds, two women who have meant a great deal to me, Simone Weil and Virginia Woolf, had an extreme aversion to food and had difficulty with physical intimacy. When Woolf suffered breakdowns she stopped eating; to "cure" her, the doctors and her husband force-fed her. Weil also stopped eating for periods: when she suffered headaches, she was physically unable to eat; at other times she refused food on the ground that others were starving. At the end of her life, rather than accept nourishment she ordered that her food be sent to the French troops at the front.

Much has been made of Weil's refusal to be touched. She was called the Red Virgin, and her biographer notes that Simone, even though physically frail, had studied some form of self-defense.

> Nothing seemed more detestable to her than to force upon a woman physical attentions that she did not desire. To speak of extreme instances, nothing filled her with more horror than rape. Mme. Weil said that she would have killed in no other situation, but perhaps she might have killed to prevent a rape or defend herself from it. This crime seemed to her even more frightful than murder. (*Simone Weil: A Life*, Simone Pétrement)

When I consider the absolute nature of Weil's hatred of violence, I am stunned by this description. What gave Weil a fury (because it seems more fury than fear) such that she might commit murder? I must also ask: Had she been raped? And, if so, knowing my own experience of rape, did she turn this fury against herself? Did she consider herself guilty because of it? When I was raped, I fantasized doing violence to the man who raped me, but more often I blamed myself. Because I had gone willingly to his apartment. Because I thought I could control the situation. Because it was the last thing I expected to happen. Because I couldn't believe it was rape.

Had Weil felt

> the other force, the force that does *not* kill, i.e.,that does not kill just yet. It will surely kill, it will possibly kill, or perhaps it merely hangs, poised and ready, over the head of the creature it *can* kill, at any moment, which is to say at every moment. In whatever aspect, its effect is the same: it turns [one] into a stone. From its first property . . . flows another, quite prodigious too in its own way, the ability to turn a human being into a thing while [she] is still alive . . . An extraordinary entity this, a thing that has a soul. (*The Iliad, or the Poem of Force*)

Does her brilliant analysis of the effects of violence, actual and potential, come from her own experience of violence? I can go no further with this — but I will always wonder about it.

Weil's mentions of Jews in her writings are few and far between, and when she refers to them she distances herself from them. She talks about the Hebrew people of the Old Testament, saying they became corrupt in what she cites as their pursuit of power. In a letter to a French authority, she constructs an intricate argument, defending herself as a non-Jew. Yet she was aware of the death camps and left France with her mother and father for New York. She says she is French and wants to form a unit of frontline nurses — she who claimed to detest nationalism; she knew that Hitler had to be defeated. But she does not say that she is Jewish. When she was refused employment as a teacher because she was a Jew, she wrote to another French authority'': . . . simply because of my name I have an original defect that it would be inhuman for me to transmit to children.'' Why couldn't she admit that being Jewish went deeper than her name?

I am not Jewish. I was not a Jew in Europe during the thirties or before or since. I feel presumptuous passing judgment on someone who may have internalized the anti-Semitism around her; on someone who was trying to survive. But she did not survive; she killed herself with a Christian hammer.

But I do know about the effects of internalized racism on the life and heart of a Black person. I know about people who cut themselves off from their pasts and their identities and so internalized racism that they ended by hating their pasts and their identities, and deeply hating themselves. Then there are others who walk through life as ghosts, holding their Blackness safe within and protecting it from anyone not like them. They may not hate themselves, but they hate the world in which they exist for the most part. Neither of these people is whole. Everything in the "larger" world has discouraged their wholeness. Some believe that assimilation is entirely possible. Others think they can assimilate to a certain degree — by using the system but remaining aloof from it. But of course any attempt at assimilation must have at its base an acknowledgment that what we are to begin with is somehow wrong. That we are "things with souls."

A French farmer's wife complained that Weil talked on and on, seemed obsessed by what she called the coming martyrdom of the Jews. This same woman complained that Weil never bathed. Milked the cows without first washing her hands. That she refused some cheese, saying she could not accept it when the "little Indochinese" were hungry. What did Weil understand by the "coming martyrdom" of the Jews? How much anti-Semitism is contained in the complaints of the Frenchwoman? Does this "obsession" of Weil's indicate some sense of her own Jewishness, and perhaps also a fear about it? Did she think that if her people were martyred they would be redeemed?

I once gave a graduate seminar on the work of Simone Weil. My professor, an intelligent and sympathetic man, turned to me, interrupting me in the middle of speaking, and said: "You do realize she was insane, don't you?" I nodded and muttered agreement, but I did not really believe him. I don't know; I have a great deal of difficulty with that particular judgment. I do think she was a woman mired in self-hatred, which she elevated to the level of metaphysics. A woman who spun herself into an isolation from which she would not emerge. She removed herself from any collective in her isolation. In her death she was released from any responsibility to the woman she was. Her absolute belief in the corruption of the individual and the hopelessness of her world view made any real political movement inaccessible to her; she joined several groups in her lifetime but never managed any sustained involvement. She probably had no choice but to die; and no doubt she saw this as good.

But self-hatred, internalized racism or anti-Semitism, can make you feel crazy, as can isolation. I fould that when I kept my identity — as a woman of color, a lesbian — to myself, I never forgot who I was, but I also isolated myself, calling it self-protection. I felt I knew the white straight world for what it was — a dangerous and hopeless place which seemed irredeemable. A place which could only hate me, in which I walked as a shadow.

Weil wrote about the Cathari, a Christian sect during the Middle Ages who lived in the Languedoc. Catharism was a heresy, and the Cathari were wiped out during the Albigensian Crusade. The central tenet of the sect was an absolute dichotomy between good and evil. The Cathari believed that there were two deities: the god of the New Testament, who ruled the spiritual world, and Satan, who ruled the world of matter. There were two classes of Cathari: the Believers and the Perfect. The Believers became perfect through a complicated rite know as *Consolamentum,* essentially a purification ceremony. The means to perfection according to the Cathari was absolute asceticism — represented, for example, by the practice of suicide through starvation.

Weil wrote in her notebooks: "The soul comes down and incarnates itself in order to know good and evil. On high it knows only good (Cathari tradition)."
This earthly life is essentially evil, the Cathari believed, and its end is to be hastened rather than delayed.

I feel that my relationship with Simone Weil has moved in a circle. I began almost in awe of her mind and imagination, ignoring what I found emotionally difficult, reminding myself always, she was a woman, an intellect. I have ended feeling that though her mind and imagination were truly extraordinary, she was caught somewhere, from there she could not move. *The Need for Roots* was the title of her last book; but she herself seems essentially rootless. Where did Weil find her roots? In the Platonic Academy of fifth-century Athens, the harmony and balance of the Pythagoreans, the mind/body split of the Cathari — all of whom held to the inferiority and danger of women and the threat of the outsider and unbeliever.
And with all this, she meant a lot to me. Her concept of interruption, that there is a continuum of human thought which is stopped, damaged, when ideas are killed; her belief in the power of violence, force, to create and maintain oppression — these are two elements in her writing that I remember and believe in. But I also regard her as a sister in some way, an isolated sister as I once felt isolated.
I am now thirty-six. I have come far from being the girl in brown who walks alone. I am still occasionally attracted by isolation, by living apart from the real world, but I also know that for me a life without engagement in a movement for change would not be worth living. She died at thirty-four, believing in the need for change, but believing also that all was lost and that the only change would be

achieved through death, bringing the separation of the soul from the thing in which it lived. That is how I read her life.

She wrote of Antigone:

> a human being who, all alone, without any backing dares to be in opposition to her own country and to the laws of that country, to the head of its government and who is naturally put to death.

Dora Carrington

J. J. Wilson

J. J. Wilson

CARRINGTON REVISITED

My first meeting with Dora Carrington (British painter, 1893-1932) was really a blind date. I was asked in 1971 to review *Carrington: Letters and Extracts from Her Diaries* for a special women's issue of the *Massachusetts Review*.[1] Book reviews had been rather casual encounters for me and I certainly had no inkling, as I settled down on an autumn day to read on my deck in a California redwood grove, that I would become involved in a long-term relationship.

Looking back (one of the pleasures of middle age!), I can see just from rereading the very first paragraph of the editor's preface by Carrington's good friend David Garnett that there was going to be trouble:

> The reader may ask: "Who was this woman Carrington anyway?" And when I reply that he should read this book to find out — for all her qualities good and bad are revealed in these letters — he may be annoyed and ask: "But to look at? Was she beautiful?"
>
> To provoke him still further I will say that he probably wouldn't have thought so, but that I enjoyed looking at her.[2]

The question Garnett starts with is a good one (though oddly phrased — "that woman Carrington") and could indeed have been addressed to me, as I knew nothing about Carrington at the time. I had been chosen to do the review only because I had done work on the British novelist Virginia Woolf and thus knew about the Bloomsbury group, that fascinating in-group of artists and intellectuals that included Virginia and Leonard Woolf, Vanessa Bell (Virginia's artist sister), Clive Bell (critic and Vanessa's sometime husband), Duncan Grant (the artist who lived at Charleston with Vanessa), Lytton Strachey (the biographer), John Maynard Keynes (the economist), Roger Fry (the art critic), and others. Carrington was a peripheral member of Bloomsbury only because of her long-term relationship with Lytton Strachey and indeed was rather intimidated by them, as we shall see. To return to the preface to her *Letters*, in 1971 I was as ignorant as anyone else about who Carrington was, and I would have agreed with David Garnett's answer to "read this book to find out," except that it was clearly not addressed to me but rather to some male reader whose response ("But to look at? Was she beautiful?") aroused in me all those latent fears of rejection I'd felt as a teenager (and still?): Are we then not worthy of attention because we are not beautiful? Suddenly I realized that I was identifying with the subject of this locker room conversation, Carrington, and not with the reader, this frivolous fellow whom the editor apparently had in mind as the primary audience. I was not even too interested in the fact that David Garnett "enjoyed looking at her" but wanted instead to know why Carrington was important enough for Garnett to have published her letters and diaries and why I should be spending my lovely autumn weekend reviewing them. Though I still felt somewhat vague about Carrington's value, I was beginning, through this first encounter with the editor, to realize my own value as a reviewer of Carrington.

Indeed, I came out as a feminist critic in that book review, recognizing for the first time (as I blush to admit) what I had to bring to scholarship that the "men of letters" could not be expected to.* And I am sure I felt emboldened by the feminist focus of the *Massachusetts Review* issue and by the warm support of its editors. But no matter what the context, I think I would have resented being left out of that invocation to "the reader" and that I would have been wary of some of David Garnett's interpretations. I did wonder why the facts that Carrington had deep attachments to her woman

---

*Interestingly, in a letter written to me in 1978, Carrington's brother Noel acknowledged that he had noticed early on "that generally the women critics were the more understanding" of his sister's life and work. A generous-minded, sensible person, he saw more easily than I the advantage of communication across time, nationality, and class lines between women.

friends, hated her menstrual periods, adored her brother, fell in love with an older man should be considered evidence that Carrington hated being a woman. My experience in many areas duplicated hers and yet I knew I enjoyed being a woman. Whatever the dangers of overidentification, these "alienation devices" in Garnett's preface forced me to try to establish my own relationship as directly as possible with Carrington herself.

I decided therefore at the outset to try to read her heavily edited letters for what was *not* there, to try to adjust for David Garnett's astigmatism of gender, and to ignore such leads as the following:

> Tens of thousands of young women have china-blue eyes, talk in little gasps and have sex trouble, but one does not want to wade through their correspondence. Carrington would have always been attractive to her friends; what makes her interesting and fascinating to subsequent generations is her relationship with Lytton Strachey, the critic who sprang into fame with *Eminent Victorians* and his biography of Queen Victoria.[3]
>
> Like a child, she . . . (phrase repeated three or four times on one page).[4]

Even at the time, I remembered that feminist critics were pointing out the similarities of language used to describe children and women and slaves in the Old South.

My urge to communicate directly with Carrington dictated the genre of my review, which was published, as you will see in the abridged version that follows, as a letter addressed "Dear Carrington" (she preferred that form of address to her Dickensian first name, Dora) and signed, "love, J. J. Wilson." As is characteristic of feminist criticism, according to our percipient editors, I had overtly deserted the so-called objective neutrality of the usual reviewer's stance. I wrote of her and to her, using her as my vehicle to understand the dilemma of women artists, past and present, who have so much trouble saying — and living — as Mary Cassatt did: "I am independent. I can live alone and I love to work."

Dear Carrington,

Who are you? I have recently been reading your personal letters to lovers and friends, and even excerpts from your diaries. What is more, I've been hearing gossip about you from Michael Holroyd

(*Lytton Strachey: The Years of Achievement 1910-1932*, vol. 2);[5] he appears to find your appeal to his friends more difficult to explain than any of their so-called deviant relationships. Your own editor, David Garnett, feels it necessary to reassure readers that though you were not a really beautiful woman, your letters are still worth considering. The male reviewers, responding predictably, almost unanimously declare you an artless and charming child, who must have resented being a woman, and whose love affairs are thus "all the more interesting" (this last curious conclusion from some Lolita fan perhaps?). There was one stand-out who preferred the pleasantly medieval epithet, "this wayward woman." Years ago in *Chrome Yellow*, Aldous Huxley called you "an exception . . . a *femme supérieure*," but that strikes me as the kind of phrase best kept in French because no one is very sure of its actual meaning. The best translation might be your own description of yourself: "I am more aware of everything than you suppose, or anyone perhaps supposes."[6]

One reason we may never know who you are is that all the primary texts are being filtered down to us through various male consciousnesses . . .

Would a woman editor have dwelled quite as much on your sexual "problems," for instance? I can guarantee that she would *not* have used the evidence that you had deep attachments to your women friends, that you hated your period, that you adored your brother, that you loved a man who couldn't/wouldn't ball you, that you married a man you didn't love, that you loved some men you didn't marry, and that you often felt guilty for spoiling the joy in a relationship, to declare you "an unconscious lesbian." While we might all agree that you experienced difficulty in deciding your sexual identity (who doesn't?), I wonder if your sexuality remained uncommitted because you fell in love with a homosexual, rather than the other way around as has been assumed.

Your love for Lytton Strachey is completely comprehensible to me, and so, alas, is your suicide after his death; he was a man who needed warmth more than he could offer it, a need you could and did fulfill. You found in Lytton an entirely absorbing *animus*, and only everyone's conviction, sadly Lytton's too, that you must not be satisfied caused you to seek satisfaction elsewhere, I suspect. Or it could be said that your Prince Charming was a split archetype: father in Lytton and husband in Ralph Partridge. Like being married to a Superego and an Id. Was your lover Gerald Brenan the ego? If so, your statement to Gerald, "And yet when it came to the point, I couldn't face giving up Ralph and Lytton for you," becomes of considerable psychological interest.[7] You don't fit patterns,

Carrington, and so people can't seem to stop gossiping about you, perhaps seeking through you as objective correlative some truer perception of their own sexual potentials. I am enough of a fatalist in such matters myself to agree with Lytton when he said: "Remember that I too have never had my moon! We are helpless in these things — dreadfully helpless."

Once entranced by Lytton, you set about becoming essential to him, and soon you are writing, as it happens in a letter to Virginia Woolf, that arch-debunker of the "angel in the house" syndrome: "How can I do woodblocks when for the last month, ever since in fact we left Northumberland, I've been a ministering angel, hewer of wood and drawer of water."[8] Later you complain that your "useful grimy hands" emptying chamber pots and making beds were all that made the elegant talk of some weekend guests possible and "I couldn't for a whole weekend do any painting."[9]

Obviously, however, domestic duties, the care of even such a household as Tidmarsh, would not be enough to deflect a true painting fervor. The process was rather more subtle than that, as I chart it in your letters and diaries, keeping my eyes open for the obstacles women find in becoming committed artists . . .

Lytton always needed a good deal of looking after, of course, but aside from his ill-health, an atmosphere of expectation prevailed around him (the general feeling being perhaps that so great an eccentricity must needs be justified by some great "work"); everything was arranged so that the future great man could produce, and produce he finally did. No one seems to have these sorts of expectations for you, Carrington; indeed all the expectations still seem to be that if you could just have gotten your sex life straightened out, you'd have been fine . . . And with a quality as fragile as creative confidence, these elements of support, expectation, belief are crucial. In a *ménage* where Lytton Strachey is accepted by all as The Creator, where Ralph Partridge's difficulties in finding a suitable career absorbed everyone's energies, a kind of credibility gap grew up around your image of yourself as a painter.

Garnett, in his preface, takes the men in your life to task for not encouraging you in your painting: ". . . and she became discouraged."[10] Strachey's biographer, Holroyd, on the other hand, writes in a footnote that "Lytton always encouraged Carrington with her painting . . . "[11] and gives it as his opinion that your inviolable shyness kept you from exhibiting. What do you say? Various revealing statements, such as "R[alph] P[artridge] is so busy tying up these books and typewriting *that I get rather merged into it* and find it interrupts my painting"[12] (italics mine). And even more ominous: "The alternative is to try to be a serious artist."[13] No "serious artist" sees that kind of commitment as an alternative, but women often do, of course. As Nancy Milford asks in the *New York Times Book Review:* "In the end is it so difficult to understand that as long as we continue to maintain the dichotomy of male as generative and female as gestative that the creative woman (as well, I believe, as the creative man) must face exceptional conflicts in her develop?"[14]

The effect of these conflicts on you, all this merging with others, this feeling the primacy of other commitments and roles, this painting of signboards and trunks and cups and dining room walls which Holroyd makes so much of,[15] was that your art did not develop. You did not give your painting the continuous plumbing, reaching, experimenting, and just time in front of the easel necessary to make it grow along with you. You begin to make decisions based on this diminished vision, as in a December 1922 entry when you choose not to start anything too big and difficult "or I know I shall then despair and give up the composition before it is finished."[16] And then later:

> I feel slightly depressed as I can't do any painting. *There is no reason* except that I feel I know what the result will be before I start on the picture and the result is so dull always it hardly seems worth beginning.[17]

Your painting had begun to bore you. In order to keep interested yourself, and I suspect, dear Carrington, to get some attention from your friends, to surprise and delight them, you began to use your superb technique in *tour de force* work such as the painting of the cook and the cat of the Biddesden wall which you refer to near the end: "perhaps one of the only pictures I have ever 'brought off'! I am glad Lytton saw it and liked it."[18] In this last reference you made to your art we have its epitaph. "Lytton saw it and liked it" is not motivation enough for being a serious painter; it is all too often the motivation behind much of women's creative activity — to dress so that someone will see and like them, to fix a meal that some will eat and like, to iron a shirt that can be worn and liked — but that kind of motivation is a limitation. Van Gogh or Kathe Kollwitz did not paint so that someone might see it and like it . . . Well, I hope my point is made, Carrington. I do not condemn the interior decorating even, except insofar as it was a sign of the deflection. After all, Vanessa Bell painted doors and walls all over her house, but the situation in Vanessa and Duncan's house, at Charleston, was quite different and the results were different too — babies were raised, lives lived, parties held, but everybody who wanted to paint, painted. The deflecting factors are complex but they worked on you, you who were "never quite so happy as when I paint."[19] You would never blame the gradual falling away from your art on anyone else, of course, and come closest to expressing the dilemma as you saw it in the following letter to Lytton:

> And yet do you know, this morning I felt these conflicting emotions are destroying my purpose for painting. That perhaps that feeling which I have had ever since I came to London years ago now, that I am not strong enough to live in this world of people, and paint, is a feeling which has complete truth in it. And yet when I envision leaving you and going like Gerald into isolation, I feel I should be so wretched that I should never have the spirit to work.[20]

Fortunately, the nice, the capping irony, is that out of your very need to "live in the world of people" has come this volume of letters, not a sublimation but a substitution perhaps for the art you did not do. As Gerald Brenan rather ingenuously exclaims in his review of the letters: "Who could ever have supposed that these rapidly scrawled, badly spelled sheets that she was continuously sending off to her friends could look so well in print?"[21] He goes on to claim them among the best letters to have been published in England in this century, however, and long ago writing to you yourself, from his mountain retreat at Yegen, he caught this essence and their importance well:

> . . . gesture, speech, walk, expression, seen through a medium of words; like the rustling of leaves, the voices of birds, the arrangement of natural forms. Education has not deadened in you this mode of expression, has not, as it has for nearly all of us, reduced speech and writing to the level of a vulgar formula, through which we can barely let our own natures be recognized.[22]

While fine poetic examples of your unique style and visual imagination leap to the eye when reading the letters (such as: ". . . with only the half-sucked acid drop of a moon for company,"[23] or "They [sensations] rush through my head like flames up a chimney"[24]), the example which sticks in my memory, neither poetic nor very visual, certainly demonstrates your originality and escape from vulgar formula: "The yellow cat has passed away. Dead as a ducat."[25] To follow the pious euphemism of "passed away" with the abrupt phrasing and startling analogy "Dead as a du*cat*" simply would not occur to someone who saw herself as a "serious writer." And yet it works. My daughter! My ducats!

So I am writing to congratulate you and to thank you, Carrington, and even here we are making literary history — think how few letters written by one woman to another have been preserved in literature (always excepting Clarissa's, which were hardly of the sisterhood is powerful variety). Would you, now at some Yegen where letters are slow arriving if at all, be surprised to know that your life has become allegory for many of us, that we know you better than we know our own friends, ourselves, that we recognize your own nature though we still wonder just who you really are . . .

love,

J. J. Wilson

Though I wrote then that Carrington's life had become allegory for many of us, I was nonetheless startled by the level on which my review was received. Instead of sinking like a stone leaving no trace other than an angry or a grateful letter from the author, the fate of any other reviews I had ever written, women began writing me letters that ran something like "Dear J.J. Wilson, I suspect you had me in mind as well as Carrington when you wrote about 'the effect of these conflicts on you, all this merging with others, this feeling the primacy of other commitments and roles' as deflections from developing our art." Friends, and even people I didn't know, took Carrington's life to heart, seeing it as a cautionary tale directed toward their own artistic potential, when of course I would never have had the confrontery to do such a thing. The reaction to my "personal" review was indeed personal, more so than I had bargained for.

These responses helped me recognize the universal dilemma of women artists, so many of whom feel, as Carrington said, "that I am not strong enough to live in this world of people, and paint."[26] I have come to honor women artists for feeling this tug, for staying with both life and work and trying through every sort of ingenuity — whether it be waking at 4 A.M. to work before the family gets up or using the lint from the dryer as *matière* for collages — to keep both going. Barbara Hepworth's studio crowded with the toys and tools of her triplet sons remains for me a more remarkable image of crea-tivity than the pristine studio of her friend Jean Arp. Even back in 1971, I questioned the advantages of Virginia Woolf's "room of one's own," having found on the basis of my own experience as well as of Carrington's that these proud citadels were too often besieged by the three demons of loneliness, laziness, and lust. I found myself able to follow with my feelings (unusual guides in those benighted days) her urge to lose herself in Lytton Strachey, to make herself essential to him, to love him in all the ways he could accept, while accepting his fatalistic view that "we're helpless in these things — dreadfully helpless."[27] I even accepted, though I mourned the life not led and the paintings not painted, her suicide after Lytton's death as the inevitable consequence of her earlier self-oblation.

In short, like many people suddenly fallen in love, I believed uncritically everything Carrington said, and here I think I paid a certain price for my partisan position. I believed her when she wrote to Virginia Woolf, "How can I do woodblocks when for the last month . . ."[28] I took her word for it when she complained that her "useful grimy hands" had been emptying chamber pots and "I couldn't for a whole weekend do any painting."[29] In a way, I fell for my own allegory, responding to our need for the cautionary tale, for a martyr perhaps. It suited my theory to see her as the victim of lack of support from society, from the Bloomsbury group (where was Roger Fry when she needed him?), and from her intimates. David Garnett too had lamented the lack of priority given her work by her husband, Ralph Partridge, and by her beloved Lytton, and one of the Sitwells wrote in 1973 that "the two or three paintings that Carrington left behind reveal her talent." Still, I should have known better, because of my feminist perspective.

After all, I know how my own letters and diaries decry my lack of productivity, my sloth, the interruptions, and so on. I am wiser now to the ways in which women artists, especially, describe themselves and their work with such self-deprecation, such diffidence, such despair, and this syndrome is particularly characteristic of someone who has been precocious as Carrington was, winning awards at the Slade Art School. The childless woman, too, rarely expects immor-tality, that anything of hers will last.

As a teacher of English composition, I should have recognized another syndrome too, from all the sly digs about Carrington's spellings. Garnett mentions that she was likely to spell *minute* as *minuet,* and Paul Levy notices that she spells her own name wrong on the cover of her journal. Carrington undoubtedly suffered from some degree of dyslexia, and while she compensated by developing strengths as an artist, she still had that image of herself as "dumb" that so many dyslexics carry around with them, though statistics actually show a correlation between dyslexia and intelligence. But to suffer this particular learning disability while seeking acceptance into a verbally hyperactive group consisting of the Stracheys, the Woolfs, and other Bloomsbury types must have put her under considerable stress at times and given her more cause to put herself down. This discovery also explains some of the original turns of phrases in Carrington's letters, by the way. Now I can see that the phrase I'd thought charming and original, the yellow cat "dead as a ducat," comes from the reading problem; she saw the word *du-cat* in pieces without its meaning attached. Dyslexia certainly added to her low self-esteem, to her lack of confidence and assertiveness, and to her frustrations.

Aside from this "discourse of the body," I should have realized as I now do, after studying the stories of more women artists who have died young, that their works are usually either collected in one memorial museum, like those of Paula Modersohn Becker, or distributed among family and friends as Carrington's were. They are rarely found in major museums or collections, because their value did not have time to become established. And, of course, Carrington was never in the art world; her isolation or at least marginality, her independence, her diffidence led to the sad fact that, as John Rothenstein recounted recently, in all the time he was director of the Tate Gallery, her work "was never mentioned by any Trustee at our meetings," resulting, as he says with "a certain shame," in her being "the most neglected serious painter of her time."[30] This being ignored, which resulted in our ignorance of her actual achievement, is a self-chosen position to some extent, as we see in an excerpt from one of her letters to fellow painter (and lover) Mark Gertler:

> The true life of an artist is, I am sure, all connected very closely with birds singing and branches against the sky, and not with Cafe Royals and intellectual people. Lately there have been the most beautiful moonlight nights. All the country and landscape looks glazed with many washes of beautiful blues and greens.[31]

She had a real painter's consciousness, as we see here, and while I can understand her distaste for the "Cafe Royals," the social pressures involved in "making it" as an artist, I do regret some of the consequences of that "princess and the pea" sensibility: no exhibits during her lifetime and that time cut short by her suicidal devotion to Lytton Strachey. Carrington, before her self-inflicted death in her late thirties, copied out the following lines from a seventeenth-century poem:

He first deceased, she for a little tried
to live without him, liked it not and died.[32]

What we all still had to learn about Carrington, I with my feminist perspective and Sir John Rothenstein with his art-world perspective, David Garnett, the Sitwells, Michael Holroyd, and so on, was that Carrington had indeed achieved a considerable body of work before her death. A recent exhibit in England of more than fifty pieces assembled from many private collections by her brother Noel, which I was fortunate enough to visit and photograph, shows us once and for all that Carrington was a fine painter and that her output was nothing to be ashamed of for someone who died so young. "It is in fact testimony to her extraordinary and dedicated energy that in a life of this kind she should have found time to pursue and develop her rare talent for painting and drawing," Rothenstein writes in his foreword to Noel Carrington's book on the exhibit.[33] Carrington said, "If I become a very good painter, no one can take that from me,"[34] but *I* almost did, with the best intentions in the world, through my ignorance and my mythmaking in that 1971 review. (Now, to my dismay, I find some people are still attached to the version of Carrington I adumbrated back in 1971 and do not even want to hear about a Carrington successful in her own and even in the art world's terms.)

What then have I learned and unlearned by this process so far? Is this essay a recantation, a retreat? It feels more like a step forward in developing my tools as a feminist critic. Certainly it cannot be considered a divergence from the personal and feminist path to set about evaluating Carrington by her actual work, now fortunately available, and not just by her own estimations of that work. Indeed, it has been an important lesson for me in my own friendships with artists and other women workers: I do not take them at their word so easily when they tell me how little they have accomplished, how muddled they are about their roles. I honor their modesty, but I also honor their work at home and in the studio. Their ambitions inevitably exceed their possibilities, with the concomitant feelings of disappointment those frustrated ambitions can engender. An unpublished letter from Carrington to novelist Rosamund Lehmann in

1928, which I read in the King's College Library, sums up this extremism of the artist:

> Dadie was charming. I enjoyed seeing him enormously, but the painting was sheer agony. [Carrington was doing some wall decorations for Dadie (George Rylands) in his rooms at Cambridge, decorations that are by the way still there.] It wouldn't come right and I got hysterical and fussed and then drank too many cocktails with Dadie, so the final results were deplorable. However — it can easily be painted over again next term. It's fatal if I work things out in detail first and think too much about them. It's rather maddening to have the ambition of Tintoretto and to paint like a diseased mouse.[35]

I think I could write another Dear Carrington letter now and it would be a better one, more positive and more accurate.

Dear Carrington:

I have just spent a wonderful afternoon at your exhibit at the Christ Church picture gallery at Oxford. It must be some satisfaction to you (despite your agony at showing people "what I have loved") to have so much of the work presented to the caring eye of those who love, as you do, the look of the fields in winter, the familiar tree in different seasons, and the people "so beautiful one quivered to look at them." Visitors have been flooding the gallery — the porters boasted to me that last Saturday was like St. Giles Fair Day!

The exhibit as a whole has a coherence and a solidity that I think would have surprised even you; it certainly surprised me! Why didn't you tell us more about the work you did do instead of the work you didn't? Well, I won't complain anymore, but really the painter who achieved Mrs. Box and Lady Strachey within a year of each other need not apologize about nonproductivity. The portraits are a lesson to me, showing the influence of Mark Gertler, of course, but giving besides — in the contrast between Annie the maid and your sister-in-law — a kind of study in class differences. Your subjects look out to us with a candor that is yours rather than theirs, I suspect. And then, as Alan Hollinghurst said in a *Listener* review, your paintings of Lytton Strachey have "none of the freakishness of the more celebrated Henry Lamb portrait" because they are seen "through the transforming light of intimacy."[36] Indeed, they remind me of Gabriele Munter's portrayals of her lover and teacher Kandinsky. Munter painted on glass, too, and her landscapes are as vividly seen as yours, though the technique is different. I wish you'd known of each other.

Why does everyone speak of Duncan Grant's influence on your decorative skills and not mention also Vanessa Bell? You enjoyed your rare visits to Charleston but did not really get much support from the artists there. And Roger Fry never encouraged you in your own work, though he did hire you to help with the highly technical restoration of the Mantegna frescoes, showing his respect for your technique.

Oh well, you are now everywhere admired, as much for your diversity of modes as for your big paintings — the Tidmarsh fantasy, the marvelous work from Yegen. The witty line drawings in your letters are compared to Picasso, but most of the viewers at your exhibit are not looking just at the caricatures but at something deeper. I heard one of them say, "these paintings have character." That seems the kind of review you would appreciate.

Your work is not "stridently personal," as Frida Kahlo's has been described, nor is it as personal and political as the great Kathe Kollwitz, but to me you too are of heroic stature, though your path did not lead to fame, long life, or social change. What others called whim, I see as choice — after all, you did choose to escape your family and live a determinedly unconventional life. Your choices may not always have been sensible, but you followed your heart. You may have betrayed yourself — and you certainly underestimated yourself — but you were ultimately true both to your art and to your other love, Lytton. You were an odd mixture of selfish and selfless, a hero and perhaps a martyr to your wish for privacy in a way different (and yet perhaps not so different) from that of Gwen John, painter sister of the almost too famous Augustus John.

I'd go on to discuss the connections I feel between her life and Gwen John's, I'd expand upon the connections I have mentioned with Munter. Oh, I'd have lots to say now that I know the work that is there. And then I'd probably end this letter with "like" instead of "love," and certainly with respect rather than pity.

I am glad to have had this opportunity to set the record straight, to "reflect publicly on my method and perspective," and to work on that "reconstruction of the Mind" that Adrienne Rich calls for in *The Will to Change*. The next change I'd like to make in developing my feminist perspective is not to be so grateful when the male critics like Rothenstein suddenly convert and make an (unprovable) over-statement such as the contrite "the most neglected serious painter of her time." I don't want to depend on having him on my side for my own conviction about Carrington's work, and Carrington's reputation should not have had to wait for his endorsement. We need to build alternative ways to identify and support nonmainstream artists and writers worthy of attention and a good balanced feminist perspective is helping to bring about this goal. I want to devote my next ten years to this task and am, of course, strengthened by all the good work I see going on around me.

Notes

1. *The Massachusetts Review* (Winter-Spring 1972). Reprinted in *Women: An Issue,* ed. Lee Edwards and Arlyn Diamond (Boston: Little, Brown, 1972), 291-96.
2. David Garnett, ed., *Carrington: Letters and Extracts from Her Diaries* (New York: Holt, Rinehart & Winston, 1970), 9.
3. Ibid., 10.
4. Ibid., 12.
5. Michael Holroyd *Lytton Strachey: The Years of Achievement 1910-1932,* vol. 2 (London: Heinemann, 1968).
6. Garnett, *Letters,* 224.
7. Ibid., 249.
8. Ibid., 106.
9. Ibid., 152.
10. Ibid., 13.
11. Holroyd, *Strachey,* 478.
12. Garnett, *Letters,* 173.
13. Ibid., 323.
14. *New York Times Book Review,* 19 September 1971, 50.
15. Holroyd, *Strachey,* 478.
16. Garnett, *Letters,* 237.
17. Ibid., 369.
18. Ibid., 496.
19. Ibid., 258.
20. Ibid., 170-71.
21. Gerald Brenan, *New York Review of Books,* 11 January 1971.
22. Holroyd, *Strachey,* 231.
23. Garnett, *Letters,* 281.
24. Ibid., 275.
25. Ibid., 337.
26. Ibid., 170-71.
27. Ibid., 183.
28. Ibid., 160.
29. Ibid., 152.
30. Sir John Rothenstein, foreword in *Carrington: Paintings, Drawings and Decorations,* ed. Noel Carrington (Oxford: Polytechnic Press, 1978).
31. Quoted in Rothenstein, *Paintings,* 11.
32. Garnett, *Letters,* 500.
33. Rothenstein, *Paintings,* 10.

34. Quoted in Michael Holroyd's review of Noel Carrington's *The Painter, The Sunday Times* 19 February 1978.
35. King's College Library, unpublished letter from Dora Carrington to Rosamund Lehmann, 1928.
36. Alan Hollinghurst, "On the River Pant," *The Listener,* 6 March 1978.

Shirtwaist Strikers, New York

Meredith Tax

Meredith Tax

I HAD BEEN HUNGRY ALL THE YEARS

I have spent the last fifteen years of my life writing about some obscure women, long dead, who were socialists, feminists, and labor organizers before World War I. I wrote about them first in a history book, *The Rising of the Women*, then in a novel, *Rivington Street*. During the same period I worked in the women's liberation movement and on the left; labored at a succession of largely menial jobs; lived in innumerable cold apartments in four cities; went through the hopeful beginnings and bitter dissolution of one marriage and, at length, began another; and raised a child. I also wrote leaflets, political manifestos, letters, unpublished short stories, songs, and children's books. But always I returned to this group of historical women, as if I could not really go on to anything else until I told their story.

In the beginning, it was their brave moments that captured me: Clara Lemlich at seventeen, standing up before the huge crowd of shirtwaist workers in New York's Cooper Union in 1909 and calling for a general strike; Elizabeth Gurley Flynn traveling back to mama in a bumpy cross-country train, extremely pregnant but unwilling to stay with her husband because he wanted her to give up organizing; Matilda Robbins, torn for many years between her work in the Industrial Workers of the World and her passion for a flashy actor who undermined her confidence and for whom she had contempt; Maggie Hinchey, the laundress-suffragist adopted and then abandoned by the feminist movement, writing to her friend Leonora

O'Reilly from a 1913 suffrage convention, "I feel as if I have butted in where I was not wanted." And Leonora O'Reilly herself, the brilliant child-laborer rescued from factory life by fascinated settlement workers. They saw her as a beacon of hope to other working girls, yet she carried with her the mementos of her class: heart disease caused by her early labors and a bitterness and unwillingness to be patronized by well-meaning ladies who didn't think before they spoke.

I loved these women for their conflicts: between work and love, politics and family, the feminist movement and the labor movement, the joys of poetry and the discipline of analysis, the grindstone of social responsibility and the illness or pregnancy or physical breakdown that forced them at last to take a rest from lives that were too hard. I loved their voices, their ungrammatical eloquence, like these words of a Chicago garment worker in 1910:

> What bothers me most is time is passing. Time is passing and everything is missed. I am not living, I am only working.
>
> But life means so much, it holds so much, and I have no time for any of it; I just work.
>
> In the busy time I work so hard . . . I am too weary for anything but supper and bed. Sometimes union meetings, yes, because I must go. But I have no mind and nothing left in me. The busy time means to earn enough money not only for today but to cover the slack time, and then when the slack time comes I am not so tired, I have more time, but I have no money, and time is passing and everything is missed.[1]

These immigrant cadences, like those of my own grandparents, were to me the true voice of feeling and moved me as great literature does.

Of course I romanticized these women at first; it was 1969 and we were all looking for heroines who could show that women knew everything even when they'd been taught nothing. Our movement needed a past. How had these earlier organizers combined the personal and the political? How had they bridged the chasm between middle-class and working-class women? We needed answers, for although the women's liberation movement seemed able to attract hundreds of members wherever it hung out a shingle, what was our program? What organizational form did we want? How could we develop a strategy? Did our inability to grasp these problems have something to do with how middle class we all were?

Was the women's movement different when it had more workers in it?

I would try to find out. I would write a history book.

It wasn't a job I'd been trained to do. I grew up in the fifties, in a midwestern suburb where excessive thinking on any subject was discouraged, expecially for girls. I never met a woman who had a career, although I understood that some of my mother's friends had had jobs before they married. The only things women did besides "homemaking" were "social" (playing bridge, going to the country club) or "community service" (being on the temple women's committee, fundraising for Israel, helping out at hospitals). I knew no way of life that seemed more meaningful to me, though I also knew I could never feel at home in Milwaukee. There would be more choices in a more cosmopolitan place. I went east to college.

There, after experimenting with theater and art, I settled down to write, only to find I could not write fiction. My goal was "self-expression," but this left me with nothing to write about, since my life seemed to me so trivial, without adventure, even boring. I could write about it cleverly, but mere wit did not interest me; I wanted to be great. This ill-concealed ambition did not sit well with most of my teachers (all male) or the boys I went out with; all made it clear that hubris was reserved for their own sex. "Why do you always have to write these long, analytical papers?" asked one boy impatiently. "Why can't you write little poems?"

Yet the only sufficiently challenging projects were the papers I set myself, grand schema of literary typologies. Did this mean I should become a graduate student? Perhaps later on, when I had gained wisdom through experience, I would be able to write fiction. I went off to London to study the great works of English literature, still hoping to find role models for an acceptable way of life if I only traveled far enough from home. In Europe I would become an aristocrat of the imagination, like Henry James's "heiress of all the ages." I did not understand that the sources of my misery were political, not geographical. I knew nothing of politics.

The sixties changed that. Politics was in the air I breathed. Reading the newspapers — the war in Vietnam, the assassinations of Martin Luther King, Jr., and Malcolm X, the riots all over the country — became unbearable. Things began to come together for me. The pain my country was inflicting on the world, the racism within it, the emptiness of my own life — all were connected and were tied to the self-satisfied, prosperous boosterism of the community I'd grown up in, where there was no room for oversensitive children or intellectual females. There was a system in all this and its name was imperialism. Feeling as I did, I had two choices. I could try to block out my own sense of reality and continue as I was, but this felt more and more like going mad. Or I could change my life by trying to change the world — starting with the war.

I plunged into the antiwar movement. Within a few months my thesis ceased to interest me; I never finished it. I found I had a talent for politics and was a natural administrator. For the first time, hard work had some point. I came back to the United States, to Boston, because it made more sense to do antiwar work here than in London. I was ceaselessly active. But I wasn't writing, except for an occasional leaflet.

The women's movement gave me a way to write. It connected me directly with an audience, a community; at last I found people like me to talk to — thousands of them. I began to find my own style, to get beyond the easy wit and academic cleverness that had served me well in school but had always felt like a con game. First in speeches, then in an essay called "Woman and Her Mind," I began to hear my voice — still raw, wordy, and full of uncontrolled pain, but reaching beyond irony to feeling. The essay was excerpted in many underground newspapers and printed as a pamphlet by the New England Free Press. It sold more copies through the mail, without advertising, than anything I've ever written since — but it cost only 35 cents and I never made a penny from it.

When I decided to write a history book, in 1970, I thought it desirable to find a more commercial publisher. I wrote an ambitious proposal, covering virtually the entire history of feminist organization in the United States, about which I knew next to nothing; and I found a publisher immediately. Shulamith Firestone's *The Dialectic of Sex*, one of the first radical feminist manifestos, had just come out and was creating a sensation, and everyone wanted a piece of the new women's liberation market. Could I get my book done in two years? Sure, why not? My organizing wouldn't stand in my way; research and social practice would go hand in hand. We had our own group in Boston now, Bread & Roses, one of the first socialist-feminist organizations, so everything seemed under control.

But two years later Bread & Roses was falling apart and all my study couldn't teach me how to put it back together. Nor was my writing zipping along. Everything around me was in turmoil. SDS had disintegrated; the Black Panthers were being destroyed; the antiwar movement was still active because of the government's bombs but was shapeless and full of contradictions. I felt abandoned and cut off. Marxists told me the workers were the most revolutionary force in society, so why didn't the working class come and rescue us from this mess? We couldn't even seem to broaden the base of the women's movement. But I knew this had been done in the past: The Women's Trade Union League, founded in 1904, had recruited workers like Leonora O'Reilly who could lead it and give it strength.

But soon I found that Leonora O'Reilly had had problems working in the league. She'd resigned three times because she resented being patronized. Other workers had similar difficulties. Did that mean a women's movement broader than the middle class was impossible? I couldn't figure it out. I had no theoretical understanding that would have enabled me to put together the contradictory bits of evidence I found.

In 1972, like many of the perplexed, I turned to the study of Marxism-Leninism, especially as it seemed to be practised in China. I found a way of thinking that held more excitement and potential than any I had previously explored. This was not the crude materialistic reductionism of the Marxists I'd previously encountered, but a supple dialectical method that could balance tensions between class and race and gender, culture and material circumstances, individual and organization. At least, it held that promise. I have never learned so much so quickly as in that year of study. Sometimes I felt as if my head would burst. And my study had a powerful impact on my ability to understand problems of women's history, such as the IWW's approach to organizing women:

> The IWW's second major contribution to work with women was its effort to integrate women's fundamental demand for reproductive freedom with the general class struggle, to take the demand for birth control into the labor movement and bring out its class aspects. Not only did the IWW agitate around the need for access to birth control information; it actively distributed such information at a time when to do so was to court arrest. This . . . stood in startling contrast to the rest of the labor movement's avoidance of the dangerous issues of reproduction and sexuality . . . IWW practice on the birth control issue showed that it could be militant about the needs of women as well as about economic issues. By bringing these two realms together, the IWW added a new dimension to both the labor movement and the movement for women's liberation.[2]

Applying Marxist-Leninist theory to the present was harder than writing history. Bread & Roses was gone by this time, and I had found people to work with who were trying to formulate a revolutionary strategy for the United States. We applied theory in a rather slapdash way, like putting on a coat of paint without examining the wall underneath, but we were in a hurry. We needed to build a movement that wouldn't fall apart so easily; to us that meant it had to be based in the working class and led by a Leninist party. Those of us who were willing should declass ourselves and go into the factories to build links with workers, learn from them, teach them Marxism, and recruit them into some future party.

I moved to Chicago and went to work in an electronics factory, where I learned a lot more than I taught. Factory work was exhausting and I wasn't very good at it, but it was fascinating. I changed in ways that brought me closer to the women in my book. I began to understand work and hardship and the long haul. But I did not become proletarian enough for my political associates. I kept wanting to work in the women's movement — clearly I was an unregenerate feminist, always backsliding. Even my husband, who had been doing factory work for years, could not understand why I was always making trouble about women's issues. Eventually I found myself alone, a single mother, with no support group of any kind.

Thrown back on my own resources, I remembered those long-dead women organizers whose groups had fallen apart or abandoned them, who had no families, who were losers, as I felt myself to be. Like Maggie Hinchey in 1918, when she lost her connection with the women's movement and went back to work in a laundry:

> I lost my bread and also lost the light or sunshine when I lost my work now I have to work long hours in darkness and take my rest in a cellor and work until 9 oclock at night for 18 a week in my last job and no work I received 32 a week . . . so we will have to find an org that will stand by the working women that we can trust wont sell us out while our nose is to the grinding stone.[3]

Or like Kate Richards O'Hare, one of the very few women to reach the exalted heights of the National Executive Committee of the Socialist Party:

> My experience on the N.E.C. gave me an excellent chance to study the antics of the male who feels that his domain has been treacherously invaded by a female. Only Shaw could do justice to the humor of the paternalistic patronage, the lofty scorn, the fatherly solicitude I enjoyed lest my weak and faltering footsteps be led astray in the dangerous quagmires of party service. I am happy to say that I managed to extract enough fun from the situation to make the annoyance bearable, though I was totally unable to be of

any service to the party. I am absolutely sure that my experience has also been the experience of every woman in the party who has ever held a position or accomplished a piece of party work that some man felt it would have been an advantage for him to have held or done.[4]

Perhaps now I could give these women a voice. I completed the second draft of my book while working full time as a nurse's aide, barely able to pay for food, child care, and carfare. I would rise at 5:30, get my baby up and to the sitter, and be at the hospital by 7. I'd get off work at 4, pick up the baby, feed, bathe, and play with her, then put her to bed. I'd sleep from 10 until 2. Then I'd write for two hours, take another nap, and begin again. It didn't leave much time for social or family life, but I had none to speak of.

In 1976, I moved back east, where I had friends, and began to rebuild my life. I submitted my book to the publisher. But my once enthusiastic editor no longer liked it. It hadn't turned out the way she'd hoped. It wasn't well written. She hired her lover, a noted left-wing authority on trade-unionism, to read it, and he didn't agree with the politics; he thought it was "too Leninist." Besides, her publishing house felt the market for women's books had peaked. Wasn't the feminist movement dead? She said I shouldn't give up hope; they might still publish the book. I should make some more revisions and, since I had quoted extensively from books and manuscript collections, I should write letters asking permission to quote.

All that fall, I spent the little free time I had writing permission letters — only to be informed that my publisher was dropping the book. Although my editor had told me to take all the time I wished, my contract specified a deadline of two years and I was late. My editor had decided to move to another publishing house and wasn't taking my book with her; it just wasn't good enough. The publishing company sent me a letter advising me that they probably wouldn't sue me to get back the $4000 advance I had gotten over the years, as long as I didn't sell the book to anyone else.

I was devastated. Years of work blown away! They were probably right that the book was no good. Nothing I'd ever done had amounted to anything. There was no solution. I sent the manuscript to two other publishers, but they weren't interested. A small alternative press was, but it didn't have $4000 to buy out the first publisher. I was working as a legal secretary, borrowing money to keep my child in preschool, and doing literary piecework — copyediting, book reviewing — at night to make ends meet. I could no more get $4000 than I could get $400,000. I put my book aside in despair.

I had obtained book-reviewing work through want ads in the *New York Times*. I was paid $25 a shot for blurbs about mass-market novels, mainly historical romances about queens and courtesans and Regency belles, books aimed at America's housewives and working women. None of it was foreign to me. I'd grown up on a slightly higher grade of the same sort of novel. When I moved from the young adult to the adult sections of the library, I went from Louisa May Alcott to Daphne Du Maurier and Annemarie Selinko without even shifting gears. I always knew there were two kinds of books, men's and women's, and while I sometimes raced through the books my father brought home — books about wars and doctors and murders — I preferred my own, about love and family. If they had some history thrown in, all the better. I even read some men's books — Kenneth Roberts and Captain Horatio Hornblower — just for the history in them.

So it was obvious to me that the main way to get history into the hands of masses of women readers was in the form of a novel. It wasn't enough anymore to get into the libraries; such a novel would have to be a mass-distributed paperback, so that people who didn't go to libraries or bookstores could get it at the drugstore, supermarket, or shopping mall.

I had thought about this idea quite a bit over the years, and now, reviewing historical novels, I knew I could do better than many of them. But I had no time. Not only was I caring for a child alone and holding down two or three jobs, but once the right-wing attack on abortion began in 1977 I became active in the women's movement again.

Then, in 1978, my situation was transformed. I had left my job as legal secretary for one at a small magazine. When the magazine changed hands after six months, I was laid off. It seemed like a miracle — I could collect unemployment! For the first time in years, I had space to read and think.

I'd been carrying around a microfilm since 1972, without having time to read it. It was from the papers of a labor organizer in Chicago in the 1880s, and I hoped it would contain information about the activities of his wife, Elizabeth Morgan, an early organizer of women's unions. It did more than that. It turned out to be an archive of clippings about an almost unknown but extremely important women's organization, the Illinois Women's Alliance, which filled in gaps that had puzzled me for years.

In my history book I had focused on the problems of alliances between working-class and middle-class women. The organizations I had studied, such as the Women's Trade Union League, demonstrated that such alliances were necessary and helpful, yet seemed to emphasize their problems — the cultural clashes, the lack of understanding of the middle-class women, the lack of workers' resources. This dialectic of class had always fascinated me, but there was little to read about it. Dimitrov, a Communist theorist of the thirties, talked about a "united front of women," but only perfunctorily. Mao Zedong's analysis of united fronts in China was meatier but said little about women. But the Illinois Women's Alliance was nothing less than a fully developed, much earlier example of such a united front between working women, socialists, and feminists, put into practice with great success between 1870 and 1890 by a brilliant group of socialist-feminist organizers.

This new information illuminated the complexity of the issues. It was not merely differences of style that determined whether such united fronts were workable; it was the political environment. The strength of the labor movement, the openness of the socialist movement to feminism, the breadth of the women's movement — these set the limits on what could be done. Things that were possible in one period were not in another, because the configuration of forces had changed. This may sound obvious, but I had not understood it clearly before, and others had not discussed it.

So I had to rewrite my history book yet again, changing it considerably. I had to pare down the vivid personal anecdotes and life stories, which had been the main commercial strength of the early drafts, and bring the analysis to the fore.

> The united front of women . . . was . . . a major factor in giving working women the social muscle to organize into trade unions . . . But its success depended on the strength of the labor movement as a whole, the strength of socialists within it, and how progressive the feminist movement was. Above all, the united front's ability to organize working women depended on who led it — what class and what kind of politics. When the working-class and left forces were strong, when they had deep enough roots among the people to be able to organize women without the help of the middle class, and when they were clear about what they were trying to achieve, they were able to lead the whole united front of women and build vital links between women's struggles at work and in the community. This was the case in the Illinois Women's Alliance.[5]

Rewriting the book solved the problem of the $4000: *The Rising of the Women* was a different book from the one rejected by my first publisher. Monthly Review Press was consequently able to publish it.

But my change in emphasis necessitated another change in my conception of the book. Throughout the early versions, I had used quotations from people's speeches, letters, and diaries in great profusion, wanting to let those women speak directly to the reader in their own voices, without my mediation. I hadn't even corrected their spelling. I wanted to make myself a vessel, a transmission belt, through which their spirits would pass and transfigure the reader.

Friends who read the manuscript didn't seem to like this. Time after time they asked, "But what do *you* think? Why are you hiding behind all these quotes?" They didn't want a transmission belt; they wanted a mind. They didn't want a camera; they wanted a historical agent — someone willing to take the responsibility not of passively presenting history, with her interpretations invisible behind a collage of voices, but of saying what she thought it all meant. I cannot tell you how much this responsibility terrified me. A chorus of invisible judges seemed to read over my shoulder as I typed, jeering at every word; they held things up considerably.

When I had finally finished *The Rising of the Women*, I had to confront the question of accessibility. No matter how well written it might or might not be, few working women would read it, few would even hear of it because, owing to the processes of book distribution, it would be available mainly in universities, movement bookstores, large metropolitan centers, and by mail order. How could I get this history out to the people who needed it most? A passage by Bertholt Brecht had been one of my sacred texts for years:

> Nowadays, anyone who wishes to combat lies and ignorance and to write the truth must overcome at least five difficulties. He must have the *courage* to write the truth when truth is everywhere opposed; the *keenness* to recognize it, although it is everywhere concealed; the *skill* to manipulate it as a weapon; the *judgement* to select those in whose hands it will be effective; and the *cunning* to spread the truth among such persons.[6]

I had often played with the idea of a historical novel. Now I developed an outline for one based on some of the events in my history book, but focusing specifically on Jews in the New York garment industry. I called the book *Rivington Street*. Two of the characters were involved in the great shirtwaist strike of 1909, and one went on to be an organizer for the union and the Women's Trade Union League. Another was a suffragist and another an early career woman, carving out a niche for herself as a designer in a Fifth Avenue department store. They all had problems with love and identity.

Through a friend in the women's movement, I found an agent who liked my outline enough to take me on, and who was skilled enough to sell my proposal for a large advance. Suddenly, in 1979, I found myself in the remarkable position of being able to write full time. Rags to riches! My good fortune was almost too much for me to grasp and I kept it virtually secret for months, afraid it would somehow be swept away.

> I had been hungry, all the Years —
> My Noon had Come — to dine —
> I trembling drew the Table near —
> And I touched the Curious Wine —
>
> 'Twas this on Tables I had seen —
> When turning, hungry, Home
> I looked in Windows, for the Wealth
> I could not hope — for Mine —
>
> — Emily Dickinson[7]

Writing fiction was a liberation. It left me free to construct characters and situations that were composites, ideal types of the contradictions that interested me. Since I knew the history so well, I could build on it and be confident I was not lying — that is, distorting what had happened — but rather creating heightened versions of the truth that people could identify with and remember. But I still needed to know as many facts as possible; since I am a realist, I feel helped rather than burdened by an accretion of fact. My research into the Kishinev pogrom of 1903, in which a government-orchestrated anti-Semitic campaign led to a two-day orgy of terror, was far more extensive than I actually needed for the novel, but knowledge of many details enabled me to select among them. I was particularly proud that nothing about the pogrom, except the ways in which it affected my central characters, was "made up"; even the names of the victims came from casualty lists. And I took the greatest pleasure in finding out and re-creating the ways our grandmothers did their work: washing clothes in a cold-water flat, working in garment factories, doing fine sewing by hand, as Ruby, one of my central characters, does:

> When she had finished, the yoke was securely backed in satin and outlined in dark pink. She then cut away the paper backing between the net and the fabric, and began her embroidery, in a pattern of peonies, chrysanthemums, and curling tendrils and leaves. She stuffed the larger flowers and leaves with cotton as she went, to give a three dimensional illusion. She worked the one large and two

small peonies in a rose and lilac satin stitch, filling their centers with mauve French knots, and did the leaves in short-and-long stitch, pale green. She used both pale green and olive for the stems, which she outlined in buttonhole stitch. The curling vines were a medium green. There were eight chrysanthemums of varying sizes embroidered in pink, beige, and old rose, with ivory highlights.

This embroidery took Ruby four weeks. When it was done she carefully cut the satin from behind the net yoke, and bound the edges underneath with more buttonhole stitch. The front of the shirtwaist was now finished: a pinky-beige satin bodice and a net yoke, transparent except for strategically placed embroidered leaves and blossoms. Her round pink shoulders would peek out from behind the pale chrysanthemums, while the shadow between her young breasts would be discreetly, erotically hinted by the curve of the darker peony, lilac and rose, and the trembling of the pale green leaves that twined around it like a lover's fingers.[8]

Including such details is a way of giving value for money. A book should be well made, like a good coat. If it's made sloppily, with big, careless stitches, it will fall apart. If the style is too extreme or fanciful, women won't be able to wear it for every day. I want to write books simple enough for everyday use but strong enough to be passed around from friend to relation, mother to daughter, and even to be read more than once and to outlast current fashions.

Since my novel, *Rivington Street*, was published, a number of my historian or social scientist friends have told me they don't need to read it because they've already read my history book, and they only like to read stories that are true. When I hear this, I am flabbergasted. Surely there is more than one kind of truth in writing: the truth of feeling, which reaches from writer to reader, moving both; the truth of provable facts, bulwarks in winds of controversy; the truth of suspenseful narrative, which can be experienced as if lived through; the truth of analysis, which can be understood and used by the intelligence. While the provable facts and analysis are more prominent in nonfiction than in the novel, I prefer books that have a bit of all these kinds of truth.

I expect to continue writing both fiction and historical-political analysis. I am still part of the women's liberation movement, seeking a history and a strategy, just as I am still a reader of popular fiction, seeking a story in which I can both lose and find myself. Doing both kinds of writing is my way of making sure the personal remains the political. It is not that my fiction is personal and my nonfiction political: both are both. How can one compartmentalize the subjective element in writing? I am no one unless I can locate myself in history. History is nothing if it is devoid of the self — yourself, myself. This is another way of saying, as Rabbi Hillel, one of the authors of the Talmud, did: "If I am not for myself, who will be for me? If I am only for myself, who am I for? And if not now, when?"

Notes

1. Meredith Tax, *The Rising of the Women* (New York: Monthly Review Press, 1980), 110.
2. Ibid., 162.
3. Ibid., 176.
4. Ibid., 197.
5. Ibid., 20.
6. Bertholt Brecht, "Writing the Truth: Five Difficulties" (1935), translated by Richard Winston, in *Galileo*, translated by Charles Laughton, edited by Eric Bentley (New York: Grove Press, 1966), 133.
7. *The Complete Poems of Emily Dickinson*, edited by Thomas H. Johnson (Boston: Little, Brown, 1960), 283.
8. Meredith Tax, *Rivington Street* (New York: Morrow, 1982), 155.

Margaret Fuller

Bell Gale Chevigny

Bell Gale Chevigny

DAUGHTERS WRITING: TOWARD A THEORY OF WOMEN'S BIOGRAPHY

Margaret Fuller's forty years of struggle for life and work of her own recently absorbed a few of my own years. Like many nineteenth-century women in the United States, Fuller was one whose gifts, needs, and values made her American contemporaries perceive her as an anomaly. Like very few, she was not content to win acceptance as an exception but sought to change the rule itself. She tried to transform the criteria — intellectual, political, and sexual — by which she was judged anomalous so as to turn such judgments on their head. An intellectual prodigy and a compelling talker, she persuaded New England ladies to break their silence and to think aloud and transcendentalist gentlemen to indulge their senses, to open the scandalous volumes of Goethe and George Sand. As the first woman of the working press, she criticized the United States for deviating from its revolutionary promise and suggested that the experience of the 1848 revolutions in Italy, and especially in France, might be corrective. As a feminist writer, in her friendships and in her clandestine liaison with Giovanni Angelo Ossoli and the bearing of their child, she publicly argued and privately acted in support of freer sexual relationships and less confining gender definition.

Of course Fuller was not uniformly iconoclastic and of course she did not succeed in revising American values, though she made a mark on them. With her death a compromise was struck. Her first biographers immortalized her as a harmless anomaly. They muted, masked, or ignored what was challenging about her. But one cen-

tury's anomaly may be the next century's vanguard, and where
Fuller had failed with her contemporaries, I felt she would succeed
with mine. Her struggle to locate and express her gifts, needs, and
values could inform our own.

Perhaps this approach to Fuller gave rise to questions that
bemused me long after I had completed my book on her, questions
that I could not lay to rest.[1] They centered on an engagement with
my subject that amounted at times to a sense of identification. I
wondered how this had affected my work, whether it had deepened
or distorted it, or both, and what the identification meant. A visit to
the library assured me that I was not alone in my dilemma. Edgar
Johnson, for example, has said that biography is "a psychological
intersection between the personality of the biographer and that of
his subject."[2] Perhaps the matter should have rested with this
wisdom. Need a feminist do more than silently — once more —
supply *her* for *his*? Was anything changed by this tiny emendation?

It seemed to me that women writing on women in a period of
deepening and accelerating growth of feminist consciousness might
experience a "psychological intersection" that could be more
sharply specified. I wrestled retrospectively with my own work,
rethinking not only my own mode of interpretation but Fuller's as
well. This time my orientation was less literary and historical than
psychological. I studied my own process pragmatically, rather than
trying to locate it in existing theory. My findings are personal, but I
feel confident that they are not unique: I suppose that it is nearly
inevitable that women writing about women will symbolically reflect their internalized relations with their mothers and in some
measure re-create them.[3] These notions did not occur to me when I
was writing my book on Fuller. I was, even then, increasingly
perplexed by the rivaling claims of my engagement, verging on
identification, and of my commitment to "objectivity" — that is, to
letting Fuller speak for herself. The voices of few writers have been
so muffled, or so changed by ventriloquists, by people who believed
they acted lovingly in her interest, as Fuller's voice was. Her treacherous confidant, William Henry Channing, stood in my mind's eye
as a warning against the perils of too interested an interpretation.[4] I
sought to honor (and elucidate) all claims by the very structure of my
book: In each of six sections I offered my analysis, writings about
Fuller by her contemporaries, and writings by Fuller.

But this strenuous attempt to be objective did not end my perplexity, which in fact increased after I had completed the book. It was not
the first time that I had been fiercely engaged by a writer, but I
experienced the intensity of this engagement as alien and as simul-

taneously troubling and promising. What was troubling was the sense that, for feminist biographers, the new engagement with feminist theory, with our subjects, and with ourselves might produce a fresh mode of distortion, might introduce a specifically feminist fallacy. I refer to the inadequately acknowledged vicariousness a biographer may feel through projection of her actual, latent, or ideal experience onto the subject. Of course, women biographers of women have no monopoly on this error. But the validating stress that feminist theory has laid on the personal, the confusions about the role of the personal in our theory, the urgency and the fervor associated with a movement to redress historical and current injustice — all make feminist biographers of women more susceptible to uncritical identification. Since a precipitating cause of feminism was our indignation about misuse of women and distortion of their reality, it would be profoundly ironic if feminists should find a new way to abuse their subjects.

What I thought promising in the process of identification is harder to describe. I believed an oportunity lay within the trouble itself: There might be a dynamic way of engaging the identification with so little qualification or inhibition that one would emerge at the far side of the experience with a deeper and clearer appreciation of the subject than usually accompanies "objectivity." My hunch was that an author might be possessed by, and in possession of, her subject in such a way that both would emerge from the embrace more autonomous than before. But this "way" eluded further description. I found myself cornering other biographers and asking them how they handled the problem of identification. Their answers only made me feel I had failed to frame the real question. Friends and readers to whom I confided my uneasiness tended to have one of two reactions. Either they pointed out that I had done my research, placed Fuller in time, and held my private associations in check, or they suggested that my anxiety stemmed from an archaic notion of objectivity and that the best biographies were informed by the author's strong personal involvement. Both responses seemed to me right, but also wrong because they failed to illuminate the mysterious link that bound the separation to the identification. I had learned more in writing the book on Fuller than I had learned about anything before, only to end facing my ignorance about the impulse and process of such learning itself. I felt my work still unfinished.

In the same period, as months passed, one aspect of Fuller's life kept recurring to mind, refusing to stay settled. It had to do with a fragment of manuscript I had discovered in a box of Fuller's miscellaneous papers at the Harvard library — a dreamlike fiction about

Fuller's childhood, which oddly distorted the facts about her mother and herself. Again, I found myself asking persons with psycho-analytical training how they would interpret this manuscript. Many shed new light, but it was not until I reached my own interpretation of the manuscript that I understood the larger implications of the dynamics of my relation to Fuller. It is as if for two or three years I carried around two puzzles — one about Fuller's relation to her mother, one about my relation to Fuller — and each held the key to the other. Such tidy dovetailing would be suspect to me were it not so illuminating.

Fuller's Autobiographical Act

Fuller's "manuscript fiction" that preoccupied me so tenaciously was only one of three extended attempts she made to account for her childhood. Her relation to each of her parents evidently remained an open and provocative question in her maturity, for she was drawn to reevaluate and reshape it again and again. The interpreta-tions and uses she made of her parents and childhood, and especially of her relation to her mother, interest me more than their "actuality" — which, in any case, we can derive only from random surviving letters and reminiscences.

Nonetheless, here, based on my reading of the letters between Fuller and her parents, is a brief interpretation of the aspects of this triadic relationship that relate to Fuller's autobiographical work. The marriage of Timothy and Margarett Fuller appears to have been marked by great affection, good humor, mutual respect, and con-fident acceptance of a conventional division of human attributes and labor by gender. A second child, Julia Adelaide, born two years after Margaret Fuller, died suddenly at the age of eighteen months. At three and a half, Margaret was greatly upset by the funeral and the loss of this sibling (the next child, a boy, was not born until she was five). With the loss of his second child, Timothy began to devote himself to the instruction of his firstborn, not yet four years old, and sustained sole responsibility for her education for several years. That none of his five sons or his other daughter received this educa-tion testifies to the singular intensity of this relationship. Timothy Fuller is widely remembered as an earnest but stiff and contentious person. He probably placed great demands on his gifted daughter. Although there is some playfulness in the letters they exchanged, their agreement that she should study and behave in a manner creditable to him is paramount.

Far from contesting this arrangement, Margarett, the mother, appears to have welcomed and reinforced it.[5] Several factors worked to diminish her contact with her firstborn: her own chronically delicate health, the care of her second child and her grief after that child's death, and the subsequent bearing of seven more children. In 1850, the year of Margaret Fuller's death, her mother (who survived her by several years) suggested that their earliest connection may have been tenuous. She begins a single page of reminiscence thus: "Why is it that I can recall so little of thy beauteous childhood my glorified one . . ."[6] It is impossible to assess the quality and degree of closeness in their relationship. On the one hand, letters indicate that Fuller was both more in her mother's company and engaged in family and neighborhood activities than her autobiographical accounts suggest. On the other hand, her position in the family, her role as her father's intellectual companion, must have set her apart from her siblings and her mother. Some evidence suggests that Fuller felt she had less access to her mother's attention than she would have liked. A letter from her mother received in illness while she was at boarding school at the age of fourteen had, as Fuller wrote her father, a marvelously curative effect. She added, perhaps wistfully, that she had never seen her mother "equalled in tenderness and assiduity with which she devotes herself to sick friends." After Timothy's death in 1835, Fuller, then twenty-five, became in effect the head of the household, and the two women appear to have drawn closer. But nowhere is the tone of their correspondence so intense as in their last transatlantic letters, after Fuller confided that she had married and borne a child; in these long-distance exchanges, the primary mutual bond, so long tacit or repressed, became explicit.[7]

Turning to Fuller's autobiographical texts, I interpret them, like those of other writers, as imaginative constructions. In Fuller's case, I read them as strategies by which the author sought to explain or justify her current sense of herself, a need that might be especially strong in a woman who felt herself moving into uncharted waters and whose sense of herself was subject to sharp shifts in direction. The "manuscript fiction" that puzzled me becomes significant in the context of two other texts, which I discuss first: an "autobiographical romance" and the "Miranda fable."

The "autobiographical romance" was written in 1840,[8] the year Fuller became thirty. Looking for ways to help support her mother and younger siblings and concerned about her own emotional and intellectual fulfillment, she suffered from a critical sense of impasse. The "romance" of 1840 is an attempt to understand the origins of that impasse.

In this text she presents her parents in gender-bound terms: While her father is a man of the world, of intellect, and of practical action, her mother is "bound by one law with the blue sky, the dew, and the frolic birds . . . She had in her most of the angelic, — of that spontaneous love for every living thing, for man, and beast, and tree, which restores the golden age." Her father's love for her mother "was the green spot on which he stood apart from the common-places of a mere bread-winning, bread-bestowing existence."[9] Her parents' nurturing of Fuller is as unconventional as their "natures" are conventional. Her mother's relatively unusual absence from Fuller's rearing is epitomized in the brevity of its mention here; and the loss of female companionship is underscored by Fuller's grief over the loss of her sister: "she who would have been the companion of my life was severed from me." (Fuller judges that her sister's character, had she lived, "would have tempered mine to a gentler and more gradual course.")[10] By contrast, the father's intense attention based on his classical (and especially Roman) curriculum and his severe habit of drilling her, often late at night, in Latin and English grammar deprived her, she judges, of a "natural childhood."

The chief refuge she describes from her father's study and from dreams of heroism inspired by the Romans was, significantly, the garden, her mother's cherished workplace. Although the mother is not described here, her presence is felt, perhaps with more power and pathos, through the plants she nurtured so tenderly. Thus the clematis-creeper becomes for Fuller "the emblem of domestic love," and she confides, romantically but tellingly, "I loved to gaze on the roses, the violets, the lilies, the pinks; my mother's hand had planted them, and they bloomed for me . . . I kissed them, I pressed them to my bosom with passionate emotions . . . An ambition swelled my heart to be as beautiful, as perfect as they. I have not kept my vow."[11] While the mother is "bound by one law" to nature, the child apparently feels that she is not. She clings to flowers as links to her mother that are also her sibling rivals, but she asserts that she cannot match them, cannot be a garden growth. The rejection is implicitly mutual: The supposedly "natural" world of women will not allow her entry, and the girl who dreams of Romans cannot become a rose.

The autobiographical romance goes on to chart the effects of this early loneliness and rigor. In describing the two worlds of her divided self (her father's books and her mother's flowers), Fuller all but names them masculine and feminine. She looks about her for an understanding and interpretive figure, a mirroring being who will also compensate for her deprived childhood and stunted emotional life. Significantly, she finds this — temporarily — in an older

woman, a visiting British woman. A more enduring effect of loneliness, beginning in the aftermath of her father's nocturnal drills but
persisting throughout her life, is the terrible nightmare of following
her mother's corpse to the grave as Fuller had traumatically
followed her sister's.[12]

Three years later, in her essay for the *Dial* on women (expanded in
1845 into *Woman in the Nineteenth Century*), Fuller presented a
second autobiography, thinly disguised in the description of
"Miranda." The "Miranda fable" gives an idealized portrait of her
father and an encomium on his teaching methods (which were
Timothy Fuller's own, freshly evaluated). What Fuller called her
father's "great mistake" in 1840 now expresses Miranda's father's
"firm belief in the equality of the sexes." In 1840, Fuller complained
that her forced education had cheated her of her female nature, but
now we read that "he addresses her not as a plaything but as a living
mind." While his legacy in the earlier version was a life "devoured
in the bud," now it was her "dignified sense of self-dependence."[13]
Clearly, Fuller had changed since she wrote the 1840 romance. This
heroic assertion of independence, equaled nowhere else in her
work, doubtless owes much to Fuller's freeing herself from a crip-
pling desire for an essentially dependent relationship on Ralph
Waldo Emerson as well as to her success in the early 1840s in
exercising and uniting her emotional and intellectual faculties in her
series of "conversations for women."

Setting these two accounts of her father side by side, we are
tempted to see the second as a symbolic act of reparation, a making
of amends for the symbolic abuse of the father in her earlier imaginative reconstruction of him. We also notice that the mother, whose
character was influential and whose absence was palpable in the
1840 version, is not mentioned here.

In the "manuscript fiction," however, the mother, by dying,
becomes the center of attention.[14] Here, Fuller takes two striking
liberties with the facts, the chief of which is the invention of the
mother's death and the father's survival with the child. The
mother's death and the child's meditation on it draw all attention
away from the father. It is as if, by construing the mother's absence
in the most ultimate way — that is, by rendering her dead — Fuller
was able to contemplate her mother's life much more freely than
ever before. That "green spot" of her father's existence is, for the
first time, imagined from a female, not a male, perspective. This
becomes problematic because the second liberty Fuller takes with
reality is to make the narrating child, Fuller's "self" here, a boy. The
beginning of the fiction is the part I find most engrossing. Plainly

drawing on the actual death of Fuller's baby sister, it opens with reference to the death of a sister:

> My mother never recovered from the death of this child. She had watched her too anxiously through her illness, and her life was a slender stem that would not bear more than one blow from the axe. Besides, her whole life was in her children, for her marriage was the not uncommon one of a lovely young girl, ignorant of her self, and of her capacities for feeling, to a man of suitable age and position because he chose her. He was an honorable, kind-hearted, well-educated (as it is called) and of good sense, but a mere man of business who had never dreamed of what such a woman as she needs in domestic life. He kept her in a good house, with a good wardrobe, was even in his temper, and indulgent to her wishes, but he did not know what it was to be companionable, the friend, much less the lover, and if he had he would not have had time, for his was the swift crowded course of an American business life. So she pined and grew dull, she knew not why, something was wanting she could not tell what, but there was a dreariness, a blank, she tormented herself that she was so ungrateful to a kind Providence, which had given her so much for want of which the many suffer: she tried to employ herself for the poor, she gave her heart to her children. Still she languished and the first blow found so little life to resist it, that she fell a speedy victim.
>
> Perhaps it was well so, and yet I know not. Beside my own feeling of infinite loss there has been a bitter sense that had she lived there was enough in me corresponding with her unconscious wants to have aroused her intellect and occupied her affections. Perhaps her son might have made up to her for want of that full development of feeling which youth demands from love.[15]

The two elements I find most striking here are the unique criticism of her father's relation to her mother and the child's fantasy of rescuing the mother as a son.[16] These elements are counterparts — like the question-and-answer design sometimes seen in dreams — which suggest a problem (the mother dies, in part through her husband's neglect) and a resolution (the son rescues the mother by arousing her intellect and occupying her affections). All interpretations of the text must take both these elements into account.

The mother's death invites us to first read the text as an oedipal parable. As such, it expresses Fuller's guilt over drawing the father's attention from the mother to herself (here Fuller is effectively the murderer). But the relation with the father is dropped, and the focus is on atonement to the mother through a superior "marriage." With the rescue element, however, the oedipal parable crosses genders: The daughter usurping the mother's place becomes the "son" usurping the father's place. Fuller's masculine persona suggests, among other things, that the intellectual tools given her by her father have desexed her, that they have also empowered her, and that only males can rescue. As rescuing "son," in any case, Fuller comes closer both to possessing and to liberating the mother. Still, what enables her to understand and satisfy the mother's needs better than the father may be vestigial female self-identification.

If we read the text as a social-psychological parable (a model that appealed to Fuller as a young woman writer), the death expresses both Fuller's rage over the father's neglect of his wife and, more broadly, her anger at society's assigning a death-in-life lot to women as wives (here the father and patriarchal society are murderous). Correspondingly, in the rescue element, Fuller supplies the mother with what the father neglected to offer and projects a richer intellectual and emotional life for women as wives.

For me, neither the oedipal nor the social-psychological reading exhausts the text. The centrality in it of Fuller's imagined relation to her mother suggests that we look for explanations centered in the actual relations of these two persons over time. The notion that the infant derives its sense of self initially from the expression it sees on the mother's face while she looks at the infant is persuasive and useful here.[17] It is natural to assume that as the child grows, this need for maternal mirroring to identify and secure the sense of self is attenuated and complicated by other factors, but it does not disappear. If we recall that at the age of three and a half Fuller not only lost her sister but also, through her father's educational intervention, effectively lost her mother, we may imagine that Fuller acutely felt the withdrawal of female mirroring presences and that her sense of self was thrown off balance. In the next several years, the mother's relative absence continued and may have deepened a sense of identity-in-disequilibrium or of a self incomplete.

In this context, the death element of the text expresses both Fuller's rage over the mother's perceived elusiveness and neglect of her daughter's needs (here Fuller is the murderer) and Fuller's sorrow because her mother's way of life could do so little to strengthen the nascent selfhood of this extraordinary child that she might as well be dead (here the mother refused life, or killed herself). In the rescue element, Fuller in a sense kills both parents in order to replace them: The father disappears and the "son" does his job better; the mother dies and the "son" resurrects her. As "son," Fuller gets complete physical, affective, and intellectual control of the newly constituted mother. What would this resurrected mother be like? She would be the reverse of the live mother of the fiction, one lovingly present and involved in intellectual nourishment — in short, a strong model or confirming mirror.

Finally, we may read the fiction as we do a dream, treating all the protagonists as aspects of Fuller herself. In this version, it both acknowledges a self divided against itself by gender and builds a fantasy that makes the self whole. Fuller's "mother," undeveloped and regressing unto death, represents Fuller's "female" self murderously neglected by both her parents. The "son" or "male" self, by contrast, is so powerfully developed that it saves, validates, and nurtures, as neither parent did, her weak "female" self. Through this rescue, with its overtones of displacement, marriage, and rebirth, Fuller creates a self in which love, thought, and action coexist. Self-creation through re-creation of her parenting sounds throughout Fuller's work. She sometimes fancied herself an orphan who needed her own adoption, as when she wrote: "I was always to return to myself, to be my own priest, pupil, parent, child, husband and wife."[18]

If the "Miranda fable" functions as a reparation to Fuller's earlier literary injury to her father, the "manuscript fiction" then presents a much more complex and reciprocal notion of reparations to Fuller's mother and to her self.[19] As "son," Fuller acts to the mother as her husband could not so that the mother might be what she was not so that the child might have a free path for her extraordinary and anomalous development. Both in writing this fantasy and in casting herself in it as a rescuer, Fuller symbolically saves and creates a mother who, in turn, should be able to act as companion, guide, and interpreter for Fuller herself.

In actuality, Fuller did something like this among her female acquaintances and friends. For as her mother was no true predecessor, so early nineteenth-century New England society offered no precedent for what Fuller was groping to become; she had to mold her own models from the material at hand. This is especially evident in her invention of "conversations" for women: weekly gatherings where women came to think aloud and together, in which Fuller worked to shape women who would understand and share her goals and consequently make them less idiosyncratic. In this reciprocal process, her own "shape" was more securely defined at the same time as the meaning of nurturing roles — mother and mentor — was redefined as subtly mutual. We can interpret this activity as a further revision of her parents' lives, a "rewriting" in which, as in the manuscript fiction, she repairs the reality.

Woman in the Nineteenth Century is the text that grew out of Fuller's reparative "rewriting" in her "conversations" for women. While the "Miranda fable," included in the volume, embodies simple reparation to the father, the book as a whole constitutes an act of reparation to the mother and child in the more complex sense I have seen in Fuller's manuscript fiction. In one of the book's crucial assertions — that "there is no wholly masculine man, no purely feminine woman," that the "two sides of the great radical dualism," male and female, "are perpetually passing into one another" — she conceives of persons not denied half their nature as she thought her parents were. And the book's chief argument for woman's unimpeded discovery and development of all her powers charts a freedom inconceivable to her mother and (therefore) still only potential and hypothetical for her daughter. Joined and mutually informing as they are, these conceptions imagine a repaired and ideal family.

The families adults make for themselves provide further opportunities for reparative activities. The family that Fuller herself fearfully created and reluctantly and tardily acknowledged in her actual life hardly meets the ideal she pointed to in *Woman in the Nineteenth Century*. But the apparent reversal of conventional gender roles constitutes an early and rough draft of it, with Fuller, ten years older, the intellectual, assuming responsibility for breadwinning and practical arrangements and the gentle Ossoli, the nature lover, nurturing both woman and child. It is also most relevant to my notion of reparations that Ossoli lost his mother early, that his tenderness toward Fuller reminded her of nothing so much as her mother's love, and that she looked forward with the greatest confidence to bringing Ossoli and her mother together.[20] Significantly, too, she was most eager to ensure both his freedom for growth and change and her own, thus articulating a repaired notion of the relations between women and men.

My Biographical Act

Retrospectively, I see that my evolving engagement with Fuller — like her several revised texts about her family, her reparations rendered on the page and in life — can be interpreted as a series of deepening endeavors to seek out and understand the sources of my position in the world, my current sense of myself. These stages corresponded roughly to my reading about her, my research on her, my writing of the book — and the aftermath which clarified the whole enterprise.

My interest in Fuller began as the culmination of a process of reeducation that began in 1963, the year I received my Ph.D. My activities in the civil rights and antiwar movements and with prisoners' rights and education all began as expressions of the moral, humanistic, and aesthetic impulses that had earlier led me to literature. Each of these carried me — as my study of literature regrettably had not — beyond literature to questions about society, history, politics, and psychology. Until my work with prisoners led me systematically to study Black history and literature, I lived a double life, with literature virtually segregated from my new social concerns. My study of Black literature in turn made me read and teach my favorite classic texts in new ways. Thoreau looked different read in the context of Frederick Douglass's life, and Ahab was transformed by the proximity of John Brown. Margaret Fuller was the only woman mentioned — and laughingly, at that — in the period that chiefly interested me. When friends, more swiftly responsive to the women's movement than I, made obvious points about the gaps in my reeducation, I began to read her. The first book I read, Joseph Jay Deiss's *Roman Years of Margaret Fuller,* astonished me, because Deiss saw Fuller's chief importance less in her quietest and literary New England transcendentalist phase than in her political activity in New York and Europe and in her unconventional emotional involvement in love (and perhaps marriage) and motherhood. There were, oddly, broad parallels (even geographical ones) between these divisions of her life and my own. I began looking at her papers at Harvard, and I wrote an essay about how Fuller effected the change between two intellectually and socially different stages in her life, changes that paralleled those I was making. But only much later did I realize that an analysis of her reeducation had drawn me because it was then my own crucial activity.

My research increasingly revealed to me the extent to which friends who believed they loved her had distorted Fuller's writing and defused the serious challenge she posed to contemporary American values. The idea grew on me of restoring Fuller's actual achievement by retrieving what I could from the original papers and peeling off the layers of legend, piety, and scandal that coated over her identity. Fuller's wish, reiterated in letters and diaries, for someone who could understand, interpret, and guide her operated as another spur. In recovering her writing for my book, I became engrossed by the task of accurately establishing the text. Being accurate about Fuller became identical with caring for her. It was as difficult for me for as anyone else to give up a hypothesis in the face of contradictory or inadequate evidence, but sometimes I had to, and there were, in my case, compensations for the reorganization of thought required by such honesty. The passion to know and understand her mattered more than the most beguiling of my theses. Only later would I ask why this passion was so strong.

After I had rescued her as best I could from the bowdlerizers, after I had established her texts and selected those that seemed most fairly to represent her, I was confronted in my analytical essays with the task of reinterpreting her. My feeling of connection with her was now so strong that I was able, after a day of teaching and an evening with my family, once the children were in bed, to turn to my writing with a freshness of energy rare in my experience. This closeness to her was so clearly a gift that I didn't worry about it or question it greatly. Margaret Fuller was so vivid before me that I did not fear I was inventing her. It seemed that she invaded and surrounded my life rather than that I was intruding on hers. The quality of connection during the writing period was not always the same. Much as I was stirred and inspired by her capacity for growth, her generosity, intelligence, and bravery, I felt closer to her on the occasions when I had to account for some less attractive qualities that showed up, especially in her earlier years. Her regal self-importance, her extravagant claims for her powers, her insensitivity toward persons who she judged did not share her appetite for freedom and those who (often wrongly) she judged did, her obsession with being understood, often on her own terms even though she could not define the terms — all these aspects of her famous arrogance (or awkwardness) I felt intimately compelled to analyze. Early temptation to explain them away or minimize them did not trouble me long, for I began to explore them as unwise or unsuccessful attempts to negotiate the distance between the situation in which she found herself and a way of life in which she deeply believed but had yet to locate or create.

This bears on the question of objectivity and subjectivity, or what might be seen as the relation between evidence and intuition (not mutually exclusive terms). My early commitment to Fuller's right to speak for herself led me to the decision to intervene minimally in interpreting her life.[21] My commitment to the independence of her and our readers made me treat interpretation as speculation and offer multiple interpretations when possible. But where Fuller was inarticulate or silent or seemed to me blind or wrongheaded, and where her other analysts were puzzled or reticent, and where general historical accounts gave slight help, more analytical intervention was called for. In discussing such moments I often drew on intuitive understanding and speculated from my privileged sense of familiarity (often experienced in its root sense: my closeness seemed familial). Not always, but sometimes, I could trace this familiarity to an analogous experience in myself. This was especially the case when Fuller's behavior was unheroic or perverse. It of course occurred to me that this bond might stem from my sharing Fuller's failings, but as hers were expressed more publicly and on a grander scale and in a relatively hostile time and environment, the sharing was not a merging or confusion of identities. In the double action of empathy, first, a flash of recognition led me to believe with some confidence that I felt her feelings and, second, historical differences helped me to delineate her peculiar situation and to analyze it. Although this was, for me, a new way of working, I believed that I was using myself without abusing her. In any case, these intuitive forays were few and were presented tentatively. I now judge this use of empathy wholly appropriate, but I failed still to understand all that drove me to employ it.

The last stage of involvement with Fuller focused on identification. It became focal when I was finishing writing the book and going through the painful separation every writer experiences when the book gains autonomy, takes its first steps, and leaves home for the dangerous outer world.

I am sure all biographers have their anecdotes of mistaken identity. When the book was published I thought I had filled my quota. (My favorite slips were the moments when, asked when I'd settled in Manhattan, I said "1845 — I mean 1961" and when I explained that "Fuller's vision of America had changed with the war in Vietnam — I mean Mexico.") But two years after completing the book, and after speaking in public several times about Fuller, I was asked to talk about her in a summer community to friends and acquaintances. Unlike previous occasions, this was an entirely relaxed atmosphere. I stood at a podium in a dimly lit wood-paneled room in an old farmhouse, with a breeze from the meadow coming in at the doors and people lounging in all the corners — a setting not unlike one in which Fuller might have conversed at Brook Farm. Time was my only constraint; other activities planned for the evening left me forty-five minutes, and I was urged not to read Fuller but to explain who she was. I put aside notes and text and described, quoted, paraphrased, and even imitated Fuller as rapidly as I reasonably could. It was very stimulating and pleasant; everyone seemed interested and wanted to know more, and several remarked afterward on how much I loved Fuller and how I had brought her to life. Instead of remaining pleased, however, I felt intolerably and increasingly agitated as the evening wore on. Attempting to analyze my malaise, I could not go beyond the feeling that I had done something tawdry in partly impersonating Fuller.I fell asleep late, only to find myself bolt upright, awakened by my own accusation: "You're as bad as Channing! You think you alone understand her!" The reader may find such shudders quaint, Gothic, or overfastidious, as I do in retrospect. But by then the notion of claiming Fuller had become deeply obnoxious to me, and I believed that impersonating her, taking responsibility for "bringing her to life," was a trespass or usurpation. The betrayal was twofold: As I had claimed her in my terms, so I had given over my identity, however briefly, to her. The "third person" in that room, the hybrid formed of both and warping each of us out of our orbits, continued to preoccupy me.

I had not come to the end of my revelations. In retelling the event a few months later, I admitted that, while I *knew* I did not alone and entirely understand Fuller, I *felt* of course that I did. Moreover, I heard myself saying, were she living now, she alone would understand me. This too persisted as feeling although it fell apart as thought (I *know* I am not inscrutable, and I can also conceive of ways that I might puzzle Fuller). But by heeding these feelings, embarrassing as they were to my understanding of the case, I grasped a dimension of my work that had been long struggling toward consciousness. Although I had realized that to explain Fuller I had drawn on unarticulated areas of my own experience, I had not before seen so clearly that I had been creating indirectly a mirroring self; that is, when I sought to explain her, especially her confusing behavior, I was generating analogous explanations or partial sanctions for aspects of my own behavior. At the same time I was working as a sanctioning mirror for her.

To put it another way, I had created a "mother" of sorts for myself at the same time as I was acting as one for Fuller, "mothers" of the sort that would nurture the difficult and unsteady growth of autonomous selves in us. This does not mean that our early developments are similar. No displacement of mother by father occurred in my childhood as it had in Fuller's. But, like Fuller, I began to make life choices that were different from my mother's, and, like Fuller, I sought supplementary models. The passion of my engagement to Fuller, especially in her struggle for her autonomy, demonstrated that a need for an active, even challenging, relation to who I was becoming — and, to a great extent, the satisfying of the need — had emerged silently and invisibly in the process of the work.

These realizations shed retrospective light on my urgent desire to know Fuller, which had grown with the work. My efforts to understand her were rooted not only in my desire for vicarious self-knowledge but also in a desire to know a precursor in ways I could not know my own mother. This is a significant cultural issue: Our education and general culture lay much greater stress on our understanding of men than of women so that we approach the lives of our mothers (and our foremothers) with few and arbitrary tools. More crucially here, it is a psychological issue. Bars to our knowledge of ourselves and our knowledge of our mothers are psychologically linked. In *The Reproduction of Mothering*, Nancy Chodorow has demonstrated persuasively that mothering practices in our culture reinforce the difficulties mothers and daughters have in finding and strengthening the boundaries that divide them.[22] She shows that for the mother-and-daughter dyad, symbiosis is more persistent while separation and individuation are more difficult than they are for mother and son, father and daughter, and father and son. The symbiotic quality of the relation between mother and daughter, whether we accept it or reject it, is such that it is difficult for us to know one another both intimately and clearly. Our difficulty in knowing our mothers dominates us as daughters and, to some extent, blocks our growth and self-knowledge. I am convinced that when, as daughters writing, we are moved to study a foremother, we are grappling with some aspect of this ignorance which is so costly to ourselves.

Here is where the two puzzles — over Fuller's manuscript fiction and over my engagement in the work — suggest a common key. The "mother" Fuller created in the manuscript fiction is as unlike her own as the "mother" I created in Fuller is unlike my own. But as Fuller in the manuscript seemed to be re-creating a mother who would sanction what she herself wanted to become, so I may have acted indirectly for myself in re-creating Fuller. My point does not depend on the biographical specifics of what Fuller and I may share. (Surely Fuller was anomalous as I am not and had greater objective need to create a sanctioning precedent than I do.) My point is that when we are the writing daughters of mothers who did not write or otherwise articulate our aspirations for autonomy, we will probably be tempted in writing to create our own maternal, mirroring sanctions and precedents.

It may be helpful, at this point, to distinguish the process I am tracing from that which Nancy Chodorow and Susan Contratto have recently discerned at work in a wide range of feminist writings — the projection into theory of the infantile "fantasy of the perfect mother." They note that much recent feminist writing presents themes that "include a sense that mothers are totally responsible for the outcomes of their mothering, even if their behavior is in turn shaped by male-dominant society. Belief in the all-powerful mother spawns a recurrent tendency to blame the mother on the one hand, and a fantasy of maternal perfectability on the other."[23] They call for new theories of mothering and of childhood that will emerge from revised analyses of child development beyond infancy and of crucial relationships over time to persons other than the mother.

Although my concerns here are tangential to those of Chodorow and Contratto, I suggest that a variant of the fantasy they criticize may be constructively experienced. In the biographical process I describe, there is a stage in which author and subject in effect become *surrogate mothers* in that they offer one another "maternal" nurture. But the fantasy of the surrogate mother differs in several ways from the fantasy of the perfect mother. It is a fantasy of reciprocity; far from being all-powerful, both "mothers" are engaged in struggle; both nurture not an infant, but a girl or woman; and for both, nurture is a sanctioning of their autonomy.[24] Ideally then, as biographers, we re-create "mothers" from whom we can integrate and separate more effectively than from our biological mothers. I say "ideally," for the working of symbiosis will intrude even in this variant fantasy. The issues of intuition and detachment, of vigilance and respect for the subjective, which dog every biographer, may be even more freighted for women biographers of women than for other biographers. Yet as women biographers are working on surrogate mothers, ideally they will enter and then separate themselves from the lives they present. The rewards for such a biography, carefully executed, may be great in that the individuality of the "foremother" and of the author may be more firmly secured.

Jane Flax, working at the same time as Chodorow on related issues, suggests a similar solution to the problem posed by the woman-to-woman identification of biographers. She argues that in patriarchal society the mother is the primary nurturer, the father the symbol of authority, and that subsequent social experience sustains the dichotomy between nurturance and autonomy.[25] Hence female autonomy cannot be experienced without a sense of abandoning the mother and, by extension, other women and even aspects of the self. Female autonomy becomes a precarious and contradictory condition until social structures are transformed wholesale, permitting women to be whole. The experience of women writing about women is one form such transformative activity potentially can take. If we borrow a term from the patriarchal side of Flax's dichotomy, we may more finely specify this activity. Authority is male, but we know that women can and do *authorize*, and we can learn to authorize the challenging and independent aspects of one another. "Mothering" as we know it remains an ambivalent activity: It perpetuates the cyclical dilemma Chodorow defines, unless women radically re-create one another. "Authorizing" is in some ways a more suggestive term, if we take it to imply not only the granting of sanction but also, and simultaneously, a re-creating ("authoring"). Of course, female authority in its most literal sense is what we are exploring in writing the biographies of our foremothers; as I have suggested, we may be subtly authorizing our own autonomy at the same time.

What is the effect of all this on our writing? How can we keep the motive of creating sanctions or mutual autonomy from dominating our other responsibilities to our subject matter? How can we be sure that this dual reparation, this giving and gaining of autonomy in the act of biography, does not distort our subject? We cannot be sure. Our interpretation will surely bear the mark of ourselves. But we will distort our subjects proportionally less as we recognize our identification and use and then move beyond it. I now believe that the fearful "third person" I had conjured up by impersonating Fuller that summer night was the spectral embodiment of the fear I had been moving toward in my nagging concern about identification. It was the figure of ultimate fusion, of regression to a seamless unity in which both Fuller and I were lost. As such, it was terrifying to me, a taboo image marking the intellectually unsound and emotionally dangerous potential at the outer limit of my engagement with Fuller. This figure of mutual usurpation was the ghost hovering just out of my sight throughout my work. For the most part, I had held it at bay with a combination of scholarly practice and instinctive caution. When I actually wrestled with the ghost, however, I did not always keep my balance. I now believe, for example, that identification at times led me to distort a side of Fuller's nature I found difficult to accept. Perhaps because I had repudiated adolescent mystical tendencies in myself, I felt distaste for her tendency to mysticism and in my book either underplayed it or smothered it in an analysis that argued it was not what it seemed. While I believe my analysis has some merit, I also think it was governed by a failure to appreciate the role of mysticism in Fuller's period. At other times, the very wrestling with the ghost seems to have ended in a confident sense of equilibrium in which Fuller and I ended on our feet, near to, but separate from, one another.

Perhaps I can now elaborate on the hunch with which I began. The trouble and the promise of the biographer's deep engagement are bound up together and necessarily remain in unresolvable tension. The trouble lies in an identification that remains uncritical of itself; such identification does violence to both subject and writer, denying each her integrity, her irreducible particularity of character. It also does violence to time and historical circumstance. "Universal truths" about female experience are failures to come to terms with historical specificity. (Even identification with contemporary figures must be tempered by historicity, that is, by attention to the modifying effects of differences in class, place, psychological formation, and so on.) Uncritical identification not only becomes an end in itself; it is also a fantasy that refuses to recognize itself as such. The very stasis and finality of uncritical identification suggest the failure of self-trust, of open-minded self-exploration.

When identification is promising, we remain relatively self-sufficient and committed to exploration. We may pass through an intense fantasy of identification, a stage which frees us to make discoveries about ourselves even as we seek explanations for our subject and in which intellectual excitement seems to be conjoined with something like solace. But it doesn't end there, for this sort of identification is dialectical rather than static. The quality we feel we share with our subject contains within itself elements of difference, for example, in the cause, the consequence, or the value assigned to the quality. The excitement of recognition bears within it the urge to scrutinize those elements that keep it from being an exact duplication. Emotional identification is potentially analytical and can produce an understanding and appreciation of separation and hence a much more finely tuned account of our subject. But for this to occur we must work for a knowledge of all relevant aspects of history nearly as intimate as our knowledge of ourselves. In my case, for example, the very discovery that Fuller and I had similar responses to our mothers impelled me to observe that her very different relationship with her father and the different meanings early nineteenth-century culture found in family relationships gave Fuller's response a meaning quite distinct from my own.

Women writing about women, I am persuaded, are likely to move toward a subject that symbolically reflects their internalized relations with their mothers and that offers them an opportunity to re-create those relations. Whether our foremothers are famous and their histories distorted, or unknown and their histories neglected, the act of daughters writing about them is likely to be, on some level, an act of retrieval that is experienced as rescue. When the work is most intensely experienced as rescue, the fantasy of reciprocal reparations is likely to become an underlying impulse in it. That is, in the rescue — the reparative interpretation and re-creation — of a woman who was neglected or misunderstood, we may be seeking indirectly the reparative rescue of ourselves, in the sense of coming to understand and accept ourselves better. In writing about our foremothers, we can be prepared to experience the specific nature for each of us of the mother-daughter dynamic, but we cannot be fully forearmed. My own experience suggests that some of our deeper motives will emerge only when the work is done; presumably others remain unknown. Nevertheless, the better we understand the functions of empathy, identification, and separation, the better we can recognize and come to terms with our motives as they emerge. Finally, if the pursuit of motive is matched with a simultaneous pursuit of historicity, the strengths of separation, as well as those of identification, may be brought into play as wisely as possible during the process; of course the process will, and doubtless must, withhold its chief mysteries.

Women's biography is simply a special case of our current study of women in which we work to recover our history and ourselves, each at least partly in terms of the other. In women's biographies, the intelligent grasp and flexible use of the dynamics of daughters' writing is essential. Clearly, womankind has not been mirrored in culture in ways that provide us with adequate and confident self-definition; but, reaching across time, we can now begin to provide that for each other when we create ourselves and our foremothers with the most scrupulous attention to each stage of our experience as it reveals itself.

Notes

I am indebted to Carol Ascher, Marcia Cavell, Paul Chevigny, Muriel Dimen, Ellen DuBois, Phema Engelstein, Evelyn Keller, Antonia Strand Meltzoff, Nancy Miller, Donald Moss, Sara Ruddick, Susan Squier, and Louise Yelin for their critical suggestions about this article.

1. Bell Gale Chevigny, *The Woman and the Myth: Margaret Fuller's Life and Writings* (Old Westbury, N.Y.: Feminist Press, 1976).

2. Johnson, quoted in James L. Clifford, *From Puzzles to Portraits: Problems of a Literary Biographer* (Chapel Hill: University of North Carolina Press, 1970), 12.

3. I say "nearly" to allow for those women writers for whom fathers or other figures functioned as "mothers." Talking about Colette and applying some remarks by Hélène Cixous, Nancy Miller has made observations that might relate to such biographers. Miller postulated that "women writers are first daughters of the mother or the father . . . depending on the power of the presence or absence of either parent in a specific biographical situation and on the way . . . that that situation is symbolized by the daughter." Moreover, I am sure that the dynamics of identification I describe in this essay apply, with slight translation, for some men writing about women or about men.

4. Ralph Waldo Emerson, James Freeman Clarke, and William Channing, who edited the two-volume *Memoirs of Margaret Fuller Ossoli* in 1852, offended not only by cutting from her letters and diaries, often with scissors, her bolder remarks, but also by penciling in conventional pieties of their own. Channing had a particularly proprietary attitude toward Fuller, and his commitment to his interpretation of her was so strong that thirty years later he tried to persuade Thomas Wentworth Higginson to reproduce, in effect, his interpretation in Higginson's biography. See Bell Gale Chevigny, "The Long Arm of Censorship: Mythmaking in Margaret Fuller's Time and Our Own," *Signs* 2 (Winter, 1976): 450-60.

5. She wrote, for example, to her fourteen-year-old daughter at boarding school (January 14, 1825): "I depend on your writing frequently and particularly to your father of the progress you make in your studies . . . You can never find another correspondent who will value all the efforts you make to gratify affection and prove yourself worthy to be loved like your father." Houghton Library, Harvard University. Fuller's papers are quoted here by permission of the Houghton Library.

6. Writing of Fuller's fourth and fifth years, Margaret recalls: " at this tender age her great pleasure was in reading, in riding with us, in gathering flowers, a love which seemed to be born with her." That mother and daughter shared a passion for flowers is remarked on by neither (Fuller papers, Houghton Library).

7. Fuller wrote that she had not wanted to pain her mother by informing her of her dangerous pregnancy while an ocean separated them. Her mother assured her (September 5, 1849) that she had been wise in this discretion: "I had thought that nothing could ever move the depths of my spirit as this did. I assure you that fervent thankfulness has come out of this tumult, that I should have suffered tortures to have known that you were to become a mother and I so far from you . . . If [Ossoli] continues to make you happy he will be very dear to me, for long have I felt in sickness great pain in the thought of putting off the body that I should leave you peculiarly lonely in delicate health and no mother to love and watch over you" (Fuller papers, Houghton Library).

8. It is so dated by the editors of the *Memoirs of Margaret Fuller Ossoli*, who also use the term "autobiographical romance." It is the fullest account of her childhood. With no surviving original text, we cannot vouch for its authenticity, but the facts we know are generally consistent with this version. See R. W. Emerson, W. H. Channing, and J. F. Clarke, eds., *Memoirs of Margaret Fuller Ossoli*, 2 vols. (1884; reprint, New York: Burt Franklin, 1972).

9. Ibid., 1:12.

10. Ibid., 1:14.

11. Ibid., 1:23-24.

12. Needless to say, her account of this dream has delighted Freudian biographers. Katherine Anthony offers it as evidence that oedipal love for the father was "the mainspring of her whole career." See Anthony's *Margaret Fuller: A Psychological Biography* (New York: Harcourt Brace, 1921), 25.

13. See Chevigny, *Woman and the Myth,* 37, 45, 249.

14. The manuscript consists of six pages of writing, without beginning (it starts on what would appear to be the fifth page) or end (it breaks off midsentence). It is clearly part of what was intended to be an extended fiction ("Chapter II" is indicated on the last extant page).

15. Chevigny, *Woman and the Myth,* 50-51. The narrator goes on to dream over the mother's portrait and to meditate on the ideal meanings of love hypostatized in a mother's death. The second chapter begins by describing the father's mourning. In its second sentence is embedded an image of bitter waste that runs counter to its otherwise pious tone: "Although he did not understand his wife, and would never have discerned the feelings that early drank the oil from her lamp, he felt her loveliness and purity."

16. Fuller's many criticisms of marriage suggest an unconfessed, perhaps unconscious, critical attitude towards her parents' own marriage.

17. See especially D. W. Winnicott, "Mirror-Role of Mother and Family in Child Development," *Playing and Reality*, D. W. Winnicott, ed. (New York: Basic Books, 1971).

18. Chevigny, *Woman and the Myth*, 111.

19. Melanie Klein's discussion of reparation may be relevant. In Melanie Klein and Joan Riviere, *Love, Hate, and Reparation* (New York: Norton, 1964), she writes: "Side by side with the destructive impulses in the unconscious mind both of the child and of the adult, there exists a profound urge to make sacrifices, in order to help and put right loved people who in phantasy have been harmed or destroyed." She continues:

> Ultimately, in making sacrifices for somebody we love and in identifying ourselves with the loved person, we play the part of a good parent, and behave towards this person as we felt at times the parents did to us — or as we wanted them to do . . . Thus, by reversing a situation, namely in acting towards another person as a good parent, in phantasy we re-create and enjoy the wished-for-love and goodness of our parents. But to act as good parents towards other people may also be a way of dealing with the frustrations and sufferings of the past. Our grievances against our parents for having frustrated us, together with the feelings of hate and revenge to which these have given rise in us, and again, the feelings of guilt and despair arising out of this hate and revenge because we have injured the parents whom at the same time we love — all these, in phantasy, we may undo in retrospect (taking away some of the grounds of hatred), by *playing at the same time the parts of loving parents and loving children*. (68-68, emphasis added)

Klein is writing here about what we do with nonparents. If, as in Fuller's fiction, the dynamic is returned and played out against the parent herself or himself, we have many kinds of reparations: atonement for the child's imagined injury to the parent, repair of the parent as a person, repair of the parent as a parent, and consequent repair of the child.

20. Chevigny, *Woman and the Myth;* see especially 484-85, 487-88, 493-94.

21. Thus I would never have ventured in *Woman and the Myth* the extensive psychological speculation I outlined in the first part of this essay, and I offer it now because it supports my notion of biography.

22. *The Reproduction of Mothering: Psychoanalysis and the Sociology of Gender* (Berkeley: University of California Press, 1978).

23. Susan Contratto and Nancy Chodorow, "The Fantasy of the Perfect Mother," in *Rethinking the Family: Some Feminist Questions*, ed. Barrie Thorne and Marilyn Yalom (New York: Longman, 1982), 55.

24. Although Chodorow and Contratto are concerned, as I am not here, with developing theories of child development, I believe that my approach to biography is consonant with their recommendations:

> We would suggest that feminists draw upon and work to develop theories of child development that are interactive and that accord the infant and child agency and intentionality, rather than characterize it as a passive reactor to drives or environmental pressures. We need to build theories that recognize collaboration and compromise as well as conflict. We should look to theories that stress relational capacities and experiences instead of insatiable, insistent drives; to theories in which needs do not equal wants; in which separation is not equivalent to deprivation, and in which autonomy is different from abandonment;

in which the child is thought to have some interest in growth and development. (70-71)

25. Jane Flax, "The Conflict Between Nurturance and Autonomy in Mother-Daughter Relationships and Within Feminism," *Feminist Studies* 4 (June 1978): 171-89.

Suffragists, 1910

Jane Marcus

Jane Marcus

INVISIBLE MENDING

Why, I wonder, has it taken me so long to see the connections between my work, feminist criticism and biography, and my mother's work, "invisible mending"? Her skill, an extremely delicate and meticulous kind of darning, the mending of moth holes and cigarette burns, is exactly like the skill I have tried to develop as a writer and historian. Both are, as Emmeline Pankhurst said of politics during the struggle for women's suffrage, simply "house-keeping on a grand scale." Preserving the fabric of history is the same job as mending the family's jackets and sweaters. My efforts to found a feminist collective of scholarship represent a wish to repro-duce the scene of my mother and my aunt in their shop in Boston in the forties and fifties. Invisible mending has now become for me a metaphor for the feminist criticism our collective produces. We want to weave women's lives and works back into the fabric of culture, as if they had never been rent. It sometimes seems as if we are like Penelope, weaving by day and undoing our work by night, though it is others who seem bent on undoing what we weave. Penelope's shuttle, my mother's needle, and my pen are implements of order. They speak — the shuttle, the needle, and the pen — in one voice, not of destruction and war but of the preservation of culture.

A second question plagues me: Why have I worked so long and so intensely on women? My dissertation began with research on the women's suffrage movement in England, and I have tried to re-create the lives of Elizabeth Robins, Rebecca West, Virginia Woolf,

Olive Schreiner, and, most recently, the composer Dame Ethel Smyth in relation to it. My first book was a collection of the writings of Caroline Norton, the poet and novelist whose personal suffering drove her to achieve passage of the Custody of Children Acts in England. *New Feminist Essays on Virginia Woolf* and *Virginia Woolf: A Feminist Slant* came out of a desire to extend the sewing circle to the writing circle of collective feminist scholarship. *The Young Rebecca: Writings of Rebecca West, 1911-1917* came out of the desire to convince historians that there was a leftist intellectual feminist component in the suffrage movement. And *One's Own Trumpet: Ethel Smyth and Virginia Woolf: A Portrait in Letters,* the book I am working on now, proves two points — that women artists influence each other more than we suspect and that not all late-Victorian lesbians internalized deviance as Radclyffe Hall did. Dame Ethel Smyth loved women and wrote memoir after memoir of her love affairs. My scholarly career is the story of the pursuit of authority in women. It is difficult to separate memory into components. What is self-indulgence and what is the political motive of proving to myself that I was always a feminist, primarily bonded to women and women's work? I tell my own tale here in the hope that in the process of reweaving the threads of my own life, it may help other women make sense of their lives and work.

In my all-girls' Catholic high school in Boston in the 1950s, we divided our heroines into two categories — hunting amazons and fishing amazons. Obviously, Joan of Arc was a hunting amazon and Saint Teresa was a fishing amazon. These appellations were applied also to ourselves and to the nuns who taught us. Before we knew that the idea of the female utopia was a historical reality and a feminist literary convention with a long history, we sensed our special circumstances. (Since then, as a critic I have needed those two figures in my working life, a Virginia Woolf, fisher of women's souls, a Rebecca West, hunter of women's hearts.)

Passing almost daily between the poles of the active life and the contemplative life, we switched allegiances to and from the frail, spiritual nuns and the fighting, achieving nuns. As white as our veils, we fainted in chapel from fasting. We wept and wailed with what my long-suffering Protestant mother called "the rosary bead clutchers," baroque religious activity that often coincided with premenstrual cramps. We briefly protested on entering our high school because the boys' schools had both Greek and Latin and we were denied Greek, an unfair division since it was our role to help the boys with their homework. Unlike Virginia Woolf, I never did get beyond the Greek alphabet.

Another protest, however, had more significance. This world, like the rest of Boston at the time, contained two kinds of Catholics, the Irish and the Italians. Often there were two churches on one block, and one never entered the other ethnic sanctuary except on Holy Thursday. Most of our nuns were Irish, and there was a statue of St. Patrick in the school hall, duly decorated by our rebellious crew one March 17 with orange crepe paper. My father, a Catholic, always claimed that the nuns in my school, the sisters of St. Joseph, had a monopoly on feminine mediocrity in the state of Massachusetts. This confused me because my father had made me compete for a scholarship to St. Joseph's to escape from the small-town high school where he taught history and coached the football team.

It was a long commute to Mount Saint Joseph Academy, by bus and train, on an empty stomach, stopping for Mass on the way, and risking the daily threat of switchblades from the boys of Brighton High, across the street, who slashed our prim, long-sleeved blue serge uniforms. In the morning there was a flurry of activity outside the gates as we rubbed off the lipstick and removed the forbidden bobby socks by which we tried to look like ordinary high school girls on our travels to and from "the Mount." In honesty I cannot claim that all vanity of dress was abolished once we were behind bars in our imitation nuns' habits, for there was a great traffic in embroidered handkerchiefs, worn in the breast pocket as a badge of our mothers' skill at starching and ironing. Otherwise the somber navy seas of serge were broken only by student council badges and medals of the Virgin Mary, to whom we idolatrously prayed in French, Latin, and English. My daughter wears a modern version of this uniform, blue jeans and a sweatshirt, and scorns the girls in Shetland sweaters and pleated skirts, descendants of the girls my friends and I envied.

Helen Keller and Anne Frank were our heroines, Amy Lowell our favorite poet. It was a world of great discipline, intellectual and emotional growth directed by female authority. We worked collectively to write and perform plays, our great success being a version of Genesis with a Greek chorus. I suppose that once you have played Joan of Arc in a homemade coat of mail at age twelve and the voice of God at age fifteen, there is no stopping you. I was exported to play the female parts in the boys' schools but we managed to do the male characters in our own.

Every day after school I crossed the street to another world of nuns — the white-robed ones of the Kennedy Memorial Hospital — to put in a full shift as a nurse's aide in a ward with twenty-three little girls with cerebral palsy. I was paid thirty-five cents an hour for the back-breaking labor of removing braces, bathing and feeding the spastic children, and scrubbing down the kitchen and bathroom. Protest over my pay was impossible because the nuns did this work for nothing (or, rather, for the greater glory of God). My sister, two years younger, worked in the mental ward at St. Elizabeth's Hospital, dividing her day between sane nuns and crazy nuns, and soon quit. Her memories are entirely different from mine, for in two years in our teens the class identity of our family changed. My identity was then and is now that of a working-class intellectual; hers is middle class. She went into the convent, like most of my school friends, but eventually left the Maryknoll Missionaries.

My attempts at blood sisterhood have always been less successful than those at political and scholarly sisterhood. My sister left the convent and lived instead the life of a Catholic wife and mother with four children. Both my left-wing politics and feminism repelled her and we have seldom been able to leap over those barriers back to the bonds of childhood. In the winter of 1981 I read with shock and disbelief the name of the Maryknoll nun who had been raped and murdered in El Salvador: She was my sister's best friend, god-mother to her children. Though they had left the convent together, the friend had gone back with the political commitment of the antiwar movement to bring a social message to the suffering peasants of El Salvador. Her cause was political and religious, but she died a woman's death. The loss of her best friend devastated my sister, and for the first time in years we were able to communicate. The last time I spoke to her the house was full of nuns preparing to demonstrate in Washington. Now she knew someone besides me who had demonstrated for a cause.

My father not only taught history and coached the local teams, he was a member of the hod-carrier's union and worked nights un-loading ships. Somewhere in between he took courses, earning a doctorate when I was thirteen in the rehabilitation of the blind. One of my clearest childhood memories is of sitting in the back of his classroom at the local high school while he lectured eloquently on labor history as an antidote to the textbook's treatment of strikes as evil plots of foreign anarchists. The father of my imagination wears a cloth cap and trudges up Summit Avenue with a lunch pail. The daughter of his imagination crosses the street and only hugs a white-collar daddy.

In my senior year at the Mount, messengers interrupted class to announce scholarships and acceptances at college. I had disobeyed my parents and the nuns by not applying to a Catholic college, but I had borrowed money from my aunt and had applied to Radcliffe. There was no announcement. I was called to the principal's office.

She called my mother; my mother cried. The nuns lectured, expressed their disappointment in me. They offered me not only tuition but board and room at Regis College. The occasion of this tragedy was my winning a scholarship to Radcliffe. I wonder what would have happened had I gone to Regis instead.

Harvard in the fifties was regarded locally as a hotbed of radicalism: I would lose my virginity. I would become a Communist. Lose my faith.

I lost my faith. I became a radical. But I hung on to my virginity for dear life. Mount Saint Joseph Academy had taught me something.

I was interviewed at Radcliffe by a well-meaning WASP dean who told me I was an experiment. Local students usually came from Girls' Latin; to take an Irish Catholic from an ordinary convent school was an event of some daring for the Boston Brahmins. While the announced Jewish quota was 40 percent, the Catholic quota was given in one figure. It was suggested that I meet my fellow experiments, and I did, making friends with a girl who was the daughter of a Cambridge policeman and a boy who worked afternoons in his father's Chinese laundry.

From my own tight community of creative women teachers and students, a separate female world of love, ritual, discipline and excellent performance, I went bewildered into a world where my religion, my sex, and my class defined me as an outsider to culture. Among the Seven Sisters, Radcliffe was not the Cinderella, but it is odd to think that the little active feminism of the day was organized by "outsiders" — commuters — and went largely unnoticed by the student body in general. In this world there were no women professors, and Amy Lowell's poetry was laughed at. I played a few parts in Eugene O'Neill plays and joined the newspaper, which was staffed by outsiders and "townies." Not only were there no fishing amazons or hunting amazons, it was hard to find any amazons at all.

Snobbery about clothes was worse than snobbery toward Irish Catholics. My jeans and pigtails were not in conformity with Radcliffe's rules and were out of place in the cashmere sweater set. I developed a passionate longing for good clothes, and for a long time I dreamed of becoming the feature editor of *Vogue*. Several years later, when the job was actually offered, I didn't take it and went to graduate school at Brandeis instead. But I must say that my being elected one of the ten best-dressed Cliffies, in the clothes of the woman whose children I cared for in a room-and-board job, meant more than I like to remember. How I scrimped to save the money to buy a Marimekko dress solely because I saw Adrienne Rich, pregnant poet, pushing a baby carriage down Brattle Street in one. It served me well, and my mother made it into a maternity dress, which I wore for three pregnancies and passed on to my sister.

Adrienne Rich was obviously both a hunting amazon and a fishing amazon, but I wouldn't have dared to approach her. While at Radcliffe, however, I met a host of interesting characters. I met a lesbian painter who urged me to write, a Greek girl and her sister from Boston University who urged me to write, and a half-Israeli, half-Italian classical archaeologist who thought writing was a waste of time. It wasn't the Mount, but things were getting better. I went to study at Widener with a friend from Louisville. A Black student sat down opposite us and my friend actually fainted. Her explanation of her fear of Black men was a revelation to me since, during high school, I had attended Father O'Connor's teenage jazz Sundays at Storyville. I had also spent many an evening alone or with a girlfriend in Black jazz bars in Roxbury, always courteously ignored. I told my new friend of my mother's ferocious and successful attempt to buy a house in Newton for a Black friend, her handling of the neighbors who threw rocks. She was astonished, and our friendship made little progress. I met an independent amazon type from Arizona who carried a rifle in the back of her car, but she got expelled. She was the stuff Republican congresswomen are made of.

Halfway through my freshman year I came home to find my mother sitting on the floor reading my letters from a Dartmouth medical student, a poet and Orthodox Jew from Providence. We had met at a high school play contest. Since he played Harvey the rabbit and I played God, we should have known the relationship wouldn't last. My mother was amused and I was outraged. In high dudgeon, I packed my belongings in a laundry bag and left home. A kindly Radcliffe dean found me a room-and-board job with a wealthy family where I became Irish maid and a governess to the children. One of the first formal dinners I served was to the master of the house and the boys being initiated into the Hasty Pudding Club. Two of them were in my English classes. I was mortified — needlessly. They didn't recognize me.

My father wrote to the dean. Obviously I had left home because I had oedipal problems. They all had to do with my father. He suggested I be sent to the Harvard psychiatrist. I went. When I walked into the office the psychiatrist looked at me; he looked at the papers on his desk. He didn't ask me to sit down, and the interview had the brevity and epiphanic power of the famous Lacanian psychiatric sessions. Instead of a discourse about my father, he said: "Young lady, have you ever lied to your mother?" "Of course not," I said. "I couldn't lie to my mother. She's my mother." "Try it," he said. "It would be a good beginning." I was mystified and shocked. Lie to my mother? I was never even going to speak to her again.

It took me twenty years, a rebirth in radical politics, marriage, three children, a miscarriage, and the sweating sisterhood of scholarship to whom I owe my deepest allegiance to figure out what the Harvard psychiatrist was up to. He perceived, as the Freudian patriarchs always do, that this eighteen-year-old's primary identification and loyalty were to her mother. He was suggesting a strategy of survival in the patriarchy, a cutting of those bonds. I've laid many another burden on my mother's lap. I've been angry and aloof and felt unloved. But I've never lied, for there is honor among women and I have inherited her fierce love of truth for its own sake.

Critics have argued that the key to women's autobiographies is self-revelation through the other — God, one's husband, or mentor. But the theory falls apart because there are so many counterexamples — Simone de Beauvoir, for example. In *Reinventing Womanhood*, Carolyn Heilbrun has shown that most of the academic women of achievement she surveyed were first children, sonsubstitutes, father's daughters. While in fact I fall into that category, more careful analysis forces me to fall out again — it is the mother who matters.

Life was hard for my mother, and we girls often got out of hand. She use to say, "I don't beat you 'cause I hate you. I beat you to show my authority." She said this in a broad brogue, imitating her grandmother. "I don't bate ye 'cause I hate ye. I bate ye to show me aw-thaw-dity." She was and is authoritative, believing in "will power" and its capacity to conquer all obstacles. One could argue that her daughters' abiding need for a circle of women of authority is a replication of the family circle in which she, her mother, and her sisters solaced each other. But what I remember is the way they worked, in the years of my childhood, my mother and her sister keeping a shop where they did "invisible mending," then working at home, heads bent in the same curve as their goosenecked lamps, over the cashmere sweaters and sport jackets delivered by the local tailors and cleaners. They both had a way of peering at us over their glasses, gnarled arthritic hands still plying the needle. Their button box was full of magic — glass buttons and shoe buttons, brass embossed buttons for naval uniforms, leather buttons for camel hair suits, lead weights for skirt hems and bits of fabric, ribbon, elastic, wool, cotton and silk threads, and sometimes a shiny penny at the bottom. The treadle of the old Singer whirred and whistled, the music of my childhood.

It was invisible mending I thought of when I first read *A Doll's House*. Nora stays up all night for years doing fine sewing to pay back what she borrowed to save her husband's life. Her sewing is invisible in more ways than one, and she gets no domestic glory from it, keeping it secret at all costs, playing Helmer's little bird for all she's worth to maintain her husband's status as a middle-class banker. Her work, though it saved his life, would expose him as something less than a good provider. By her chivalrous code Nora has a right to expect that her husband will protect her honor when her debt is revealed. But his conscience is capitalist and patriarchal; his class identity cannot bear the fact that it was she who supported him. His is a social system where men achieved respectable middle-class status by keeping their wives out of the marketplace and by denying that housework and the raising of children were work, robbing women of their self-respect.

Invisible mending is delicate, necessary, skilled labor, mending and preserving the fabric of society. The measure of a woman's skill is the degree to which the work can't be seen. The holes are darned to perfection. Now it is impossible to maintain middle-class standards without two salaries; divorced or single mothers find it difficult to provide for their children. But for my father and his contemporaries, limiting a wife's work to the family's needs was a kind of status to struggle for. The shop itself provided my mother and her sister with a network of self-respect that they never achieved in the isolation of their homes, where the differentiation of labor was not clear and where shame was attached to having to work at all.

My own situation — as an academic in the seventies, jobless for four years, working in a study off the kitchen, a seven-by-seven-foot space — showed me how depressing working at home, piecework for small amounts of money, must have been for my mother. The intellectual piecework I did for small amounts of money — writing book reviews and essays — amounted in essence to the same thing. If I were in a shop with my sisters — the university — a paycheck would give me self-respect and the definition of the collective identity of "working." As it was, the space I occupied, transformed by my husband's effort of building bookshelves to the ceiling, retained the warm damp smell of its previous existence as the laundry. I wrote at a desk looking out the same window where I folded diapers and patched blue jeans, letting out, taking in, the rather coarse and very visible mending of a mother with growing children.

My overworked colleagues used to tell me how lucky I was to be there when the children came home from school, to have time for making jams and jellies and for keeping a garden. It was by any measure a good life compared to my mother's or grandmother's or the lives of most women in the world, spent in backbreaking physical labor. Writing was a luxury for which I could thank my husband's job. If I were inside the system or had a hope of it, they argued, I would be less bold; as a critic I would not attack Quentin Bell or Nigel Nicolson; I would know which side my bread was buttered on.

In 1974 after my first year of teaching, I went to the English Institute at Radcliffe/Harvard to hear papers on Virginia Woolf. I hadn't been back to Cambridge for years, and it was an important emotional and political experience. I shared a room with Moira Ferguson, a feminist critic and author of a book on Mary Wollstonecraft, and we stayed up all night telling life stories, variations on "how I became a feminist critic." We were housed in a Radcliffe dormitory, and I was overcome with nostalgia. As a commuter, a "townie," and then a "room-and-board girl" in the days when students were required to live on campus, I had ached with longing to live in a dorm. I had romanticized this ideal sisterhood of gracious living and scholarly endeavor beyond the bounds of decency. At thirty-five I finally slept in a Radcliffe dormitory and, sure enough, it was magic. There was a sisterhood of scholarship in Virginia Woolf studies and I had joined it.

The place was full of hunting amazons and fishing amazons. They hissed and booed when Quentin Bell's letter was read aloud denouncing Ellen Hawkes's feminist work on Virginia Woolf. They gave a similar response to the paper of a professor from a famous university when his facts and dates were wrong. Obviously they could hunt or fish at will, these accomplished amazons.

One of them had been two years behind me at Radcliffe. When we compared notes, she said she'd read *Mrs. Dalloway* in a course. I hadn't, though my field was modern British literature. A professor had told me the novels were too full of death and despair to count as major works. It turned out that she was one of the first women to write for the *Harvard Crimson* and had married the editor. I said I had edited the Radcliffe newspapers and that we had conducted a campaign against women writing for the *Crimson* (and a similar, unsuccessful campaign against letting men into the Radcliffe library). She swore that she never knew the Radcliffe paper existed. And we had thought ourselves such a brave lot of feminists.

The events I remember from my Radcliffe days all concern women or politics. Helen White in her purple suit came from Wisconsin for a semester to lecture on the metaphysical poets.

Young women hung from the rafters and sat on the floors and windowsills to hear her. Isak Dinesen read in a hoarse whisper, her huge coal-black eyes staring out of an almost naked skull, only thinly veiled with flesh. Walter Jackson Bate gave his new course in the history of criticism. Like all the other students, I had wept yearly with him over Samuel Johnson. I went to protest a low grade on a paper on T. S. Eliot's right-wing politics and criticism, a commonplace enough subject nowadays but fraught with danger when we were being taught how sensible and objective and right he was. I was breathless in the T. A.'s office. My friend the Cambridge cop's daughter worked as a waitress in Schrafft's. Recently T. S. Eliot had been there drinking tea. My friend had dared me to ask him in person whether his political and literary views could properly be called conservative and right wing. Graciously, he had bought me a pot of Schrafft's tinny tea and for an hour had discoursed on his conservative philosophy. "Just ask him yourself," I exclaimed to the astonished T. A. "He's proud of being right wing." She changed my grade, and I learned to fight back when reactionary social views are paraded as objective reality. The low grade was not for pointing out that Eliot was a reactionary but for daring to disapprove of the great man's ideas.

In my time at Radcliffe, the Irish Catholic "experiments" seemed to work. My friend and I graduated with honors and went off to study Yeats at Trinity College, Dublin. What a farce: Everyone but us knew that you could earn a master's degree there without lifting a finger. We insisted on meeting with our tutors. If there were no lectures, could we at least write papers? We lived in a filthy, cold basement flat on bacon and eggs and foolish hope. Every time we went to tutorial, the slightly drunk, superior young man would fling us to the floor, pinch, pull, and pant at the sight of what to him was fair game, American girls. Fainthearted, we retired from the fray.

Back in Boston I went to work for Jerome and His All Girl Press, which is what we called the rattrap in Scollay Square where I edited *Panorama*, the Boston guide magazine, and theater programs. Then I began to do public relations for a junior college while earning a degree at Brandeis. I had done all but the dissertation, in seventeenth-century religious literature, when we went off to Santa Monica. I had married a left-wing Jewish mathematician. *Time* and *The New Yorker* disappeared from the bathroom shelves, replaced by the *Guardian* and the *Monthly Review*. He rode a motorbike, went mountain climbing, worked in civil rights, and started the first antiwar teach-ins at M.I.T. In California he and his friends organized the Peace and Freedom party, an alliance of antiwar people, socialists, and Black Panthers. He was fired from Rand Corporation for publicly urging draft resistance. I registered people out of the Democratic party into the Peace and Freedom party on the beach with my babies and belly. Off we went to Northwestern University — three babies in three years, born in Boston, Los Angeles, and Chicago. More antiwar activities.

When Ben was two, the Northwestern English Department broke its rules — I was married, over thirty, and had children — and let me in, refusing to accept my Brandeis credits and insisting that I begin all over again. Northwestern boasted a few amazons who urged me on, and Florence Ross, of blessed memory, a black woman from the South Side of Chicago, baby-sat and cleaned the house so I could go to class. I never would have gone at all if it hadn't been for Elaine Shinbrot, who gave me Doris Lessing's *The Golden Notebook*. She would squirm at the thought of being called a hunting or fishing amazon, but there was never anyone like her for bouncing a baby, stirring a pot, washing your kids' diapers, all the while carrying on hot political debate. I began to study the history and literature of English feminism. The antiwar movement had forced the universities to accept unheard-of dissertation topics. (Black studies and women's studies were relatively easy for the university to allow. It is getting them to stop investing in South Africa we haven't been able to achieve.) It was 1969-70 — Christopher Lasch encouraged Ellen Du Bois to work on American suffrage and me to work on English suffragettes. There was little to go on and we did primary bibliographies and drove the Inter-Library-Loan people mad. I wanted to write on Virginia Woolf. But my advisor said that everything had been done on Virginia Woolf and directed me to Elizabeth Robins, an American actress, novelist, and playwright who had brought Ibsen's plays to London and had been an active suffragette, serving on the board of the Pankhursts' Women's Social and Political Union. I spent 1970-71 in London on a fellowship, tracking down Robins's papers and letters and reading women's papers, letters, diaries, and political pamphlets in the Fawcett Library and the British Museum. Here was the whole history of women, practically invisible. I felt the same thrill Virginia Woolf felt in researching the lives of the obscure, the eccentrics, our ancestresses and their mothers and aunts. "One likes romantically to feel oneself a deliverer," Woolf wrote of the stranded ghosts of history — women and the working class.

It was, I think, the only romantic indulgence she allowed herself. It was a grand indulgence, and I allowed it to myself in London and I allow it to myself now. We women scholars are our own redeemers.

We do rescue and deliver our people — women — from the obscurity of history. Is this a shared messianic feminist delusion of grandeur? There are, Woolf pointed out, no lives of maids in the *Dictionary of National Biography*. The work of feminist scholarship gives one a remarkably clear conscience. One is definitely not old Professor Z of *A Room of One's Own*, inditing the millionth work on Miltonic inversion. We are amazons, fishing and hunting in our own past with the political motive of changing possibilities for the future. We may seem to outsiders both frantic and smug. But we work and write zealously in passionate haste, those of us who know the history of women. How long will it last? Like Septimus Smith in *Mrs. Dalloway*, we hear the heavy breathing. How soon will Holmes and Bradshaw (the psychiatrists and the social police of society) be upon us? Patriarchy's winged chariot is hurrying near. If it were not for the commands of women like Rebecca West, we would hearken to the voices of our patriarchal professors and not write essays of our own.

Steeped as she was in Elizabethan travel literature, Virginia Woolf described her own work of reviving obscure lives as an adventure. She would lead "a relief party" to rescue the reputation of Mrs. Radcliffe. She would lead a search party to ferret out lives of the obscure. It is a great adventure to continue this search into the unexplored continent of woman's past, to plant our flags on domestic territory that men have ignored. It allows us a voyage out into a literal no-man's-land without a suspicion of patriotic or imperialist motives.

On our scholarly adventures, we rend the veils that cover the lives of women of the past, and thousands of us are presently at work darning the myriad holes in the history of culture. This garment itself is so worn, fragile, tattered, moth-eaten, with great gaps where the lives of women were, that often we cannot do more than patch hurriedly, darn crudely, and move on. Our work will not always be invisible, for some of those holes in our history were made deliberately by violent men. They were burnt in anger, stained in the blood of rape and torture, slashed by knives. But our object in this labor is to make a usable past, to make the cloak of history wearable so our daughters may fling it over their shoulders and go off on tracks of their own.

There's more to my story, and more to ours, but the very telling of our stories helps us onward. Adrienne Rich has said that we ought to ask ourselves exactly at what moment women became de-eroticized for us? I hardly know the answer but sense instinctively that it is one of the right questions for feminist scholars. Undoubtedly there is an erotic component in the excitement of women's research into the lives and work of other women, and the bonds that hold together the sisterhood of feminist scholarship have more than a few erotic threads. The intellectual challenge of our collective task is itself erotic. But as a socialist feminist I do not like to see lesbian feminists splinter off into a separate movement. As a mother of sons I feel it is just as important to work against the draft as for passage of the ERA.

As a feminist literary critic I believe that we should write as truthfully as we can, singly and collectively for the sake of the future. Our task is clear. But I worry. Will our feminist literary critical efforts be as lost to our descendants as the work of earlier feminist critics has been lost to us? Is this whole process doomed like housework to go on forever? Will they always be ripping holes in our work, leaving us to sew them up again, always rending while we are mending? And how can we work out an alliance between women and oppressed peoples everywhere, with our working-class brothers, across the lines of race and class that divide us? We need not only take back the night from rapists but take back the day from those who exploit working people.

I have not told here the sordid stories of personal oppression I've experienced. Sometimes they seem ridiculous in comparison to the daily indignities suffered by one Black cleaning woman who comes from the South Side of Chicago to the suburbs. Professional ethics, that old-boy code, advises silence. The advice of Tillie Olsen is better. We should break the silence with an axe if necessary, and working women will then break theirs. I have not told of the professor, drunk and red with rage in my Ph.D. orals, slamming his fist on the table, shouting, "It's my job in this department to see that women don't get Ph.D.'s!" Or the story of the exam committee, refusing to read my list of books on the history of English feminism, my field, and forcing me to write for two hours on Irish history instead. The feminist scholar's humiliations in trying to get books needed for research, finally getting a library card as a faculty wife in the university where she earned a Ph.D., seem trivial compared to the daily lives of secretaries. But as Virginia Woolf wrote, these stories should be told. We owe a debt of gratitude to the obscure who wrote biographies and autobiographies. How much of my own life and work owes to Marie Bashkirtseff's diary, the memoirs of the mathematician Sophie Kovalevsky, Jane Ellen Harrison's *Reminiscences,* Ethel Smyth's eight volumes on music and friendship with women, Elizabeth Robins's *Both Sides of the Curtain* and *Ibsen and the Actress, Theatre and Friendship,* the autobiography in *Of Woman Born, Reinventing Womanhood,* and Tillie Olsen's novels and stories? But it is not only the life stories of heroines and great women that we need. Woolf thanks ordinary women, like ourselves, for adding to the collective history that allows us to "think back through our mothers."

I confess that I don't read men anymore, that even my favorite poets annoy me as a women, though I can't extinguish the flames of some lines from Donne and Yeats that still burn in the memory. It is Alice Walker's story "Everyday Use" that tells my life story. I wince with the pain and truth her tale exposes of my own experience. The young Black woman has gone north to be educated and comes back to her mother and sister to reclaim the grandmother's quilts she was ashamed to bring to college. Now they are works of art, part of the history of Black culture. Just as the mother resents her daughter's new name and language, my mother felt patronized by my "Radcliffe accent." Just as Walker's heroine-mother keeps the quilts for her more loyal daughter, I didn't get my grandmother's Irish cut glass (I remember how the celery dish caught the light at all our festive dinners). The cut glass went to my sister, though there is a further irony in the fact that she sold it in a garage sale.

Autobiographies act as moral tales, exempla, like the lives of the saints to the religious, the lives of revolutionaries to radicals, the life of Einstein to scientists. Woolf thanks the obscure and ordinary for preserving their lives as well:

> for persisting, in spite of their invincible mediocrity, in writing their memoirs; for providing precisely that background, atmosphere, and standing of common earth which nourish people of greater importance and prevent them from shrivelling to dry sticks or congealing to splendid pinnacles of inaccessible ice. For imagine a literature composed entirely of good books . . . starvation would soon ensue. No one would read at all.[1]

Woolf's argument is a serious one, despite its graceful and mocking tone; it poses a radical alternative to the great men/great books attitude toward history and literature. We do persist, despite our invincible mediocrity, in writing these memoirs, convinced by another theory of Woolf's that Shakespeare's sister will live and write because we have lived and written and she will consciously stand on our backs. Memoirs, Woolf wrote,

> do not merely break the ascent and encourage us to mightier efforts. They have a more important office. They are the dressing-rooms, the wings, the sculleries, the bubbling cauldrons, where life seethes and steams and is forever on the boil. By sousing ourselves in memoirs we keep our

minds supple, and so when at last we tackle the finished product — *Hamlet* for example — we bring to the understanding of him fertile minds imbued with ideas, at once creative and receptive. So we can never approach Ajax and Electra; and in consequence they are never taken into the depths of our beings, but remain always a little craggy, a little indissoluble, an inch or two beyond our grasp. For literature did undoubtedly once lie down with life, and all her progeny, being the result of that mis-alliance, are more or less impure.[2]

Woolf was a fishing amazon who often joined the hunters. Perhaps she felt, looking back at the little purple volume in which she wrote her feminist utopia for Violet Dickinson, the way I feel when I look back on my days in a girls' school. She herself wrote a brilliant introduction to a collection of lives of working women and published their memoirs. When some of the contributors criticized her, she took their advice in good part. Then she suggested that the memoirs of herself and her friends ought to be collected and introduced by the members of the Working Woman's Cooperative Guild. She paid her own debt to working-class women by including the figure of the charwoman in all her work. The pen is not the penis, and when we women critics lift it we lift it like the needle of my mother and my aunt, mending our way over the uneven hemline of the out-skirts of history.

This is a success story. I am now teaching at the University of Texas while continuing the invisible mending of literary criticism and history. So far, I have not been tempted to suppress my feminist writing or to stifle the voice of my pen. But recently I found a moth hole in my husband's suit. I am told that there is no one in town who can do invisible mending. If the skills of my mother can be lost in one generation, can the skills of feminist criticism disappear as well? We are not as different from working-class women as we sometimes think. Because we want to make the holes invisible in the fabric of society, we must keep our pens and needles sharp against the cloak of invisibility that our culture would still like to fling over us.

Notes

I dedicate this essay to my mother, Ruth Healy Connor, and my aunt, Marion Healy Wilson, and their work at the craft of invisible mending in their shop and in their homes.
1. Virginia Woolf, "The Eccentrics," *Athenaeum*, 25 April 1919, 230-31.
2. Ibid.

Crystal Eastman

Eleanor Roosevelt

Blanche Wiesen Cook

Blanche Wiesen Cook

BIOGRAPHER AND SUBJECT:
A CRITICAL CONNECTION

Who do we choose to write about? What moves us? What do we care
about? For biographers, I think, all choices are autobiographical.

Biographers traffic in individual sensibilities. We seek to understand change and process through individual lives and how they are
lived. We believe in the influence and impact of the individual on
the political, economic, and social forces of society. We have
chemical, emotional, and profound connections to our chosen subject. We may not always like our subject, but there is no reason for
selection unless there is a basis for identification — for real understanding.

As a journalist and historian, I have been attracted to biographical
subjects whose ideas and politics seemed to me not merely influential but unusual and imaginative. As an historian I am concerned
with the process of social change. My own commitment to peace
research, economic justice, and human rights influence always my
choice of focus. My subjects reflect my interests. I am moved deeply
by what moved them. The initial contact is strengthened when I
notice that a subject stands apart, assesses circumstances critically,
imaginatively, and well (from my point of view), and offers new
bases upon which to build alternative visions. A relationship develops as I seek to investigate and analyze why my subject made the
decisions he or she did and came to follow the path he or she
followed.

I studied Crystal Eastman (1881-1928) at first because she was an antimilitarist during a period of heightened international tension. During the early years of the war in Indochina (1962-1964), my professional interests turned from foreign economic policy to peace research, and Crystal Eastman emerged significant. That she was also a feminist and a socialist in the World War I era concerned me only later, when my own vision and priorities changed and developed as a result of the contemporary feminist movement. Similarly, Dwight David Eisenhower appealed to me as the war throughout Indochina continued to rage, because he had set limits. Of all post-World War II presidents, only Eisenhower insisted that there are real fiscal and political dangers to America's imperial commitments; there are actually limits beyond which the United States cannot afford to go. His warning against the growing influence of the military-industrial complex was not the coda of his career but a theme that ran through it. I was fascinated also by his diverse use of power, both strategic and covert. Currently, my work on Eleanor Roosevelt enables me for the first time to combine my interests — the role of women in society, the importance of and potentials for women's support networks, human rights, international relations, and the various forms of power.

Although there are many reasons to select a subject for study, including the need to understand the bestial and violent as well as the virtuous and noble, most biographers choose to write about people they care about and can identify with. In my opinion, the best biographies are those, written with passion and intensity, that seek to redress the wrongs, reconstitute the spirit, restore and celebrate the subject.

For me the process of writing is itself a time of joy. During the course of research I develop very personal, intimate relations with my subjects. They grow and change and are generally full of surprises. I dream about the people I write about — they enter my conversations, intrude on the privacy of my bath, join me in the ocean and the garden. They tell me stories, give me feedback, disagree, suggest new sources. I listen very carefully. Frequently a great flirtation emerges. In the process of writing about several radical women, two presidents, and Eleanor Roosevelt, I am aware that vastly different relations emerged with each. Except for Woodrow Wilson, who bored me (although he was the subject of my dissertation), all the women and men I have written about interest me personally and politically. And I have had personal and political relations with them.

Still ignorant of the truths beneath and the complexities of the myths of U. S. history, I landed originally on Woodrow Wilson because he seemed a liberal internationalist rather decently committed to peace and progressive reform. But when I was a graduate student in diplomatic history and foreign economic policy at the Johns Hopkins University, my career plans were altered by U.S. military policy in Vietnam.

One of my mentors, Charles A. Barker, a long-time pacifist and antinuclear activist, talked about creating what was to become the Conference on Peace Research in History (CPRH). This organization grew rapidly, became international, combined activism with research, and introduced a pacific or anti-war perspective to professional international studies. I became executive secretary of the CPRH, edited the first *Bibliography on Peace Research in History* (1969), and was senior editor of the Garland Library on War and Peace, a 360-volume reprint series that supplied students and scholars with a basic library of books on the history of the organized peace movement, the political economy of war, international law, arms limitation and arbitration, and nonresistance and nonviolence. At the same time, my interest in Woodrow Wilson was transformed. He was not only boring, but disingenuous. I disliked him and ultimately focused on the loyal opposition to him. That was my first meeting with Crystal Eastman. The Wilson Papers at the Library of Congress contain angry, vigorous letters of admonition and protest signed by Crystal Eastman, executive secretary of the American Union Against Militarism.

The American Union Against Militarism (AUAM) was organized in 1915 by Jane Addams, Lillian Wald, Crystal Eastman, Paul Kellogg, Max Eastman, Oswald Garrison Villard, and other pre-World War I reformers to keep the United States neutral and, after 1917, to protect civil liberties during the war. Of all the people involved in the AUAM, I felt most closely connected to Crystal Eastman. Her style attracted me. Direct, provocative, and dashing, she never walked away from a fight. She appreciated the complexities of all struggles. She taught me much about women in society that I now take for granted. Although I was not a feminist as a graduate student, my current conviction that we can have it all, demand it all, work for it all derives from her vision that it was all connected. There would be no social change without peace, no peace without feminism, no feminism without absolute sexual freedom. More than any other woman activist of the World War I era she combined a commitment to radical social change with militant feminism. A dedicated and independent socialist, she never subordinated her commitment to equal rights for women and sexual freedom to any misogynist version of social change. She understood

that ultimately feminism and socialism are about freedom —
freedom to work, to grow, to know, to play, to live in security, and
to live well.

My identification with the views and style of Crystal Eastman
became key to my ongoing work. Personal involvement is central for
me. If it fails to emerge in the course of research, I change subjects.
My writings on the progressive activist women have focused more
on Lillian Wald, Emma Goldman, and Crystal Eastman than on Jane
Addams.[1] When I consider future projects, I never consider Jane
Addams. Objectively that is too bad, since no full biography of Jane
Addams exists to date. On the other hand, I have never felt sufficiently engaged by Jane Addams to flirt with her. I flirt regularly
with Lillian Wald, a champion flirt. More precisely, I fancy that she
flirts with me — as is only appropriate given her daring and
prowess. She excites my imagination. She is bold. Her letters are
forthright. Her presence in any group is stirring. I can imagine with
ease the scene of a conference or an argument between Wald and
Eastman. They are alive for me. I identify with them both. But my
imagination tucks in when I try to imagine Addams in the room. A
brooding, quiet presence emerges, and I know I will never write
deeply about her. I may write accurately, but not deeply. Her
failure, in the words of Virginia Woolf, to "stir my imagination"
renders it impossible to write with the kind of intense and caring
understanding required. I am mindful of a range of connection.
Emma Goldman, for example, does excite my imagination. Her
presence is always vivid. I like to quote her. It is always thrilling
when she enters the page. But I do not identify with Emma
Goldman. Although I often admire her, her ways are not my ways,
even when her choices might be mine. Then, all too often her
choices are not mine. She is mendacious, cruel, self-stuffed.
Occasionally delightful and flamboyant, she is ultimately narrow-
minded and vicious to both enemies and allies. As a result, I will
never commit myself to the time needed for a serious study of her life.

On the other hand, I have been involved with Crystal Eastman
since I read her antimilitarist correspondence twenty years ago. On
occasion, the identification became total. While I was writing the
biographical essay for *Crystal Eastman: On Women and Revolution*
(1978), I drank too much, as she did, became red-faced with rage,
wrote vigorous letters to editors, and thought that, like Crystal
Eastman, I was dying of nephritis. I had kidney pains until I turned
in my manuscript — months before it was due because I believed I
was in a race with death. There were some aspects of identification
more difficult to achieve. I never grew taller, for example, and
Crystal Eastman was, after all, over six feet tall.

"Life is a big battle for the complete feminist," Crystal Eastman wrote in 1918, entirely convinced that the complete feminist would ultimately achieve total victory. In 1923, as one of the founders of Alice Paul's Congressional Union and National Women's Party, which introduced the ERA, Crystal Eastman wrote that this is a battle worth fighting even if it takes ten years. Although her time-table clearly required adjustment, her legacy is ongoing. She was in the vanguard of every major movement for social change. From her student days at Vassar (1903) and New York University Law School (1907), she was a radical feminist and suffragist.

Suffrage was for Crystal only a part of the power that women were denied and needed to reclaim. Tall, athletic, and robust, she sought to extend the contours of women's strength and women's sphere far beyond the vote. In 1909 she and Annette Kellerman, a champion swimmer and diver from Australia, then in New York to dive before Broadway audiences, attempted to work out a program for the physical regeneration of the female sex. At that time, Crystal spoke before large audiences on "women's right to physical equality with men." Freda Kirchwey, long-time editor of the Nation, recalled that Crystal pictured a utopia of athletes, with women "unhampered by preconceived ideas of what was fit or proper or possible for their sex to achieve." Crystal believed that "when women were expected to be agile, they became agile; when they were expected to be brave, they developed courage; when they had to endure, their endurance broke all records."

From adolescence on, Crystal recognized that fashion served to confine and limit women's ability to move freely. In matters of style — from short hair and short skirts to bathing suits without the customary stockings and skirts — her guiding principle was the achievement of greater and easier activity. Freedom involved discarding antique and unnecessary encumbrances. She never rode sidesaddle but careened about her home town "on a man's saddle in fluttering vast brown bloomers" that shocked polite society. When her neighbors complained to her father about her swimming clothes, she received her family's support. Although her father never said a word to her, Crystal believed that he was "startled and embarrassed to see his only daughter in a man's bathing suit with bare brown legs for all the world to see."

She was a pioneer in the field of labor legislation and industrial safety. Her book Work Accidents and the Law, published as part of the massive Pittsburgh Survey, became an international classic and was reprinted by Arno in 1970, when occupational safety and health seemed once again on the American agenda. In 1911 she drafted New York State's first workers' compensation law, a model law that

was used by many states thereafter. Before World War I she was
appointed to state and federal commissions of labor. During the war
she committed her vast energies to the international peace movement. She founded the Women's Peace Party, which became the
Women's International League for Peace and Freedom, and served
as executive director of the American Union Against Militarism,
which parented the American Civil Liberties Union.

After the war Crystal and Max Eastman copublished and coedited the *Liberator,* which was the only American journal to print
information about the new Communist governments and parties
of Russia and Europe. In March 1919 she was the first U.S. journalist to visit and report from Communist Hungary. In 1922 she
moved to England to live with her second husband, Walter Fuller,
and their two children. She remained identified with radical equal-
rights feminism and wrote regular columns for Lady Rhondda's
Time and Tide.

The writings of Crystal Eastman's later years relate to issues and
visions that concern all who seek a better, more humane environment. They relate to visions of socialism that would end poverty,
racism, and privilege; visions of feminism that would end dependence and subservience; visions of internationalism that would end
imperialism and devastating warfare.

"Freedom is a large word," she wrote in 1920. It demanded a large
struggle, a long battle. Personally, Crystal Eastman was dedicated
to freedom. She loved life and was surrounded by family and
friends. Protected and fortified by the support of women and men
who shared her ideals and battled beside her, she was free and bold.
Her close friend Jeannette Lowe once said, "You wouldn't believe
how free she was." Her brother wrote that she "poured magnetic
streams of generous love around her all the time" and boldly
plunged into new experiences. She was impulsive and passionate
and, evidently, consulted Dr. A. A. Brill, the first psychoanalyst to
practice in America, to bring her intense "libido down."

Crystal Eastman appeals to me both as historical figure and
private personality. I consider the challenge of her legacy my current work: work for women, civil liberties, and international peace;
the quest for individual freedom and public control over a self-
aggrandizing state. Her visions remain brave and distant. She
demanded radical change and committed herself to the long, many-
front struggle required for its achievement. The dynamism of her
feminist, socialist, and antimilitarist visions are a challenge to further explorations.

Today, part of my work involves organizations and political
activity. As a journalist and historian, however, I regard writing as

my core political work. My columns, short essays, and radio program, "Women and the World in the 1980s," reach large and diverse audiences and represent the major thrust of my political activity. It was out of this political activity that my original connection to Eisenhower emerged. In 1972 I wrote a column widely syndicated by the *Los Angeles Times,* originally called "Dwight David Eisenhower: Antimilitarist in the White House." In this column I argued that General Eisenhower believed that war was an outmoded strategy and that he prayed that World War II might be the last civil war to tear civilization apart. Not only did he believe there was no alternative to peace but for eight years he actually found alternatives to war. Basically, I concluded, George McGovern was the real heir to Eisenhower's vision, and "the real conservatives of America" would do well to vote for him.

This column had two immediate and long-term consequences. Clare Coss and I agreed to write "puff pieces" for a small outfit called Republicans for McGovern, and Sam Vaughn, then president of Doubleday, offered me a book contract asking only that I be "fair to Eisenhower." Since I had already decided that Eisenhower was the most undervalued president in U.S. history, I considered that an acceptable condition.

My eight years with Dwight David Eisenhower were not without emotional upheaval. Not passion precisely, but warmth, as well as respect for his principles and scruples; affection for his loyalty to friends (men do have support networks — we know them as command posts for power); and anguish over those aspects of his foreign policy that have left us a legacy of bloodshed, torture, and tragedy in global politics generally and in Central America particularly. The great betrayal of the peaceful aspects of Eisenhower's vision was a continual source of distress that informed my daily relationship to my book. In the end, I wrote of a "divided legacy" of peace and political warfare. Did I like Eisenhower? Very often. I identified with what I considered his honest struggle to pursue basic precepts that involved détente and human rights. Ultimately, his personal ambition and insistence on America's dominance truncated and distorted his pursuit of global stability. When I finished my book, after almost a decade of research, political growth, and personal change, I wrote in my journal — with some weariness — "I have now spent most of my vital youth with one dead general."

As I considered new projects, I longed above all to obtain Crystal Eastman's papers to complete a full biography. The status of Crystal Eastman's papers is, in part, a result of my own belated feminist awareness. My relationship to Crystal Eastman, it must be noted, began very slowly. In 1966, when I visited her brother Max Eastman,

I was writing about World War I, "hard history." When Max Eastman suggested that I might want to write about Crystal Eastman and showed me her letters to her mother and to him, an enormous collection, as well as the manuscripts of her feminist writings, I politely refused his offer. Reflecting my culture and socialization, I did not fully realize Crystal Eastman's importance until the women's movement altered my own consciousness and I began to think about all the women — activists and writers — who came before and whom we were until recently programmed to deny.

That programming not only caused us to lose contact with our foremothers but also contributed to our loss of control over the very sources of our history. Currently the quest for sources, the documents of our heritage, is a primary battlefield upon which knowledge — or truth — lays frequently a bloodied corpse. The battle for sources has much to do with property law and copyright law. But much more than who owns which words is involved. Issues of censorship and sensibility dominate the situation.

These are fundamental issues for writers. Who knows? Who controls our access to information? How do we assess historical facts without historical documents? What about privileged access? Are we to be limited once again to the genre of the court biography? Because our access to information determines who we write about, what we write, and the accuracy of our effort, it is essential that we fight the battle for access boldly and publicly.

World War I-era radicals and feminists, Crystal Eastman included, intended to have their words used as widely as possible. They asked only that copiers cite the journal of first printing and sent their words blithely off into the public domain. Had we their words, therefore, we would have full use of them. But history is more capricious. Writers have descendants, by marriage or blood, who intend either to protect the ancestor or profit from her or his good words. All of us who write, who have lovers and friends and relatives who write, can appreciate the situation. I do not mean to trivialize the rights and privileges of the descendants. But this is an essay about biography and how we know our subjects.

To be specific: When Max Eastman was alive he offered me his sister's papers. He had them in his possession, although legally Crystal Eastman's daughter, Annis Young, owned the rights to them — to quote from them, or to print them. When Max Eastman died, his widow, Yvette Eastman, removed from the Max Eastman Collection sold to Indiana University all letters and manuscripts written by Crystal and her mother, Annis Ford Eastman. Yvette

Eastman had decided to write about the women in the family. For the past fifteen years she has refused to let these papers be seen. In 1981 Annis Young died suddenly. Presumably the legal copyright passes on to her husband and children. But first Yvette Eastman must permit them to be seen, since she still has them in her possession. This is not a case of copyright or censorship, but of access and ownership. And for that there is no recourse for the fact-hungry historian.

Dwight David Eisenhower's only son, John S. D. Eisenhower, controls the copyright for, as well as access to, his father's papers. He reviewed my manuscript and presumably could have demanded deletions, even from Eisenhower's letters and journals while he was president. He made no such request. But his right to do so is the issue. What constitutes the "private papers" of a president? In 1975 I participated in an American Assembly, "The Records of Public Officials," which argued that no presidential documents were private papers.[2] That opinion became law. Ronald Reagan will be the first president whose papers as president are deemed public documents. But it is not retroactive. I am not referring to security classifications relating to military or international affairs. (Security-classified documents cover a vast range of material, and now that Reagan's papers are legally "public" property, this strategy for secrecy is being used more than ever before.) I am referring to papers that are quite ordinary in the daily run of governmental, bureaucratic, or political business, the very stuff of partisan, economic, or policymaking life. When I was doing research at Abilene, the papers of Vice-President Richard Nixon and White House aide Nelson Rockefeller, as well as of other controversial personalities, were simply sealed. Issues of "sensitivity" rather than security were involved, as were all issues relating to the personal and campaign finances — and that in a nation whose business is business.[3]

The issue of security classification is different from issues of "sensitivity," be they financial or affectional. Moreover, issues of security classification are covered by laws — notably the Freedom of Information Act, as amended in 1972 and 1974. My eight-year effort to get information relating to covert activities of major significance such as the CIA-State Department "destablization" of the Arbenz government in Guatemala in 1954, about which there was not one document of verifiable fact available, led me to activities on behalf of freedom of information that remain central to my work. Today President Reagan has declared war on the Freedom of Information Act. His newly staffed Classification-Declassification Center (CDC) has actually reclassified thousands of documents released during the Nixon-Ford-Carter years. Over thirty volumes of *Foreign Affairs* covering the 1950s, scheduled to be published by the State Department, have been suspended and are being rereviewed. The entire volume relating to Central America has as of this writing been reclassified. While the situation in Guatemala has become "resensitized," the situation regarding historical documents is unprecedented.

While the situation regarding public or government documents is covered by law, and the "law" has been abridged by Reagan's executive order of April 1981, the issue of access to private papers is even more complex — capricious in fact. In the case of Eleanor Roosevelt, for example, the family kept the papers closed to historians until the chosen family biographer completed his study. Hardly an isolated or unique case. The Communist party, which owns and controls Elizabeth Gurley Flynn's papers, also controls who sees them and what is seen — conveniently "losing" them entirely on occasion. In the absence of family heirs who have financial or personal concerns, or political interests, there are examples of libraries and archives that choose to keep sensitive or controversial information under lock and key. One recent example, with a happy ending, is the case of Miss Marks and Miss Woolley.

During the 1970s, Anna Mary Wells was the first to use the papers of Mary Woolley, president of Mount Holyoke College, and Jeannette Marks, chair of the English department then. Housed at Mount Holyoke, the papers document the forty-seven-year relationship between the two women. For the fact that Anna Mary Wells saved this valuable correspondence from obscurity or the shredder we will always be grateful. Committed to reclaiming the pioneering president of Mount Holyoke from oblivion, Wells was at first "shocked and embarrassed" by the letters. "I had supposed myself to be open-minded and tolerant about sexual deviation, but it now appeared that I was not so at all when it occurred in women I admired and respected."

When she described the contents to the archivist, David Truman, then president of Mount Holyoke, decided to close the collection until 1999 and to hide the fact that Mount Holyoke possessed the letters. Regardless of Wells's initial upset, and to her everlasting credit, she appealed for continued access to the material and for the right to use her notes — temporarily denied — and contacted archivists and historians for support. I was then a member of an American Historical Association committee on research that protested this attempt at prepublication censorship. Following appeals from many archivists and historians, the decision was reversed. Except for a "packet" of letters of unknown content and size, still closed until 1999, the correspondence is now available.

I am cheered when I consider that the people I choose to study favored freedom of information, preserved their correspondence with diligence, and intended every word to be read and used. Both Eisenhower and Eleanor Roosevelt were self-conscious about history, their role in it, and their future status at the hands of biographers. They both wrote with an eye to forthcoming books. They fully expected to be studied, analyzed, and understood. Both Eisenhower and Eleanor Roosevelt lived long lives. They each reviewed their papers. They chose to preserve what they deposited in the archives. Eisenhower regularized classification procedures in 1953, putting the emphasis on the right to know, and he declassified all World War II documents within ten years. Eleanor Roosevelt did not burn her thirty-year correspondence with Lorena Hickok. That she intended these letters to be read is clear by the fact that she encouraged her daughter, Anna Roosevelt Halsted, to go through her own papers and remove any she might not want read after they were deposited at Hyde Park. Great gaps in the correspondence between mother and daughter consequently exist. Also, before Lorena Hickok deposited her collection in the library, she wrote to Anna Halsted telling her that she removed those letters that related to her and that Mrs. Roosevelt would not have wanted included. People work hard at shaping the fullness of their lives and generally want us to know and appreciate their effort. Their descendants might choose to seal their words regarding some "sensitive" person, relationship, or policy; but we do them no honor by acquiescing in this truncation of their lives.

For the biographer, the fight over access to documents is just the beginning. Then comes selection, understanding, impact. To date, Crystal Eastman has had the most abiding impact on my life. My ongoing work, whether related to foreign policy or feminist issues, reflects her influence. For me, there is a connection between Eastman's life of relative freedom, Eleanor Roosevelt's struggle for fulfillment and identity, and my own present need to understand them both.

Eleanor Roosevelt's life is part of a personal continuum that embraces all of my interests — going beyond Eisenhower, who opposed her vision of international human rights, and touching my own life specifically. I met and worked with Eleanor Roosevelt between 1959 and 1962 when I was a student activist and, for a time, a vice-president of the National Student Association (NSA). In those years Eleanor Roosevelt's vision stood in marked contrast to the prevailing "better dead than red" winds that froze student politics to cold war America. She encouraged student leaders to think boldly about the future, about a world in which competing economic systems would in fact "coexist." Her support for human rights and civil rights was passionate and absolute, at a time when NSA, the voice of America's student leadership, endorsed segregation. I was suspended by the southern president of my college for "misappropriating" the student funds that paid for our bus to the sit-ins in North Carolina. The college president spoke of "breaking the law"; but Eleanor Roosevelt spoke of natural law, the laws of justice and humanity. There was in my mind no contest — just the ongoing struggle between good and evil. At graduation, I received the Roosevelt Memorial scholarship for academic excellence and service. The college president, upon shaking my hand and presenting the awards, hissed between her clenched teeth: "You know how this hurts me." But whenever Eleanor Roosevelt shook my hand, she smiled. I was very proud. I saw her in those years as warm and gracious but also firm and uncompromising. Her manner and her vision were inspiring. Now, after reading through much of her correspondence, I am also amazed by her incredibly complex days of political work and social whirl and her ongoing ability to change over time.

Most of the information available about Eleanor Roosevelt derives from her own words: her remarkably frank memoirs *This Is My Story* (1937), *This I Remember* (1949), and *Autobiography* (1961), her frequent columns and essays, and, more recently, her letters. Her own words remain the best source for the details of her lonely, soon-orphaned childhood, her years at Allenswood (the famed school near Wimbledon Common for the daughters of the *fin de siècle* smart set), and the early years of a marriage we now know to have been a bruising disappointment. According to Eleanor Roosevelt, the early phase of her life was highlighted by her experiences at Allenswood and her association with its cultured and cosmopolitan headmistress, Marie Souvestre, about whom she wrote: "Whatever I have become since had its seed in those three years of contact with a liberal mind and a strong personality."

But Eleanor Roosevelt's quest for personal independence and fulfillment evolved slowly, as did her political vision. Her sense of social responsibility and consideration for political activism were only partially awakened during her school years at Allenswood. Similarly, she did not become the kind of independent spirit that Marie Souvestre had encouraged her to become until the last third of her life. It was not until Eleanor Roosevelt was nearly the age that her teacher was when they first met that Mrs. Roosevelt defined fully the contours of her own life and creativity.

One is stunned, for example, to read that the woman who stands above all others in her generous support for Jews during and after the holocaust wrote an Allenswood classmate in Germany that although "there may be a need for curtailing the ascendancy of the Jewish people," she deplored Hitler and, she wrote, "it seems to me, it might have been done in a more humane way by a ruler who had intelligence and decency."[4] During the 1930s she identified with the women of the South as portrayed in *Gone With the Wind*. She called black adults "darkies" and children "pickaninnies," until she received a letter of protest from a Black woman who was stunned because Mrs. Roosevelt had spoken so sincerely on behalf of civil rights. Eleanor Roosevelt explained that her Georgia family had always used those words as terms of "affection." "What do you prefer?" she asked her correspondent. From her early refusal even to walk with her suffragist cousins for votes for women to her celebrated demand for all-women press conferences and her general call for power for women in public life, Eleanor Roosevelt's personal and political journey reflects the full range of the contradictory tides of the twentieth century.

It is too early to define my relationship with Eleanor Roosevelt as it will unfold during this project. In vision, purpose, strength, and ability to change, she is remarkable. I admire her physical stamina and her intensity. And when I cringe at her choices or disagree with her decisions or wonder at her activities, she sits down beside me and tries to explain her evolving sensibilities. Unlike Crystal Eastman's, her life was not generally joyful. She was not surrounded by loving, trusting relatives and friends who from childhood supported her visions and her life. Given her tragic childhood, her abusive and alcoholic relatives, the intensity of her warmth is extraordinary. I feel very close to her, even when I disagree with her. And I occasionally do try to please her. Unlike Crystal Eastman, Mrs. Roosevelt abhorred liquor, and I obligingly stick to coffee while studying the complexities of her changing enthusiasms over time. Moreover, she made lists — lists of things to do, to read, to inquire about. I now compile lists as never before. It is not that I am a chameleon or a dutiful daughter, although I may in fact be both. But I aim to understand, to feel profoundly, to absorb the flavors as far as possible and to learn from my subjects. This can of course be dangerous, and tiring. Both Crystal Eastman and Eleanor Roosevelt worked twelve to eighteen hours a day on a regular basis. All the women who interest me did. And some, like Eastman, worked themselves into a needlessly early grave. I am beginning to get self-protective. But most of the joy of discovering is in feeling and experiencing; in knowing the essence of the subject's life as deeply as possible. Twenty years ago it was fashionable to warn students, would-be historians, and biographers to be "objective." I once had a professor (who became the college president referred to above) who barked: "An intellectual thinks! Think, don't feel!" But she wrote about Cotton Mather; and she was wrong. I would advise: Think and feel — in order to know fully — with emotion and caring.

Notes

1. See especially my "Female Support Networks and Political Activism" (*Chrysalis* 3; reprint, Out and Out Books, 1980). This is also the theme of my *Tough Ladies: Peace, Politics and the Power of Love,* to be published by Oxford University Press.
2. "The Records of Public Officials," Forty-Eighth American Assembly, Arden House, Harriman, New York, 3-5 April 1975.
3. See B. W. Cook, "The Dwight David Eisenhower Library: Manuscript Freedom at Abilene," in *Access to the Papers of Recent Public Figures: The New Harmony Conference,* ed. Alonzo Hamby and Edward Weldon (AHA-OAH-SAAC, 1977).
4. Although it is unclear whether Mrs. Roosevelt mailed this letter to Carola von Schaeffer-Bernstein, it was drafted as late as 6 September 1939.

May Sarton and Martha Wheelock

Martha Wheelock

MAY SARTON:
A METAPHOR FOR MY LIFE,
MY WORK, AND MY ART

On a February New England day in 1977 — a day curiously blessed by the sun's most intense light, the earth closest to the sun yet its northern axis at the apogee — I was en route to meet and interview May Sarton. For the hour I drove along Route 101 toward York, Maine, where Sarton lived, I considered my own road and the junction I had come to. I was in my mid-thirties, four years separated from a childless marriage in which I questioned myself and distrusted my self-worth. The elder daughter of a Harvard classics scholar and professor, with a dozen years of high school English teaching experience, I had completed my M.A., which was required for me to remain in teaching.

Now I was pursuing a Ph.D. in American literature. But why? To enable me to advance, teach in college, and be "one of the boys"? To compensate for having no children? To please my father? To train myself in academic rhetoric? To become proficient in using note-cards? How did playing the patriarchal game of separating people into groups and judging them by their educational merits fit in with my newly found feminism, which extolled equality? How could I possibly believe in exalting the rational and mental above the emotional, spiritual, and intuitive; in receiving credentials for conformity to the standards of an institution; in being rewarded with money and status for the title before and the letters after my name?

Maybe I could use the discipline that went into earning the Ph.D. for the development of my own discipline. Or perhaps I could expose the academic world to new feminist viewpoints. I might eventually even infiltrate the ranks by playing the boys' game to win sacred entrance into the temple, and then I would be able to upset traditional male-dominated criticism and criticize works of literature in my own way. Perhaps I even believed in intense study for its own sake and for its own rewards. Whatever the results of my efforts, and for whatever mysterious reasons, I knew I would at least feel stronger with a Ph.D. after my name.

If I was to obtain a Ph.D. — for the feminist cause, for humanism, and for my own greater good — I must find a topic that would suit these aims, that was compatible with my thoughts, experiences, lifestyle, and being. Norman Mailer just wasn't the answer. Other people's dissertation topics looked grim to me: the significance of color in Spenser's *Fairie Queene,* Ernest Hemingway's castration complex. The critically acclaimed mainstream writers would be safe, but did I want to wade among the myriad dissertations to find one small question that had not been treated? What writer would challenge me to spend intense and concentrated time in eating and drinking her words and in abandoning most of my own pleasures for inquiring into the nature of her works? I was convinced that the right topic was the most salient requirement, not only for starting a thesis but also for determining whether I would be able to muster the love, respect, and energy necessary to finish the project.

I had already decided that I must work with a woman author rather than a male, especially because my traditional education had insisted that I read the major male writers while only permitting me a glimpse at a handful of women writers such as Jane Austen. My search for Ms. Right Author was extensive. I found either that a woman writer I became interested in was *au courant* — Woolf, Lessing, Chopin — and therefore being devoured by many voracious graduate students or that she had written only a few excellent books, so that the body of work was limited. I was idealistic. I wanted my dissertation to contribute something to the world. I wanted to uncover or rediscover some lost genius. I wanted to expose someone who had fought the darkness with a strong, self-made sword — a woman who needed celebration because she had been eclipsed and overlooked by male critics and by the academic world but who had developed a personal and unique view of life that should be recognized. Furthermore, I wanted to challenge the traditional modes of criticism by infusing my own work with the feminist attitude of "appreciation."

I found such a writer in May Sarton. I responded to her view of life immediately and rejoiced in what she wrote and lived. "Look for affinities," my inner voice had cried out, and in May Sarton I found that connection, and the food that could nourish me. Sarton needed critical attention. For more than fifty years, Sarton had been writing, not only poetry but also novels and nonfiction memoirs. She had struggled against the critical current and yet continued to produce work that nurtured many people of diverse backgrounds.

Did I dare contact Sarton herself? Her journals tell often about how intrusions from people interrupted her work and invaded her hermitage. But I humbly wrote her that I had read hundreds of authors and everything that *she* had written at least three times, and it was she and only she whom I wanted to study, to celebrate. Could she find a few minutes to meet with me and hear my dissertation plans? When I looked at my letter, I wondered if I, a woman, could confer honor on Sarton in the way that a man could, as prominently as a man could. Why, even in the presence of this woman, was I so self-effacing and apologetic for the work I was willing to do?

Sarton agreed enthusiastically to my visit. So in February 1977 I was on my way to talk with her. Like the two interviewers in Sarton's novel *Mrs. Stevens Hears the Mermaids Singing*, I was excited. But I was alone, with no one to help me, to buffer me from a woman I expected to be formidable, to be grand and idiosyncratic. May Sarton had graciously asked me for dinner and, since I had traveled all the way from New York City, I was also invited to spend the night.

In that narrow afternoon, the sun almost down at 3:30 P.M., I stopped in the small town of Raymond, New Hampshire, to pick up some dinner wine to accompany my gift of homemade bread. We were to meet at Cox's Store in York Village proper at 4:30, and she would show me the way to her house, as snow had blocked the main road.

At Cox's Store, we knew each other immediately — she, a cheery bustling woman with snow hair and perky smile, who hurriedly said, "Martha? Just follow me." In the few minutes that I was trailing her gray Audi through the Maine winter landscape, I felt on the trail of my own scent. I was not just following someone blindly. I was pursuing an ideal of my own choosing, according to my own blood. And what ensued was supervenient, leading me into paths beyond my immediate one.

Once inside her spacious yet cozy and tastefully and personally decorated home on the coast of Maine, a house and appointments I had come to know from details she had shared as a writer, I felt exhilarated and anchored. May Sarton masterfully lit a fire in the grand fireplace, the huge logs held by Hessian soldier andirons, and we settled down for introductions. She told me that we could not have a drink until 6 P.M. because, as one who lived alone, she must have a ritual to help control any indulgences; even without a drink, I relaxed as our conversation turned easily.

Sarton affably asked me what I wanted to propose as my thesis topic and whether I had an advisor. It hurt me to have to tell her that I had gone to several American literature professors who were all unfamiliar with her work. However, my search finally led to a professor who had at least heard of May Sarton and who had even met her during their mutual days at a social function at a New England college. He had remarked that the only work of hers he had read, *Faithful Are the Wounds,* had stayed with him, unlike most books. Yet he really did not consider Sarton to be an important writer and did not know what in her work could be the subject of a thesis. Although the academic disregard for her work had annoyed me, Sarton was "amused" at a situation she had expected and accepted yet about which she, too, could not help feeling annoyed.

Our conversation energetically spun on and on. I shared my indignation at critics' dismissal of her works as "simple," whereas the works really possess a deceptive clarity, a clarity Sarton only attained after many, many drafts, and, in the case of certain poems, after as many as a hundred. What the reader finally receives is the understanding available in the moment of experiencing the poem, not the struggles that Sarton underwent to reach that understanding.

We talked about the nature of the woman writer and her differences from a male writer. Sarton feels that the woman writer works primarily from her inner life but finds the sources for her creativity in her real, mundane world. Men can write epics, for example, because they readily live in their imaginations and transform the real world through their creativity. Sarton acknowledged that ordinary things and situations are exciting, that simple events can cause us to grow. Therefore, her responsibility as an artist is to deal with ordinary life — an unfashionable subject. She does not want to imitate the books, primarily written by men, that depict extreme crisis and violence but rather wants to deal in the lives of human beings and in the discovery of the self, a topic that she writes about with tenderness and compassion, not sentimentality. As Virginia Woolf wrote in her essay "Women and Fiction,"

> It is probable, however, that both in life and in art the values of a woman are not the values of a man. Thus, when a woman comes to write a novel, she will find that she is perpetually wishing to alter the established values — to

make serious what appears insignificant to a man, and trivial what is to him important. And for that, of course, she will be criticized; for the critic of the opposite sex will be genuinely puzzled and surprised by an attempt to alter the current scale of values, and will see in it not merely a difference of view, but a view that is weak, or trivial, or sentimental, because it differs from his own.[1]

In the course of that piquant and personal evening (dinner finely done and served simply and then each of us retiring to bed early), we talked of beginnings, of her parents whom she felt she had to integrate into her being: her mother, artistic and sensitive; her father, disciplined, pioneering, and scholarly. We shared the ways our love affairs and relationships with women had influenced and inspired us. (For Sarton the Muse has always been a woman.) I felt comfortable revealing my newly found identity to May Sarton, for even as she recounted the cost of living authentically she nonetheless affirmed her lifestyle.

That night in my guest room, I felt that Sarton the artist and May the person were one, integrated and whole. Should they be separated? But I resolved to go about the thesis as an objective critic, to be a detached Sarton scholar for my academic role and to keep my admiration, respect, understanding, and love for Sarton in my journals and in my dialogues with myself.

As I was about to leave the next morning, after breakfast, watching birds feed (May had ritualistically eaten early that morning in her bedroom), Sarton received a phone call. The caller reported the death of Anne Longfellow Thorpe, a beloved teacher from May's Shady Hill School days (when poetry first took root in her) and later a close friend. When Sarton shared this sad news, I offered to depart immediately so as not to intrude on her private grief. But instead, she showed me around her house and through the corridors of her life, sharing realities and memories of Anne Thorpe. As in her poems, she wove what she had learned and experienced with Thorpe into the texture of her being, into that synthesis where art is everyday life. "We can never stop learning, never cease exploring the mysteries of life in which human relationships are the greatest mystery." Here, in one moment, before I left her alone in the middle of winter, I felt again Sarton's strength and her remarkable vision of life and her art. As I drove off, the sun refracted many colors off the prismatic sea.

For less than a day, I had had a privileged glimpse of May Sarton's life and I had heard her talk about her creative process. In that day, I guessed why my university rarely promotes the idea of Ph.D. dissertations on living writers and why critical biographies of them are not encouraged: The personality and the presence of the writer are too pervasive and too powerful. They overcome the so-called objective stance that the academy requires. Yet this same possibility for knowing first-hand the writer I was working on, this very possibility for intimacy, was the reason I had chosen a living woman writer, someone I could get to know on my own, whose work and being I respected enough to spend years of my life studying. It was precisely this need to encounter a powerful presence that had led me to May Sarton. Why, I thought, can't criticism be enriched by the personal and include unabashed appreciation of the writer's work and person? Should artists only be deferred to, as gods, and remain personally remote? *I* was determined to integrate, as I believed Sarton had, my own self and my experiences with my work — the subjective and the objective — an integration that I felt was the only possible stance appropriate to me and to my values as a feminist.

In the months that followed that first meeting, I poured energy and study into my work. My topic was "Sarton's Approach to Growth," an attempt to show how Sarton's characters created growth experiences out of day-to-day life. One of my themes was Sarton's own growth and change as a result of writing each novel: "If you are not changed by your novel, if it does not teach you something you did not fully understand until you came to grips with it through setting your characters to work it out as if they really live and you lived through them all, then there is small chance that it will magnetize readers to the troubling questions it has asked," she wrote in "Design of a Novel."[2]

After several chapters, however, I found my theme collapsing. How to arrange Sarton, her changes, her life, and her works in a cause-and-effect pattern? Life and art, I had come to believe, are not that simple. When I shared my problems, my advisor said that I was not being "critical." I tried to keep my momentum and my spirits up by beginning again, on another tack, determined to find a way through the exterior to the heart. I persevered.

In the years that have followed my first visit to May Sarton in 1977, we have created a friendship, a trust, a familial bond. On two occasions, when Sarton was away on lecture tours, I stayed in her house to care for it and its flora and fauna. I subsequently lived, for the month of August 1978, in a rented cottage next door to May while I worked on my thesis, resisting the temptation to show her my work or to ask her questions. I modeled my discipline and work habits after hers, in the hopes of experiencing her experiences.

During that month, my friend Marita Simpson (who was vacationing there with me and writing a film script) and I shared a wide variety of experiences with Sarton — from simple meals, daily phone calls, and errands we ran together, to moments of frustration, pain, fear, anger, and Sarton's apprehension about the impending reviews of her latest novel, *A Reckoning*. I was writing painstakingly but understanding more about her works than could ever become part of my academic criticism. I could "feel" who had written these poems and novels in ways deeper than any part of my penetrating study could possibly reveal.

Together, Marita, a filmmaker, and I conceived the idea that we would make a film about May Sarton to celebrate her. We proposed our project to May, who temperately gave her consent. She reminisced about a video tape that a Boston TV station had made of her when she lived in Nelson, New Hampshire; when she saw it, she cried. But the station was no longer operating, and the tape was lost. That evening, Sarton gave both Marita and me a great challenge — through her tacit faith that we would do it and through the example of her own life in taking risks.

The project and May's approval compelled us to establish a business to raise money, which we called Ishtar Enterprises. We were attracted to that moon goddess's name because Ishtar had been a most powerful matriarchal figure in early Babylonia. According to one description, Ishtar had a hundred breasts and was "the mother of all." We felt protected and enlightened by the image of Ishtar and gave her homage.

Sometime soon after, I met Liz Van Patten, a woman in market research who wanted to move into film production. I told her of our idea for a Sarton film. A week later, Liz called to say that she was ready, willing, and able to help with the film and to raise the money. Liz's additional impetus and input contributed to Marita's and my convictions that this film must be made and that the project already had a special energy of its own and was taking off. With May Sarton as inspiration and our desire to make this film on our own, we infected others with enthusiasm.

The ordinary financial avenues — grants, rich uncles, or our own "large" savings — were not available, so we ventured forth to find backing elsewhere. Our first fundraiser was on a dismal snowy evening at the end of November 1978, at Marita's loft in New York City. A few people we had reached through a mailing gallantly showed up. We wined and fed them, dramatized a scene from Sarton's book *Mrs. Stevens Hears the Mermaids Singing,* and read some of her poems.

After the literary presentation, I started to tell the gathering that we were about to embark on a film and we wanted to elicit their support in the form of investments. I could hardly speak. Seeing my hesitation, a long-time friend, Barbara Murphy, spoke up and said, "What Martha is trying to say is that we want to make a film about May Sarton and we have called you all together to ask for your support and investment." Then it all became easier. By the end of the evening, we had raised $1,000 in $100 shares and donations. Marita had estimated that *without salaries,* we could make this film for just under $10,000. We promised our shareholders that we would return their investment if all the necessary monies were not raised — a thought too horrible to contemplate.

With these few dollars and more momentum, we invaded the Modern Language Convention in 1978 in New York City to interest people in the film and to hold another fundraiser. Since we could not afford a hotel suite for our function, our "hall" was a small, second-story malodorous dance studio, with mirrors and no atmosphere but overlooking the Christmas tree in Rockefeller Center — a sure drawing card for out-of-towners! There again, we wined and dined them, performed another reading of Sarton's works, and asked for donations, all more proficiently than before. Unfortunately, after all our work, only thirty people showed up, and no one contributed. The compensation for the event, however, was that a newspaper covered the evening and reported the dreams we had for our film. From that article alone, another $1,000 eventually came.

This slow, pedestrian, and laborious manner of fundraising continued. An investor gave us her swanky apartment for an evening in which we showed the fruits of an afternoon's filming — May Sarton in the Maine winter, surviving the snow and cold. That teaser of three minutes showed May's energy, demeanor, and environment and endeared her to viewers and investors at once. We did a direct mail appeal, pleading that we needed only $2,000 to reach our budget. The money came in, from ex-students and strangers, from as far away as Kansas and England. An account was set up for tax-deductible donations, and more money came in. By May 1, 1979, the deadline, all production money had been raised and Marita and I were off to "house-sit" for May Sarton, a grand opportunity to study the environment and to do some preliminary filming.

When the June weekend for our shooting with May arrived, we had the crew (all people we knew) and equipment ready. Although the crew did not possess much expertise, they had a spirit of cooperation and a belief in the film and were willing to work for the experience and a share in the film. We drove or flew up on our own and by the evening before the first day of filming had all managed to find our way to the small cottage, next door to May Sarton, which was to be our location quarters. The crew consisted of Marita Simpson, cinematographer, gaffer, and director in charge of the entire production; Liz Van Patten, production manager and assistant sound; Barbara Murphy, assistant camera; Felipe Napoles, sound and assistant gaffer; John Simpson, cook and accountant; and me, scriptwriter, interviewer, and director "in charge of May."

We would begin shooting the next afternoon, and since the weather was in our favor we would start with the outdoor sequences. That morning we gathered around a family breakfast on the porch and conferred about our individual duties and about the particular personality we were working with. In order to be sensitive to Sarton's needs and the rhythm of her work, we had to be punctual, as May is; we had to be efficient and not waste her time or cause her to wait, as she was busy and wanted time to write and do her own work.

Filming was like creating a home and family; every member was indispensable, so that indeed the whole was greater than the sum of its parts. We as a crew had to work confidently and calmly together because we wanted to create a supportive and nurturing environment in which May would feel comfortable, peaceful, and authentic. We all cared about reducing tensions a d technic interruptions, working unobtrusively, keeping Sarton's sacred space unruffled, and evolving as a unit through ongoing group analysis. We believed that only through doing this would the film be harmonious.

To introduce the crew to May, we worked that first day outside without interview, filming May gardening, planting, and taking her walk with Tamas, her Shetland collie, and Brambles, her speckled cat. Because the weather was still glorious, the third segment on the second day was an interview with May outside on her terrace. There I asked her to talk about her relationship with her readers and her critics:

> Sarton: I do get about fifty letters a week. I love hearing from people and the letters have helped me very much because many times when I felt that the work wasn't getting through, that neither I nor it existed, people from all over . . . wrote me to thank me . . . and this is of course very moving to me and very heartening and helpful, since I still lack serious critical attention.

That first interview unnerved us all. Bugs and airplanes disturbed the peace; trouble with loading the camera held up the flow; our failure to explain to May the length of each film roll stopped her in

the middle of a response. Since May Sarton is fresh and spontaneous, we found that the most genuine replies and reactions came
on the first takes; in the second take, something was lost and
formalized.

In the first interview, the crew had its first encounter with sound
syncing and group coordination, problems that were intensified by
our mutual endeavors to be professional yet humanly involved with
our subject. May soothed our frazzled souls, after the session, with
tea and *causerie*. Marita took the opportunity to film her European
ritual of tea preparation.

We invited May to join us that evening for a Maine lobster dinner
in our cottage. She came promptly at 6 P.M. and we celebrated with
Scotch (her drink) and wine and enjoyed being in a nonfilmic
relationship. It was the first extended period of time that we were all
together outside the "set." Such informal times together were
necessary to maintain the human experience of the film.

As dinner neared its end, May Sarton suddenly and dramatically
exploded about her discomfort during that interview sequence, how
she wanted this film to *really* represent her and to be something that
she could be proud of; how during the afternoon she had felt that
she was not at her best or focused on what we wanted her to say.
Through her generous and honest sharing and criticism of our
methods, we all saw the experience from her viewpoint, and she,
after all, was the star! She was directing us to direct her and give her
structure.

When she left that evening, I felt like a failure, as if I had antag-
onized her and as if I had forgotten all the research and preparation I
had done for the film. That outburst from May, however, was a
catalyst for all of us, including May, because it pulled us more
together to meet this challenge and to revise and refresh our
methods. Without the love and trust between May Sarton and us
and within the crew itself, that confrontation could have been coun-
terproductive rather than cleansing and supportive. After May left,
the crew gathered around the fireplace and conferred about how to
provide a secure framework for May's reactions and feelings
through the questions that we asked.

Reborn from our evening of communion and support not only
with May Sarton but also among ourselves, we met May the next
morning for a day of shooting two interviews. We approached the
task with renewed vigor and the conviction that we would work
with her to make the best possible film. The first sequence, in
Sarton's study, about her creative process and being a woman
writer, went smoothly, even though a few questions still felt flat.

> Sarton: I am at my desk for three to four hours every day
> and I try to keep that very much a sacred time, because it's
> the time when I have energy . . . when the door to the
> subconscious is still open . . . That's the creative time for me.
> Because you want that primary intensity. This is what my
> life is all about — creating a frame in which I can have that
> primary intensity for three hours a day.

The results of our experience of the night before and of May's
growing ease showed up that afternoon in "the library interview."
There Sarton, dressed in her black "poetry suit," reviewed her
accomplishments, shared her philosophy of growth, feelings, love,
and aging. She was facile, interesting, vulnerable, honest, and
provocative, clearly at home with herself and the filming, an evolution that shows in the film itself.

> Sarton: So I am just hoping that when it is all added up
> what will come true is a vision of life, and what does one
> mean when one says that? It is simply that every single
> human being sees life for himself, if he's honest, in a way no
> one else sees it . . . There is a vision of life in my work which
> is a combination partly of my European background plus
> the America I know, and plus the temperament, the sort of
> passionate temperament which is accompanied by a rather
> critical mind; and this also the critics have not given me
> credit for, I mean, for being intelligent as well as sensitive.

We left May to a quiet and recuperative evening, and we went
home feeling that we were closer to the form and content that May
had wanted.

We finished the shooting the next day with two different scenes.
In the morning we filmed May reading poems. We wanted to depict
how those myriad actions and scenes and questions and answers
actually culminated in The Poem. She read beautifully and
genuinely, even breaking into tears during "A Hard Death," a poem
about her mother's death, despite the camera's eye. At that time we
were not only filmmakers but also the poet's audience. Later that
afternoon, leaving Sarton's home, we ventured into town to film
May at the post office, a scene that represents another evolution,
from the private poet to the public person — a symbolic place for us
to end our filming.

After Felipe and John had left for New York, the rest of us,
including May, got together for a girls' night out. Sarton generously
reminisced about her early years and expressed interest in each of
our lives; the evening flowed into new terrains and to new levels.

What was particularly fine about that last evening together was its contrast with the gathering two nights before, when, nervous and eager to please and do our best, we shared our anxiety about the filming.

One week after we had returned to New York City, May called to say that she was going into the hospital for a mastectomy. Of course, we were shocked; she had given us no inkling about her illness because she did not want to disturb the filming. I offered to come up and care for her; she thought that someone else nearby would come. I reiterated that I would come whenever she needed me. A few days later, she called and asked me to come. She was giving me the opportunity to help the woman who had given and still gives so much to me — as inspiration, as a writer whose words and experiences have helped and centered me, as a source for my thesis, as the star of her own film, as a friend, as a muse.

The fact that just three weeks before, May Sarton had trusted us to present her in a film portrait and that we all had worked together as a family, as a whole, must have made it easier for her to accept our offer of care, love, protection, and openness, to share her fears, her pain, and her situation; she let us be "her family," rather than insisting that she be her usual self-sufficient self.

The experience of sharing May's operation and recovery was truly inspirational. She had decided that she would not have chemotherapy if the cancer had spread and was malignant; she wanted to be her own hero. Like the heroine of her latest book, *A Reckoning*, published a year before, May wanted to be in charge of her own life and death. The novel portrays a woman dying of cancer who chooses to die consciously in her own manner, in her own home, and who finds her life's real connection not in her family but in her friend Ella. May Sarton, the woman, lived through the very experience that she had written about earlier.

Fortunately, however, the cancer had not spread and soon May returned from the hospital to her big house, wanting to be her "ole" self immediately. It was difficult for her to let me care for her, but she acquiesced appreciatively. In a few days, May was driving her car and managing well and I was on my way back to New York City to begin editing the film. In one month, my relationship with May and my work on her had taken on new dimensions: a creation of art around her and an opportunity — a most primal one — to care for her lovingly on the real, the physical plane. This is how May herself described those days in her journal, which she later published under the title *Recovering: A Journal, 1978-1979.*

Tuesday, June 26th

The operation was on the eighteenth and I came home yesterday welcomed by dear Martha and Marita who have been holding the fort here.

The York hospital, small, intimate, and kind, was an ideal place for me to be, especially as I was on their new plan, Joint Practice, where nurses are given unusual powers and work closely with the surgeon. The operation was not bad at all, a modified radical mastectomy, modified meaning that they found no malignancy in the lymph glands. It looks as though I am in the clear.

I had a room of my own until the last night, and it was soon full of flowers, glorious flowers, among them a bunch of many sprays of delphinium, several blues, and white peonies. Another was a basket with six African violets of shades of pink and lavender. The first day Heidi brought a little bunch from her garden, and later on Martha and Marita brought me samples from my garden, one day two clematis, one deep purple and one white, another day, Siberian iris. The flowers were a constant joy. I opened my eyes to find them there, silent presences, and I slept a lot, grateful for the loss of consciousness.

The flowers helped, the visible sign of the love of many, many friends, and the great elm tree I looked at from the window helped too, its long branches waving gently in the wind. One evening an oriole came to rest there and sing. The changing skies and the admirable steadfast tree did me a lot of good. I needed it for I had imagined that the loss of a breast would create catharsis, that I would emerge like a phoenix from the fire, reborn, with all things made new, especially the pain in my heart. I had imagined that real pain, physical pain, and physical loss would take the place of mental anguish and the loss of love. Not so. It is all to be begun again, the long excruciating journey through pain and rejection, through anger and not understanding, toward some regained sense of my self. I have in the past six months been devalued as a woman, as a lover, and as a writer. How to build back to a sense of value, of valuing myself again?

At least I have proved that I have some resilience. Today I had a bath and changed the bandage myself, not without terror as a lot of fluid spurted out. But what bliss to sleep last night with Tamas and Bramble on each side of me!

Thursday, June 28th

Perhaps there has been a greater inward change than I can yet measure, and if so, it has to do with the miracle of human trust and lovingness that Martha and Marita have created here for and with me. They are leaving today. Yesterday they installed the air conditioner up here, and we waited all day for the telephone company to come and extend telephone cords so I can be saved from getting up to answer calls. That will be a great help. They have watered the garden, cooked a delicious dinner each night, and we have had long talks about their lives and hopes and mine, sometimes with tears flowing down our cheeks. They say they are my family (they each have living parents but this is something else, for it is they who mother me though they are twenty years younger).

It was very hard to ask Martha to come . . . she had offered three times, had insisted that she would "come at the drop of a hat" if needed. But she and Marita are just settling in to a country place they have bought along the Delaware river; they are hard at work putting the film together; and Martha still has a lot to do on her thesis. I hated to ask, but I did it finally when it was clear that Karen, who was with me through the operation for the first two days, would miss her California trip if she stayed on. So I did ask, and the only hard thing about these days was having to ask for help from the young. I should have remembered what Jean Dominique taught me long ago, that accepting dependence with grace was one of the last lessons we all have to learn. With the help of such tact and understanding, it has turned out to be revelatory. Perhaps it is teaching me to bury the one-pointed heart, that fierce infant demand that there must be one person, my person, on whom I could and must depend. Perhaps it is teaching me to rest lightly on the palms of the many hands that have been lifting me so gently all these days, an ever present sense of thought flowing toward me. I felt when I went into the hospital that I was carrying with me an invisible bunch of flowers, each flower a dear friend.

As Marita and I spent three months editing the volumes of material and the footage, we lived concentratedly and intimately with Sarton. Her words and intonations, her face and its protean expressions, her movements and gestures (I studied and absorbed them all) became a part of me, as had her writings. We were challenged as filmmakers and editors to find the image and the form that best expressed and portrayed not only the woman we had come to know and love but also the process and style of her creative life — the creator's life as art.

The gala premiere of our film *World of Light: A Portrait of May Sarton* was on October 16, 1979, in New York City, less than a year after we started our adventure. The guest of honor was May Sarton herself, who courageously was seeing the film for the first time, and at a public showing — another example of her trust in us! Our investors, contributors, friends, and the press were invited for the two screenings that evening. The hall was full. My big fear and question was: Would Sarton like it? Had we met the challenge she offered us that evening when she passionately asserted, "It's my life and I want this film to be something I am good in and feel proud about."

At the end of the first showing, we heard applause through the doors, but froze with worry about May's reaction. Then, during the intermission, May finally reached us and said, sincerely, "It's beautiful." (I let out my breath.) "It's amazing how much you captured of me." At a subsequent showing a few months later for her friends in Maine, where we were not present, May was reported as saying, after she had seen the film again, "Now I can die." Certainly Sarton's work will bring her her own immortality. But perhaps as her protegée and progeny, I can contribute to that in my own way.

From that launching, *World of Light: A Portrait of May Sarton* has moved into the world with a life of its own. The film sells itself; it rents and reaps on its own and drives us to expose it as much as we can. It was a finalist in the American Film Festival and in the Connecticut Film Festival. Its life is a collection of vibrations: May Sarton's real and honest performance, a rich and interesting text, Marita's exquisite cinematography, Marita's and my collective, harmonious, and companionable editing, and the love and energy of people who gave to the film in every possible way. Audiences, too, give to the film through their appreciative and emotional responses.

After the film had been produced and released, my work on my thesis plodded along. My academic approach to May Sarton, however, was neither as lively nor as rich to me as were the real experiences that I had shared with her. May Sarton too found my thesis flat and lifeless and even contested its accuracy and validity. When I offered to withdraw my chapter on her theater years, she applauded the decision: "The film has done more than your thesis could; your creative product is more successful than your critical, academic one."

After this confrontation with Sarton, the decision to abandon my Ph.D. thesis took still another year. I was Sarton who first urged me to forgo the thesis and concentrate on films, words that I first took as a painful criticism and rejection, but later as a revelation.

Other reckonings followed — with my family, my advisor, and myself — and they all brought me new direction. I experienced my family's supportive and understanding recognition of my strengths and energies in the creation of the film and of my struggles within the academic world. And instead of being disappointed and con-demnatory for my dropping my thesis, my family helped me with the distribution of the film and with our subsequent book based on the soundtrack.

When I eventually packed up cartons of notecards, chapters, and books, I laid my thesis to rest and allowed myself to accept the film and book as my gifts and labors of love for my beloved muse, May Sarton.

I was released.

What have I learned from the whole experience? I had chosen to work on Sarton because she illuminated and enriched my own life. From her model, I garnered the discipline for hard work and a dedication to following the path to who I am. As May herself said, "You begin, as you get older at least, to know who you are and to choose not to follow paths which go against that image you have of yourself, not the image *projected* necessarily, but the image *you have of yourself.*"

The road I took in February 1977 was not toward the Ph.D. thesis but to another destination — a film, a new career, and a friendship with May Sarton. I emulate Sarton's energy and persistence, her ability to forge ahead even without support. Because she believes what she has to say is important, she is driven to create. From her, I have relearned that life is art — and so much more — when one is fully awake and open.

The film itself is a metaphor for what Sarton has given and taught me. It could never have been made without energy, hard work, and dedication. To be completely involved in such a vision and project, I — we — had to believe in the subject. I had to believe that I was creating something that represents who I am as well as who May Sarton is. And from the life, from the experiences and relationship with Sarton, came the art and the future life.

I have "retired" from teaching to become a fulltime filmmaker. Marita and I have produced *Kate Chopin's "The Story of an Hour,"* narrated by Elizabeth Ashley, which was filmed in part at Kate Chopin's home in Louisiana. Our film on Chopin was a natural outgrowth of our work on May. Chopin, like Sarton, was unheralded in her lifetime because her works were daring and often shocking to audiences in the 1890s.

Marita and I are now embarked on another project, to record and celebrate on film the disappearing ancient tribes of Kahunas on

Hawaii. In the early months of 1983, we descended into the rain forests and ascended the crater of Kilauea to do research for our film on one of the last great spiritual and healing Hawaiian Kahunas, Morrnah Simeona. In Hawaiian culture, the Kahunas teach how to revere and worship nature, how to respect others, and how to call up from within ourselves spiritual power and communion with the divine Creator.

In New York City, I had been a student of the Huna way, but New York City was not a Huna environment. Finding Morrnah Simeona in person, in Hawaii, was like finding fresh water in a lava field. What beautiful peace and spiritual power emanate from her strong, time-worn face. She has healed, helped, and inspired thousands of people in Hawaii and around the world since she was three years old. Meeting the challenge and earning the privilege of working and creating with this magnificent woman demand the journey to, and the exploration of, our own inner and spiritual life forces. For Marita and myself, this film is a new adventure, but it is also a natural outgrowth of our work on the creative and personal world of May Sarton and the historical and literary milieu of Kate Chopin. Through the process of steeping ourselves in the history, culture, and nature of Hawaii will come the idea and the vision. Only then can we create the art.

Notes

1. Virginia Woolf, "Women and Fiction," in *Granite and Rainbow* (New York: Harcourt Brace Jovanovich, 1958), 8l.
2. May Sarton, "The Design of a Novel," in *Writings on Writing* (Orono, Maine, 1980), 37.

Zora Neale Hurston

Alice Walker

Alice Walker

LOOKING FOR ZORA

On January 16, 1959, Zora Neale Hurston, suffering from the effects of a stroke and writing painfully in longhand, composed a letter to the "editorial department" of Harper and Brothers inquiring if they would be interested in seeing "the book I am laboring upon at present — a life of Herod the Great." One year and twelve days later, Zora Neale Hurston died without funds to provide for her burial, a resident of the St. Lucie County, Florida, Welfare Home. She lies today in an unmarked grave in a segregated cemetery in Fort Pierce, Florida, a resting place generally symbolic of the black writer's fate in America.

Zora Neale Hurston is one of the most significant unread authors in America, the author of two minor classics and four other major books.

— Robert Hemenway,
"Zora Hurston and the Eatonville Anthropology,"
in *The Harlem Renaissance Remembered*

On August 15, 1973, I wake up just as the plane is lowering over Sanford, Florida, which means I am also looking down on Eatonville, Zora Neale Hurston's birthplace. I recognize it from Zora's description in *Mules and Men:* "the city of five lakes, three croquet courts, three hundred brown skins, three hundred good swimmers, plenty guavas, two schools and no jailhouse." Of course I cannot see the guavas, but the five lakes are still there, and it is the lakes I count as the plane prepares to land in Orlando.

From the air, Florida looks completely flat, and as we near the ground this impression does not change. This is the first time I have seen the interior of the state, which Zora wrote about so well, but there are the acres of orange groves, the sand, mangrove trees, and scrub pine that I know from her books. Getting off the plane I walk through the hot moist air of midday into the tacky but air-conditioned airport. I search for Charlotte Hunt, my companion on the Zora Hurston expedition. She lives in Winter Park, Florida, very near Eatonville, and is writing her graduate dissertation on Zora. I see her waving — a large, pleasant faced white woman in dark glasses. We have written to each other for several weeks, swapping our latest finds (mostly hers) on Zora, and trying to make sense out of the mass of information obtained (often erroneous or simply confusing) from Zora herself — through her stories and autobiography — and from people who wrote about her.

Eatonville has lived for such a long time in my imagination that I can hardly believe it will be found existing in its own right. But after twenty minutes on the expressway, Charlotte turns off and I see a small settlement of houses and stores set with no particular pattern in the sandy soil off the road. We stop in front of a neat gray building that has two fascinating signs: EATONVILLE POST OFFICE and EATON-VILLE CITY HALL.

Inside the Eatonville City Hall half of the building, a slender, dark-brown-skin woman sits looking through letters on a desk. When she hears we are searching for anyone who might have known Zora Neale Hurston, she leans back in thought. Because I don't wish to inspire foot-dragging in people who might know something about Zora they're not sure they should tell, I have decided on a simple, but I feel profoundly *useful*, lie.

"I am Miss Hurston's niece," I prompt the young woman, who brings her head down with a smile.

"I think Mrs. Moseley is about the only one still living who might remember her," she says.

"Do you mean *Mathilda* Moseley, the woman who tells those 'woman–is–smarter–than–man' lies in Zora's book?"

"Yes," says the young woman. "Mrs. Moseley is real old now, of course. But this time of day, she should be at home."

I stand at the counter looking down on her, the first Eatonville resident I have spoken to. Because of Zora's books, I feel I know something about her; at least I know what the town she grew up in was like years before she was born.

"Tell me something," I say. "Do the schools teach Zora's books here?"

"No," she says, "they don't. I don't think most people know anything about Zora Neale Hurston, or know about any of the great things she did. She was a fine lady. I've read all of her books myself, but I don't think many other folks in Eatonville have."

"Many of the church people around here, as I understand it," says Charlotte in a murmured aside, "thought Zora was pretty loose. I don't think they appreciated her writing about them."

"Well," I say to the young woman, "thank you for your help." She clarifies her directions to Mrs. Moseley's house and smiles as Charlotte and I turn to go.

> The letter to Harper's does not expose a publisher's rejection of an unknown masterpiece, but it does reveal how the bright promise of the Harlem Renaissance deteriorated for many of the writers who shared in its exuberance. It also indicates the personal tragedy of Zora Neale Hurston: Barnard graduate, author of four novels, two books of folklore, one volume of autobiography, the most important collector of Afro-American folklore in America, reduced by poverty and circumstance to seek a publisher by unsolicited mail.
>
> — Robert Hemenway

> Zora Hurston was born in 1901, 1902, or 1903 — depending on how old she felt to be at the time someone asked.
> — Librarian, Beinecke Library,
> Yale University

The Moseley house is small and white and snug, its tiny yard nearly swallowed up by oleanders and hibiscus bushes. Charlotte and I knock on the door. I call out. But there is no answer. This strikes us as peculiar. We have had time to figure out an age for Mrs. Moseley — not dates or a number, just old. I am thinking of a quivery, bedridden invalid when we hear the car. We look behind us to see an old black-and-white Buick, paint peeling and grillwork rusty — pulling into the drive. A neat old lady in a purple dress and white hair is straining at the wheel. She is frowning because Charlotte's car is in the way.

Mrs. Moseley looks at us suspiciously. "Yes, I knew Zora Neale," she says, unsmilingly and with a rather cold stare at Charlotte (who I imagine, feels very *white* at that moment), "but that was a long time ago, and I don't want to talk about it."

"Yes, ma'am," I murmur, bringing all my sympathy to bear on the situation.

"Not only that," Mrs. Moseley continues, "I've been sick. Been in the hospital for an operation. Ruptured artery. The doctors didn't believe I was going to live, but you see me alive, don't you?"

"Looking well, too," I comment.

Mrs. Moseley is out of her car. A thin, sprightly woman with nice gold-studded false teeth, uppers and lowers. I like her because she stands there *straight* beside her car, with a hand on her hip and her straw pocketbook on her arm. She wears white T-strap shoes with heels that show off her well-shaped legs.

"I'm eighty-two years old, you know," she says. "And I just can't remember things the way I used to. Anyhow, Zora Neale left here to go to school and she never really came back to live. She'd come here for material for her books, but that was all. She spent most of her time down in South Florida."

"You know, Mrs. Moseley, I saw your name in one of Zora's books."

"You did?" She looks at me with only slightly more interest. "I read some of her books a long time ago, but the people got to borrowing and borrowing and they borrowed them all away."

"I could send you a copy of everything that's been reprinted." I offer. "Would you like me to do that?"

"No," says Mrs. Moseley promptly. "I don't read much any more Besides, all of that was *so* long ago. . . ."

Charlotte and I settle back against the car in the sun. Mrs. Moseley tells us at length and with exact recall every step in her recent operation, ending with: "What those doctors didn't know — when they were expecting me to die (and they didn't even think I'd live long enough for them to have to take out my stitches!) — is that Jesus is the best doctor, and if *He* says for you to get well, that's all that counts."

With this philosophy, Charlotte and I murmur quick assent: being Southerners and church bred, we have heard that belief before. But what we learn from Mrs. Moseley is that she does not remember much beyond the year 1938. She shows us a picture of her father and mother and says that her father was Joe Clarke's brother. Joe Clarke, as every Zora Hurston reader knows, was the first mayor of Eatonville; his fictional counterpart is Jody Starks of *Their Eyes Were Watching God*. We also get directions to where Joe Clarke's store *was* — where Club Eaton is now. Club Eaton, a long orange-beige nightspot we had seen on the main road, is apparently famous for the good times in it regularly had by all. It is, perhaps, the modern equivalent of the store porch, where all the men of Zora's childhood came to tell "lies," that is, black folk tales, that were "made and used on the spot," to take a line from Zora. As for Zora's exact birthplace, Mrs. Moseley has no idea.

After I have commented on the healthy growth of her hibiscus bushes, she becomes more talkative. She mentions how much she *loved* to dance, when she was a young woman, and talks about how good her husband was. When he was alive, she says, she was completely happy because he allowed her to be completely free. "I was so free I had to pinch myself sometimes to tell if I was a married woman."

Relaxed now, she tells us about going to school with Zora. "Zora and I went to the same school. It's called Hungerford High now. It *was* only to the eighth grade. But our teachers were so good that by the time you left you knew college subjects. When I went to Morris Brown in Atlanta, the teachers there were just teaching me the same things I had already learned right in Eatonville. I wrote Mama and told her I was going to come home and help her with her babies. I wasn't learning anything new.

"Tell me something, Mrs. Moseley," I ask. "Why do you suppose Zora was against integration? I read somewhere that she was against school desegregation because she felt it was an insult to black teachers."

"Oh, one of them [white people] came around asking me about integration. One day I was doing my shopping. I heard 'em over there talking about it in the store, about the schools. And I got on out of the way because I knew if they asked me, they wouldn't like what I was going to tell 'em. But they came up and asked me anyhow. 'What do you think about this integration?' one of them said. I acted like I thought I had heard wrong. 'You're asking *me* what *I* think about integration?' I said. 'Well, as you can see, I'm just an old colored woman — I was seventy-five or seventy-six then — and this is the first time anybody ever asked me about integration. And nobody asked my grandmother what she thought, either, but her daddy was one of you all.' " Mrs. Moseley seems satisfied with this memory of her rejoinder. She looks at Charlotte. "I have the blood of three races in my veins," she says belligerently, "white, black, and Indian, and nobody asked me *anything* before."

"Do you think living in Eatonville made integration less appealing to you?"

"Well, I can tell you this: I have lived in Eatonville all my life, and I've been in the governing of this town. I've been everything but mayor and I've been *assistant* mayor. Eatonville was and is an all-black town. We have our own police department, post office, and town hall. Our own school and good teachers. Do I need integration?

"They took over Goldsboro, because the black people who lived there never incorporated, like we did. And now I don't even know if any black folks live there. They built big houses up there around the lakes. But we didn't let that happen in Eatonville, and we don't sell land to just anybody. And you see, we're still here."

When we leave, Mrs. Moseley is standing by her car, waving. I think of the letter Roy Wilkins wrote to a black newspaper blasting Zora Neale for her lack of enthusiasm about the integration of schools. I wonder if he knew the experience of Eatonville she was coming from. Not many black people in America have come from a self-contained, all-black community where loyalty and unity are taken for granted. A place where black pride is nothing new.

There is, however, one thing Mrs. Moseley said that bothered me.

"Tell me, Mrs. Moseley," I had asked, "why is it that thirteen years after Zora's death, no marker has been put on her grave?"

And Mrs. Moseley answered: "The reason she doesn't have a stone is because she wasn't buried here. She was buried down in South Florida somewhere. I don't think anybody really knew where she was."

> Only to reach a wider audience, need she ever write books — because she is a perfect book of entertainment in herself. In her youth she was always getting scholarships and things from wealthy white people, some of whom simply paid her just to sit around and represent the Negro race for them, she did it in such a racy fashion. She was full of sidesplitting anecdotes, humorous tales, and tragicomic stories, remembered out of her life in the South as a daughter of a traveling minister of God. She could make you laugh one minute and cry the next. To many of her white friends, no doubt, she was a perfect "darkie," in the nice meaning they give the term — that is, a naive, childlike, sweet, humorous, and highly colored Negro.
>
> But Miss Hurston was clever, too — a student who didn't let college give her a broad "a" and who had great scorn for all pretensions, academic or otherwise. That is why she was such a fine folklore collector, able to go among the people and never act as if she had been to school at all. Almost nobody else could stop the average Harlemite on Lenox Avenue and measure his head with a strange-looking, anthropological device and not get bawled out for the attempt, except Zora, who used to stop anyone whose head looked interesting, and measure it.
>
> — Langston Hughes,
> *The Big Sea*

What does it matter what white folks must have thought about her?

— Student,
black women writers' class, Wellesley College

Mrs. Sarah Peek Patterson is a handsome, red-haired woman in her late forties, wearing orange slacks and gold earrings. She is the director of Lee-Peek Mortuary in Fort Pierce, the establishment that handled Zora's burial. Unlike most black funeral homes in Southern towns that sit like palaces among the general poverty, Lee-Peek has a run-down, *small* look. Perhaps this is because it is painted purple and white, as are its Cadillac chariots. These colors do not age well. The rooms are cluttered and grimy, and the bathroom is a tiny, stale-smelling prison, with a bottle of black hair dye (apparently used to touch up the hair of the corpses) dripping into the face bowl. Two pine burial boxes are resting in the bathtub.

Mrs. Patterson herself is pleasant and helpful.

"As I told you over the phone, Mrs. Patterson," I begin, shaking her hand and looking into her penny-brown eyes, "I am Zora Neale Hurston's niece, and I would like to have a marker put on her grave. You said, when I called you last week, that you could tell me where the grave is."

By this time I am, of course, completely into being Zora's niece, and the lie comes with perfect naturalness to my lips. Besides, as far as I'm concerned, she *is* my aunt — and that of all black people as well.

"She was buried in 1960," exclaims Mrs. Patterson. "That was when my father was running this funeral home. He's sick now or I'd let you talk to him. But I know where she's buried. She's in the old cemetery, the Garden of the Heavenly Rest, on Seventeenth Street. Just when you go in the gate there's a circle, and she's buried right in the middle of it. Hers is the only grave in that circle — because people don't bury in that cemetery any more."

She turns to a stocky, black-skinned woman in her thirties, wearing a green polo shirt and white jeans cut off at the knee. "This lady will show you where it is," she says.

"I can't tell you how much I appreciate this," I say to Mrs. Patterson, as I rise to go. "And could you tell me something else? You see, I never met my aunt. When she died, I was still a junior in high school. But could you tell me what she died of, and what kind of funeral she had?"

"I don't know exactly what she died of," Mrs. Patterson says. "I know she didn't have any money. Folks took up a collection to bury her . . . I believe she died of malnutrition."

"*Malnutrition?*"

Outside, in the blistering sun, I lean my head against Charlotte's even more blistering car top. The sting of the hot metal only intensifies my anger. "*Malnutrition,*" I manage to mutter. "Hell, our condition hasn't changed *any* since Phillis Wheatley's time. *She* died of malnutrition!"

"Really?" says Charlotte. "I didn't know that."

> One cannot overemphasize the extent of her commitment. It was so great that her marriage in the spring of 1927 to Herbert Sheen was short-lived. Although divorce did not come officially until 1931, the two separated amicably after only a few months, Hurston to continue her collecting, Sheen to attend Medical School. Hurston never married again.
>
> — Robert Hemenway

"What is your name?" I ask the woman who has climbed into the back seat.

"Rosalee," she says. She has a rough, pleasant voice, as if she is a singer who also smokes a lot. She is homely, and has an air of ready indifference.

"Another woman came by here wanting to see the grave," she says, lighting up a cigarette. "She was a little short, dumpy white lady from one of these Florida schools. Orlando or Daytona. But let me tell you something before we gets started. All I know is where the cemetery is. I don't know one thing about that grave. You better go back in and ask her to draw you a map."

A few moments later, with Mrs. Patterson's diagram of where the grave is, we head for the cemetery.

We drive past blocks of small, pastel-colored houses and turn right onto Seventeenth Street. At the very end, we reach a tall curving gate, with the words "Garden of the Heavenly Rest" fading into the stone. I expected, from Mrs. Patterson's small drawing, to find a small circle — which would have placed Zora's grave five or ten paces from the road. But the "circle" is over an acre large and looks more like an abandoned field. Tall weeds choke the dirt road and scrape against the sides of the car. It doesn't help either that I step out into an active ant hill.

"I don't know about y'all," I say, "but I don't even believe this." I am used to the haphazard cemetery-keeping that is traditional in most Southern black communities, but this neglect is staggering. As far as I can see there is nothing but bushes and weeds, some as tall as my waist. One grave is near the road, and Charlotte elects to investigate it. It is fairly clean, and belongs to someone who died in 1963.

Rosalee and I plunge into the weeds; I pull my long dress up to my hips. The weeds scratch my knees, and the insects have a feast. Looking back, I see Charlotte standing resolutely near the road.

"Aren't you coming?" I call.

"No," she calls back. "I'm from these parts and I know what's out there." She means snakes.

"Shit," I say, my whole life and the people I love flashing melodramatically before my eyes. Rosalee is a few yards to my right.

"How're you going to find anything out here?" she asks. And I stand still a few seconds, looking at the weeds. Some of them are quite pretty, with tiny yellow flowers. They are thick and healthy, but dead weeds under them have formed a thick gray carpet on the ground. A snake could be lying six inches from my big toe and I wouldn't see it. We move slowly, very slowly, our eyes alert, our legs trembly. It is hard to tell where the center of the circle is since the circle is not really round, but more like half of something round. There are things crackling and hissing in the grass. Sandspurs are sticking to the inside of my skirt. Sand and ants cover my feet. I look toward the road and notice that there are, indeed, *two* large curving stones, making an entrance and exit to the cemetery. I take my bearings from them and try to navigate to exact center. But the center of anything can be very large, and a grave is not a pinpoint. Finding the grave seems positively hopeless. There is only one thing to do:

"Zora!" I yell, as loud as I can (causing Rosalee to jump). "Are you out here?"

"If she is, I sho hope she don't answer you. If she do, I'm gone."

"Zora!" I call again. "I'm here. Are you?"

"If she is," grumbles Rosalee, "I hope she'll keep it to herself."

"Zora!" Then I start fussing with her. "I hope you don't think I'm going to stand out here all day, with these snakes watching me and these ants having a field day. In fact, I'm going to call you just one or two more times." On a clump of dried grass, near a small bushy tree, my eye falls on one of the largest bugs I have ever seen. It is on its back, and is as large as three of my fingers. I walk toward it, and yell "Zo-ra!" and my foot sinks into a hole. I look down. I am standing in a sunken rectangle that is about six feet long and about three or four feet wide. I look up to see where the two gates are.

"Well," I say, "this is the center, or approximately anyhow. It's also the only sunken spot we've found. Doesn't this look like a grave to you?"

"For the sake of not going no farther through these bushes," Rosalee growls, "yes, it do."

"Wait a minute," I say, "I have to look around some more to be sure this is the only spot that resembles a grave. But you don't have to come."

Rosalee smiles — a grin, really — beautiful and tough.

"Naw," she says, "I feel sorry for you. If one of these snakes got ahold of you out here by yourself I'd feel *real* bad." She laughs. "I done come this far, I'll go on with you."

"Thank you, Rosalee," I say. "Zora thanks you too."

"Just as long as she don't try to tell me in person," she says, and together we walk down the field.

> The gusto and flavor of Zora Neal[e] Hurston's storytelling, for example, long before the yarns were published in "Mules and Men" and other books, became a local legend which might . . . have spread further under different conditions. A tiny shift in the center of gravity could have made them best-sellers.
>
> — Arna Bontemps,
> *Personals*

> Bitter over the rejection of her folklore's value, especially in the black community, frustrated by what she felt was her failure to convert the Afro-American world view into the forms of prose fiction, Hurston finally gave up.
>
> — Robert Hemenway

When Charlotte and I drive up to the Merritt Monument Company, I immediately see the headstone I want.

"How much is this one?" I ask the young woman in charge, pointing to a tall black stone. It looks as majestic as Zora herself must have been when she was learning voodoo from those root doctors in New Orleans.

"Oh, *that* one," she says, "that's our finest. That's Ebony Mist."

"Well, how much is it?"

"I don't know. But wait," she says, looking around in relief, "here comes somebody who'll know."

A small, sunburned man with squinty green eyes comes up. He must be the engraver, I think, because his eyes are contracted into slits, as if he has been keeping stone dust out of them for years.

"That's Ebony Mist," he says. "That's our best."

"How much is it?" I ask, beginning to realize I probably can't afford it.

He gives me a price that would feed a dozen Sahelian drought victims for three years. I realize I must honor the dead, but between the dead great and the living starving, there is no choice.

"I have a lot of letters to be engraved," I say, standing by the plain gray marker I have chosen. It is pale and ordinary, not at all like Zora, and makes me momentarily angry that I am not rich.

We go into his office and I hand him a sheet of paper that has:

ZORA NEALE HURSTON
"A GENIUS OF THE SOUTH"
NOVELIST   FOLKLORIST
ANTHROPOLOGIST
1901   1960

"A genius of the South" is from one of Jean Toomer's poems.

"Where is this grave?" the monument man asks. "If it's in a new cemetery, the stone has to be flat."

"Well, it's not a new cemetery and Zora — my aunt — doesn't need anything flat, because with the weeds out there, you'd never be able to see it. You'll have to go out there with me."

He grunts.

"And take a long pole and 'sound' the spot," I add. "Because there's no way of telling it's a grave, except that it's sunken."

"Well," he says, after taking my money and writing up a receipt, in the full awareness that he's the only monument dealer for miles, "you take this flag" (he hands me a four-foot-long pole with a red marker on top) "and take it out to the cemetery and put it where you think the grave is. It'll take us about three weeks to get the stone out there."

I wonder if he knows he is sending me to another confrontation with the snakes. He probably does. Charlotte has told me she will cut my leg and suck out the blood if I am bit.

"At least send me a photograph when it's done, won't you?"

He says he will.

Hurston's return to her folklore-collecting in December of 1927 was made possible by Mrs. R. Osgood Mason, an elderly white patron of the arts, who at various times also helped Langston Hughes, Alain Locke, Richmond Barthe, and Miguel Covarrubias. Hurston apparently came to her attention through the intercession of Locke, who frequently served as a kind of liaison between the young black talent and Mrs. Mason. The entire relationship between this woman and the Harlem Renaissance deserves extended study, for it represents much of the ambiguity involved in white patronage of black artists. All her artists were instructed to call her "Godmother"; there was a decided emphasis on the "primitive" aspects of black culture, apparently a holdover from Mrs. Mason's interest in the Plains Indians. In Hurston's case there were special restrictions imposed by her patron: although she was to be paid a handsome salary

for her folklore collecting, she was to limit her correspondence and publish nothing of her research without prior approval.
— Robert Hemenway

You have to read the chapters Zora *left out* of her autobiography.
— Student, Special Collections Room,
Beinecke Library, Yale University

Dr. Benton, a friend of Zora's and a practicing M.D. in Fort Pierce, is one of those old, good-looking men whom I always have trouble not liking. (It no longer bothers me that I may be constantly searching for father figures; by this time, I have found several and dearly enjoyed knowing them all.) He is shrewd, with steady brown eyes under hair that is almost white. He is probably in his seventies, but doesn't look it. He carries himself with dignity, and has cause to be proud of the new clinic where he now practices medicine. His nurse looks at us with suspicion, but Dr. Benton's eyes have the penetration of a scalpel cutting through skin. I guess right away that if he knows anything at all about Zora Hurston, he will not believe I am her niece. "Eatonville?" Dr. Benton says, leaning forward in his chair, looking first at me, then at Charlotte. "Yes, I know Eatonville; I grew up not far from there. I knew the whole bunch of Zora's family." (He looks at the shape of my cheekbones, the size of my eyes, and the nappiness of my hair.) "I knew her daddy. The old man. He was a hard-working Christian man. Did the best he could for his family. He was the mayor of Eatonville for a while, you know.

"My father was the mayor of Goldsboro. You probably never heard of it. It never incorporated like Eatonville did, and has just about disappeared. But Eatonville is still all black."

He pauses and looks at me. "And you're Zora's niece," he says wonderingly.

"Well," I say with shy dignity, yet with some tinge, I hope, of a nineteenth-century blush, "I'm illegitimate. That's why I never knew Aunt Zora."

I love him for the way he comes to my rescue. "You're *not* illegitimate!" he cries, his eyes resting on me fondly. "All of us are God's children! Don't you even *think* such a thing!"

And I hate myself for lying to him. Still, I ask myself, would I have gotten this far toward getting the headstone and finding out about Zora Hurston's last days without telling my lie? Actually, I probably would have. But I don't like taking chances that could get me stranded in central Florida.

"Zora didn't get along with her family. I don't know why. Did you read her autobiography, *Dust Tracks on a Road?*"

"Yes, I did," I say. "It pained me to see Zora pretending to be naive and grateful about the old white 'Godmother' who helped finance her research, but I loved the part where she ran off from home after falling out with her brother's wife."

Dr. Benton nodded. "When she got sick, I tried to get her to go back to her family, but she refused. There wasn't any real hatred; they just never had gotten along and Zora wouldn't go to them. She didn't want to go to the county home, either, but she had to, because she couldn't do a thing for herself."

"I was surprised to learn she died of malnutrition."

Dr. Benton seems startled. "Zora *didn't* die of malnutrition," he says indignantly. "Where did you get that story from? She had a stroke and she died in the welfare home." He seems peculiarly upset, distressed, but sits back reflectively in his chair. "She was an incredible woman," he muses. "Sometimes when I closed my office, I'd go by her house and just talk to her for an hour or two. She was a well-read, well-traveled woman and always had her own ideas about what was going on . . . ."

"I never knew her, you know. Only some of Carl Van Vechten's photographs and some newspaper photographs . . . What did she look like?"

"When I knew her, in the fifties, she was a big woman, *erect*. Not quite as light as I am (Dr. Benton is dark beige), and about five foot, seven inches, and she weighed about two hundred pounds. Probably more. She . . . "

"What! Zora was *fat!* She wasn't, in Van Vechten's pictures!"

"Zora loved to eat," Dr. Benton says complacently. "She could sit down with a mound of ice cream and just eat and talk till it was all gone."

While Dr. Benton is talking, I recall that the Van Vechten pictures were taken when Zora was still a young woman. In them she appears tall, tan, and healthy. In later newspaper photographs — when she was in her forties — I remembered that she seemed heavier and several shades lighter. I reasoned that the earlier photographs were taken while she was busy collecting folklore materials in the hot Florida sun.

"She had high blood pressure. Her health wasn't good . . . She used to live in one of my houses — on School Court Street. It's a block house . . . I don't recall the number. But my wife and I used to invite her over to the house for dinner. *She always ate well,*" he says emphatically.

"That's comforting to know," I say, wondering where Zora ate when she wasn't with the Bentons.

"Sometimes she would run out of groceries — after she got sick — and she'd call me. 'Come over here and see 'bout me,' she'd say. And I'd take her shopping and buy her groceries.

"She was always studying. Her mind — before the stroke — just worked all the time. She was always going somewhere, too. She once went to Honduras to study something. And when she died, she was working on that book about Herod the Great. She was so intelligent! And really had perfect expressions. Her English was beautiful!" (I suspect this is a clever way to let me know Zora herself didn't speak in the "black English" her characters used.)

"I used to read all of her books," Dr. Benton continues, "but it was a long time ago. I remember the one about . . . it was called, I think, 'The Children of God' [*Their Eyes Were Watching God*], and I remember Janie and Teapot [Teacake] and the mad dog riding on the cow in that hurricane and bit old Teapot on the cheek . . ."

I am delighted that he remembers even this much of the story, even if the names are wrong, but seeing his affection for Zora I feel I must ask him about her burial. "Did she *really* have a pauper's funeral?"

"She *didn't* have a pauper's funeral!" he says with great heat. "Everybody around here *loved* Zora."

"We just came back from ordering a headstone," I say quietly, because he *is* an old man and the color is coming and going on his face, "but to tell the truth, I can't be positive what I found is the grave. All I know is the spot I found was the only grave-size hole in the area."

"I remember it wasn't near the road," says Dr. Benton, more calmly. "Some other lady came by here and we went out looking for the grave and I took a long iron stick and poked all over that part of the cemetery but we didn't find anything. She took some pictures of the general area. Do the weeds still come up to your knees?"

"And beyond," I murmur. This time there isn't any doubt. Dr. Benton feels ashamed.

As he walks us to our car, he continues to talk about Zora. "She couldn't really write much near the end. She had the stroke and it left her weak; her mind was affected. She couldn't think about anything for long.

"She came here from Daytona, I think. She owned a houseboat over there. When she came here, she sold it. She lived on that money, then she worked as a maid — for an article on maids she was writing — and she worked for the *Chronicle* writing the horoscope column.

"I think black people here in Florida got mad at her because she was for some politician they were against. She said this politician *built* schools for blacks while the one they wanted just talked about it. And although Zora wasn't egotistical, what she thought, she thought; and generally what she thought, she said."

When we leave Dr. Benton's office, I realize I have missed my plane back home to Jackson, Mississippi. That being so, Charlotte and I decide to find the house Zora lived in before she was taken to the county welfare home to die. From among her many notes, Charlotte locates a letter of Zora's she has copied that carries the address: 1734 School Court Street. We ask several people for directions. Finally, two old gentlemen in a dusty gray Plymouth offer to lead us there. School Court Street is not paved, and the road is full of mud puddles. It is dismal and squalid, redeemed only by the brightness of the late afternoon sun. Now I can understand what a "block" house is. It is a house shaped like a block, for one thing, surrounded by others just like it. Some houses are blue and some are green or yellow. Zora's is light green. They are tiny — about fifty by fifty feet, squatty with flat roofs. The house Zora lived in looks worse than the others, but that is its only distinction. It also has three ragged and dirty children sitting on the steps.

"Is this where y'all live?" I ask, aiming my camera.

"No, ma'am," they say in unison, looking at me earnestly. "We live over yonder. This Miss So-and-So's house; but she in the horspital."

We chatter inconsequentially while I take more pictures. A car drives up with a young black couple in it. They scowl fiercely at Charlotte and don't look at me with friendliness, either. They get out and stand in their doorway across the street. I go up to them and explain. "Did you know Zora Hurston used to live right across from you?" I ask.

"Who?" They stare at me blankly, then become curiously attentive, as if they think I made the name up. They are both Afroed and he is somberly dashikied.

I suddenly feel frail and exhausted. "It's too long a story," I say, "but tell me something: is there anybody on this street who's lived here for more than thirteen years?"

"That old man down there," the young man says, pointing. Sure enough, there is a man sitting on his steps three houses down. He has graying hair and is very neat, but there is a weakness about him. He reminds me of Mrs. Turner's husband in *Their Eyes Were Watching God*. He's rather "vanishing"-looking, as if his features have been sanded down. In the old days, before black was beautiful, he was probably considered attractive, because he has wavy hair and light-brown skin; but now, well, light skin has ceased to be its own reward.

After the preliminaries, there is only one thing I want to know: "Tell me something," I begin, looking down at Zora's house. "Did Zora like flowers?"

He looks at me queerly. "As a matter of fact," he says, looking regretfully at the bare, rough yard that surrounds her former house, "she was crazy about them. And she was a great gardener. She loved azaleas, and that running and blooming vine [morning glories], and she really loved that night-smelling flower [gardenia]. She kept a vegetable garden year-round, too. She raised collards and tomatoes and things like that.

"Everyone in this community thought well of Miss Hurston. When she died, people all up and down this street took up a collection for her burial. We put her away nice."

"Why didn't somebody put up a headstone?"

"Well, you know, one was never requested. Her and her family didn't get along. They didn't even come to the funeral."

"And did she live down there by herself?"

"Yes, until they took her away. She lived with — just her and her companion, Sport."

My ears perk up. "Who?"

"Sport, you know, her dog. He was her only companion. He was a big brown-and-white dog."

When I walk back to the car, Charlotte is talking to the young couple on their porch. They are relaxed and smiling.

"I told them about the famous lady who used to live across the street from them," says Charlotte as we drive off. "Of course they had no idea Zora ever lived, let alone that she lived across the street. I think I'll send some of her books to them."

"That's real kind of you," I say.

> I am not tragically colored. There is no great sorrow dammed up in my soul, nor lurking behind my eyes. I do not mind at all. I do not belong to the sobbing school of Negrohood who hold that nature somehow has given them a lowdown dirty deal and whose feelings are all hurt about it . . . No, I do not weep at the world — I am too busy sharpening my oyster knife.
>
> — Zora Neale Hurston
> "How It Feels to Be Colored Me,"
> *World Tomorrow*, 1928

There are times — and finding Zora Hurston's grave was one of them — when normal responses of grief, horror, and so on do not make sense because they bear no real relation to the depth of the emotion one feels. It was impossible for me to cry when I saw the field full of weeds where Zora is. Partly this is because I have come to know Zora through her books and she was not a teary sort of person herself; but partly, too, it is because there is a point at which even grief feels absurd. And at this point, laughter gushes up to retrieve sanity.

It is only later, when the pain is not so direct a threat to one's own existence, that what was learned in that moment of comical lunacy is understood. Such moments rob us of both youth and vanity. But perhaps they are also times when greater disciplines are born.

SUBJECTS' BIOGRAPHIES

HANNAH ARENDT is the author of *Rahel Varnhagen, The Origins of Totalitarianism, The Human Condition, On Revolution, Between Past and Future, Eichmann in Jerusalem, Men in Dark Times, Crises of the Republic, On Violence, The Life of the Mind,* and many philosophical articles on issues of political importance. She was born in Germany, studied with Heidegger and Jaspers, lived in exile in France, and became a widely respected and controversial thinker in America. She was a thinker and a friend in the world. She died in 1975 at the age of 69.

SIMONE DE BEAUVOIR was born in 1908 to a bourgeois family residing in the same district in Paris in which she continues to live. Her mother was a devout Catholic and her father an agnostic; family disharmony about religion became the source for her independent thinking and, in adolescence, for her total break with Catholicism. At the end of World War I, with their father's decline in economic standing, Simone and her younger sister lost their chance to have the doweries they needed for "proper marriages"; as they began to look toward their own careers, they also won a certain freedom not available to other girls of their class. Still, de Beauvoir attended Catholic schools until she had exhausted that educational system, and only then was she allowed to enter the Sorbonne. There she soon met Jean-Paul Sartre, who became her life companion. In addition to *The Second Sex*, Simone de Beauvoir has written several philosophical works, a book on aging, five volumes of fascinating memoirs, and a number of novels, of which the best is surely *The Mandarins*.

CHARLOTTE BRONTË was born in 1816 and died in 1855 at the age of thirty-nine, when she was pregnant for the first time. She was raised in the Yorkshire hills, isolated, for the most part, from society and intimately involved with her sisters and her brother. She began writing as a very small girl. Her intense imagination, combined with a life in which she carried a heavy burden of loss, bereavement, guilt, and pain, resulted in a passionate commitment to writing for release and self-definition. She created female heroes whose passionate natures were very threatening to the critics and public of Brontë's day. Her novels are *The Professor, Jane Eyre, Shirley,* and *Villette*.

JULIA DE BURGOS was born in Carolina, Puerto Rico, in 1917. She studied at the University of Puerto Rico and worked during the 1930s as a rural schoolteacher and for the PRERA (Puerto Rican Economic Rehabilitation Agency). During that period she also began writing political poetry and prose. She left Puerto Rico, never to return, in 1940. She lived in Cuba for two years and then in New York until she died in 1953. She published three books on poetry: *Poema en veinte surcos* (1938); *Canción de la verdad sencilla* (1939); *El mar y tú* (posthumous, 1954). Very few of her poems have been translated, but those that have are usually included in anthologies of Puerto Rican poetry. A valuable biography was written in 1966 by Yvette Jiménez de Baez, *Julia de Burgos, Vida y Poesia* (San Juan, Puerto Rico: Editorial Coquí, 1966).

DORA CARRINGTON, or Carrington, as she preferred to be called, was born in England in 1893, fourth child in a family of five. Her family was middle class with no cultural aspirations, but the children were encouraged in their hobbies — Carrington's being drawing. Her art teacher persuaded her family that she should try for art school, and she was accepted at the Slade in 1910, where she won prizes and came to admire Cézanne. Many new influences made themselves felt in her life, though she was always seen as an "original" and was determinedly unconventional. Mark Gertler, a talented young painter, became a friend and lover, but their relationship, a difficult one at best, was broken off when she came under the spell of the then not very well known writer Lytton Strachey, whom she met in 1915. Their considerable difference in age, education, vocation, temperament, and, indeed, sexual inclination (Strachey was a homosexual) did not deter Carrington from her determination to devote the rest of her life to his service, and they became constant companions. In 1917 they moved together into a picturesque house Carrington found for them, Tidmarsh Mill, and here, despite domestic duties, she continued to paint seriously, secretively, and self-critically. In 1921, for complicated reasons, she married Ralph Partridge, who shared her devotion to Lytton, and they became a *ménage à trois*, though the number was often augmented by the various friends and lovers they attracted, as they were all three of them very attractive and unconventional people. In 1924 they moved to Ham Spray in Berkshire, Lytton now being more affluent from the success of *Eminent Victorians*, and Carrington's artistic talents became increasingly absorbed in interior decorating. She was also doing craft work for Omega, a Bloomsbury-inspired artists' collective. In the late twenties, her attention fell less to her painting, and when Lytton Strachey died of cancer in 1931, Carrington took her own life; she was thirty-eight years old. The full extent of her artistic output has only recently become known, thanks in the main to the efforts of her brother Noel Carrington, who arranged an exhibit of her work at Oxford in 1978 and prepared a catalog, published by the Oxford Polytechnic Press, from which most of this biographical material has been taken.

ISAK DINESEN was born Karen Dinesen in Denmark in 1885. She was gifted, rebellious, very different from her bourgeois family. She married her cousin, Bror Blixen, and they set out to a farm in Kenya where they grew coffee. During the seventeen years Karen Dinesen — or the Baroness Blixen — spent there, her marriage failed and eventually, much later, so too did her beloved farm. But no series of sorrows could possibly encompass what she found in Africa. Of that luminous time, and what she made of it, she wrote her 1938 book *Out of Africa*.

When Karen Dinesen returned in her forties to Denmark, to the house of her mother Ingeborg, near her brother Thomas, she slowly fashioned out of that defeat a new life: a new vocation, a writer; a new public name, Isak, in Hebrew "the one who laughs."

As Isak Dinesen, she wrote *Seven Gothic Tales*, first widely rejected by publishers but then a major international success, and *Anecdotes of Destiny*, *Winter's Tales*, *Ehrengard*, *Shadows on the Grass*, and others.

Twice nominated for a Nobel Prize in literature, a lionized celebrity when she visited America in 1958, she remained loyal until her death in 1962 to the story — to the search for pattern and to the clarification of the pattern through the distancing of art. As she has said, "Without repeating life in imagination, you can never be fully alive."

The photograph of Dinesen is by Peter Beard, who has spent much of his life recording aspects of the old Africa and of Isak Dinesen's world. Peter generously allowed Janet Sternburg to use his photographs for her performance, and it is this particular image that she describes in "Farewell to the Farm."

ALICE DUNBAR-NELSON, poet, playwright, journalist, short-story writer, anthologist, lecturer, club woman, and activist, was born to working-class parents in New Orleans, Louisiana, on July 19, 1875. Always busy in social and literary circles, she first came to national prominence as the wife of the famous Black poet Paul Laurence Dunbar, with whom she lived from 1898 to 1902. She was an ambitious, enterprising, almost indefatigable woman who published two books of short stories (the better known being *The Goodness of St. Rocque* [1898]), edited two collections of platform speeches, saw her poems appear in all of the major publications of the Harlem Renaissance, and wrote numerous articles and syndicated newspaper columns. Among her many other activities were teaching high school English (1902–1920), organizing for women's suffrage and World War I, founding the Delaware Industrial School for Colored Girls, and being executive secretary of the American Friends Inter-Racial Peace Committee (1928–1931). She died of a heart attack on September 18, 1935, at the University of Pennsylvania Hospital, Philadelphia, where she had moved from Wilmington, Delaware, three years before with Robert J. Nelson, her husband of nineteen years.

CRYSTAL EASTMAN was born in 1881 in Seneca Lake, New York. Daughter of suffragist parents, she claimed feminism as her birthright. She was the sister of Max Eastman, editor of *The Masses*, and influenced him politically until her death in 1928, when he began his ongoing turn toward reactionary politics. She graduated from Vassar College in 1903, received an M.A. in sociology from Columbia University in 1904, and graduated second in her class from New York University Law School in 1907. She lived in and became a leading member of the feminist and radical community just then emerging in Greenwich Village. Appalled by poverty, she was a socialist by temperament and conviction. Her pioneering sociological investigation of industrial accidents won her the position of commissioner on the Employer's Liability Commission; she was New York's first woman commissioner and drafted New York State's first workers' compensation law. In 1911, shortly after her mother died, Crystal Eastman married Wallace Benedict. The marriage ended in divorce and was followed in 1916 by a happier marriage to Walter Fuller, a British pacifist and publicist. They had two children, Annis and Jeffrey.

Crystal Eastman lectured widely for women's suffrage and equality. In 1914, she called the first meeting of the Woman's Peace Party, the parent organization of the Women's International League for Peace and Freedom, and was instrumental in creating the American Union Against Militarism, the parent organization of the American Civil Liberties Union (ACLU). Throughout her life, both in the United States and Britain, she worked for women's equality, workers' rights, and peace. She died of nephritis when she was 47.

Although there is to date no biography of Crystal Eastman, many of her essays are reprinted in Blanche Wiesen Cook's *Crystal Eastman on Women and Revolution* (Oxford University Press, 1978); Eastman's analysis of the legal politics of workers' health in industrial America before World War I, *Work Accidents and the Law*, was reprinted by Arno in 1970.

CHARLOTTE FORTEN GRIMKÉ was born in 1837, the daughter of free Black abolitionists who lived in Philadelphia. In 1854 she moved to Salem, Massachusetts, to complete her education, and she subsequently became the first Black teacher in the Salem public school system. She is best known to us through her journals, which vividly describe teaching in the Sea Islands educational experiment during the Civil War.

In 1878 Charlotte Forten married Francis J. Grimke, the mulatto nephew of white abolitionist sisters Angelina and Sarah Grimke. With the exception of four years in Florida, the couple lived in Washington, D.C., where he was pastor of the Fifteenth Street Presbyterian Church. They worked energetically with former abolitionists and civil rights advocates, forming close friendships that Charlotte Forten Grimke enjoyed until her death in 1914.

The Journal of Charlotte L. Forten, edited by Ray Allen Billington, has been reissued in paperback (Norton, 1981). On its new cover are the words "A young black woman's reactions to the white world of the Civil War era." Two articles by Forten titled "Life on the Sea Islands" were published in *Atlantic Monthly* in 1864. Moorland-Spingarn Research Center at Howard University has her journals and personal papers as well as a complete collection of Charlotte Forten's published poetry and articles.

MARY E. WILKINS FREEMAN was born on October 31, 1852, in Randolph, Massachusetts. She spoke of her ancestry as "straight American with a legend of French lineage generations back." Freeman's parents were orthodox Congregationalists and expected their daughter to conform to often rigid and constraining codes of behavior. After completing high school in Brattleboro, Vermont, Mary Wilkins attended Mount Holyoke Female Seminary (1870–71) where she had difficulty accepting what she called "too strenuous goadings of conscience." She left the Seminary after one year, feeling "somewhat confused," and turned to self-education through avid reading and discussions with her friend Evelyn Sawyer. When both her parents died, Freeman was twenty-eight, poor, and unmarried. She had begun to sell poems and stories to magazines such as *Harper's Bazaar,* and gradually, through her career as a writer, she was able to support herself. For years she ignored the pressure to marry by turning to writing. At the age of fifty, after a lengthy and unstable engagement, she married Dr. Charles Freeman. Her letters indicate that marriage quickly demanded changes that affected the quality of her writing. The marriage dissolved as her husband's alcoholism worsened.

Freeman published fourteen novels and fifteen short-story collections. She received a medal from the American Academy of Arts and Letters in 1926. Her novels *Pembroke* (1894) and *The Shoulders of Atlas* (1908) are among the most interesting and are particularly striking for their exploration of both repression and rebellion. Her most notable short-story collections are *A*

Humble Romance and Other Stories (1887), *A New England Nun and Other Stories* (1891), and *The Best Stories of Mary E. Wilkins* (1927). She died in 1930.

MARGARET FULLER was born in 1810, the first child of Timothy Fuller, a lawyer and politician, and Margarett Crane Fuller, who bore nine children. Fuller's rigorous education at home by her father was followed by brief attendance at a girls' school in Groton, Massachusetts, and then by a remarkably broad program of study designed by Fuller herself. For tutoring her younger siblings, her father promised her a trip to Europe in 1835, but his death in that year obliged her to stay home to help support her family. She became acquainted with Ralph Waldo Emerson and other transcendentalists and worked with them as editor and writer for the *Dial;* she was a teacher in experimental schools, translator of German books, and leader of "conversations for women." This last activity contributed to the first book-length feminist tract in the United States, *Woman in the Nineteenth Century,* published in 1845. Her travel journal *Summer on the Lakes in 1843* led in 1844 to a position on the *New York Tribune* writing social commentary and literary criticism. Her *Papers on Literature and Art* were published in 1846, when she left for Europe as a foreign correspondent for the *Tribune.* After traveling in England, Scotland, and France, she settled in Italy to report on the unfolding revolution. She bore the child of the partisan soldier Giovanni Angelo Ossoli in 1848, and she continued to work in Rome until the fall of the short-lived Roman Republic in 1849. The family of three lived in Florence before sailing to the United States, where Fuller, the breadwinner, hoped to publish a book about the revolutions in Europe. On July 19, 1850, Fuller, Ossoli, and child died in a shipwreck off Fire Island, New York.

EMMA GOLDMAN (1869–1940) was born poor in czarist Russia. At eighteen she fled to the United States and by twenty had joined the anarchist movement in New York City. By the time she was deported at fifty to the Soviet Union, during the Red Scare of 1920, she had become an acknowledged leader of the international anarchist movement, a legendary speaker, agitator, and organizer, and had served three prison terms for her political work. She left the Soviet Union in 1922 for two more decades of political activism and writing in Europe. Her books include *Anarchism and Other Essays; My Disillusionment in Russia; The Social Significance of the Modern Drama;* and *Living My Life,* Selections from each are collected in *Red Emma Speaks: An Emma Goldman Reader* (Schocken, 1983).

ZORA NEALE HURSTON — novelist, journalist, folklorist, and critic — was, between 1920 and 1950, the most prolific Black woman writer in America. The intellectual and spiritual foremother of a generation of Black women writers, Hurston believed in the beauty of black expressions and traditions and in the psychological wholeness of Black life.

Hurston was born around 1901 in Eatonville, Florida, an incorporated Black-run and Black-populated town that was rich in Black folk tradition and uniquely free from contact with racial prejudice. Hurston wrote about and out of this experience in novels, essays, and ethnographies. Her insistence that she was not "tragically colored" was to bring her into controversy with black (male) writers of the twenties, thirties, and forties, who protested and portrayed the oppression of Black people.

Hurston's work includes an autobiography, *Dust on a Road* (1942); a folklore collection, *Mules and Men* (1935); reportage from Jamaica and Haiti, *Tell My Horse* (1938); essays and articles, "How It Feels to Be Colored Me" (1928), "My Most Humiliating Jim Crow Experience" (1944); short stories, "The Eatonville Anthology" (1926), "Sweat" (1926), "The Gilded Six Bits" (1933); *Their Eyes Were Watching God* (1937), *Jonah's Gourd Vine* (1934), and *Moses, Man of the Mountain* (1939).

Zora Neale Hurston died impoverished, her grave unmarked, in 1960.

GEORGIA DOUGLAS JOHNSON was born in 1886 in Atlanta, Georgia. After graduating from Atlanta University, she studied music at Oberlin College Conservatory. Initially she intended to be a composer. Although she later focused her energies on lyrical poetry, her intense interest in music is evident in her writing. Johnson taught school until her husband, Henry Lincoln Johnson, was appointed recorder of deeds in the Taft administration. Johnson moved with her husband to Washington where she, too, frequently held government posts. Her home became a center for literary life and discussion.

In her lifetime, Johnson published three volumes of poetry, *The Heart of a Woman* (1918), an intensely personal statement echoing the springtime of young womanhood, *Bronze* (1918), which explores the joys and pains of motherhood, and *An Autumn Cycle* (1928), which summons up the mood of the older woman whose "love's triumphant day is done." *And Share My World,* her final book of poems, was privately printed in Washington, D.C., in 1962. Johnson died in 1966.

DING LING is the pen name of modern China's most famous and controversial woman writer. She is important not just for the outstanding body of fiction she has produced but also because her career exemplifies the critical ways in which politics has shaped both the individual fate and the literary practice of writers in twentieth-century China. Her early stories, which established her reputation, focused on the subjective feelings and search for identity of young women who were breaking away from traditional social structures. But political developments, including the radicalization of literature and the martyrdom of her husband, Hu Yepin, soon turned her fiction toward the exploration of the external social world. She joined the Chinese Communist party in 1933, later becoming the center of many of its literary and political controversies. Although for many years one of the most prominent members in the cultural hierarchy of the People's Republic of China, in 1957 Ding Ling was the target of the antirightist campaign and was stripped of her party membership. For more than twenty years her books were banned, her fate unknown. She was rehabilitated in 1979 and was thus allowed to resume her writing career.

Her works available in translation include her novel on land reform, *The Sun Shines on the Sanggan River;* her short stories "The Diary of Miss Sophia," "One Certain Night," "When I Was in Hsia Village," and "In the Hospital"; and her essay "Thoughts on March 8." In 1981 Ding Ling visited the United States for the first time, spending two months at the International Writing Program at the University of Iowa and two months touring and visiting cities and college campuses.

ROSA LUXEMBURG (1871–1919) was born in Zamosc, Poland, and graduated from Gymnasium in Warsaw. Exiled at eighteen, she represented the revolutionary socialist party of Poland at the Socialist International at age twenty-two. She studied philosophy, then law, at the University of Zurich, where she received her doctorate in political science with a dissertation on the industrial development of Poland. From 1898 when she joined the German Social Democratic party until her assassination in 1919, she was one of the foremost intellectual and political leaders in the Marxist world. Imprisoned for her opposition to World War I, she wrote passionate, stinging articles for *Die Rote Fahne*, organ of the Spartacus League, which she founded in 1914 with Karl Liebknecht, Clara Zetkin, and Franz Mehring. Her prison letters are astonishing in their high spirits and deep inward confidence; they demonstrate what Mehring called "the finest brain among the scientific successors of Marx and Engels." Her major contribution to theory is *The Accumulation of Capital*. Her posthumously published *The Russian Revolution* describes tendencies within the thought and practice of Lenin and Trotsky which, Luxemburg predicted, would lead to a mechanistic and authoritarian society.

BERTHA PAPPENHEIM, pioneer feminist, social worker, and author, was born in Vienna on February 27, 1859. Also known as Anna O., Pappenheim was the first female to be psychoanalyzed. From 1895 to 1907 she was the head worker at an orphanage for Jewish girls in Frankfurt. In 1904 she founded the Jüdisher Frauenbund (Association of Jewish Women). In 1907 she established Isenberg, the first home for unmarried Jewish mothers and delinquent and disturbed girls. In 1909 she visited the United States and in particular observed Lillian D. Wald's settlement house in New York City. Pappenheim attended the International Conferences for the Suppression of the Traffic in Women and Children in 1902, 1913 (at which a paper of hers was presented), and 1930. In 1926 Pappenheim appeared before the League of Nations protesting the extent of Jewish prostitution. In 1954 the German government commemorated her contributions in the field of social work with the issuance of a stamp.

Although a writer of shadow plays, essays, prayers, and fact-finding reports, she is best known as the German translator of Mary Wollstonecraft's 1792 polemic *Vindication of the Rights of Women*. In 1924 she published her report concerning the involvement of Jews in the white slave trade based on observations she made during her travels in the Balkans, Russia, and the Middle East in 1911 and 1912. Pappenheim died at Isenburg, Germany, on May 28, 1936.

ANNA ELEANOR ROOSEVELT, U.S. reformer and humanitarian, was born in New York City in 1884. She was a distant cousin of Franklin Delano Roosevelt, whom she married in 1905. She worked for social causes both before and after her marriage and raised a large family. After she became First Lady in 1933, she was active in the National Association for the Advancement of Colored People and other social reform organizations, was a lecturer, peace activist, human rights advocate, and was assistant director of the Office of Civilian Defense in 1941–1942. Her daily column "My Day" was nationally syndicated for almost thirty years. She visited battlefronts in World War II and after the war became the U.S.

ambassador to the United Nations. Her books include *This Is My Story* (1937) and *This I Remember* (1949). These works and her recently opened correspondence reflect the full complexities of her ever-changing private and public life. She died in 1962.

MAY SARTON, now seventy-one, has written twelve volumes of poetry, seventeen novels, and six books of memoirs and journals. She was born on May 3, 1912, in Belgium to two extraordinary parents. Her father, George Sarton, was a historian of science, an author, and a Harvard professor; her mother, Mabel Elwes, an artist and designer. The family moved to America when May was two years old and settled in Cambridge, Massachusetts. After high school May Sarton joined Eva Le Gallienne's Civic Repertory Theatre Company. Two years later, Sarton formed her own theater company and worked as director, actress, and producer for four more years. During this time, Sarton was also writing poetry; once her first book of poems, *Encounter in April,* was published, in 1937, Sarton was totally committed to writing. She now resides and writes on the coast of Maine.

ETHEL MARY SMYTH, the English composer, was born April 22, 1858, at Marylebone and died May 9, 1944, at her home, Coign, near Woking, Surrey. After studying composition at the Leipzig Conservatory in 1877, where her first works were published in 1887, she traveled in Europe and finally settled in England again in 1908. The universities of Durham (1910) and Oxford (1926) awarded her honorary degrees in music, and she was made Dame of the British Empire in 1922.

Her major works include *Mass in D* (1891), the operas *Fantasio* (1892–94), *Der Wald* (1899–1901), *The Wreckers* (1903–04), *The Boatswain's Mate* (1913–14, written after two years devoted to the suffrage movement), *Fête Galante* (1923), and *Entente Cordiale* (1925), and her last work, the choral symphony *The Prison* (1930). She wrote various songs and lieder; organ and keyboard pieces; chamber music (sonatas, trios, a string quintet, and several string quartets); choruses; orchestral pieces; songs and choruses with orchestra (*March of the Women* and *Hey Nonny No* in 1911 and *Three Moods of the Sea* in 1913); and a *Concerto for Violin, Horn, and Orchestra* (1927).

After World War I and with the onset of deafness, she began to publish her memoirs, *Impressions That Remained* (2 vols., 1919), *Streaks of Life* (1921), *As Time Went On* (1935), *What Happened Next* (1940), and books of critical and political polemics and portraiture including *A Three-Legged Tour in Greece* (1927), *A Final Burning of Boats* (1928), *Female Pipings in Eden* (1933), and *Beecham and Pharaoh* (1935). Her fame was enhanced by frequent public appearances as a conductor, broadcaster, and speaker.

ALICE STEVENS was born in Chatham, New Brunswick, Canada, in 1895. Coming to the United States as a young woman she worked in factories in Athol, Massachusetts, later as a salesgirl and waitress in Boston. She bore two children, losing her son at 15 to pneumonia. Her daughter became an artist and poet who transmits some of Alice's humor and grace in her work.

SIMONE WEIL was born in 1909 in Paris of secular Jewish parents. Her father was a physician and her older brother André became a renowned mathematician. Simone Weil was a gifted student, a protegée of the French philosopher Alain at the École Normale Supérieure. Because of Weil's self-imposed moral code, she was known as the "categorical imperative in skirts," a nickname that also indicates that she was one of a very few women in a primarily male student body.

Upon her graduation in 1931 Weil took a job as a teacher in a lycée; this period of her life resulted in *Leçons de Philosophie,* a book compiled from lecture notes by Anne Reynaud-Guérithault, one of the students in her class. While a teacher, Weil was involved in labor demonstrations and leftist politics. She later spent a year as a factory worker in Paris in order to experience the oppression of such labor firsthand. Weil was also involved in the Spanish Civil War and published widely in socialist and Communist journals. Accompanying this activism and involvement, however, was Weil's growing attraction to the spiritual and her eventual mystical affinity with Christianity, although she never actually converted to the Church of Rome. She wrote a great deal during her very short life; her works include *Waiting on God, La Condition Ouvrière, Oppression and Liberty,* and *The Need for Roots.* Her essays have been collected and published, as have her notebooks.

It has been said, even by Weil herself, that she lacked moderation. She invested her whole self in any belief or activity which she thought right; she died of tuberculosis and malnutrition in 1943, having refused to take more nourishment than that allowed the French troops at the front during World War II.

THE WOMEN IN THE PRE–WORLD WAR I LABOR MOVEMENT Meredith Tax writes about were socialists and feminists active in the labor movement before World War I. Most were first-generation Irish or Russian-Jewish immigrants who went to work as children. Among them were Clara Lemlich Shavelson, Elizabeth Gurley Flynn, Mary Kenney O'Sullivan, Matilda Robbins, Lizzie Swank Holmes, Elizabeth Morgan, Leonora O'Reilly, and Maggie Hinchey. Only one, Elizabeth Gurley Flynn, wrote a book; the rest wrote only letters, or articles in long-vanished newspapers. They laid the foundations for women's participation in the labor and socialist movements, but they are prophets without honor in their own country.

WOMEN IN LYNDA KOOLISH'S PHOTOGRAPHS

MARGIE ADAM, a feminist musician and cultural worker, formed her own record company, Pleiades Records, which has produced three records: *Margie Adam: Songwriter, Naked Keys,* and *We Shall Go Forth.* She has worked on such issues as lesbian child custody, the Equal Rights Amendment, and freeing Inez Garcia.

DOBIE DOLPHIN lives in Albion, California, in a small communal household. At the time that photograph was taken of her, she was an abalone diver and carpenter. She is now a commercial salmon fisher.

SUSAN RAPHAEL is a poet and musician who lives in Mendocino, California. She is the author of a letterpress volume, *Coming Up the Hill from the River: Collected Poems 1969–1974.*

SLIM (NANCY) TE SELLE is a graduate student in speech pathology at San Francisco State University. At the time the photograph was taken of her, she lived at Salmon Creek and Black Sheep Farm, in Albion, California, and worked at Corners of the Mouth, a natural foods store in Mendocino, California.

RUTH ANN CRAWFORD is a carpenter with Seven Sisters Construction in Oakland, California. She describes herself as "a softball fanatic." She has been an actress and dancer with Lilith Theater. At the time the photograph was taken of her, she lived in Albion, California.

ELSA GIDLOW'S first collection of lyric love poems, *On a Grey Thread*, was published in Chicago in 1923. Now eighty-five, Elsa is in the midst of several writing projects as well as maintaining an extraordinary garden in her Muir Woods home, Druid Heights. Her *Sapphic Songs: Eighteen to Eighty* was recently reissued.

SUSAN LEIGH STAR is a sociologist specializing in the sociology of knowledge, work, and science. A poet, she was the first poetry editor of the lesbian/feminist journal *Sinister Wisdom*. She lives in San Francisco with her cat Maude Elizabeth, and the author of this essay.

CAROLYN KIZER has published several volumes of poems, including *The Ungrateful Garden, Midnight Was My Cry*, and *Knock Upon Silence*. She lives in Berkeley, California, and has taught all over the country, including a period as poet-in-residence at the University of North Carolina at Chapel Hill.

TILLIE OLSEN is a writer. Her works include *Yonnondio: From the Thirties*, the novellas *Tell Me a Riddle* and *I Stand Here Ironing*, and the collection of essays *Silences*. She has profoundly affected contemporary feminist thought and a great many writers as well as readers of American literature.

JUNE JORDAN is a poet, critic, and novelist who has also worked in city planning and in film. Her most recent volumes of poems are *Things That I Do in the Dark* and *Passion: New Poems, 1977-1980*. A fierce and articulate essayist, she is the author of a collection of essays, *Civil Wars*. She currently teaches in the English department of the State University of New York at Stony Brook.

PAULE MARSHALL, like the heroine of her novel *Brown Girl, Brownstones*, grew up in Brooklyn during the Depression. She is the author of two other novels, *The Chosen Place, The Timeless People* and *Praisesong for the Widow*, as well as a collection of short stories, *Soul Clap Hands and Sing*.

ADRIENNE RICH is a major American poet and feminist theorist. She has published eight books of poems, including *Diving into the Wreck* (cowinner of the 1974 National Book Award for poetry), *Poems Selected and New: 1950-1974, The Dream of a Common Language*, and *A Wild Patience Has Taken*

Me This Far. She is also the author of two compelling book-length prose works: *Of Woman Born: Motherhood as Experience and Institution* and *On Lies, Secrets, and Silence.* She coedits the lesbian/feminist journal *Sinister Wisdom.*

AUDRE LORDE is a poet, biomythographer, and essayist. Her volumes of poetry include *The Black Unicorn, Coal, Between Our Selves, From a Land Where Other People Live* (cowinner of the 1974 National Book Award for poetry), *New York Head Shop and Museum,* and *Chosen Poems, Old and New.* A professor of English at Hunter College, Lorde is also the author of *The Cancer Journals* and *Uses of the Erotic: The Erotic as Power,* as well as *Zami: A New Spelling of My Name,* a work she calls a "biomythography" because it combines history, biography, and myth.

JUDY GRAHN is a poet whose work powerfully explores themes essential to contemporary feminist thought: the transformation of language, issues of power and powerlessness, spirituality, and redefinitions of love and survival. Her books include *The Work of a Common Woman, A Woman Is Talking to Death, Edward the Dyke and Other Poems, The Common Woman Poems, She Who,* and *The Queen of Wands,* the first of a four-part series of poems that will form a sequence called *A Chronicle of Queens.*

ALICE WALKER is a novelist, essayist and poet. Her most recent novel, *The Color Purple,* won the 1983 Pulitzer Prize for Literature. Other published works include two earlier novels: *The Third Life of Grange Copeland,* and *Meridian,* three volumes of poetry: *Once, Revolutionary Petunias and Other Poems,* and *Goodnight Willie Lee, I'll See You in the Morning,* as well as two collections of short stories: *In Love and Trouble,* and *You Can't Keep a Good Woman Down.*

VIRGINIA STEPHEN WOOLF was born in London in 1882. Until her adolescence, Virginia Stephen led a family-centered existence with her two brothers, her sister, and four, much older half-brothers and half-sisters from her parents' first marriages. From an early age her father, Leslie Stephen, gave her the run of his library. She was given Greek lessons at home and took Greek and history classes at King's College, London, but otherwise she had no formal education. She suffered a poignant succession of losses — at thirteen her mother died, at fifteen her step-sister, at twenty-one her father, at twenty-four her older brother.

During her twenties, Virginia Stephen taught at Morley College, an evening institute for working men and women, worked for women's suffrage, wrote essays and reviews, and began her novel, "Melymbrosia," which became *The Voyage Out.* Although she intended to earn her living by writing, she was greatly helped by a legacy of 2500 pounds left her by her aunt Caroline Emilia Stephen when she was twenty-five, an indebtedness she later immortalized in *A Room of One's Own.*

In 1912, when she was thirty, Virginia Stephen married Leonard Woolf, "a penniless Jew," a Cambridge University graduate, and, in the years preceding his marriage to Virginia, a colonial administrator in Ceylon. He became a writer, editor, and Labor Party organizer. In 1917 the Woolfs bought a printing press and started the Hogarth Press. During the years of their marriage the Woolfs lived in London and Sussex. The marriage lasted until Virginia's suicide in 1941, at age fifty-nine.

Virginia Woolf's literary output was enormous. She wrote none novels, many short stories, two famous feminist political pamphlets, a biography of artist and critic Roger Fry, a mock biography of Elizabeth Barrett Browning's dog Flush, several lengthy critical essays, numerous short critical reviews, letters, and a diary. Her criticism was first collected in four volumes, but new essays as well as new stories are continually appearing. Her letters have been collected in six volumes, her diary in four volumes, with a fifth volume promised.

In addition to writing and publishing, Woolf led an active social life and had several intensely close friendships and a love affair with Vita Sackville-West. She lectured and organized lectures for the Women's Co-operative Guild and a women's branch of the Workers Educational Alliance. Her politics — anti-authoritarian, antimilitarist and feminist — shaped her work, finding its fullest expression in *Three Guineas* and *The Years*.

CONTRIBUTORS' BIOGRAPHIES

CAROL ASCHER: "I was born in Cleveland, Ohio in 1941, three months after my parents had come to this continent. My father had been a literature professor in Vienna until the early 1930s, when Jews were no longer allowed to teach in the university, and then had turned to a second career as a psychoanalyst. My mother, ten years his junior, was from an upper-middle-class family in Berlin but had been unable to complete the equivalent of high school because of the Nazis. The two met in a refugee camp in England in 1939.

"I spent my childhood in Topeka, Kansas, where my father found work at the Menninger Clinic. But even in America the Nazi devastation hung heavily and in indiscernible ways on my immediate and extended family. Jews without belief or ritual, my two younger sisters and I lived in a heavily Christianized environment. My mother was a housewife who always acted on her belief that "until prejudice is lifted from all peoples, it is not lifted from any of us." Sometimes, because of her outspoken stance on civil liberties and integration, a tree would be angrily chopped down in our front yard.

"I attended Vassar and Barnard Colleges, then spent six years as a free-lance editor-writer. In a moment of caution, I entered Columbia University and earned a Ph.D., which I have only peripherally used. I now live in New York with my husband Robert Pittenger, a painter, and our two cats, and I make my living once again as a free-lance writer. In addition to *Simone de Beauvoir: A Life of Freedom*, I have written a number of articles and stories as well as two novels, *Reparations* and *The Flood*, about the complexities of secular, post-Holocaust Judaism."

MYRTHA CHABRÁN: "I studied at the University of California, Berkeley, and at the University of Alberta, Edmonton and started a never-ended thesis titled 'The Theme of Hatred Between Lovers as Presented by Contemporary Women Authors.' I taught at the University of California, the University of Alberta, San Francisco State College, and the Inter-American University of Puerto Rico. I coedited the book *Cuentos: Stories by Latinas* (Kitchen Table Women of Color Press). These days I read, edit, translate and generally worry about grammar and syntax."

BELL GALE CHEVIGNY: "My parents, Virginia Caldwell Gale and Marland Gale, descended from families that fought respectively on the Southern and Northern sides of the Civil War. My mother, a housewife, taught me to admire travel, and my father, a lawyer, to swim and paddle a canoe. For both, the values of life were bound up with good storytelling, wherever it might be found. They settled on Staten Island after my birth in 1936. At Wellesley College, reading Melville persuaded me to pursue graduate study in English at Yale, where I wrote a dissertation on another seaman, Joseph Conrad. I have taught in a variety of places — Queens College, Sarah Lawrence, and an experimental college in a black community Mount Vernon, New York, Westchester County Penitentiary, and the State University of New York at Purchase — and I have developed a variety of fields of interest. An interest in European literature has been largely displaced by Afro-American literature, women's literature, and comparative study of North and South American literature. I have written as a free-lance journalist as well as a literary critic. I am married to Paul Chevigny, a law professor and writer; we live in Manhattan with our daughters, Katy and Blue."

MICHELLE CLIFF was born in November 1946 in Kingston, Jamaica. Her childhood was spent in Jamaica and in New York City. She attended undergraduate college in New York, graduating with a B.A. in European history, and graduate school at the Warburg Institute, University of London, earning an M.Phil. in comparative historical studies of the Renaissance and concentrating on neo-Platonic philosophy and social customs. She began to write after she became involved in the feminist movement in the seventies. She has published a collection of the writings of the antiracist activist Lillian Smith, *The Winner Names the Age* (Norton, 1978), and a collection of prose poems, *Claiming an Identity They Taught Me to Despise* (Persephone Press, 1980). Her forthcoming novel is entitled *Abeng* (Crossing Press, 1984). In 1982 she was awarded a National Endowment for the Arts grant in creative writing.

BLANCHE WIESEN COOK is a journalist and historian. Professor of history at John Jay College, City University of New York, her columns have appeared in the *Los Angeles Times*, the *New York Times*, and *New Directions for Women*, and have been syndicated nationally. She hosts and produces "Women and the World in the 1980s," broadcast over WBAI, Radio Pacifica in New York. Her books include *Crystal Eastman on Women and Revolution* (Oxford University Press, 1978), *The Declassified Eisenhower: A Divided Legacy of Peace and Political Warfare* (Doubleday, 1981; Penguin paperback edition, forthcoming). She is currently writing a biography of Eleanor Roosevelt, contracted by Viking-Penguin.

She writes: "When asked to consider my own life in terms of the concept 'between women,' my thoughts turn first to my mother, Sadonia Ecker Wiesen, who from my early childhood always told me that I could do anything that I wanted to do. Her constancy and her own zest for life continue to inspire me. With my sister, Marjorie D. W. Lessem, I first experienced the full intensity, generosity, and fun that accompany our ongoing sisterhood.

"The academic and learned women of Hunter College, still a woman's space when I was a student, groomed 'their girls' for their version of success; and their own lives expressed a great range of possibilities. It was at Hunter that my lifelong friend Audre Lorde helped me to expand my understanding of friendship and love. Although my academic and political involvement have intensified and changed, the academic women of Hunter College, concerned above all with power and scholarship, continue to serve as touchstones for my visions and sensibilities — whether in agreement or struggle. Their prejudices are still there to fight against, their use of influence and achievement still central to my notions of purpose.

"Over time, I have felt empowered by a support network of allies and friends at John Jay College, where I have taught for almost two decades, and especially by Gerald Markowitz and William Preston and that community of women that I believe makes active and creative work possible in our culture. This community includes many of the women in the Columbia University Seminar on Women and Society who gave me valuable feedback on this essay and much of my other work, as well as Michelle Cliff and Adrienne Rich, and my loving friend and living partner Clare Coss whose vision and analyses continually refine and enhance my understanding of the world we live in."

LOUISE DESALVO was born in Jersey City, N.J. in 1942, to Louis and Mildred Sciacchetano, whose parents were born in Italy. Her father stayed home until her first birthday, reenlisted in the navy, and spent World War II in the Pacific, while Louise and her mother worried about him in their apartment in Hoboken, N.J. After the war, her sister Jilda was born, and her father resumed his trade as a machinist. In 1949, they moved into an old house in Ridgefield, N.J., in Bergen County, the "promised land" of suburbia.

Louise DeSalvo graduated from Douglass College in 1963, began teaching high school English immediately after, married Ernest DeSalvo, and returned to graduate school after the birth of their first son, Jason. Their second son, Justin, was born while she was still at New York University, where she was an Anderson Fellow. She completed her Ph.D. in 1977, writing a dissertation on the composition of *The Voyage Out*, Virginia Woolf's first novel. She is the author of *Virginia Woolf's First Voyage: A Novel in the Making*, and she has edited *Melymbrosia*, an early version of that novel, and has recently completed her own first novel. Louise DeSalvo is associate professor of English at Hunter College in New York City where she teaches students, many of whom are, like her, the first in their families to attend college.

YI-TSI MEI FEUERWERKER is a lecturer in comparative literature at the Residential College of the University of Michigan. She was born in 1928 in Boston. Her early years were spent traveling between the United States and China, but in 1936 the family returned to China, where her father, Mei Guangdi, was professor of English literature and later dean of the School of Arts and Sciences at National Chekiang University. The War of Resistance against Japan began shortly after their return, and for the next several years, during which the family was separated for long periods, they moved and lived as refugees in many parts of southern and southwestern China. Mei Guangdi died in 1945, leaving his wife, Ida Lee Mei, with the sole responsibility for the four children. Through the help of American friends, the three oldest children came to the United States to continue their schooling and were joined by their mother and youngest brother two years later. Yi-tsi Feuerwerker's first trip back to China, except for a month in 1973 as part of a U.S. scientific delegation, was in 1981, after an absence of thirty-three years. She returned on a grant from the Committee on Scholarly Communication with the People's Republic of China, to interview Ding Ling, the woman writer who has been the subject of her research. Her book *Ding Ling's Fiction: Ideology and Narrative in Modern Chinese Literature* was published by Harvard University Press in 1982.

Her husband, Albert Feuerwerker, is a professor of modern Chinese history at the University of Michigan and director of its Center for Chinese Studies. They have two children, Alison and Paul.

LEAH BLATT GLASSER was born in 1951 in Brooklyn, New York, where her mother was a school secretary and her father a postal supervisor. She is the youngest of three daughters; growing up with two older sisters, she discovered the meaning of sisterhood in all of its complexity.

Leah Glasser completed her dissertation on Mary Wilkins Freeman and received her Ph.D. from Brown University in 1981; currently she is an assistant professor of English at Mount Holyoke College. "The energy I channel into teaching is not unlike the energy I invest in mothering my daughter. It has the steady rhythm of giving and receiving." She is working on a revision of her critical biography "In a Closet Hidden: The Life and Work of Mary Wilkins Freeman," which she is submitting for publication. As contributing editor to the forthcoming anthology *Reconstructing American Literature* (Feminist Press), she will select and introduce works by Mary Wilkins Freeman. She also writes fiction and is putting together a short-story collection. She lives in Holyoke, Massachusetts, with her husband, Gerald, and her daughter, Rachel, and can be found at odd hours in the room in the attic, her place for work.

GLORIA T. HULL: "I love sun, the sea, and Black people — three traits I share (to varying degrees) with Alice Dunbar-Nelson. I was born in Shreveport, Louisiana, to a domestic-worker mother and laborer father. After undergraduate school at Southern University, Baton Rouge (1962-66), I eventually received my Ph.D. in English from Purdue University in 1972 and began teaching at the University of Delaware, Newark. My self-education in Afro-American literature led to my intense interest in Black women writers, a pursuit that has sustained me both professionally and personally. My work on Dunbar-Nelson is part of a larger study of the women poets of the Harlem Renaissance. I am also coeditor of *All the Women Are White, All the Blacks Are Men, But Some of Us Are Brave: Black Women's Studies* (Old Westbury, N.Y.: Feminist Press, 1982). Unlike Dunbar-Nelson, who bore no children (but helped to raise six), I am the mother of fifteen-year-old Adrian Prentice Hull."

ANN H. JACKOWITZ: Teacher, filmmaker, and writer, Ann H. Jackowitz, born in Troy, New York, in 1945, was raised in Hudson, New York, the second-oldest city in New York State, chartered in 1785. A cum laude graduate of Simmons College with a B.A. in history, she also has an M.A. in history from New York University.

She is an active member of NOW, the Institute for Research in History, the Leo Baeck Institute and the Dramatists Guild. She is a free-lance writer, has completed a screenplay, *The Case of Anna O.*, and is working on her first novel, *Who Can I Tell?* and a romantic stage comedy, *Playing for Keeps.*

LYNDA KOOLISH: "I have steadfastly refused the choice of a single career as *either* a photographer *or* an artist *or* a poet *or* a critic and teacher. Sometimes I feel as though I am walking on a balance beam, not in one direction but in many. Having selected several areas of work, commitments multiply. But teaching and writing feed the visions of my photographs, and photographing the women I love makes me passionate about writers and ideas in the classroom.

I was born in Los Angeles in 1946 and moved to Berkeley in 1965. I now live in San Francisco. I received my doctorate in Modern Thought and Literature from Stanford University. I have taught literature, art, and feminist theory at San Francisco State University, Stanford University, and Goddard College.

"Presently, I teach in the Women's Studies Program at California State University, Sacramento. My photographs have appeared on book and record jackets and in books, magazines, and newspapers. I review poetry for the *San Francisco Chronicle* and I am currently writing a book on contemporary Black feminist poets."

JANE LAZARRE: "I was born in 1943 and raised in New York City, in Greenwich Village, within the supportive and confusing subculture of American communism. When I was twelve my father was assigned to what was called 'the cultural region' and I spent the rest of my adolescence under the influence of artists and writers who were also political activists. These people had a great effect on my development. I became a full-time writer just as I became a mother and conscious feminist. Trying to earn my living as a writer for the past fifteen years has provided me with important lessons and strengths as well as difficulties. I have written memoirs, essays, articles, especially for the *Village Voice,* and fiction. My books include *The Mother Knot, On Loving Men, Some Kind of Innocence* (a novella), and a recently completed, not yet published novel entitled *Home Girl.* I have also been a teacher of women's studies over the past seven years, at City College and Yale, and this has been a very precious experience for me."

JANE CONNOR MARCUS was born in St. Albans, Vermont, in 1938, grew up in Winthrop and Newton, Massachusetts, and attended Mount Saint Joseph Academy and Radcliffe College. She holds an M.A. from Brandeis and a Ph.D. from Northwestern University. She is married to mathematician Michael Marcus and has three children. She has taught at the State University of New York at Stony Brook and the University of Illinois, Chicago Circle, and is now associate professor of English at the University of Texas at Austin and director of women's studies. She has held fellowships from the National Endowment for the Humanities, the Newberry Library, and the American Council of Learned Societies. Her books include an edition of Rebecca West's early socialist and feminist writing — *The Young Rebecca* (Viking) — and three volumes of Virginia Woolf criticism — *New Feminist Essays on Woolf* (Macmillan/University of Nebraska Press), *Virginia Woolf: A Feminist Slant* (University of Nebraska Press), and *Virginia Woolf and Bloomsbury: A Centenary Celebration.* She is completing *One's Own Trumpet: Ethel Smyth and Virginia Woolf: A Portrait in Letters* and her own book on Virginia Woolf, *We Are the Words and Music: Virginia Woolf and the Politics of the Family.* Her essays, in *Art and Anger,* are on Ibsen, Wilde, Meredith, and Woolf. Yet to be written is her biography of the Ibsen actress and feminist Elizabeth Robins, the subject of her 1973 Ph.D. dissertation.

ELIZABETH KAMARCK MINNICH is a feminist philosopher. She holds a Ph.D. in philosophy from the Graduate Faculty of the New School for

Social Research in New York City, where she studied and worked with Hannah Arendt as a student and teaching assistant. She has been dean of the Union Graduate School, associate dean of faculty at Barnard College, and director of studies at Hollins College, as well as a teacher. In addition to working with graduate students in the Union Graduate School, she writes, speaks, and consults on the transformative implications of feminist scholarship for the curriculum and for pedagogy.

SARA RUDDICK: "I was born in 1935 and grew up in Ohio where my parents have lived all their lives. My father was a lawyer; my mother took primary responsibility for their three children and was an active community volunteer. My parents took an enthusiastic interest in my education, supporting my ambitions even when they could not understand them. Fairly early I began moving "East," arriving in New York City sixteen years ago. I live there now with my husband, William Ruddick, and our two rapidly departing children, Hal and Elizabeth.

"Virginia Woolf helped me to see and love my city as she loved hers. In return, the city made it possible for me to transform a vague interest in Virginia Woolf into serious study. Among New York's many distinctive institutions, three have been central to my work: the New York Public Library, where I read Virginia Woolf's diaries and manuscripts; the New School for Social Research, especially its Seminar College where I teach; and Womanbooks at 92nd Street and Amsterdam Avenue, which has always provided me with the books and spirit I need.

"In 1977 Pamela Daniels and I edited *Working It Out: 23 Women Writers, Artists, Scientists, and Scholars Talk About Their Lives and Work* (Pantheon, 1977). I am finishing a book on the relation between maternal thinking, pacifist theory, and feminist politics."

ALIX KATES SHULMAN was born and educated in Cleveland, Ohio. At twenty she moved to New York City for graduate study in philosophy and mathematics. She earned her living as an encyclopedia editor, editing such works as the *Encyclopedia of Philosophy*, until the late 1960s, when she became a feminist activist. Since 1968 she has published two books on Emma Goldman, several books for young people, numerous essays and short stories, and three novels. In 1983 she received a grant from the National Endowment for the Arts for her fiction. She teaches fiction writing at New York University.

JANET STERNBURG was born in Boston in 1943. She spent two important years, at age twelve and thirteen, at Girls' Latin School, which gave her a sense of what women could do in a public environment where mind and spirit were valued. She attended Connecticut College on a writing scholarship but left to come to New York, where she studied for her degree in philosophy at night at the New School for Social Research. During the day she worked in film, eventually becoming a producer for National Public Television. One of her films, *El Teatro Campesino*, was featured at the 1970 New York Film Festival; another, *Virginia Woolf: The Moment Whole*, won a Cine Golden Eagle. The short film on Woolf focused on being a woman and an artist; after making it Sternburg returned to writing her own poems, fiction, and essays, which have been widely published in anthologies and magazines. Between 1972 and 1980 she taught courses in film and writing at the Graduate Media Studies Division at the New School, did extensive work through the Poets in the Schools program, and directed the Writers in Performance Series at the Manhattan Theatre Club. For the series, she produced hundreds of readings and also wrote and directed theatrical evenings on such writers as Colette, Louise Bogan, H.D., Raymond Chandler, S.J. Perelman, and, most recently, Isak Dinesen. In 1980, her book *The Writer on Her Work* was published by W. W. Norton. Of that book, she writes, "It changed my life. I keep hearing from people who speak of it as a friend, and it has also been that to me." Currently, she works as a program officer at the New York Council for the Humanities, continues to write and teach, and recently received a National Endowment for the Humanities grant to write a feature-length film on the life and work of Virginia Woolf.

ERLENE STETSON: "Each time my college-educated aunt lost another maid job, my mother invariably cocked her head in a 'didn't I tell you' position and said, 'Little foxes jump and fleas leap, but they both occupy the same holes and nest.' It's like that with us women. Though some leap and others jump, we're in this thing together. And for God's sake let us stay crazy! It keeps us sane, and really that's what gets the work done. Black women's studies helps me to get the work done. I think back to December 24, 1949, when I was born, and I am singularly grateful that my mother contributed to the feminist cause by giving me ten other sisters. Like my two daughters, I can't help but love this crazy woman."

MAY STEVENS is an artist who is working on poems to be published as the *Book of Alice*. Her autobiographical essay, *My Work and My Working-Class Father*, is included in *Working It Out: 23 Women Writers, Artists, Scientists, and Scholars Talk About Their Lives and Work*, edited by Ruddick and Daniels (Pantheon, 1977). Her paintings are in the Whitney Museum of American Art, the San Francisco Museum of Modern Art, and other public and private collections. She was a founding member of the *Heresies* Collective and contributed an essay to *Issue 15* on racism.

MEREDITH TAX was born in Milwaukee in 1942, to a family of second-generation Russian Jews. Her father was a doctor. She spent her adolescence in the suburbs and attended Brandeis University and the University of London. She has been politically active since 1967, principally in the women's liberation movement, in Bread and Roses in Boston, the Chicago Women's Liberation Union, and the Committee for Abortion Rights and Against Sterilization Abuse (CARASA) in New York. She has three books in print: *The Rising of the Women* (Monthly Review Press, 1980), *Families*, a children's picture book (Atlantic-Little, Brown, 1981), and *Rivington Street*, a novel (Morrow, 1982; Jove paperback, 1983). She is working on a sequel to *Rivington Street*. She has one daughter, Corey, by her first marriage and is now married to Marshall Berman, the writer. They live in New York City.

BONNY VAUGHT: "I was born in 1932 and was raised in a traditional midwestern home with Danish and Norwegian background.

"My husband John and I were married when I was twenty. At that time a woman often defined herself in terms of her husband's career. I called myself — in succession — a navy wife, seminary wife, pastor's wife, and corporation wife. Today I am still John's wife, but I call myself a writer.

"During thirty years of marriage John and I have moved sixteen times. Despite the problems of such frequent uprooting, I am glad to have experienced both West and East Coast lifestyles. (Even though the Southwest was difficult for me, I did find Charlotte Forten there!) My husband and I now live in Malverne, New York.

"It seems appropriate for a picture to show me standing in front of rows of books in our home. No matter where we've lived, books have been a sustaining presence for me, as well as a great joy. The neck brace is an obvious reminder of the radically changed lifestyle required to cope with a severe, disabling injury.

"Writing two books on religious education and one on industrial history gave me unusual opportunities to serve an apprenticeship in the craft of writing. Interviews and articles on social issues have been continuing efforts over many years. Now they have become ongoing projects in conjunction with my work on a book about Charlotte Forten Grimke."

ALICE WALKER was born in Eatonton, Georgia, in 1944. She attended Spelman and Sarah Lawrence colleges and has lived and worked in Mississippi, New England, and New York. Her published work includes two collections of stories, *In Love and Trouble* and *You Can't Keep a Good Woman Down;* three volumes of poetry, *Once, Revolutionary Petunias,* and *Goodnight, Willie Lee, I'll See You in the Morning;* two earlier novels, *The Third Life of Grange Copeland* and *Meridian;* and a biography of Langston Hughes for children. She is contributing and consulting editor to *Ms.* magazine and to *Freedomways* and has taught literature and writing at Jackson State University, Tougaloo College, Wellesley College, the University of Massachusetts, and Yale University. "Looking for Zora" previously appeared in a Zora Neale Hurston reader, edited by Alice Walker, entitled, *I Love Myself When I Am Laughing . . . And Then Again When I Am Looking Mean and Impressive,* (Feminist Press, 1979).

Alice Walker's father was born in Georgia and worked most of his life on farms. Her mother, Minnie Tallulah Walker, who had eight children before her thirty-second birthday, "labored beside — not behind" her husband on the farms. Alice Walker has one daughter and now lives in San Francisco. Her most recent novel is *The Color Purple,* for which she received the Pulitzer Prize.

MARTHA WHEELOCK: "I was born September 24, 1941, and came to filmmaking out of many years of high school and college English teaching and the frustration of working on my Ph.D. dissertation at New York University. Fortunately, my thesis subject was May Sarton, whose life and writings led and moved me, with my friend and partner Marita Simpson, to make the film *World of Light: A Portrait of May Sarton.* The thesis is yet to be completed.

"I thank May Sarton for inspiring me to the vision, dedication, and hard work that independent filmmaking demands; for allowing us the opportunity to work with her; for her friendship and support; and, above all, for the generous and open gift of herself.

"From this rich experience with Sarton and with film, I continue to strive to be an independent filmmaker in New York City with dreams of making consciousness-raising feature films. I am also a professional astrologer and an English instructor at Elizabeth Seton College.

"Information about the film *World of Light: A Portrait of May Sarton* can be obtained from Martha Wheelock, Ishtar Films, 305 East 11th St., 2D, New York, NY 10003."

J. J. WILSON: "I was fortunate to have many fine women teachers as I was growing up, from my grandmother, Lillian Hancock Reed, to "Aunt Susie" Lansdown, to "Ardie" Hopkins and Dorothy Montgomery. Alas, no women teachers in undergraduate school at Stanford, which may have partially accounted for my sleepwalking through that portion of my education. In graduate school at Berkeley, Josephine Miles, acknowledged by so many as an inspiration, helped me too. All these teachers taught me not only how to teach, but why. Since the early days of women's studies, we have all been learning from one another, thank heavens.

"My principal work in women's studies was my book, coauthored with Karen Petersen, *Women Artists: Recognition and Reappraisal from the Early Middle Ages to the Twentieth Century* (New York: Harper & Row, 1976), one of the first art histories to stress influences between women. We have also packaged a number of inexpensive slide sets on women artists that are distributed through the same publisher. I am one of the founding editors of the *Virginia Woolf Miscellany*, a newsletter that strives to keep scholars of Woolf and the Bloomsbury group in communication with one another. I also helped to start in my community a women's library called *The Sitting Room*. I am currently a professor of English at Sonoma State University in California."

ELIZABETH WOOD was born in 1939 in Manly, New South Wales, Australia, and has lived in New York with her four children since 1978. A musicologist and free-lance writer, she teaches and writes about women and music. Her recent work has appeared in *The Musical Woman, Massachusetts Review,* and *Ms.* magazine, on such musicians as Polish composer Grazyna Bacewicz, Bach specialist Rosalyn Tureck, and performance artist Laurie Anderson. She also writes short stories, is completing a first novel, and is preparing a new biography of the life and work of Dame Ethel Smyth.

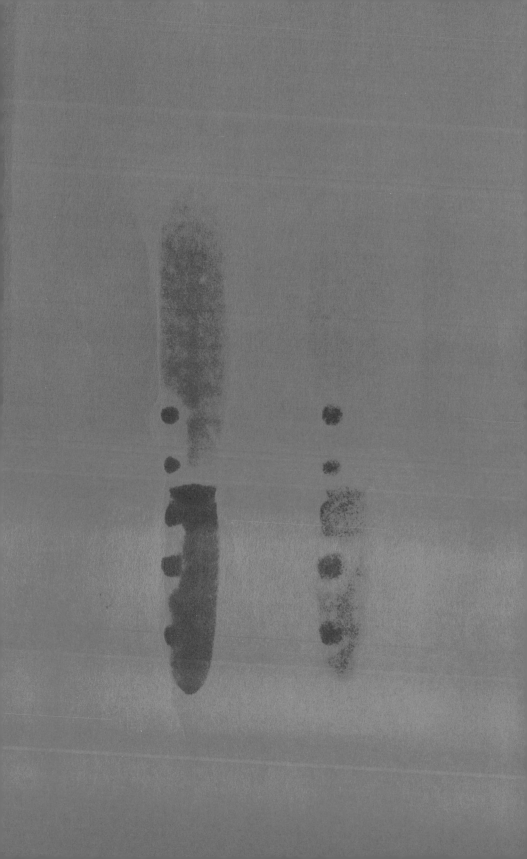

305.42   Between women   840735
Bet

305.42   Between women   840735
Bet

DATE	ISSUED TO